INCO
COMES TO LABRADOR

Library and Archives Canada Cataloguing in Publication

Goldie, Raymond, 1948-
  Inco comes to Labrador / Raymond Goldie.

Includes bibliographical references.
ISBN 1-894463-75-7

  1. Inco Limited. 2. Nickel mines and mining--Newfoundland and Labrador--Voisey's Bay. I. Title.

HD9539.N52I58 2005   338.7'6223485'097182   C2005-905918-4

Copyright © 2005 by Raymond Goldie

ALL RIGHTS RESERVED. No part of the work covered by the copyright hereon may be reproduced or used in any form or by any means—graphic, electronic or mechanical—without the written permission of the publisher. Any request for photocopying, recording, taping or information storage and retrieval systems of any part of this book shall be directed to the Canadian Reprography Collective, 379 Adelaide Street West, Suite M1, Toronto, Ontario M5V 1S5. This applies to classroom use as well.

PRINTED IN CANADA

FLANKER PRESS
ST. JOHN'S, NL, CANADA
TOLL FREE: 1-866-739-4420
WWW.FLANKERPRESS.COM

Cover Design: Adam Freake - Consumer Quest

We acknowledge the financial support of: the Government of Canada through the Book Publishing Industry Development Program (BPIDP); the Canada Council for the Arts which last year invested $20.3 million in writing and publishing throughout Canada; the Government of Newfoundland and Labrador, Department of Tourism, Culture and Recreation.

INCO
COMES TO LABRADOR

RAYMOND GOLDIE

FLANKER PRESS LTD.
ST. JOHN'S, NL
2005

*Dedicated to Bruce Ryan and Dan Lee,
who put Voisey's Bay on the map*

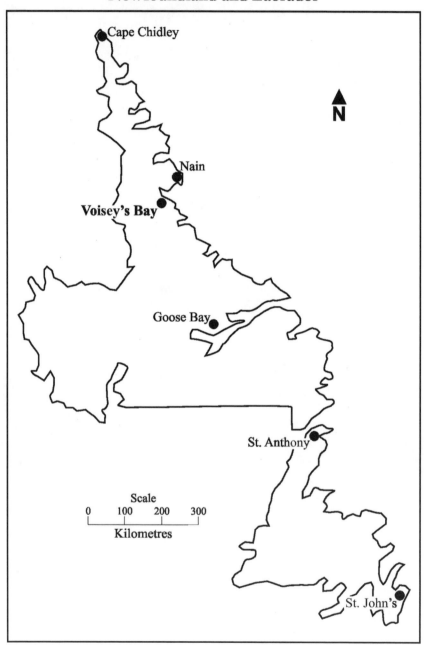

Table of Contents

Preface XIII

Prologue: Challenging Corporate Power 1

Chapter 1 — A Geological Economist 7
Chapter 2 — Discovery of Voisey's Bay 12
Chapter 3 — Keeping Up With Liz 25
Chapter 4 — Beyond Our Wildest Dreams 36
Chapter 5 — Visiting Voisey's 44
Chapter 6 — A Very Public Bet 54
Chapter 7 — Political Posturing 65
Chapter 8 — A Beautiful Woman in a Bar 73
Chapter 9 — Selective Disclosure 83
Chapter 10 — The Government Prepares to Challenge Inco's Corporate Power 85
Chapter 11 — The Caliban of Canada 90
Chapter 12 — Tobin Versus Toronto 95
Chapter 13 — Burning Inco's Bird 140
Chapter 14 — A Copper Smelter, Too? 144
Chapter 15 — Step One of the Environmental Assessment of Voisey's Bay 148
Chapter 16 — Lost Visions, Forgotten Dreams 150
Chapter 17 — Judge Marshall Impedes the "Impetuous and Heedless Pace of Man" 156
Chapter 18 — Woman of Labrador 163
Chapter 19 — Pragmatists, Finger Pointers, Tricksters, and the Big Clumsy Guy 169
Chapter 20 — Impact Benefit Agreements to the End of the Tobin Era 174
Chapter 21 — Native Claims to the End of the Tobin Era .. 181
Chapter 22 — 1997: Crisis? What Crisis? 201
Chapter 23 — What Did the Biggest Business Story of 1998 Have in Common With a Belly Dancer? 205
Chapter 24 — Soirée '99 217

Chapter 25 — A Challenge From Australia: One Man and the Starter's Pistol 227
Chapter 26 — A Challenge From Siberia: Huge Stockpiles of Nickel? 238
Chapter 27 — A Challenge From Quebec: Voisey's II? 257
Chapter 28 — A Challenge From New Caledonia: Tropical Nickel 261
Chapter 29 — Buy on Mystery – Sell on History 273
Chapter 30 — Grimes Takes Charge 288
Chapter 31 — Deal! 300
Chapter 32 — Whoa, Goro! 316
Chapter 33 — Enter Altius 319
Chapter 34 — Ahead of Schedule 327

Appendix 1: Valuing Mining Stocks 341
Appendix 2: Price Charts 343
Appendix 3: Terry Creb's Reminiscences, By Email, of Early 1995 344
Endnotes 346
Bibliography 361
Acknowledgements 365

THE PLAYERS

Aggek, Edward
Alcan Inc.
Altius Minerals Corporation
Ambachtsheer, Keith
American Metals Market
Anaconda Nickel Ltd.
Andersen, Chesley
Andersen, William
Anderson, David
Anderson, Toby
Andre, Chief Taddé
Angelyys, Kalayra
Archean Resources Ltd.
Argentia, Newfoundland
Armitage, Frank
Ashini, Daniel
Australian Financial Review
Aylward, Hon. Joan
Bacon, Dr. Gordon
Bagi, Dan
Baird, Moira
Baker, John
Baker, Max
Baldry, Julian
Bank of Montreal
Barbour, William
Barnes, Greg
Barr, David
Bart, John
Bennett, Premier Bill
Best, Anita
Beunderman, Willem
Bielski, Wiktor
Boliden Ltd.
Bonnell, Heidi
Boulle, Jean-Raymond
Brokenshire, James
Broomfield, Mayor Wayne
Bulong, Western Australia
Butler, Ed
Butler, Roland
Butler, Steve
Butt, Margaret
Byrne, Hon. Edward
Canadian Environmental
  Assessment Agency
Canadian Investment Review
Canadian Press
Canadian Shareholders Association
Canadian Society of New York
Canavest House Limited
Canico Resource Corp.
Carson, Cliff
Cassiar Asbestos of Canada
Cawse, Western Australia
CBC Newsworld
Cerro Colorado mine, Chile
Chevron Corp.
Chislett, Albert
Citizen's Mining Council of
  Newfoundland/Labrador
Clarke, Herb
Codelco (Corporatión Nacional
  del Cobre) Chile)
Colonial First State Fund
  Managers, Australia
Cooke, John
Crebs, Terry
Cresson, Mme. Edith
Crosbie, Hon. John
Crowley, Brian Lee
CS First Boston Corp.
Dallaire, Réjean
Dalton, Brian
Daly, Chris
Dean, Paul

Denison Mines
Deutsche Morgan Grenfell
Diamond Fields Resources
Dicks, Hon. Paul
Dillistone, Don
Dome Petroleum Ltd.
Doyle, Pat
Duncan, Robbie
DuPont Canada Co.
Dutton, Chris
Dynatec Corp.
El Teniente mine, Chile
Emslie, Ron
Eramet Group, France
Estrategia
Evans, Peter
Exdiam Corporation
The Express
Falconbridge Limited
Figgy Duff
Financial Post
Finlayson, Eric
Flanagan, Chris
FNX Mining Company Inc.
Forrest, Andrew
Fowler, Professor David
Francis, Diane
Franco-Nevada Mining
    Corporation
Friedland, Robert
Frogier, Pierre
Furey, Hon. Chuck
Gadsby, John
Galactic Resources Ltd.
Gallagher, Jack
Garnett, Richard
Garritsen, Peter
Gauld, Greg
Gendron, Stewart
Geological Survey of Canada
Gibbons, Dr. Rex

Gill, Derrick E. (Rick)
The Globe and Mail
Goldcorp Inc.
Gorbachev, Nikolai
Goro Nickel Co., New Caledonia
Goudie, Peter
Government of Newfoundland
    and Labrador
Gray, John
Gray, Rodger
Green, Rich
Greer, George
Griffiths, Lesley
Grimes, Premier Roger
Gwyn, Sandra
Halley, Judge Raymond
Hand, Scott
Harquail, David
Harris, Hon. Jack
Hatch Associates
Haye, Richard
Heretaunga College, New Zealand
Heron Resources Ltd.
Hewlett, Hon. Alvin
Hodkin, Ted
Hollett, Bruce
Holmgren, Janet
Holwell, Mayor Rex
House, Lieutenant-Governor
    Dr. Maxwell
Howlett, Karen
Hume, Douglas
Innu
Inuit
Iron Ore Company of Canada
Jones, Andy
Jubilee Mines NL
Kavanagh, Paul
Kennecott
Komsomolsky mine, Russia
Koniambo project, New Caledonia

Labrador Inuit Association
Labrador Inuit
    Development Association
Langdon, Hon. Oliver
Lapous, Jean-Pierre
Lazarovici, Victor
Lee, Daniel
Lime and Marble Ltd.
LionOre Mining International Ltd.
Lydall, John
Mallick, Heather
Mallory, Manford
Mameanskum, John
Marshall, Gerald
Marshall, Judge William
Masterman, Michael
Matthews, Hon. Lloyd
Maynard, Brian
McAuslan, Dave
McEwen, Robert
McLellan, Anne
McMurrough, Mike
McNish, Jacquie
McOuat, Jack
Mercaldo, Ed
Mergott, Jack
Metis
Mi'kmaq
Miller, Ralph
Minerals Resource Analysts Group
MMC Norilsk Nickel
Moore, Rosie
Moravians
Morin, Roger
Morse, Stearns
Morton, Roger
Murrin Murrin, Western Australia
Naldrett, Professor Tony
Napier, William
Naskapi Band
The National Post

NDT Ventures
Nesbitt Burns
New Caledonia
Nikkelverk A/S, Norway
Nochasak Jr., Paul
Noranda Inc.
Noril'sk Nickel Company
Nui, David
Nui, Joachim
Nuinsco Resources Ltd.
Nuke, David
Nutter, Ernie
O'Flaherty, Patrick
Oktyabr'sky mine, Russia
Ortslan, Terry
Osmium Holdings
Pain, Isabel
Paterson, John
Penashue, Peter
Peters, Emery
Phillips, Fraser
Pickard, Frank
Pidjot, Raphael
Pinch-point™
Pirie, Jim
Platts Metals Week
Power, Lee-Anne
Powis, Alf
Prospectors and Developers
    Association of Canada
PT Inco
Ramu River project, Papua
    New Guinea
Ranieri, Santo
Redstone, John
Regent, Aaron
Reguly, Eric
Reuters
Richardson, George
Richardson Greenshields of
    Canada Ltd.

Rich, Lloyd
Rich, Monique
Rich, Paul
Rideout, Hon. Thomas
Rio Algom Ltd.
Roberts, Hon. Ed
Robinson, Alan
Roman, Stephen B.
Rorke, Harvey
Roth Investor Relations
Rowat, Bill
Russell, Todd
Ryan, Bruce
Rylkova, Galina (Galya)
Schulich, Seymour
Scotia Capital
Scott, Sandra
Scott-Taggart, Roger
Selco Mining Corp. Ltd.
Shaheen, John
Sharpe, Bill
Shell Canada Ltd.
Shelley, Hon. Paul
Sherritt International Corp.
Shnier, Mitchell L.
Skye Resources
Smallwood, Premier Joseph R.
SNC-Lavalin Group Inc.
Snow, Hon. Alec
Solar, Maurice
Sopko, Mike
Sparkes, Grace
Storer, Robyn
Stratton-Crawley, Dr. Richard
Sudbury
The Sudbury Star
Sullivan, Hon. Loyola
Summerville, Paul
Tapper, Gayle
Teck Corporation
The Evening Telegram

Texasgulf Inc.
Thurlow, Geoff
Toronto Geological
    Discussion Group
Tuglavina, Jerry
Usher, Dr. Peter
Valdmanis, Alfred
Verbiski, Chris
Verbiski, Mort
Verge, Hon. Lynn
Voisey's Bay
Voisey's Bay News
Voisey's Bay Nickel Company
Wagner, Fred
Walsh, Jim
Walsh, Mary
Walsh, Nancy
Wangersky, Russell
Webb, Henry
Webster, Tom
Wells, Premier Clyde
White, Winston
Williams, Premier Danny
Winsor, Hon. Neil
Young, Vic

PREFACE

You've probably seen financial analysts interviewed on TV, confidently commenting on the value of the shares of this company or the future prospects of that industry. You may have wondered, "Do they really know what they're talking about?" The purpose of this book is to answer that question using, as an example, how one financial analyst on Bay Street in Toronto watched the discovery, exploration, and development of the Voisey's Bay nickel-copper-cobalt deposit in Labrador from 1993 to 2004.

When analysts value the shares of mining companies, we use a variety of techniques (see Appendix 1). In applying these techniques, I have uncovered anomalies which are both persistent and difficult to explain. For example, one method, "Option-Pricing," often indicates values for diversified base metal companies which are considerably greater than their share prices. This suggests "the option-pricing valuation is generally an indicator of the highest share price available under a management policy of auctioning the firm,"[1] which means that stocks are usually priced at less than their true value, unless they are the object of a takeover.

As well as crunching numbers, financial analysts must also consider issues beyond those traditionally covered in financial texts. Two such issues at Voisey's Bay were:

(a) The company which developed Voisey's Bay, Inco, was painfully slow to realize the extent to which challengers of corporate power — governments, aboriginal groups, and environmentalists — had usurped control of its future.

(b) Strategic considerations can override strict investment criteria. For example, although it was having difficulties in finding enough feedstock for its existing nickel refineries, Inco agreed to develop and build a new hydrometallurgical ("hydromet") refinery to process ores from Voisey's Bay. This investment was, in part, an insurance policy: if Inco didn't develop an appropriate hydromet process, a competitor might. And that competitor might discover that hydromet was so cheap and so efficient that Inco's existing smelting and refining operations would become uncompetitive.

All of the people mentioned in this book are real people, whose words and actions I have tried to record as faithfully as possible. Some of those who watched the Voisey's Bay drama with me — "Donny," "Harry," "Liz," and "Patricia" — are composite characters. They are composites for two reasons:

(a.) because I have had many employers, many colleagues have successively filled similar roles;
(b.) when I noted the questions asked at analysts' meetings with management, I usually did not record who had asked them.

Nevertheless, the statements and questions which I attribute to the composite characters were made, and were made at the times stated.

All dollar amounts in this book are Canadian dollars unless otherwise specified.

Raymond Goldie
Toronto, Ontario

June, 2005

PROLOGUE: CHALLENGING CORPORATE POWER

In Ontario in the late 1970s, [New Democratic Party] leader Stephen Lewis was becoming increasingly frustrated by his party's ... Floyd Laughren and Elie Martel [members of provincial parliament], who regularly stood up in the legislature and demanded the nationalization of mining firms Inco and Falconbridge.

In a desperate gesture, he [Lewis] flew them out to meet secretly with Eric Kierans, the respected left-leaning Liberal minister and economist whose death we all mourned last month. ... [Kierans] had recently persuaded Allan Blakeney's Saskatchewan NDP government that state ownership was a bad idea, and made a similar case to the Parti Québécois; now he sat down with the Ontarians, showed them the numbers, and persuaded them to abandon the cause of nationalization.

... Mr. Kierans, through hard experience and rational calculation, had realized that governments could influence business more by passing laws and regulations than by actually owning them.
— Doug Saunders, *The Globe and Mail*,
Toronto, June 26, 2004

Men prize the thing ungained.
— *Troilus and Cressida*, William Shakespeare

At 12:35 p.m. on September 28, 1998, a group of mining analysts is sitting around a U-shaped table in the dark-panelled heart of Toronto's financial district. I'm a nearsighted near-vegetarian, so I sit close to the front and far from the sliced-meat sandwiches. I spear an assortment of cheese cubes and grapes with my fork, and sit back to listen to the presentation. At least I get to eat. The presenters do not.

International Nickel Company (Inco) President Scott Hand and Chairman Mike Sopko are outlining their company's prospects in a dismally declining nickel market. Dr. Hand is a white-haired, patrician lawyer from California; Dr. Sopko is a shorter, rounder man, a metallurgist who has worked his way up Inco's operations. Their audience, the Mineral Resource Analysts Group — M.R.A.G. — is a self-selected body of some thirty mining analysts. M.R.A.G. meets irregularly to listen to the senior executives of mining, metals, and fertilizer companies explain to us why they believe our clients — institutional fund managers and individual investors — should invest in their firms.

Both of Inco's representatives are understandably wary; the previous meeting between Inco and M.R.A.G. was a bitter confrontation in 1988 in the old, now demolished, and much mourned Engineers' Club. That meeting ended with Inco's legal counsel, incongruously attired in a tuxedo, ushering a shaken and shaking chairman out of the room. They left behind a group of analysts, several of whom had lost their tempers in their frustration with what they thought was a stupid decision on Inco's part: to borrow money in order to pay a special dividend of US$1,059 million to the holders of its common shares. With one abstention, the group voted unanimously to censure Inco's proposal, and issued a press release to that effect. I was the abstention because I sensed a conflict of interest. I worked for a firm controlled by the Richardson family of Winnipeg, and George Richardson was on Inco's board. My abstention had a surprisingly useful effect. Some of M.R.A.G.'s members worked with corporate financiers who would have been annoyed if one of their colleagues had irritated such a big client as Inco. My abstention allowed each M.R.A.G. member to suggest to their corporate finance department that they might have been that one abstention.

Reporters at *The Globe and Mail* had picked up M.R.A.G.'s press release but recognized that the true story was that a group of analysts had agreed on something. A box on the front page of the next day's *Globe* carried a quote from one of M.R.A.G.'s members, Manford Mallory, to the effect that the only thing mining analysts could usually agree upon was to order a beer.

Now, ten years later, Inco is meeting M.R.A.G. again, and the program chairman, the resourceful Terry Ortslan, has even got Inco to pick up the tab. Dr. Sopko and Mr. Hand walk us through a well-organized, coherent presentation. Their main messages are:

1. They mean what they had said to the Government of Newfoundland and Labrador: that it was no longer feasible to build a smelter and refinery in Newfoundland to process ores from the Voisey's Bay nickel deposit in Labrador.

2. That there's a lot more to Inco than Voisey's Bay.

I'm convinced that Inco means what it says. I wonder what my colleagues think. So, during the question period, I ask for a show of hands from M.R.A.G. members: Does anyone think Inco is bluffing? Not one hand goes up.

Two and a half hours later, M.R.A.G. reassembles around the same table. Thanks to magical timing on the part of Mr. Ortslan, we are now to hear from the Government of Newfoundland and Labrador. Bill Rowat and Bruce Hollett walk us through another well-organized, coherent presentation. Their main message is that, if Inco is not prepared to live up to its promises and build a smelter and refinery in Newfoundland, the province will not grant it the right to mine Voisey's Bay ore. Again, I poll my colleagues: Does anyone think the government is bluffing? No one.

After the meeting, I bump into Bruce Hollett in the washroom, say I'll see him in St. John's in a few weeks at the Voisey's Bay environmental hearings, and walk out into an unseasonably warm day. I think of a telephone conference call Inco hosted on March 27, 1996. Inco's senior executives were then looking forward confidently to emerging triumphant from a battle with their archrivals across the street at Falconbridge Limited. Dr. Sopko said that he was about to consummate "one of the most important transactions in Inco's history," the acquisition of Diamond Fields Resources. Diamond Fields owned the 75% of the Voisey's Bay deposit that Inco did not already own. Dr. Sopko was optimistic that he could complete the acquisition that May. He was also confident that Inco could be processing Voisey's Bay ore as early as 1998.

May 1996 came and went. Inco was not able to complete its takeover of Diamond Fields until August of that year.

It was now September 1998, and the subsoil of Voisey's Bay remained undisturbed.

Inco had won the contest, but it didn't seem to know how to unwrap its prize.

What had gone wrong?

INCO

CHAPTER 1

A GEOLOGICAL ECONOMIST

Mrs. Wright, you sure would please us,
By noting we don't sit like cheeses.
— *Panui*, 1965 yearbook of Heretaunga College, New Zealand

After a few good years of ... pounding stakes into mosquito-ridden moose pasture, the romance of the field starts to pale. So seasoned miners head back to school, get their MBAs, then flock to Bay Street.
— Andrew Willis, *The Globe and Mail*, July 5, 2005

Organisms "discount the future" when they value imminent goods over future goods.
— Wilson and Daly, 2003

Ralph Miller, M.Sc., Vice-Principal, strode along the corridors of Heretaunga College, preceded by a bristling moustache and closely followed by a billowing black academic gown. His bright eyes flicked from side to side in search of transgressions of the college's intricate code of conduct, but his mind was probably on greater matters. A man whose vision and imagination were not fully appreciated by the students in his charge, he may have been contemplating his plan to expand Heretaunga College's annual rummage sale into a southern hemispheric equivalent — smaller, mind you, but as exciting as the original would be — of Montreal's Expo '67. Or perhaps he was planning his political career in which, under the inspired slogan "Vote for Ralph Miller, M.Sc.," he would stand for election as member of parliament for Heretaunga. Or perhaps he was contemplating his reorganization of the college's daily morning assembly.

When I first entered Heretaunga College (a co-educational high school), we lowly Third Formers stood at each morning assembly in the front of the sweaty, smelly school gym, facing the teaching staff and closely watched by prefects for signs of motion, talking, slouching, or slovenliness. As the years passed and we advanced through the ranks of the school, our position in the gym moved toward the rear. By the time I was in the Sixth Form, I had gained both an impressive set of varicose veins and the right to stand at the very back of the gym, where one was generally observed by neither teachers nor prefects. At least, I *would* have had this right but, after years of rummage sales, the college had been able to construct a proper assembly hall which, unlike the gym, was equipped with seats. Each morning, the teaching staff would traipse onto the stage of the assembly hall and, despite some jostling for spots partially concealed by curtains and therefore preferred, sat on display to some 800 students.

Ralph Miller, M.Sc., thought it a shame that the school's most prestigious pupils, those in the Upper Sixth Form,[2] were not also on display. Thus, early in the school year he announced that the Upper Sixth Form would henceforth occupy the front row at assembly so that our mature demeanour would commend itself to the members of the lower forms who, admittedly, could see only the backs of our heads. We Upper Sixth Formers, jealous of our hard-won privileges, were understandably outraged by Mr. Miller's directive. Through our favourite teacher, Mrs. Wright, we conveyed our concerns to Mr. Miller, who agreed to a frank exchange of views.

"The real reason that you are opposed to this change," said Mr. Miller, "is that you, as is typical of young people, are a bunch of hidebound conservatives!"

"Sir," rejoined Upper Sixth Former Ross Wilson, "the real reason for our aversion to sitting in the front row is, in fact, that we find ourselves staring up at Mrs. Wright's legs."

I would like to report that, the next day, we found ourselves seated in the back row of the assembly hall. But we were not. Dustin Hoffman had yet to perform in *The Graduate*, a movie about a relationship between a young man and a fortyish babe, and Ralph Miller, M.Sc., apparently did not perceive that there could be anything improper in Ross Wilson's gaze.

I had written an essay in primary school in which I stated that my ambition in life was to become an industrial chemist and emigrate to America, and I believe I still held this ambition as I entered the Upper

Sixth. That year, however, I discovered that my favourite subject was geography. It was also the subject in which I earned my best marks in the year-end, nationwide exams, which was astonishing because the geography teacher had been absent for most of that year. In fact, his absence allowed me to pursue a growing interest in the geology of the country around Heretaunga, a distant suburb of Wellington. Although Wellington is blessed with astoundingly boring rocks, its landforms are some of the most interesting on the planet: faults major and minor; terraces marine and alluvial; grabens, half-grabens, and horsts; peneplanes dissected, buried, and partially exhumed.

In the mid-1960s, Victoria University of Wellington's programs were table d'hôte rather than the cafeteria style more popular today. Still with a career as an industrial chemist in mind, but wavering, my first-year university program consisted of Mathematics I, Physics I, Chemistry I, and, because of my experience in the Upper Sixth, Geology I. By the end of my second year at Victoria, I knew that I no longer wanted to be an industrial chemist, and, in my third and final year, I needed only to complete a third-year geology course to graduate with a Bachelor of Science. This left room for another course, so, in part encouraged by a cute red-haired economics student, I added a course in economics. This turned out to be my best subject, and my unheard-of combination of courses prompted my relatives to jest that I was going to be a geological economist or an economic geologist or some damn thing. This eventually turned out to be the case, although my interest in economics lay dormant for more than a decade while I undertook employment and further studies in geology.

In 1977, my red-haired wife tapped me on the shoulder and said it was time to choose between her and the bush and the bogs of northern Canada. I made the right choice and, with her help, found a job as a financial analyst with an investment dealer, Canavest House Limited in Toronto. Canavest was dedicated to quantitative analysis of stocks and stock markets and, in fact, had on its board a future Nobel laureate in economics, Bill Sharpe. I had to learn, very quickly, a lot more about economics and finance.

There are many ways to value stocks, but the approach I learned at Canavest is the one I use in this book. One of Canavest's principals, Keith Ambachtsheer ("take it one syllable at a time and it's easy to pronounce") explained it as follows: "We're not going to pay you very much now." (I silently dissented, knowing that Canavest was offering to pay me more than my last employer, a mining exploration company. But what seems like a big salary on Troisième Avenue, Val d'Or, shrinks on Bay Street, Toronto.)

"Say I withhold a dollar of your salary this year and promise to pay you more next year, how much more should I give you in twelve months?"

I contemplated interest rates, then rising through the teens, and the risk that poor markets might force Keith to go back on his word, and said, "Oh, about $1.25."

"OK," said Keith, "if you think a dollar in your hand today is as good as an offer by me to pay you $1.25 a year from now, you're saying that the discount rate appropriate to my promise to pay is 25%.[3] Or, another way to put it is that my offer to pay you $1.25 next year has a Net Present Value — its value today — of $1.00 at a discount rate of 25%. Net Present Values are just a mathematical way of saying 'the sooner, the better.' And a stock is just a package of implied promises to make a series of future payments to the owner of that stock."

"How so?"

"Through dividends. If a company promised to pay you a dividend of a dollar a year for the next ten years, and then wind itself up with a residual value of zero, the value of your share of the company would be the sum of the Net Present Values of those ten dividends. And if another company were to promise to pay you a dollar dividend every year forever, the value of your share of that company would be the sum of the Net Present Values of that infinite number of dividends."

I didn't question Keith's last comment because I recalled, from maths class at Heretaunga College, that the sum of an infinite series of numbers need not be infinitely large. (Indeed, the net present value of a dollar to be paid more than a couple of decades in the future becomes vanishingly small.) But I did ask "How would you value Dome Petroleum?" Dome Pete was a prominent company whose flamboyant chairman, Jack Gallagher, had vowed to pour all available cash into the Beaufort Sea and to never pay a dividend.

"Same idea," said Keith. "You assume that eventually someone will take him over and estimate how much the acquirer will be willing to pay Dome Pete's shareholders for those shares. Find the Net

Present Value of that payment, and you have the true value of Dome Pete's shares today.

"So, Ray, this is what I want you to do. No company will make you promises about the size of dividends they're going to pay between now and the end of time. And they certainly won't tell you when they expect to be taken over and at what price. So your job is to *estimate* those future payments, then select an appropriate discount rate so you can calculate the Net Present Values of each of those payments, then add up all those Net Present Values. If that sum is more than the current price of the stock, you tell people to buy it. If it's *less* than the price of the stock, you tell them to sell it. Simple process, right?"

That "simple process" is the basis of this book.

CHAPTER 2

DISCOVERY OF VOISEY'S BAY

The Provincial Geologists Medal is awarded to recognize major [scientific] contributions ... [by] Canada's provincial and territorial Geological Surveys. Each Survey may nominate a candidate each year ... the winner of the inaugural Provincial Geologists Medal was A. Bruce Ryan of the Geological Survey of Newfoundland and Labrador. Bruce's landmark 1990 geological map of the Nain region, together with a remarkably prescient model for the origin of the Voisey's Bay nickel-copper-cobalt deposit, formed the foundation for the exploration rush that followed the discovery.
— Press Release by the Department of Mines and Energy, Government of Newfoundland and Labrador, from the 56th annual Energy and Mines Ministers Conference, Charlottetown, P.E.I., September 13, 1999

February 3, 1996

"May I speak to David Barr, please?"

"Speaking ... is that you, Ray?"

"Greetings, Dave! Is now a good time for that chat?"

"Perfect! As I pointed out in my letter, Ray, I've been working on my autobiography. I have a draft in front of me."

"Glad you don't mind my tapping your brain, Dave. Your idea that there might be a big copper-nickel deposit in Labrador seems awfully prescient, given what's been happening there in the past two years."

"Yes, before our trip there in 1970, I don't think anyone had thought it worthwhile to prospect for base metals on the coast of Labrador."

"So, how did you come up with the idea, Dave?"

"Well, like you, the first job I had after graduating with a geology degree was a summer job with Kennco.⁴"

"Uh huh, I'd worked with Kennecott in New Zealand a year or so before you hired me for a summer job with Kennco in Canada."

Dave continues. "My summer job in 1950 was to supervise a small field party searching for copper-nickel mineralization in northwestern Ontario.⁵ Planning for the project had not been particularly thorough, to say the least. When we assembled in Port Arthur to initiate the program, we found that none of us had a driver's licence! So we were delayed for two days while I learned to drive. Fortunately, my examiner overlooked a few minor deficiencies in my rather brief experience and passed me. The rest of my recollections of that summer are mostly of days spent trying to push myself through thick groves of alders."

"I remember when you called me in July 1970, Dave, telling me that you wanted me to work with you in Labrador. I was so relieved because I'd just spent six weeks cursing alders on that project you sent me on in northwestern Ontario! Anyway, we didn't find any mineralization there .... Did you?"

"Oh, yes, we found three prospects that I thought were worth further exploration by diamond drilling. One of them was eventually picked up by another company, Great Lakes Nickel, which proved up some 100 million tonnes grading 0.4% copper and 0.2% nickel plus precious metals. If it ever does go into production, it will probably be because of those precious metals — platinum, palladium, and gold.

"Anyway," continues Dave, "by 1969 I had long been working for Kennco full-time. The company sent me to South Africa to see the Bushveld Igneous Complex, which is a vast mafic intrusion that hosts mines that produce platinum, palladium, nickel, chrome, and iron, as well as other metals. I began to wonder: Could there be a Bushveld in Canada that everyone has missed? When I returned home, I began to search the geological literature, and I found that there were three large mafic intrusions in eastern Labrador – Kiglapait, Harp Lake, and Michikamau – all of which seemed to have the same shape and the same kinds of rocks as the Bushveld. I couldn't find much information on their exploration potential, which was great news — it meant the field was open to us! I decided to start by visiting the Kiglapait intrusion, the smallest and most northerly of the three, with a surface area of about 500 square kilometres. Now, a fellow called Stearns Morse, who was a geologist from Franklin and Marshall College in Pennsylvania, had mapped the area in the '60s. From his reports, we found that there was a shack that we could probably use in a place called Village Bay, on the east side of the Kiglapait intrusion."

"As I remember it, Dave, when I got your call, I left my assistant, Max Baker, behind in Thunder Bay and flew to Toronto."

"Max ... ah, yes, Max. He was a Newfoundlander, wasn't he?"

"Yes, from bonny Botwood, the first Newf I'd met and a true gentleman."

"Have you kept in touch with him?"

"Sad story. I met his cousin in St. John's, John Baker, who does some legal work for mining companies. John said that Max went to work for the feds in Ottawa; they moved him out your way, to Vancouver, where he died around 1990. Always a shock to find that someone you think of as a contemporary has not been with us for years."

"It is. It makes me wonder if I'll be around by the time you finish your book on Voisey's!"

"Now, Dave, the party leaving Toronto consisted of you, Dave McAuslan, Tom Webster, and me, right?"

"Right," says Dave, "we flew from Toronto to Goose Bay on ... on August 1, 1970, on Eastern Provincial Airlines. And thank you, Ray, for sending me that stunning photo."

I chuckle, recalling my photograph of a leggy Eastern Provincial Airlines stewardess at work in a microminiskirt.

"Everyone who sees that picture today, Dave, is astonished that stewardesses dressed like that in 1970!"

"And the next day we chartered a float plane from Eastern Provincial, an Otter, to fly us up to Nain ..."

"... and we loaded it with so much stuff, the pilot needed to use several miles of Lake Melville to take off!"

I recall that flight, beginning over flat, timbered land just like the country west of Thunder Bay where Max and I had been working. As the Otter ground its way north, steep-sided, flat-topped hills began to appear and, on the flat-tops, the trees began to shrink and disappear.

Then a maze of steep cliffs, fjords, and forested valley bottoms, splashes as the plane's floats hit the sea, and we'd reached Nain.

"When we were in Nain, Ray, it had a population of 800 people, mostly English and Inuit. It seemed that most of them came down to the dock to look us over!"

"There seemed to be almost as many sled dogs as people — the poor dogs were sweltering in the 10°C heat when we were there."

"We docked at a long pier extending into the bay," says Dave. "At the foot of the pier was a church - though probably not the original building.[6] In my later research, I found that the original church would've been built in 1771 by the Moravian missionaries — Protestants. My dominant impression of Nain was a huddle of white buildings with red, blue, and occasional green roofs, all within a few hundred metres of the shore, surrounded by spruce trees, then scrub and bare rock on the higher ground.

"We found a local fellow," he continues, "Henry Webb, who agreed to transport our barrels of aviation gas in his dory, 'down the shore,'[7] as he put it, to Village Bay."

"He and his wife had just got back from their first week 'outside,'" I add. "It was supposed to have been three weeks in Florida, but they came back after two because they missed Nain so much!"

"And then we continued flying north in the Otter without the av. gas. We landed and beached the Otter at Village Bay. Village Bay was uninhabited, but the shack was still there. Tom Webster immediately began to set up a kitchen and bedroom in the shack; the rest of us slept in a couple of tents."

"Marvellous setting, wasn't it?"

"Oh, yes, spectacular!" replies Dave. "There was a little iceberg floating in the bay and, immediately to the west, the central part of the Kiglapait intrusion rising to an elevation of about 1,000 metres. The campsite itself was a broad, grass-covered area, partly surrounded by boulders and sandhills, with a profusion of wildflowers, cotton grass, and Labrador tea. There were still broad patches of snow scattered throughout the mountains to the west, and on the ancient, raised beaches, which ran along the coast like flights of stairs.

"The next morning Henry Webb arrived with our load of av. gas — probably before you'd got up!"

"Well, there *is* a two-hour time difference between Labrador and the part of northwestern Ontario I was in, Dave."

"And our helicopter hadn't arrived, so I decided to make use of Henry Webb and his dory on his return journey to Nain."

"You'd been in the exploration business long enough, Dave, to know that late helicopters get later!"

"True. Henry agreed to take me back along the shoreline to the south to a point about 10 kilometres south of our camp, near the southern end of the Kiglapait intrusion. We stayed close to shore, as I wanted to be sure that, if I had to follow parts of it back to Village Bay, I would recognize where I was. Henry was somewhat apprehensive about dropping me off. 'Are you sure you'll be all right?' he asked. I assured him, appreciating his concern, but assumed that it was a natural reaction for a seafaring man considering a landlubber contending with the vagaries of terra infirma. I set off, equipped with my usual field gear, which included aerial photos.

"By the end of the day, I was within a kilometre of camp and looking forward to dinner. With a steep mountain rising above me, I was eventually forced to traverse immediately above the shoreline until I reached a cliff face dropping into the sea. Checking the air photo, I realized that there was a 50- to 100-metre-wide cliff spur separating me from what I recalled to be accessible ground beyond.

"I couldn't believe what I was seeing. Finally it dawned on me that I was looking at high tide, compared to low tide earlier. I considered my options. I could wait for low tide when it would be dark. And I had no flashlight. I could walk back to the south, climb the mountain above me, then descend to camp, without any guidance as to the distances and time involved. I finally gambled on what I could see on the aerial photos and recollection of what I saw from the dory.

"So I put my camera, aerial photos, and compass in my pack and I lowered myself into the sea, which was fortunately quite tranquil, and set off holding my packsack above my head and paddling vigorously with my other arm. At what I believed to be the halfway point, I thought 'I'm not going to make it.' It was so cold. The alternative must have seemed worse, because I kept going and, by good fortune, reached a spot where I could wade ashore.

"Again I was most fortunate, for it was still sunny. I stripped quickly and was still wringing out clothing when I heard a *whissh!* to seaward. I turned and saw the spray from the blowhole of a whale not more than 70 metres away. I put my clothes back on and continued back to camp. I remember you were all very concerned."

"Yeah, we were wondering who would sign our paycheques."

"I think that the helicopter, a G-2 with floats, arrived the next day. We'd chartered it from Universal Helicopters out of Gander, Newfoundland."

"Just looking at the picture you took of me in front of that machine makes me shudder. I flew around in that?"

"Yes, you did, Ray! I remember the pilot, Fred Wagner, kept making reference to the 'Jesus nut' at the top of the rotor, which allegedly kept the whole thing from falling apart. He mentioned it whenever the wind was blowing hard. There must have been a mechanic with Fred, but I don't recall his name."

"There *was* a mechanic — he's in a group photo I took — but I don't remember his name either. Universal Helicopters is still in business, and I sent them a copy of my picture, but they weren't able to help. So we know the names of only five of the six people in the first exploration party to look for the Voisey's Bay deposit."

"And that party was blessed with six clear days, enough to cover the entire Kiglapait. Fred would drop off each of us individually on one side of the intrusion and would pick us up later on the other side."

"Then it was my turn, Dave, to worry you!"

"Oh, yes, the watch incident!"

I had been wearing a watch, which I'd just had repaired at a real bargain price on Yonge Street in Toronto. On our second or third day at Kiglapait, I wandered across the mountains, sampling and mapping, entranced by the bonsai trees and cotton grass bogs, snowbanks with icicle-lined caves and crevices, curious "deer,"[8] whales breaching, icebergs, and the beautiful glacial erratic boulders of glossy blue chatoyant (iridescent) labradorite. I failed to notice that the watch was running at — oh, about a quarter of the speed it was supposed to be running. So, when my 4:45 helicopter pickup time came, I was missing in action. All evening I heard and saw the helicopter flying long traverses over my work area and wondered what the pilot was doing. But it was only as the sun began to set that I realized he was looking for me.

"On our way back in the Otter we must have stopped in Nain because I recall we gave a woman with a sick baby a lift to Goose Bay."

"And I took a picture of you on the plane: scruffy, unshaven, and asleep."

"Funny, women I show that picture to today say 'Oh, Goldie, you looked so cute!' How come none of them expressed that opinion at the time?"

"Beats me," deadpans Dave.

"Before we left Village Bay," says Dave, "Fred Wagner caught several Arctic char, up to nine pounds. Fred kindly donated one of these to me, caught the day before we left Village Bay. I had the fish frozen overnight in Goose Bay ..."

"And," I interject, "on the flight out of Goose, you seized the official Eastern Provincial Airlines ice bucket from the stewardess, stowed the fish inside, and sat with it all the way back to Toronto. As soon as you reached TO, you called your wife and suggested she make appropriate reservations with her favourite seafood restaurant."

"Funny, I don't remember the ice bucket. I remember only wrapping it up in my sleeping bag for insulation ... I must have done that once I'd reclaimed my sleeping bag at Toronto airport. Boy, did we have an incredible amount of camping equipment! Tom Webster and I managed to stuff it all into his station wagon and drove off on Highway 401 en route to my home in Etobicoke. As Tom drove, both of us became aware of the odour of decaying fish. We immediately attributed it to the char in my sleeping bag, but before we committed ourselves to action, the truck in front of us turned off and the odour disappeared. And, yes, it *was* a memorable dinner! How about you, Ray, did you bring back any souvenirs?"

"In those long evenings in northwestern Ontario, Dave, I'd been writing letters and arranged to get myself married! So while you were getting your fish frozen in Goose, I was out the back buying a couple of bottles of 'Screech'[9] for the wedding punch. But, I guess, other than fish and rum, we returned empty-handed ..."

"No, we ... oh, you'd gone back to school by the time the assays[10] came back. Ray, we found mineralization grading 0.1% to 0.2% copper and 0.04% nickel, no precious metals, across thicknesses of 8 to 15 metres. That's not economic, but it wasn't bad for a week's reconnaissance in an area where no one had ever before found copper-nickel mineralization. I was encouraged that coastal Labrador had the potential to host copper-nickel-platinum ore bodies and, since getting my feet wet at Kiglapait, I focused on the Harp Lake mafic intrusion, which covered an area twenty times greater than Kiglapait. Harp Lake is about 150 kilometres south of Nain. I assigned Dave McAuslan to supervise a month-long helicopter reconnaissance program at Harp Lake, which David ran in August and September of 1971. Dave identified 13 mineralized zones at Harp Lake; the best graded 0.6% copper, 0.08% nickel, and 0.03% cobalt over 4 feet. He also noted that all the mineralized samples had been partially leached of their mineralization, so surface samples weren't a reliable indicator of grade."

I sit up sharply in my chair. "That's fascinating! Dave, you know, the surface mineralization at Voisey's Bay was leached too. I didn't appreciate that when Diamond Fields found it. And because of that, I didn't believe in Voisey's right away."

"Well," says Dave, "Dave McAuslan and I were encouraged by these results, and we approached the Newfoundland Government with the intent of obtaining a concession over the Harp Lake mafic intrusion. They granted it to us on June 3, 1972. But history had intervened."

"Allende?"

"Yes," says Dave.

"In July 1971, Chile's Allende government had completed the nationalization of the Chilean mines and smelters of Kennco's parent, Kennecott. Although Kennecott had been compensated for a previous, partial nationalization, Allende did not compensate Kennecott in the final phase. So, in November 1971, when it came time for Kennecott's annual budget exercises, money was tight. Kennco's 1972 Harp Lake project was not approved. So I offered a joint venture proposal to seventeen companies. Chevron Oil and Selco Mining Corp. Ltd. accepted, and work continued under Dave McAuslan's supervision in the summers of 1972 and 1973 from a base camp established at Dave's Pond in the east-central part of the intrusion."

"Nice coincidence in the name!"

"No coincidence. Ron Emslie of the Geological Survey of Canada was mapping the area while we were there, and Kennco gave him some helicopter support. In return, he officially named the lake after Dave McAuslan. I sent you a copy of a letter I had from Dave McAuslan. Has it reached you yet?"

"Yes, I have it in front of me," I say. "My favourite story was the one about the camp cook!"

Dave McAuslan's letter read:

> Ed Butler from St. John's was the cook at Dave's Pond in 1973. I hired him on the recommendation of Canada Manpower in St. John's. He arrived with two very heavy suitcases which I lugged to the cook tent. He was an alcoholic and the suitcases were full of Screech. He did his drinking secretly at first but was eventually found out by Réjean Dallaire the helicopter mechanic. Réjean was in camp during the day and found Ed incapable to make lunch. Réjean somehow sobered Ed up whereupon Ed asked him for help. Ed told Réjean that he was terrified of the bush and if the booze was put somewhere out in the woods he would not touch it. Réjean hid the screech a mere 50 feet from the tent and Ed never went near it for the rest of the summer. He was thereafter an acceptable cook with an amazing collection of jokes and was an incredibly crooked cribbage player (things like "15-2, 15-4 and a pair make 8" ... but so quick you would never notice). Ed once in a while after dinner would say "party tonight Dave?" and if it seemed appropriate a bottle would be fetched.

"It was a busy program," says Dave Barr. "From the air McAuslan and his crew looked for 'gossans' — rusty zones, the same thing that led Albert Chislett and Chris Verbiski to the Voisey's Bay discovery more than twenty years later. They found about 70 mineralized gossans, which they followed up with geophysical surveys, trenching and sampling.

"I visited Harp Lake in 1972 and 1973," he continues. "It was similar to, but less austere than, Kiglapait, with far more vegetation and lakes — well, we'd call them 'lakes,' the Newfoundlanders called them 'ponds.' Harp Lake itself had impressive cliffs on the very edge of the lake.

"On one occasion, Dave McAuslan and I visited two prospectors who were working for us in a partly timbered area. One commented ironically on his and his colleague's bush-beaten appearance: 'Yes, boy'oh; we's s'wave and d'bonner!' Dave and I sat chatting around a fire at their camp and Dave commented on the size of the firewood they had been able to cut from a spruce they had felled. Trees were quite scarce, so we were surprised to see blocks 30 centimetres wide. We cut several slabs off one of the blocks and I later sanded and polished one of them to accentuate the growth rings. The tree was over four hundred years old! I also took a sample of one of the stakes which the prospectors had cut to mark survey lines. It was young: only a hundred and fifty years old! After that, we cautioned everyone to cut as few trees as they could."

"Dave, what happened to the program after 1973?"

"I don't know. The joint venture agreement on the Harp Lake project was terminated, oh, I don't know when — 1974 or 1975. I'd left Kennco to join DuPont Canada in January 1974."

"Oh, that's right, you found the Baker gold mine for them, didn't you? In northern B.C.?"

"Yes, I was *one* of those involved with the discovery and early exploration of Baker, but my role was more in arranging for Dupont to option the property from Kennco in 1974; then I saw it through to production in 1980. And, of course, Dave McAuslan went on to work for Shell Canada, and to discover the East Kemptville tin deposit in Nova Scotia. How about you, Ray; did you ever find anything which became a mine?"

"I'm afraid the short answer is 'no.' But I came close! In the summer of 1974 I was again a summer student — this time with Texasgulf — and I worked on a series of projects in northwestern British Columbia. Texasgulf had hired me because I was writing my thesis on the Noranda mining district of Quebec, and TG's management thought they had Noranda-type geology at a place called Tom Mackay Lake on the Prout plateau. At least, *we* called the property 'Tom Mackay Lake.' In 1991, I went to a talk at the Prospectors' Convention about the hottest new discovery in Canada — an incredibly rich gold-silver deposit called Eskay Creek — and, when they showed a geological map of Eskay Creek, I nearly yelled from my chair, 'That's my map! Of Tom Mackay Lake!'"

"And *was* it your map, Ray?"

"Well, it could have been. Nothing to stop anyone from copying it once it's made its way into the government's assessment files. But the rocks wouldn't have changed since 1974, and another geologist could well have come up with the same map as me. Anyway, my biggest consolation was that the ore body was nowhere exposed at surface, so at least I hadn't stepped on it and not seen it."

"Did Texasgulf drill it?" asks Dave.

"I thought that they should. I did find the geology to be similar to Noranda's geology, and we now know that the ore body is located where you might expect to find a Noranda-type deposit. But I went back to school in October and, like you at Harp Lake, I don't know what happened, but I've heard they put in just one hole.

"And my experience with Kennecott in New Zealand had an interesting ending, too. We'd been looking for metals, but found asbestos. I never gave any thought to the possible economic value of asbestos and, again, I lost touch after I left the company. But I've since found out[11] that Kennecott withdrew in 1972."

"Allende, again."

"Yes," I say, "but Kennecott returned in a joint venture much like the one you set up at Harp Lake. In 1973, Kennecott came back with Cassiar Asbestos of Canada and Lime and Marble Ltd., a local New Zealand firm. Apparently, they carved out a substantial road before the project ran out of steam. I don't know what finally killed the project — probably a combination of local environmental opposition and the collapse of asbestos markets as people realized what filthy stuff it is."

"Well, to go back to the Labrador story," says Dave. "As far as I know, there was no more geological or mining exploration in the area until 1984, when the Geological Survey of Newfoundland and Labrador mapped a large part of north-central Labrador and discovered a large, previously unrecognized mafic intrusion, which they named the 'Reid Brook intrusion,' midway between the Kiglapait and Harp Lake mafic intrusions. The Survey released its maps, and mining companies responded with a total lack of interest. Everyone 'knew' the coast of Labrador had no mineral potential. So, in 1993, when two struggling prospectors, Albert Chislett and Chris Verbiski from St. John's, Newfoundland, were grubstaked by Diamond Fields Resources to look for diamonds, as well as gold and base metals in eastern Labrador, they had no competitors.

"In September, Chislett and Verbiski were prospecting on the northwest side of Voisey's Bay about 35 kilometres southwest of Nain when they noticed a gossan: rusty rocks. Within fifteen minutes of reaching the gossan, they had chipped away the leached zone and found fresh rock with copper mineralization .... Ray, when did you hear about the discovery?"

"It was that winter, 1994. There's always exploration going on somewhere. It usually amounts to nothing, but you keep up with the press releases and every now and then something catches your eye. My competitor and colleague, John Lydall over at First Marathon Securities, knew Diamond Fields's management well and made sure I followed this one. Because of my experience in Labrador with you, Dave, I was predisposed to believe that Voisey's Bay was real even though the firm I worked for was not comfortable with Diamond Fields's promoter, Robert Friedland."

"You know, changing the subject a bit, the one thing that's made me unhappy about this discovery is how mean-spirited some people can be. Eric Finlayson, who was the Western Manager for Kennco's successor, Kennecott Canada Inc., has told me that he has heard several unflattering comments about how Kennco 'missed' Voisey's Bay. I was a little annoyed by this, so I wrote a letter to the editor of *The Northern Miner*, which they published on September 25, 1995, describing Kennco's contributions to the ultimate discoveries."

"And I've heard similar comments about Bruce Ryan," I respond. "He worked on that government geological mapping project in 1984 to 1987. He sampled the gossan on the ridge where Chislett and Verbiski later made their discovery, but Ryan's assays came back zero ... he seemed to have been bedevilled by that same leaching process that Dave McAuslan referred to.

"People forget two things," I continue. "Firstly, Bruce Ryan wasn't looking for a mine; he was a government geologist making a map. And secondly, that map was of enormous help to Chislett and Verbiski once they'd discovered the mineralization, because it occurred in troctolite,[12] and Ryan and his co-workers had carefully distinguished troctolites in blue on their map. Essentially, all Diamond Fields had to do to tie up all the prospective ground was to go to the mining recorder in St. John's and claim all the areas underlain by 'blue' rocks! I was at a Diamond Fields meeting in June 1995 when Ed Mercaldo, the company's Chief Financial Officer, said that that was exactly what Diamond Fields did. Before announcing the discovery, they staked claims on all of the known troctolites in Labrador."

"Have you ever been back to northern Labrador, Ray?"

"So far, just once, Dave."

CHAPTER 3

KEEPING UP WITH LIZ

The miner ignorant and unskilled in the art digs out the ore without careful discrimination while the learned and experienced miner first assays and proves it, and when he finds the veins either too narrow and hard or too wide and soft, he infers therefrom that these cannot be mined profitably and so works only the approved ones.
— Agricola, 1556

There's another story that says the Great Creator made this earth in six days and spent the seventh day tossing rocks at [Labrador].
— White, 2003

Late November 1994; Diamond Fields's share price at $8.60.[13]

"Ray, can you come over here sometime soon? Himself has become agitated by this Diamond Fields thing in Labrador and he wants you to give me your opinion. Says you're the only person on Bay Street who can't tell a lie."

"Gee, *thanks*, Liz ... I think! Ah ... yes, I do have some problems with that discovery ..."

"We don't. Can you come over and show me how you'd value a mining property, and the Diamond Fields one in particular?"

"Well, Diamond Fields is a Friedland company, and it's been made pretty clear to me that, given Robert Friedland's background — he once promoted Galactic Resources and, as one journalist put it, he's famous 'for being in no way responsible for the financial and environmental mess which Galactic left behind' — we don't want to publish recommendations on any of his stocks."

"I hear you. You're saying that any work you do for me can only be for me. OK. We'll make sure you get paid somehow. Don't worry. When can you come over?"

"Um, tomorrow, at 10?"

"OK. Bye!"

Interesting. "Himself" — Liz's boss — had become wealthy by prudently and patiently investing in mining stocks whose potential he recognized while others didn't. I get to work.

The next day, I sit in Liz's waiting room clutching a bag full of papers, pens, and a calculator. Promptly at 10:20, the receptionist ushers me into the boardroom, where I lay out my materials. A few minutes later Liz, breathless, bangles jangling, joins me.

"What do you have here, Ray?"

"This is the most recent press release from Diamond Fields, the one dated November 17, 1994. Blah, blah, blah ... 'Diamond Fields is pleased to report that assay results of core samples recovered from the four drill holes confirm a significant nickel, copper, cobalt discovery at the Voisey's Bay, Labrador project. The Company's discovery is located 35 kilometres southwest of Nain on the east coast of Labrador and is approximately 10 kilometres from deep tide water.' Then they give the assays, which I've plotted up on this extra-long piece of graph paper: Hole 1 intersected 40.5 metres of 0.83% nickel, 0.63% copper, and 0.042% cobalt. Three hundred metres away, Hole 4."

"Guess they didn't drill the holes in any kind of order."

"Actually, I think they had an idea that this was a long, thin structure they wanted to test, so they poked down Holes 1 and 2 at each end and, when it looked like they'd hit something, put down Holes 3 and 4 in between to test its continuity: Hole 4 intersected 10.5 metres of 0.74% nickel, 0.45% copper, and 0.038% cobalt. Another 200 metres and you come to Hole 3, 36.0 metres grading 0.87% nickel, 0.62% copper, and 0.046% cobalt. Finally, 200 more metres along the structure, Hole 2 with 71.0 metres of 2.23% nickel, 1.47% copper, and 0.123% cobalt."

"How do you evaluate all that?"

"Well, the grades are interesting. In Sudbury, INCO is mining ore which averages about 1.2% nickel, 1.1% copper, and something like 0.04% cobalt. But these results worry me. If the mineralization is real, it stretches for 300, plus 200, plus 200 — 700 metres — and in all cases it's less than 60 metres below the surface. It's pretty hard to believe that anything could be that long and that shallow without parts of it being exposed at the surface. Ore bodies don't have straight edges; they twist and bend and bulge."

"How do you know it *doesn't* come to the surface?"

"Well, there's a rumour that what they're drilling is bare rock with no glacial overburden. The usual practice would be to blast some trenches in that bare rock and take samples from them. But there's no mention of surface samples. It would be a lot more comforting if there were, and you could see the mineralization in place."

"What if the surface samples were so — what's the word you use — weathered?"

"Yes."

"So weathered that all the mineralization had been washed away?"

"That's pretty unlikely, Liz. That area has been scraped clean and polished by glaciers, and I'll bet the glaciers left not much more than 10,000 years ago.[14] Any time I've seen this kind of mineralization — I assume it's sulphide mineralization — in glaciated areas, it's sitting at the surface nice and clean."

"Humour me, Ray. Himself has an old friend in the business who assures him that there really are those kinds of grades in those drill cores. What would that mineralization be worth?"

Hmm. Himself's friends in the mining industry rarely lead him astray.

"I did do some work on the assumption that it's real."

I lay out sheets showing my calculations.

"There are several steps: estimating how much mineralization you have; approximating a mine plan based on what you have; calculating the cash flows from such a mine, and finally; calculating the Net Present Value of those cash flows."

"OK, first step. Estimate how much mineralization you have."

"Er — I should have said 'guess.' You can't *estimate* the size of a three-dimensional body based on four holes poked through it."

"Well, *guess*, Goldie."

"If the mineralization is continuous — a big 'if' — what they've drilled so far is long and thin, like a bootlace. Not many ore bodies are shaped like that. It's more likely that they've just pierced the top of it and the whole thing is shaped more like a thin vertical slab, like the black slab in the movie *2001*, or like a slim book balanced on its spine.

We know the slab is *at least* 700 metres long; let's just say 700. How thick is it?"

"The length of the drill intersections, surely."

"Not if they cut the slab at an angle. If you drill a hole into a book at an angle, the hole is longer than if it goes through perpendicularly. But from the press release it looks as if they hit the mineralized zone pretty well at right angles, so let's use the length of the drill intersections to approximate the thickness of the slab. So that's two dimensions. The third dimension is tougher. How deep is it? If it *is* shaped like a book, it could be hundreds of metres. I think we should just consider that which could be easily reached from an open pit — say, 100 metres. That means you've got 700 metres times the average thickness of the intersections ... which is?"

"Thirty-nine point five metres," says Liz, "times 700 metres times 100 metres, uh, 2.8 million cubic metres."

"Actually, my number was 2.3 million cubic metres because I put more weight on the lengths of the intersections in Holes 1, 4, and 3, since they're spread over a larger area and so are more likely to be representative than Hole 2 down at the end. I added on a few per cent to allow for the fact that the miners will inadvertently mine some waste rock along with the ore. Now, to turn that into a tonnage figure you need to know the density of the mineralized rock, which the press release says is a 'basic intrusive.' 'Basic' means the same thing as 'mafic.' The density of a 50:50 mixture of a 'basic intrusive' rock and sulphide mineralization would be about 3.93 tonnes per cubic metre."

"Three point nine three times 2.34 million cubic metres is 9.17 million tonnes of mineralization."

"Yeah, that's what I got. And the grade of that 9.17 million tonnes is the average of the assays, weighted for the lengths of each intersection and the spacing of each hole, and reduced by a few per cent to allow for that waste rock: 1.25% nickel, 0.85 copper, and 0.07% cobalt."

"Which is worth what?"

"There's a school of thought that says the best estimate of future metal prices is today's metal price ... so if you multiply those grades by today's metal prices, you get a gross value of $240 Canadian per tonne of this stuff ..."

"Not bad!"

"But a mine doesn't get paid for the gross value of its ore. Its revenues are based on something called 'Net Smelter Returns.' Here's a paper I've written on Net Smelter Returns.[15] A mine like Voisey's will treat its ore in a mill to produce what are called concentrates. Concentrates are the feedstock for smelters. Net Smelter Returns are what the smelter will pay the mine for its concentrate, once you allow for what's lost in processing, and once the shipping companies have taken their cut. For the kind of mineralization that Diamond Fields appears to have found, the average Net Smelter Return is 57% of the gross value of the mineralization."

"Are you sure it's that low? That means if I mine ore containing $100 worth of nickel I get paid only $57."

"Even lower than 57% if there are 'nasties' in the mineralization — things like arsenic, antimony, mercury, and selenium, which are toxic and expensive for a smelter to remove. A smelter will charge you penalties if the stuff you send them has lots of nasties. And just be thankful it's not a lead-zinc deposit. Lead-zinc Net Smelter Returns are usually around 33% of the gross value of the mineralization."

"Ouch. OK — 57% of $240 per tonne is ..."

"There's more, Liz. The press release says that someone else gets a 3% royalty on the Net Smelter Return."

"Which brings us down to $132 per tonne. Still not bad, actually. So you've completed your first step: You have 6.5 million tonnes of stuff worth $132 per tonne. What's next?"

"The 'mine plan.' The mineralization is shallow, so we'll assume an open pit mined over seven years. It'll take a while to get it permitted and financed, so I assume a start-up in 1998."

"Why a seven-year mine life?"

"Mostly because you want to get good use out of your equipment, and a lot of it tends to wear out after about seven years."

"Fine. Where's your valuation?"

"Here, on this spreadsheet. I've used some engineering manuals to very roughly estimate the costs, both of setting up the mine and concentrator and the costs of operating them."

I hand over the spreadsheets. Along the bottom line I had tabulated, year by year, estimates of the amount of cash thrown off by the project. In 1996 and 1997 those figures were negative, as the construction of the mine and mill eat up cash. Subsequently, the figures were positive. Then, following Keith Ambachtsheer's "simple process," I took the Net Present Value of these cash amounts, and found the project to be worth $358 million.

"What discount rate did you use in calculating this Net Present Value, Ray?"

"I used the historic rate of return on Canadian stocks, which has been the yield on long-term Government of Canada bonds plus 5.6 percentage points. That's about 15% per annum right now."

"Did you make any correction for beta?" Beta is a measure of the riskiness of a stock. Liz is referring to the Capital Asset Pricing Model, a means of valuing stocks which takes riskiness into account.

"I know you learn in school that you're supposed to do that, but I've seen some studies of returns on investment in Canadian stocks that show that risky stocks have *lower* rates of return than less risky stocks."

"Which is the opposite of what you'd expect."

"Which is the opposite of what the Capital Asset Pricing Model says, so I just use the average rate of the Canadian stock market as a whole, plus 5.6 points as a discount rate for all Canadian stocks, regardless of beta."

"Hmm. And you find the project to be worth $358 million. There are some 25.75 million Diamond Field shares outstanding ... um," she says and taps her calculator, "that's $13.90 per share. Is there anything else in the company besides this project?"

"There's some cash; doesn't seem to be any significant debt, and there are some diamond operations. I just assumed that the market wasn't paying anything for Voisey's Bay before this discovery, so the rest of the company is worth the price of the stock just before the discovery was announced: $5.63 per share."

"Giving you a total value of $13.90 plus $5.63," ... tap, tap, ... "or $19.53 per share."

I put up my hands. "Whoa. We're adding apples and oranges. Stocks — at least Canadian mining stocks — tend to trade at only about 70% of their Net Present Values. The best way I could demonstrate that to you would be to look at a company whose ore body has been mined out — the latter years of Steep Rock Iron Mines or Consolidated Rambler, for instance — and all that's left in the company is cash. If such a company was to have $1.00 per share in cash, its shares would trade at only about $0.70.

"I've never figured out why this is the case, but it is. The only time that stocks seem to trade at or near their Net Present Values is when they're the object of a takeover. It's a paradox: if a stock trades at $0.70, but is worth a dollar and is taken over at a dollar, why shouldn't it have traded at a dollar before the takeover? I don't know the answer, Liz."

"OK, then, your target price is 70% of $13.90 plus $5.63 — do you take 70% of that too?"

"No. Since it's where the stock was trading before they announced the discovery, the market should already have priced in that discount."

"So, $9.73 plus $5.63, equals $15.36. So you think this thing is worth something north of $15?"

"That's what it'd be worth if I had full confidence in my assumptions about the size of the deposit."

"But if they find more ore, it's worth more, right?"

"Ah, right."

"And if it gets taken over, it's worth $15.36 divided by 0.70, or $21.94. So why is the stock so cheap? Mr. Friedland's past?"

"It's not just the Friedland factor, Liz. Everyone 'knows' that the best place to find a nickel mine is beside another nickel mine, and there are no nickel mines in Labrador. That's the common wisdom, but don't buy it. I was on an exploration party which tried to find the damn thing back in 1970."

Liz's lips form a question.

"I was a summer student with Kennecott," I explain, "and one of the Kennecott people got the bright idea that Labrador seemed to have the right geology for South African–style copper-nickel-platinum mineralization. Unfortunately, we turned left at Nain. Shoulda turned right. ... And I guess the other reason why the stock is cheap, Liz, is that some people have the same concerns as me: if the mineralization is so extensive and so shallow, why don't the press reports tell us what it looks like at the surface? That's my biggest worry. So tell me, Liz, have you yet to buy the stock, or was this an exercise in making you feel more comfortable about something Himself has already bought for your fund?"

Wicked smile. "No comment. The main thing I needed to know was that the stock hasn't got ahead of itself, so as long as they keep finding more mineralization the stock'll keep going up."

On my way out of Liz's offices, I go over in my mind the factors which, I think, will drive Diamond Fields's stock in the future:

(a) Indications that the mineralization was larger than the slab I assumed would help the price.
(b) Indications that average grades were higher than I assumed would help.
(c) Because the "best estimate of future metal prices is today's metal price," higher metal prices should help.
(d) Indications of the presence of "nasties," like arsenic, would hurt.
(e) Indications of bonus metals, like platinum, would help.
(f) Indications that the costs of the project were higher than I'd assumed would hurt.
(g) Expectations that start-up of the mine would be delayed would hurt the stock, because the Net Present Value of cash in the future is less than the Net Present Value of cash in the hand.
(h) Higher interest rates would hurt because the Net Present Value of cash in the future declines when interest rates rise.
(i) Hints that another company was interested in taking over Diamond Fields should help the stock because it would erase some of the discount at which stocks trade when they are not the object of acquisition.
(j) And, finally, the stock would be helped by increased confidence that the discovery was real, despite the Friedland factor and despite my own concerns about the apparent failure of the mineralization to make an appearance at the surface.

In summary, what drives the price of the stock — any stock — is the expectation of how much money the stock is going to put in investors' pockets and how quickly it will put it there.

Early December 1994;
Diamond Fields's share price at $11.00[16]

A call, from John Lydall of First Marathon Securities, underwriters to Diamond Fields. John is an elongated engineer from Midlands of England, and has a pragmatic approach to life. Once, at a one o'clock meeting for mining analysts in the bowels of Toronto's Hilton Hotel, I wandered in expecting lunch, but found that our host, a junior mining company, had provided only coffee and cookies at the back of the room. As we sat waiting for the presentation to begin, clutching our coffee and cookies, all eyes turned to John Lydall and the big chicken salad sandwich in his hand.

"Hey, Lydall, where did you get that sandwich?"

"Oh, I got it from the software meeting across the hall."

John is the only person I know who can take a seven-hour nap on a six-hour flight, and who can sleep through all the dull bits of an annual meeting, waking up just in time for any quarrels or revelations.

John says that First Marathon has decided to address the Friedland factor by bringing in gruff, tough, crew-cut Jack McOuat, a veteran mining man, to talk to analysts and brokers about Voisey's Bay. Am I interested? Sure!

John stands at the entrance to First Marathon's boardroom wearing his customary attire of a blue blazer and a big smile. He ushers me inside. Mr. McOuat begins his presentation by assuring us that the drill cores in front of him, threatening to mar First Marathon's elegant boardroom table, are very real. So are the geophysical surveys. (The geophysical surveys, a series of measurements made by instruments similar to the metal detectors which people use to find lost jewellery on the beach, suggest that the mineralization is much more extensive than that drilled so far.) And Bruce Ryan, one of the Newfoundland government geologists who had mapped the area, had given Mr. McOuat the confidence that the geology at Voisey's Bay was favourable for more discoveries of nickel-copper-cobalt mineralization. I ask why there appear to be no surface indications of mineralization. Mr. McOuat replies that it is heavily weathered. Heavy weathering in rocks fresh from under a glacier puzzles me, but Mr. McOuat's squeaky-clean reputation is reassuring.

* * * * *

"Hi, Liz, it's Ray. I'm going to start recommending that our clients buy Diamond Fields shares."

"Great to have your support for something we own. Can you send me a copy of your report?"

"Ah – I still don't think it would politically be a good move to put into print a report favouring a Friedland stock. But I will verbally recommend Diamond Fields at our morning meeting, both for our institutional sales and trading people and for our retail sales people."

Daily morning meetings have been a fixture of every firm I've worked for on Bay Street. Morning meetings are held in a boardroom, with traders, analysts, and salespeople in attendance. Traders speak in shorthand. Analysts speak as if we were paid by the word. Salespeople ask awkward questions.

After the morning meeting at which I first recommend Diamond Fields, Donny the trader is fired up. "So, Ray, you're a fucking geologist and you think the DFR is real? [DFR was Diamond Fields's ticker symbol.] That's good enough for me. I'm going to get our clients into this fucking thing." He sways back to the trading desk, croaking "Everything's coming up roses."

But the skepticism continues. On December 13, 1994, the leader of the New Democratic Party in Newfoundland and Labrador's House of Assembly questioned the "Diamond Mines Corporation [sic] find in Labrador ... maybe the whole thing is designed as a share promotion on the Vancouver Stock Exchange." Which is helpful to those investors who hadn't yet bought Diamond Fields's shares — as long as investors are doubtful that Mr. Friedland has stumbled across a very real and very rich deposit, Diamond Fields's share price will continue to be a bargain.

January 25, 1995

"Good afternoon, Ray. Well, I suppose it's still morning over there." The starched voice belongs to the anglophilic Canadian who is our institutional salesman in London.

"Good morning, Geoff! How are you?"

"Good, good ... um, Ray, this Voisey's Bay thing you were talking about at the morning meeting. Do you really believe it? This Friedland chap has a bit of a dodgy reputation ..."

"Geoff, the drill core I saw ... "

"Ah, but that's just it, isn't it? One of my clients saw a Diamond Fields presentation last week given by their fellow Richard Garnett. Showed off some pretty spectacular pieces of drill core. Afterwards my client marched up to him and said 'most impressive, Richard — now, tell me, which mine in Sudbury is that *really* from?'"

"And Richard replied?"

"Chap didn't say. But what do you think, Ray?"

"Mmm, it's not from Sudbury. Grain's too coarse. Noril'sk in Russia maybe ... but I doubt very much that anyone could fool Jack McOuat with a switch like that. Voisey's Bay is real, Geoff."

March 29, 1995, Miami, Florida

At the "Investing in the Americas" conference, Canada's Federal Energy Mines and Resources Minister, Anne McLellan, describes Voisey's Bay as "an elephant" with 30 million tonnes of ore.

May 19, 1995

Dr. Rex Gibbons, Minister of Natural Resources, Newfoundland and Labrador, tells the House of Assembly: "The Voisey's Bay discovery is beyond our wildest dreams."

CHAPTER 4

BEYOND OUR WILDEST DREAMS

There is some ill a-brewing towards my rest
For I did dream of money-bags tonight.
— *The Merchant of Venice*, William Shakespeare

January 3, 1995

"Fax from Diamond Fields for you, Ray!" I pick up the press release from Jean-Raymond Boulle, Diamond Fields's Co-Chairman. It includes a geophysical sketch map of the Voisey's Bay project showing a long, skinny, shaded area representing a zone of high electrical conductivity, running east from the area where Chislett and Verbiski had made their initial discovery. At its eastern end, this conductive zone widens into what Mr. Boulle described as a "large ovoid feature," which occupies an area of, perhaps, 300 metres by 300 metres. In the middle of the Ovoid, the geophysicists' map shows a series of question marks subtly outlining an elliptical area, approximately 100 metres in diameter, that is unshaded, thus representing rocks which apparently did not conduct electricity. This suggests that the Ovoid is doughnut-shaped, with a plug of non-conductive rock at its centre. Mr. Boulle's text does not refer to this non-conductive zone.

To the east of the Ovoid, the zone of high electrical conductivity appears to jog to the south, then continue eastward, terminating in a series of question marks and the word "open." Mr. Boulle comments that Diamond Fields will begin further geophysical work on January 5.

Diamond Fields's first four holes have already convincingly shown that the long, skinny zone of metallic mineralization, which Liz and I had discussed in November 1994, is the cause of the long, skinny easterly trending zone of high electrical conductivity. Mr. Boulle reports that Diamond Fields's fifth drill hole, which apparently cut the northwestern fringe of the Ovoid feature, had also intersected metallic mineralization, and adds that he will release assays of this mineralization "when available."

Liz calls. "You've had time to digest the DFR press release, Ray. What do you think?"

"It leaves me with three questions, Liz. Number one — is this 'ovoid feature' caused by metallic mineralization? Number two — if so, is there a 'hole' of non-conductive and therefore waste rock in the middle of the Ovoid? And three — is metallic mineralization also responsible for the electrically conductive zone which jogs off to the south and east of the Ovoid?"

"So, overall, positive, negative, or a wash?"

"Oh, positive. The most likely explanation of the Ovoid is that it's a continuation of the mineralization they've already found. Even if there is a hole in the Ovoid, this map seems to imply that the mineralization gets better to the east of where they've already drilled."

"Anything else?"

Somewhat self-consciously, I reply, "Well, Liz, there is a stock market myth — which is actually supported by some serious academic studies — that the prices of stocks, especially stocks representing small companies, usually go up in January!"[17]

January 31, 1995

"Your track record is not looking too good, Goldie."

"You're right, Liz. Diamond Fields has dropped $2.00[18] from $13.50 at the end of last month. Not a very good call on my part."

"What's gone wrong?"

"We've been waiting for assays from that Hole Number 5, the one that seemed to have kissed the northwestern edge of the Ovoid. There's been enough time for the core to have been analyzed, but not a peep from the company. I think people are beginning to wonder if the mineralization has petered out."

"But there was another press release, Ray. January 18th."

"Yeah, that was a funny one. Mr. Boulle said they'd drilled 'the first of two geophysical conductor zones' within the Ovoid. He seems to be saying that they really do think that there is a hole in the middle, with the electrically conductive zone bifurcating and sweeping around the hole.

"There was no mention of Drill Hole 5, which makes me suspect that 5 was a dud. Mr. Boulle said that they're drilling Drill Hole 7. Whatever happened to Drill Hole 6? There's an old market adage with more than an element of truth to it: 'Bad news travels slower than good news.'"

"Time for us to think of bailing out?"

"Hmmm. ... I don't think so, Liz. That last press release spoke of 'at least 90 metres of massive mineralization.' By hanging on, you're taking a gamble that the Ovoid conducts electricity for the same reason that the long, skinny zone conducts electricity: that it's composed of metallic minerals."

"Well, what the hell else could it be, if it conducts electricity?"

"I guess I should have said *economic* metallic minerals. It could just be fool's gold — fool's nickel — iron pyrite with no nickel or copper or cobalt. Or it need not even be metallic. Graphite — carbon — conducts electricity. Professor Ambrose at Queen's used to say that, in northwestern Quebec, some of the conductive zones picked up by the geophysicists have had so many holes poked in them that, when the wind blows from the east, they play 'O Canada.' Yet all that the poor benighted geologists ever found in most of those holes was tens of metres of dirty black graphite."

"As I said, time to bail?"

"No, Liz. The press release says it's metallic mineralization, not graphite. And the likeliest explanation is that the same kind of metallic mineralization explains the electrical conductivity of both the long, skinny, east-west zone and of the Ovoid zone. They're probably really a single continuous zone."

As Diamond Fields was deducing the nature of the "Ovoid," something happened which was to completely change the way I looked at Voisey's Bay.

February 7, 1995; morning

"Ray, what's this about vandalism at Voisey's Bay?" It's Liz.

"Ahh ... I'm going to have to get back to you, Liz; I don't know." I check the websites of both the Canadian Broadcasting Corporation and the St. John's *Evening Telegram*. A few minutes later, I leave a voice message.

"Liz — about 100 Innu — Indians — mostly from Davis Inlet, have ridden into Diamond Fields's camp on snowmobiles and shut down operations. They call themselves the Innu Nation and say they own the land and want Diamond Fields to leave. It's a bit of a surprise to me because Robert Friedland has encouraged his people to consult the aboriginal people. But it gets more complicated. The L.I.A. — the Labrador Inuit Association — Eskimos — which, I think, also claims to own the land — says it supports mining exploration and has asked the *Innu* to leave. The Inuit and Innu have long had an uneasy truce along their traditional mutual border. Unfortunately for Diamond Fields, the Voisey's Bay deposits lie *on* that border."

The Innu's protest petered out, and, on February 26, Diamond Fields resumed drilling. But the Government of Newfoundland and Labrador realized that if unhappy Innu could block Diamond Fields from spending money at Voisey's Bay, they could also block Diamond Fields from *making* money at Voisey's Bay. And if Diamond Fields couldn't make any money, it couldn't pay any taxes. And so the province's premier, Clyde Wells, told Peter Penashue of the Innu Nation that the government wished to negotiate land claims with the Innu Nation. He added that the negotiations would be "speeded up" by comparison with those the government had commenced "a couple of years or so ago" with the Labrador Inuit Association.[19]

February 7, 1995; evening

"I don't get it, Goldie. They looked like pretty good results to me ..."

"Just fabulous, Liz! Drill Hole 7, right in the middle of the Ovoid, hit 104 metres grading 3.9% nickel and 2.8% copper, with some cobalt. So much for the 'doughnut hole' in the Ovoid! And Drill Hole 8, a bit to the south, was just as good. I'll wait for more results, but I'm certainly going to have to increase the tonnages I'm assuming in my model. By a lot. Mr. Boulle now thinks the Ovoid is the geophysical expression of a wine glass-shaped body 450 metres by 250 metres by over 110 metres deep, and he tells us that the density of the mineralization is not the 2.8 tonnes per cubic metre that you and I assumed in December, but 4.9 tonnes per cubic metre."

"Yes, what's all that about?"

"They're trying to tell us the potential tonnage of the Ovoid, but in a fashion that won't run them afoul of any securities regulators. If you approximate their 'wine glass' by an inverted cone with an average diameter at the surface of 350 metres and a depth of 110 metres, you have a volume of about 3.5 million cubic metres. Times 4.9 is 17 million tonnes. But it's still a bit of a stretch to infer that kind of tonnage from two or three drill holes, especially since the doughnut hole could still be lurking in there somewhere. Still, my tonnes will be up and I'm going to have to increase the nickel grades above that 1.25% nickel that you and I assumed before. ... Wow! What results!"

"But the fucking stock is *down*, Ray. It ran up to $13.13 yesterday, but today it's down a quarter. Those Innu ..."

"Let's be fair, Liz. The market's probably more pissed with Diamond Fields than with the Innu."

"Yes, you're right, you're right. They waited till now to let us know that Hole 5 was mediocre and Hole 6 was a duster. Buried the bad news in with some good news, hoping we wouldn't notice."

"Bet on the ore body Liz. Buy more."

February 22, 1995

"Thought I'd let you know, Ray, that John Lydall over at First Marathon says there's over 15 million tons of high-grade mineralization in the Ovoid."

"Hey, Liz, good for John! It sounds like the sort of number we talked about a coupla weeks ago, doesn't it? 'Fraid I still haven't had the OK to put anything on paper. Pity. Those holes that came out yesterday have certainly given me more confidence. Number 9 was nothing to write home about, but it seems to have been right on the fringe of the Ovoid, and 10 and 11 were remarkably similar to Holes 7 and 8 — each a hundred-odd metres of over 3% nickel. Number 10 was right where the doughnut hole's supposed to be."

"Such a relief that the market's started to believe this story. The stock's over $19 now, well past your old target of $15.18. Do you have a new target, Ray?"

"Just done some rough figures. Something in the mid-30s!"

"Good, good."

March 21, 1995

Diamond Fields announces that all of the 17 holes drilled into the Ovoid had intercepted massive mineralization. Furthermore, the Company has poked two holes into the electrically conductive zone that jogs south and east of the Ovoid. They encountered troctolite and "significant" mineralization. Diamond Fields's shares close the day at $22.375.

March 27, 1995

Mr. Boulle announces assays from Drill Holes 12 to 19, all confirming that the Ovoid comprises high-grade mineralization as much as 110 metres thick. Its surface extent has grown from the 450 metres by 250 metres, reported on February 7, to 450 metres by 300 metres, presumably as the result of the more detailed geophysical surveys which Mr. Boulle had announced on January 3.

Diamond Fields's shares close at $24.00.

April 13, 1995

Mr. Boulle reports new, remarkably consistent assays from holes in the Ovoid. He also reports three from the new discovery to the southeast, with grades of around 1% nickel, 0.5% copper, and some cobalt — similar to those from the long, skinny zone of the initial discovery.

Diamond Fields's shares close at $33.00.

April 17, 1995

Diamond Fields announces that it has issued 3,000,000 new shares and that it is selling them to Teck Corporation of Vancouver. Teck is to pay $36 per share, partly with cash and partly with shares of Teck Corporation. Teck also agrees to prepare a preliminary study of the feasibility and means of bringing Voisey's Bay into production.

Teck's investment, the first concrete expression of interest by a major mining house, helps to remove lingering doubts about the reality of Voisey's Bay, and Diamond Fields's shares end the month at $45.38.

"Ray."

A call from the boss.

"You cover Teck, don't you?"

"Yes."

"Well, you can't really give an opinion on Teck now without having a view on Diamond Fields."

"So, is this an OK to publish on Diamond Fields?"

"Yes."

May 3, 1995

"And so," I tell the morning meeting, "I seem to be alone in worrying that it will be at least ten years before Voisey's Bay can begin production, thanks to the lack of infrastructure, possibly acrimonious land claims, and environmental concerns. Nevertheless, Diamond Fields's shares are a 'Buy.' It's likely that the market will become more enthusiastic both about Diamond Fields's exploration potential and its takeover potential long before it starts to worry that I might be right about the timing of the project."

June 29, 1995

Cliff Carson announces that Teck Corporation has calculated that, at Voisey's Bay, in the Ovoid and adjacent parts of the long, skinny zone to the west, there are 31.7 million tonnes of ore which could be mined via an open pit. Allowing for dilution due to unavoidable mining of waste along with the ore, these reserves contain 2.83% nickel, 1.68% copper, and 0.12% cobalt.

CHAPTER 5

VISITING VOISEY'S

The three key things in this science are travel, travel, and travel ... geology is legitimized tourism.

— J. McPhee, 1983

Toronto's mining industry is a village. It has several clubs with: overlapping memberships; regular get-togethers; its own newspaper, *The Northern Miner*; and its own official photographer. Some contend it is large enough to have several village idiots.

In the 1980s and early 1990s, I ran one of the village's clubs, the Toronto Geological Discussion Group. I was the group's Secretary/Treasurer, its highest executive position. Its only executive position. Once, when I was trying to find a speaker for the Group's Christmas dinner, I enlisted the help of John Cooke, a genial, silver-haired village elder who was Publisher Emeritus of the village newspaper.

"Why don't we try another student?" asks John. "It must have been in the late '70s that we brought this student in from Queen's to give us a slide show on volcanoes. It was really good, light, entertaining holiday fare! Maybe someone up at the U of T has some likely candidates ..."

"John," I blurt, "that student was me!" And I thank him for his complimentary review.

My main memory of that slide show was that Professor Tony Naldrett from the University of Toronto had heckled me. He had feigned outrage that I should represent myself as an authority on volcanoes. For some reason, the fact that I'd been born on the side of a volcano wasn't good enough. Every time I uttered a volcanological term, Tony's cultured ex-RAF voice would loudly remind the audience that I had written my thesis on *granites*, a notably non-volcanic family of rocks. One of Tony's students introduced me to him afterwards, confiding, "You know, people who have encountered Tony over the phone are always astonished to meet him in person. When they hear his cultured voice, with its slight, endearing stutter, they imagine a Cambridge don. They can't believe that this big bear of a man is Professor Naldrett!"

By mid-1995, Toronto's mining village has become intensely interested in Voisey's Bay. I decide to arrange a seminar for the Geological Discussion Group, featuring Bruce Ryan and Canada's — the world's — reigning expert on the geology of nickel deposits, Tony Naldrett.

June 2, 1995

"Ray? It's Kalayra Angelyys. I'm investor relations for Diamond Fields Resources. I have a couple of things for you. Firstly, you're Chairman of the Toronto Geological Discussion Group, right?"

"Right."

"I understand that, on June 27, you're bringing Bruce Ryan in from the Geological Survey in St. John's and Professor Naldrett from the University of Toronto to tell the geological community in Toronto about Voisey's Bay? Well, we'd be delighted to sponsor an open bar. But we understand geologists are thirsty people, so we should put a limit on it. Fifteen hundred dollars, OK?"

"Why, yes! Thank you, Kalayra!"

"And I have an invitation for you. How would you like to be our guest at Voisey's Bay?"

"Hey, I certainly would! Tell me more!"

"If you can arrange your own transportation to Goose Bay on June 7 and back again on June 9, we'll take care of everything else."

"Done!" I say, hoping my boss will agree.

Kalayra has touched on a delicate ethical issue. In the bad old days, a promoter would charter a train or a plane to take a party of brokers and analysts to visit his property, and generously lubricate them en route, in the expectation of subsequent favourable interest in his stock. By the 1990s, it was generally expected that brokers and analysts should pay their own way to and from some convenient collection point, but the extent to which the host company covered intervening expenses, without jeopardizing their guests' independence of thought, was a matter of debate. On August 10, 1984, I was part of a group of bankers and investment dealers from Toronto who had been the guests of Denison Mines' chairman, Stephen B. Roman. Mr. Roman had flown us to Vancouver, put us up at the Four Seasons Hotel, and then on to Tumbler Ridge in northeastern British Columbia, where we watched Mr. Roman and Premier Bill Bennett depress the plunger for the opening of the Quintette coal mine. The reception which followed was lavish, and so well-stocked with Torontonians that the only voters the Premier could find were the members of the band. As he chatted with the musicians, one of Mr. Roman's assistants teetered across the floor on spiky heels and tapped the Premier on the shoulder. "Mr. Roman says it's time to go."

Before we left, the organizers thought it appropriate for the analysts to view the operation whose opening we were celebrating, so we bustled onto a bus and roared across the open pit. I'd read Quintette's promotional literature, and had been expecting to see thick, flat-lying seams of coal. That's not what I saw.

"Er, driver, can you stop so that we can look at the pit walls?" I asked.

"Can't stop — might be hit by a truck."

"Could you perhaps slow down a little so's I can take a photo?"

"No."

I jotted down what I saw — coal seams that were contorted, swollen, and pinched to nothingness. Clearly, this ore body was going to be tougher to mine than its planners had believed. But Mr. Roman's hospitality had been effective — when I returned to Toronto, it was difficult, but fortunately not impossible, to write critically about what I'd seen.

On June 8, 1995, Rosie Moore, an impressive and articulate geologist who has taken on managing geological and technical services for Diamond Fields, welcomes twelve mining analysts to Goose Bay, Labrador. In a grimly fluorescent-lit basement bar at the Labrador Inn, she briefs us on the plans for the morrow and introduces us to two of her fellow Diamond Fields employees: Cliff Carson, recently lured from Falconbridge Limited to advise on marketing nickel; and Richard Garnett.

"Spring weather in northern coastal Labrador is unpredictable," says Rosie, "but tomorrow looks as if it will be clear and sunny!"

It is. We, and stacks of empty drill core boxes, fly to Nain, where I remark on the changes since my previous visit twenty-five years earlier: an airstrip and a breakwater; new fish plant, caribou-processing plant, and school; no curious, shy locals come to see what we look like. Then, by helicopter to the exploration camp: the duckboards that link the tents give us a sense of being behind the lines on the Western Front, but the continual helicopter traffic is more reminiscent of Vietnam.

"We want to respect the environment," shouts Richard above the roar, "so all our drill moves are done by chopper."

Accent. English?

"Isn't that expensive?"

"It certainly is!" English. But South African overtones. "However, we think it will pay off. Moving the drills on land would leave scars for decades."

I've seen pictures of tundra disturbed by all-terain vechicles. Richard is right. What a mess. I give Robert Friedland's environmental policy a mental thumbs-up.

Several of the workers are Innu. I ask them whether Diamond Fields is a good employer. They have no complaints. Some of the other employees are Inuit. Do they get on with each other?

"They don't sleep in the same tents as we do, but we work with them OK."

When I evaluate an exploration property, I bear in mind that promoters may tell the truth and nothing but the truth — but not necessarily the *whole* truth. I've visited properties that looked fine on paper but which may be, for reasons that their promoters neglected to mention, worth less than the paper evaluations would indicate. I once passed a very thirsty day on a copper-gold prospect. After hours of crawling over boxes of drill core laid out in the desert sun, and peering through a hand lens, I concluded that most of the gold was locked up in very fine grains of pyrite. Conventional metallurgical techniques might be able to recover only 25% of that gold. Other analysts' valuations were based on the assumption that most of the gold could be recovered and, therefore, their valuations and the price of the stock were too high.

Two other deposits I have looked at were, as their promoters suggested, rich in copper, zinc, silver, and gold — but both were also rich in the 'nasties' which had concerned me when I presented my Voisey's valuation to Liz. One of the two properties became a mine. The mine sent its output to smelters that levied severe penalties to compensate for the removal of two "nasties," arsenic and antimony, so the mine was never the bonanza it initially appeared to be.

As Richard Garnett hurries me along the duckboards, I tell him that I'd seen Jack McOuat's drill core and that it looked coarse-grained and hence likely to be easy to treat.

"Is all the deposit like that, Richard? And have you looked for nasties?"

"Nasties? Well, we've looked for them, notably arsenic and selenium, and found nothing. Grain sizes? Here's your answer."

We lift the flap of one of the tents and find tables covered with drill core — slim, cylindrical samples of rock. And, standing before the tables is a beaming University of Toronto Emeritus, Professor Anthony Naldrett.

"Welcome to Voisey Bay! Or Voisey's Bay, as we're now supposed to call it."

One easy way to tell that a person is a geologist is to hand her a piece of rock. If she licks it, she's a "geo." (Moisture makes minerals stand out more clearly.) Tony's approach is more elegant — he is using a spray bottle.

Tony outlines the geology of the deposit and its likely metallurgical characteristics. He reiterates Richard's observation of the lack of nasties.

"How about pleasant surprises, Tony? Any PGE[20] like at Sudbury or Noril'sk?"

Richard interjects. "PGE are very difficult to measure and Diamond Fields doesn't want to issue assays for them, then run the risk of having to retract them. So we haven't published them. But, Ray, the fact that we've hired John Paterson, who's a specialist in hydrometallurgy, ought to tell you something."

It does. There are two main processes for treating nickel-copper-cobalt ores: pyrometallurgy (fire and brimstone like the smelters at Sudbury); and hydrometallurgy (pressure cookers, like Sherritt International's plant in Alberta). Hydrometallurgy is cheaper and less messy, but more finicky to operate. And, unlike pyromet, it can't recover PGE.

Tony chips in. "I wouldn't be surprised to find peripheral ore bodies rich in PGE. You do get that situation at Sudbury."

We walked out of the coreshack to find Cliff Carson standing on a doorstep, trying to stop a sheet of fax paper from flapping in a stiff breeze, and preparing to make an announcement.

"Ladies and gentlemen, I have here a press release which has just gone over the wires. Let me read it to you:

"Jean Raymond Boulle and Robert M. Friedland, co-chairmen of Diamond Fields Resources Inc., today announced that Diamond Fields has entered into an agreement with Inco Limited to sell a 25% interest in the Voisey's Bay nickel, copper, and cobalt project and related claim areas in Labrador to Inco for consideration of $525 million plus a further contribution of $25 million by Inco for feasibility study and related expenses.

"Inco will issue US$386.7 million of 15-year 6.5% preferred shares in return for the 25% interest. The preferred shares will be convertible into Inco common shares at a price of US$29.00 per share. The shares will be non-callable by Inco for a minimum of five years.

"Under the terms of the agreement, Inco will have the right and obligation to market 100% of Voisey's Bay nickel and cobalt production in the first five years of production and a minimum of 133 million pounds of nickel per year for a further 15-year period. Inco will provide technical and managerial assistance as requested, free of cost to Diamond Fields, until the completion of the feasibility study of the mine and processing facilities.

"Separately, Inco has advised Diamond Fields that Inco has entered into agreements to purchase 2 million common shares of Diamond Fields from three existing shareholders. Inco and Diamond Fields have also entered into a standstill agreement, which limits the acquisition and disposition of shares held by each company in the other. Inco and Diamond Fields have also entered into voting arrangements which govern the voting of all such shares."

And then there are some warm comments from Messrs. Friedland and Boulle "Yes, we're all pretty happy about this deal!"

A pause, while we contemplate the news. Inco showing some interest! Finally! I can almost read my colleagues' thoughts: "Typical stodgy slow Inco, wakes up two months after the nimble guys at Teck Corp. What took Inco so long?"

Cliff can also read our thoughts. "I'm glad it came about when you were actually on the site, but that's not the way we planned it. It took my colleagues six weeks of intense negotiations. We didn't expect that it would take that long, but Inco's lawyers kept trying to add vetoes, and we kept on deleting them. So now, ladies and gentlemen, you're as up-to-date as anyone on Bay Street. Any questions?"

"Cliff, will it really be Inco running the show now?"

"Harry, there will be two committees: a technical committee and an operating committee. Votes will be by simple majority, and Diamond Fields will have a majority on each committee."

"Cliff, you'll mine and concentrate ore here and then ship it off to a smelter. Does it have to be an Inco smelter?"

"No, in fact the most likely place to treat the concentrated ore might be with my former employer, Falconbridge, at its Nikkelverk refinery in Norway. After all, we're on the shores of the North Atlantic here and so is Nikkelverk, whereas Sudbury is in the middle of the continent. Or we could send it to Australia or even Russia. Inco's marketing rights cover refined metal, not concentrated ore."

"And it's just refined nickel and cobalt — you can do what you want with the copper you produce?"

"Yes."

"Cliff, you, or at least John Paterson — you're looking at building your hydrometallurgical smelter. What if that smelter produces something other than refined metal?"

A twinkle in Cliff's eye. "Ray, we just might build a plant to produce ferronickel.[21] And ferronickel just might not be classified as 'refined nickel' for the purposes of our agreement with Inco."

"Can Inco restrict your rate of production?"

"No way."

"Cliff, this feasibility study: what rate of production would it consider?"

"The target is a 20-year mine life, producing 100 to 200 million pounds of nickel [45,000 to 90,000 tonnes] per year."

"Might not even the low end — 100 million pounds a year — be enough to destroy nickel markets?" asks one of the analysts.

"Harry, with initial production of 100 million pounds a year, scaling up to, say, 220 million pounds [100,000 tonnes] by 2004, I believe that nickel markets can still maintain average prices of US$4.00/lb. After all, nickel markets survived 1992, when Russia added 220 million pounds [100,000 tonnes] to world markets."

"And when would you be in production?"

"The critical path is likely to be the environmental impact study, which may take three years, which is how long it took Raglan[22] to be permitted. Admittedly, Voisey's permitting will be done under the new federal legislation, which did not apply to Raglan. However, I believe, and this is very aggressive, that we could be in production two years from today."

Rosie takes advantage of a break in the questioning to beckon us to follow her.

"And behind this door," she says, hoisting a tent flap, "is my favourite geophysicist, Terry Crebs!"

A welcoming smile behind a beard. Terry enthusiastically shows off rainbow-coloured maps which capture Diamond Fields's dreams of the future.

"Now see her?" He stabs his finger at a psychedelic doughnut. "That's the Ovoid — named by Rosie, by the way."

Rosie grins. "I remember arguing with Robert Friedland about my choice of name. 'The letter *O* looks too much like zero, which is nothing,' he said, 'and '"void"' definitely doesn't sound good, I don't like it! Hey wait a minute — two negatives make a positive, don't they? '"Ovoid,"' '"Ovoid"' ... yeah, I like it — '"Ovoid"' it is!'"

"Terry," said Harry, "that new zone, off to the south and east of the Ovoid — on the geophysical map that Diamond Fields published, this zone terminated in little question marks. Have you now done the geophysics to tell if it keeps going to the east?"

Richard responded. "Harry, if there is mineralization to the east, and if it's at the same altitude as the known mineralization, it would be 600 feet under that hill off behind the camp. That's too deep for the geophysics to pick up."

"But the Ovoid was shallow enough to be picked up by geophysics," adds Terry, "and Diamond Fields's geophysical data from over the Ovoid was very good. Good enough that Crebs could show that geophysicists don't need drills to measure tonnages. I used a frustrum-of-cone approximation and came up with 23.7 million tonnes in the Ovoid. Adding in the mineralization to the west, I calculated 'reserves' to be about 28 million tonnes. Pretty close to the 32 million tonnes that Teck later calculated! My model even anticipated that the thickest part of the Ovoid would show up as a hole. The hole in this doughnut is not real; it's apparent and due to the dipolar effect." The physics escapes me, but Terry's skill does not. Richard pats his shoulder.

"Crebs is the only geophysicist to have correctly interpreted the doughnut shape of the geophysical data from over the Ovoid."

In November 2001, I contacted Crebs via email.

"Am I correct, Terry, in deducing that the map that Diamond Fields published on January 5 1995 wasn't completely accurately labelled? What you said at Voisey's Bay that summer suggests to me that the EM data, which measures electrical conductivity, did not imply a 'hole,' only the magnetic data did. But the January 2, 1995 map represented itself as showing EM, not magnetic data."

"I never saw the Jan-2-95 map," he replied. "Could you please fax it to me? Thanks."

I faxed it.

"Got it, Ray. You're right, the Jan-2-95 map's question marks do imply that the 'EM Anomaly' may have a hole in it. I'm afraid that this was a misinterpretation.

"Sadly, this problem is common in mining exploration. Press releases are written more for people in the securities business than for their science. There were (and are) a lot of fuck-ups involving labelling on exploration press releases. Especially, it seems, when geophysics is involved.

"What can I say? Always get a second and third opinion if you think you have a world-class ore body by the tail? I'm sure glad they called me when they did."

Crebs went on to explain the map of the Ovoid's magnetism.

"The ground-magnetic response over the Ovoid yielded a circular magnetic high with a local magnetic low — hole — at its centre. The 'hole' occurs because the magnetic intensity increases around the Ovoid's edges."

"Terry, do you mean that the Ovoid is like a giant bar magnet, and magnets have two poles, and in some places the attraction of one pole is just balanced by the repulsion of the other?"

"That is not quite accurate," Terry replied, "but it will do for the time being."

Crebs emailed further reminiscences of early 1995 (reproduced in Apendix 2).

"Right," says Rosie, "we have to move along. If anyone's interested, we can hike up to the discovery outcrop and, since it's late, the helicopter can pick us up there to take us back to Nain."

We skirt the Ovoid, which lies under an unwelcoming bog, and in brilliant sunshine puff up a line cut through the sparse spruce and onto bare, rusty rock. Rosie leads us to the western edge of the ridge where the prospectors Chislett and Verbiski had made their discovery.

I am still puzzled by the absence of ore metals in the samples taken by government geologists years before Chislett and Verbiski's visit, and why there was no mention of surface mineralization in any of Diamond Fields's press releases. So I hammer off a piece of rock, the size of a loaf of bread, and lug it onto the helicopter and back to my office in Toronto.

Whenever I walked into my office in the weeks that followed, I could smell acid, and I realized that the sample was leaching itself. Sulphides, plus oxygen in the air, plus the water inside the sample, made sulphuric acid, and this acid was dissolving the remaining mineralization. Indeed, once the sample had fully dried out the smell stopped. Later, I sliced apart the sample with a diamond saw and could see abundant cavities marking the former locations of ore minerals.

Why did the Discovery Hill leach itself when other, similar, zones I've encountered, and which had been exposed to the atmosphere for longer, did not? There are probably two reasons. Firstly, Voisey's Bay's unusual mineralogy: iron sulphide is present in the form of pyrrhotite, rather than the more common and less reactive pyrite. Secondly, the sea air of coastal Labrador probably has the same effect on ore minerals as it has on automobile bodies.

CHAPTER 6

A VERY PUBLIC BET

When sun rays crown thy pine-clad hills
And summer spreads her hand,
When silvern voices tune thy rills,
We love thee smiling land.
— *Ode to Newfoundland*, Sir Cavendish Boyle

<u>Morning Meeting, June 14, 1995;</u>
<u>Diamond Fields's share price at $69.75</u>
($17.438 allowing for the subsequent 4:1 share split)

"Ray, your turn. Any comments?"

"Yes, on Diamond Fields, DFR. Yesterday, I was one of a group of sixty or seventy mining and financial people at a meeting sponsored by DFR here in Toronto. I also talked with Inco about DFR, and I had a call from DFR's co-chairman, Robert Friedland, in Beijing.

"Firstly, I calculate that the price of the DFR shares bought by Inco implies that DFR's shares are worth somewhere in the low 70s. Furthermore, I've worked out that the price that Inco paid for 25% of the Voisey's Bay property also implies that DFR's shares' value is in the low 70s.

"Now, Mr. Friedland says that 'a South African mining company' — which, I suspect, he wants us to believe to have been Minorco — offered what Mr. Friedland says was 'lots more' than Inco did. There were rumours at the DFR meeting of a figure as high as $100.

"Secondly, Inco said it did not know if Voisey's Bay would have its own smelter and refinery. If it did not, the project would use third-party tolling arrangements and Inco would have first dibs on providing those arrangements.

"There's a lot of excess nickel smelting and refining capacity in the world, and I assume in my modelling that DFR decides *not* to build its own smelter and refinery."

"Ray — hasn't DFR hired a technical whiz to plan its smelter and refinery? Why would they do that if they intended to use someone else's smelter?"

Hey, the sales people are awake.

"A cynic might say that DFR really is for sale, and the best way to sell the company is to say that you are not for sale and to give every appearance of planning to go into production and becoming a serious rival to other nickel producers."

"OK."

"Thirdly, DFR told us that it was considering a listing on the New York Stock Exchange, a stock split, and a dividend policy."

"*Dividend policy,* Ray? For a *junior exploration* company?"

"Yes, Patricia. *Why* would they do it? It's part of wanting to be seen as a big, serious company. *Could* they do it? Certainly — with that Inco paper they now own, they have an income of $34 million in tax-free dividends!"

Several pairs of eyebrows lift from the *Report on Business.*

"Fourth, DFR's Ed Mercaldo noted that the company wanted to avoid the social consequences of a boom-bust operation. He wants a production level low enough to be able to sustain a mine life of at least twenty years.

"Fifth, although Mr. Friedland assured me that Inco wants to buy even more of Voisey's Bay, he and his colleagues 'wrestled with ourselves long and hard, before selling even 25%' because, as Inco said, they've 'only scratched the surface of exploration.' In fact, they are currently drilling a new geophysical anomaly and plan to test five more.

"Sixth, Inco says that DFR had set up a 'data room' containing drill core logs, samples, and so on; and that any company was welcome to enter, provided it first signed a confidentiality agreement and a 'standstill' agreement — that is, an agreement not to try to take over DFR, without DFR's permission, in the next two years. That was probably pretty good protection against a takeover, because just about every major mining company has showed up.

"My conclusion for investors: If DFR doesn't find any more mineralization at Voisey's Bay, the idea of stretching production over 20 years would reduce the Net Present Value of the deposit because it would spread cash flows over a longer period of time than I've assumed in my modelling. So that's a possible negative.

"The standstill agreements mean that, if someone wants to take over DFR, it must be on DFR's terms — but they would likely be pretty attractive terms for the DFR's shareholders. So that could be a positive.

"The exploration potential is excellent, and the talk about getting a New York listing and paying dividends should bring in more U.S. interest. American investors seem to place more importance on dividends than Canadian investors. I think we'll see the stock at $85.00 within the next twelve months, implying a gain of 22%, which is just shy of what you need to make the stock an outright, pound-the-table 'Buy.' So, it's an 'Accumulate': between a 'Buy' and a 'Hold.'"

After the meeting, Donny supports himself on the knob of my office door. "Ray, remind me. Why is a stock with a 22% upside — *22%* — why is it not a fuckin' *'Buy'*?"

"Donny, to me, 'Buys' are stocks whose performance you expect to be in the top 10% of all stocks. At least, that's what the fellow who introduced me to this business, Keith Ambachtsheer, used to say. Keith is a pretty quantitative guy, but he likes to keep things simple. Rates of return on stocks follow something like what the statisticians call a 'normal' distribution."

"The old bell curve, right?"

"Right. Keith said that you can approximate a bell curve by dividing stocks into the best 10%, the next best 20%, the 40% in the middle, the next 20%, and the worst 10%."

"Howzat?"

"The top 10% of stocks beat the market by at least 28% in an average year.[23] Call them 'Buys.' The next best 20% of stocks beat the market by between 12% and 28% in an average year. Call them 'Buy/Holds' or 'Accumulates.' At the other end of the spectrum, the worst 10% of all stocks — 'Sells' — well, the market beats *them* by at least 28%. The second worst, the second worst 20% — we call them 'Reduces' — underperform the market by between 12% and 28%."

"Which leaves: 100% minus 10%, 20%, 10%, and 20%. Forty per cent of all stocks."

"Yes. That 40% of stocks — they give wishy-washy rates of return, all within 12%, either way, of that of the market overall. They're the 'Holds.'"

"Forty per cent of all stocks are 'Holds.' What a fucking concept. Thank you, Ray."

"Donny, you're very welcome."

Halfway on his march back to his desk, he stops, turns, and yells over his shoulder, "Ray, on the trading desk there are only two kinds of stock: 'Piece-a shit' and 'To the moon!'"

St. John's, Newfoundland, June 22, 1995; Diamond Fields's share price at $66.25 ($16.563 allowing for the subsequent 4:1 split)

My first visit to the island of Newfoundland, a guest of the St. John's branch of my employer Richardson Greenshields. Excited because it is a sparkling day, because I'd found and bought two "Figgy Duff" tapes that were new to me, and because my rental car has a tape player. Life doesn't get much better than driving up Signal Hill in the sun, listening to Figgy Duff singer Pamela Morgan. A whisky critic might describe her voice as like a Western Highlands single malt: "beautifully rounded, warming, enveloping, deliciously smooth and confident, hints of honey, a whiff of peat smoke, and a faint tang of salt."

That evening, I stand before two huge screens in a ballroom of the Delta Hotel in St. John's in front of 200 investors eager to hear Diamond Fields's Richard Garnett and me talk about Voisey's Bay.

Richard outlines the history of the Voisey's Bay discovery. In response to questions, he dismisses the idea of joint ventures — "We don't want to share our hard-earned expertise with juniors. Anyway, our agreement with Inco does not permit such co-operation without Inco's agreement." He also says that he thinks Voisey's would have its own smelter and refinery. "Economic good sense indicates that the chances of treating it in Sudbury are very slight."

Then it is my turn.

"I am making this presentation tonight in my role of financial analyst, a job whose central element is forecasting. And when we make forecasts, we must be brave, bold, and fearless. We must have big crystal balls." I pause, waiting for appreciative chuckles. But, as my mother used to say, not a sausage. I stumble on. "I'm going to tell you what I see in my crystal ball. The first thing is a mine, or several mines. This sounds trivial, but there are still people who don't believe Voisey's Bay is real. After all, the old adage is that the likeliest place to find a new mine is beside an old one, and there are no old mines near Voisey's Bay. At the other end of the spectrum, some observers see dozens of Labradorian nickel mines in their crystal balls.

"Well, Voisey's Bay is certainly real. A well-respected commodity research house in London, CRU International, calls it the world's 'most exciting nickel discovery this century.'"

I go on to explain why my experience with Dave Barr in 1970 had made me an early believer that the discovery was real, but add: "I don't see dozens of mines in my crystal ball. That's because, if there *were* dozens of deposits exposed at the surface, more of them would have been found by now. Future discoveries will be more difficult and will probably all be discovered by drilling.

"But I do see several mines, as well as Voisey's Bay, in my crystal ball, and I do think Diamond Fields has a better shot at finding them than anyone else. That's not only because of the quality of Diamond Fields's people, it's also because, once it realized what it had — a nickel-copper deposit in a rock called troctolite — Diamond Fields was able to use the government's geological maps to identify and stake most of the troctolites of this area; including, I'm gratified to see, the Kiglapait intrusion, which I walked over twenty-five years ago.

"In my crystal ball, I do not see commercial production at Voisey's Bay before January 1, 2000. I understand that Dr. Garnett may not entirely agree with this — if so, I'd be willing to bet a bottle of Lammerlaw, which is a fine New Zealand single malt whiskey, against a bottle of Screech.

"Here's why I don't see commercial production before the year 2000 ..." I hold up one finger. "Voisey's Bay lacks infrastructure and has a shipping season of only four months."

A second finger. "Voisey's Bay is largely virgin wilderness. Environmental and native groups will want all the i's dotted and t's crossed before development proceeds. Developers and politicians cannot try any shortcuts, as environmental groups in British Columbia have taught us. In B.C., environmentalists didn't like the way Alcan's

Kemano power scheme was proceeding and, with a series of court orders, they've been able to shut down construction for the past four years. That's US$500 million worth of construction sitting idle; sitting useless, because environmental groups thought it was being built too fast."

A third finger. "There's a three-way debate on the future of native claims at Voisey's Bay. The area is populated both by Inuit, i.e. Eskimo, and Innu, i.e. Indians. The natives are negotiating with the provincial government and, to some extent, with each other, since one of the traditional dividing lines between Inuit and Innu is the treeline. Voisey's straddles the treeline.

"The two mines that have most recently come on stream in Canada, Louvicourt in Quebec and Eskay Creek in British Columbia, have a lesson for Voisey's. Although these are underground mines, which are more time-consuming to develop than open-pit mines (and Voisey's Bay will be initially an open-pit mine), both had advantages that do not, or may not, apply to Voisey's. Louvicourt was essentially an extension of an old mine, and it had an established mining town nearby, so getting permits was relatively easy. Furthermore, in Quebec, environmental permitting is more streamlined than in Newfoundland and Labrador. At the other new operation, Eskay Creek, they didn't build a concentrator and so they didn't need to construct a tailings dam either. And yet, from discovery to commercial production at Louvicourt and Eskay Creek, each took five to six years.

"How about the operating costs at Voisey's Bay? Some people say they will be zero. My crystal ball says, 'No — they will be *negative*!' The copper and cobalt and precious metals at Voisey's Bay should *more* than cover expenses, meaning that you have a profit even before you add in the value of the nickel!

"A lot of observers have worried that Voisey's Bay's low cost and high volume will ruin the world's nickel markets. Some of this concern has been alleviated by Diamond Fields's recent deal with Inco, which gives Inco both the right and the obligation to market the output of refined nickel and cobalt produced from Voisey's Bay. Some observers have interpreted this arrangement to mean that Inco has some control over Voisey's Bay's level of production.

"I don't share these concerns, but it's not because I believe Inco has control over Voisey's Bay's level of production. Indeed, Inco will have no veto over the ultimate rates of production at Voisey's Bay.

"Here's *why* I don't share these concerns. Firstly, as I've said, I believe that Voisey's Bay will come on stream later than many people expect. Secondly, the likelihood that other producers will adjust their production plans in recognition of Voisey's Bay's potential."

I make my hand into the shape of a pistol, point it into the bright lights that are dazzling me, and say that Voisey's is a weapon with which Diamond Fields and Inco could threaten any of their competitors who were contemplating constructing a new nickel mine.

"And, thirdly, nickel markets will probably remain sturdy enough to accommodate Voisey's Bay.

"Let's look more closely at the likelihood that other producers will move to accommodate Voisey's Bay's output. In my view, the best assurance of this comes from Diamond Fields's appointment of a marketing whiz, Cliff Carson, as president. Mr. Carson is keenly aware that Diamond Fields would do itself no good by seriously disrupting nickel markets. After all, Potash Corporation of Saskatchewan has shown us that, in a commodity business, price is a more important determinant of profitability than is the amount of the commodity that you sell. Mr. Carson's strategy seems to be to ensure that other producers are aware of Voisey's Bay's potential, and that they will accordingly adjust their expansion plans in a fashion that will permit the orderly introduction of Voisey's Bay nickel to world markets.

"Let's turn to look at nickel markets. In the past year, the Western world's demand for nickel has risen by about 170,000 tonnes per annum. For comparison, Diamond Fields and Inco have targeted a production rate of something in the range of 45,000 to 90,000 — say 60,000 tonnes of nickel per year from Voisey's Bay. In other words, Voisey's Bay would accommodate only about a third of the recent growth in nickel demand. 'Ah,' say the skeptics, 'but is the current level of demand sustainable?' Well, this worries me too; especially since my fellow crystal-ball gazer, Paul Summerville, who is Richardson Greenshields's chief economist, says that North America will suffer a significant economic slowdown in 1996. However, the producers of stainless steel use 60% of the world's nickel, and North

America represents only about 16% of the Western world's stainless steel industry. Since we're expecting 1996 to be much like 1986, when North America suffered a near-recession while the rest of the world kept growing, this is not a big worry."

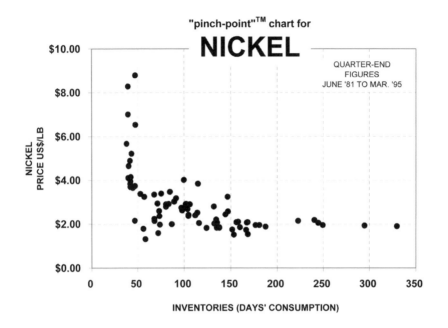

I then show a slide of what I call a "Pinch-point™"[24] chart, which relates nickel prices to nickel inventories in the world's warehouses.

One way to understand Pinch-points™ is to imagine that you have a job buying nickel for a company which produces stainless steel. Your work has two challenges.

First, you have to get the best price.

Second, you have to make sure that your employer always has enough nickel on hand to keep its plant running. Every day you tour town, shopping basket in hand, picking up some nickel from the Noril'sk big box outlet here, maybe a little from the WMC boutique, then you cross the street to the Inco department store and put in an order to have some nickel delivered to your plant next month. The stores you visit always seem to have lots of nickel in stock, neatly laid out in the aisles and for years your shopping expeditions are routine. But one day, in the Noril'sk outlet, you recognize a fellow from Inco. Is he *buying* nickel? Could Inco be running short? You look around. A lot of the shelves are empty. Then, in the Falconbridge shop, you notice a bunch of Asian shoppers you've never seen before. They're *lining up* at the cashier and the shelves are not as full as you remember. By the time you get to Inco, you begin to think about that order you were about to place for next month. You start to worry. Is it possible that some of the stores may be sold out by then? Do you want to take the risk that your employer may have to curtail production because you haven't bought enough nickel? Just to be on the safe side, you give the clerk an order to deliver twice your usual quantity of nickel. "Well," she responds, scratching her ear with a pencil, "to guarantee delivery next month, we're going to have to charge you 15% more." A vision of an angry plant manager enters your mind. "Um ... OK," you say.

You have just reached the Pinch-point™: the point at which buyers become more worried about security of supply than about prices. Beyond the Pinch-point™, nickel prices can soar. As the chart above shows, the Pinch-point™ occurs when inventories drop to a level equivalent to about fifty days' consumption.

"When inventories are high," I tell the audience, "prices stay mostly around $2 to $4 (US) per pound. But when inventories drop below fifty days' consumption — the Pinch-point™ — prices usually soar: $5, $6, $7, $8, or more. Today, nickel inventories are equivalent to about seventy days' consumption. We could be down to fifty days' within a year. Nickel prices are currently around $4 per pound. In 1996, we could see them as high as $8 per pound."

As well as nickel prices, I mention three other potentially positive influences on Diamond Fields's shares. "Firstly, increased investor interest. Now that Diamond Fields is part of the Toronto Stock Exchange 300 Composite Index, mutual funds and pension funds have to pay attention because they measure their performance against that of the Composite. Investors' interest will also be encouraged by the prospect of a listing on a U.S. exchange this year. Moreover, Diamond Fields has also announced that it is contemplating passing through to investors, in the form of dividends, some of its income from its holdings of preferred shares of Inco Limited. The prospect of such a dividend may also increase investors' acceptance of Diamond Fields's shares.

"Secondly, exploration. This summer's exploration results will be largely from drills at the western end of the deposit. My guess is that these results will confirm what most of us suspect: that the deposit here is extensive, both downwards and horizontally; though with grades lower than in what is called the "Ovoid." By the fall, however, we may start hearing news from some of Diamond Fields's other, virgin, targets.

"Thirdly, more deals. Diamond Fields's recent deal, selling 25% of the deposit to Inco, wasn't necessarily the last one; and there's no reason for future deals to be at the same price as the Inco one.

"My conclusion? Voisey's Bay is a WIN-WIN-WIN: it is a boon for the Province of Newfoundland and Labrador; it is not a killer of nickel markets; and it still offers profit potential for potential investors — my six- to twelve-month target price is $85, or $21.25 if the shares are, as proposed, split four for one."

Polite applause. My face sweaty under the bright lights. Richard walks over, shakes my hand, and says, "Ray, Voisey's will start up before 2000. I'll take your bet!"

I haven't heard from him since.

* * * * *

Another geologist on the rubber chicken circuit in 1995 is Roger Morton, a geology professor at the University of Alberta, who has signed up with NDT Ventures, one of the junior companies looking in Labrador for more Voisey's Bays. He is well-equipped to be a stock promoter. His professorial title and English accent give him credibility, and his loud, hoarse voice ensures he can be heard in large groups.

On May 30, 1995, I squeeze into an overflowing Toronto hotel dining room stuffed with retail stockbrokers, mining analysts, and journalists who have been invited by NDT to eat a free lunch and listen to Dr. Morton. He points out that nickel deposits typically occur in clusters, that only one deposit has so far been discovered at Voisey's Bay, and that, of all the companies looking for the rest of the deposits that made up the hypothetical Voisey's Bay cluster, his client has the best chance of finding them. "I can guarantee," he adds, "five to ten announced discoveries by the end of this summer." He also speculates that Diamond Fields is holding back some impressive platinum assays.

A question period follows.

"What, realistically, is the chance of multiple discoveries at Voisey's Bay?"

"Well," roars Dr. Morton, "multiple discoveries are like multiple orgasms. We've all heard of them, but I very much doubt if anyone in this room has ever had one!" Thereby demonstrating that, not only does he not really believe his client's story, but also that Mme. Edith Cresson, formerly and briefly the Prime Minister of France, had a point when she said that Englishmen know nothing about women.

Dr. Morton whirls around and points a wagging finger at *The Globe and Mail*'s mining reporter, Alan Robinson. "I dare you ... I dare you NOT to print that!"

Alan folds his arms, crosses his legs, and says, "Don't worry. I won't." And he doesn't.

The next day, Dr. Morton repeats his presentation at a breakfast in New York. It has an unexpected effect. Worried Wall Street brokers, panicked by the thought that Labrador is about to set the world awash in an unstoppable flood of nickel and platinum, knock about a dollar off Inco's share price. To the best of my knowledge, this constitutes the only occasion on which a professor of geology has, in one morning, erased more than $100 million dollars from the value of a company.

* * * * *

In the summer of 1995, most observers saw no enormous obstacles to the development of Voisey's Bay. I seemed to be alone with my worries that native groups and environmental concerns would delay production until after 2000. However, none of us in the financial community seem to have anticipated that the Newfoundland Government was about to trigger a series of events that would ultimately call into question the very viability of Voisey's.

CHAPTER 7

POLITICAL POSTURING

"How can a 'local legislature,'" a critic inquired, "influence the price of fish in a foreign market?" This was a hard question to answer. In a sense, the whole history of Newfoundland would hang on it.
— Old Newfoundland: A History to 1843, Patrick O'Flaherty

"Those who believe that I launched a squeeze play against Inco over Voisey's Bay are mistaken. In reality, I was maintaining the same justifiable position that my predecessor [Clyde Wells] had taken: Voisey's Bay should be developed in a manner that was fair to both the company and the people of Newfoundland and Labrador."
— Brian Tobin, 2002

Mr. A. Snow, PC Opposition MHA for Menihek: "Mr. Speaker, I find it passing strange that ... the Minister of Finance says he doesn't know how much revenue is going to be accruing from the greatest mineral deposit in this Province in our history [Voisey's Bay]."

Mr. P. Dicks, Minister of Finance and Treasury Board: "Mr. Speaker, I don't find it strange at all. ... [If] the honourable member ... can tell me with exactitude what exactly the world nickel price will be, copper prices, and the price for cobalt, then we can apply a regime, too, and probably tell him what the royalties will be."
— Hansard, Newfoundland and Labrador House of Assembly, November 29 1995

On March 18, 1993, the Government of Newfoundland and Labrador announced that, to encourage mining, it intended to put a tax incentive into the Mining and Mineral Rights Act. This announcement may have encouraged the prospectors, Al Chislett and Chris

Verbiski, to carry out the program which led to the discovery of Voisey's Bay late that summer.

Nevertheless, it was not until November 28, 1994, twenty-five days after Diamond Fields Resources had announced the discovery of a "potentially significant occurrence of base metal mineralization containing nickel, copper, and cobalt" at Voisey's Bay, that the government introduced a bill to amend the Mining and Mineral Rights Act. The bill proposed partial tax relief for the first ten years of a new mine's operation, improved allowances to encourage capital spending and exploration, and a scheme to encourage – but not compel – mining companies to construct smelters in the province. On December 16, 1994, the Lieutenant-Governor passed this bill into law.

On the same day, the Lieutenant-Governor also passed into law an "Act to Promote Economic Diversification and Growth Enterprises ('EDGE') in the Province," which offered ten-year tax holidays to new businesses of any kind. The relief offered by EDGE was more generous than the relief offered in the amended Mining and Mineral Rights Act.

On May 24, 1995, five days after Rex Gibbons, the Minister of Natural Resources, had proclaimed Voisey's Bay to be "beyond our wildest dreams," Premier Clyde Wells rose in Newfoundland's Parliament, the House of Assembly, to announce that he was "confident that the EDGE incentives are not required to proceed with" the Voisey's Bay project and that he would, therefore, refuse to allow these incentives to be applied to that project. With a nod to Mr. Gibbons, he went on to point out that it now seemed that the amendments to the Mining and Mineral Rights Act, which he had passed into law the previous December, would also be "overly generous" to Voisey's Bay, and that he therefore proposed further revisions to the Act. He suggested that these revisions would include a cap on tax relief.

Mr. Wells's announcement should have dampened expectations of Voisey's Bay's future, after-tax cash flows. For example, his decision to exclude Voisey's Bay from the EDGE program was a surprise because there was nothing in the EDGE legislation that required new ventures to be disqualified should they promise to be both large and profitable. Was the stock market concerned, or did it even notice? Evidently not: Diamond Fields's shares rose by $2.00 (before allowing for the subsequent split) on May 24 and by another $4.00 the next day, despite an absence of other news from Voisey's Bay. Whether other participants in the stock market had been cynical like me (I had always assumed that there would be a tax regime similar to that which prevailed before the EDGE program and before December 1994's amendments to the Mining and Mineral Rights Act.), or ignorant, either of the existence of the tax incentives or of Mr. Wells's proposed changes in their application, I do not know.

Five months passed with no sign of the proposed amendments to the Mining and Mineral Rights Act. An internal report in June by Willem Beunderman, an analyst with CRU International in London, entertained the possibility that provincial mining taxes would be waived altogether. On October 24, 1995, the Leader of the Opposition challenged the Premier to table the legislation. The Premier responded, "I can confirm for the Leader of the Opposition that Voisey's Bay mineral discovery is probably the richest, certainly the richest in Canada in recent generations. ... We have let the mining company know that the Province will require that all further processing of those minerals will be done within the Province, wherever in the company's judgment it is most appropriate to do it. We will leave that to them to decide, but we will require that it be done within this Province."

Mr. Well's comments may have confused some observers. They certainly confused me. Did the company have the option of processing Voisey's Bay ore outside the province or not? The next day, Rex Gibbons attempted to clarify matters. "For the first time in 498 years we have finally discovered a mineral deposit in this Province that is big enough to justify us requiring that the processing be done in this Province. ... Let it be clear to anybody who is listening that smelting is included in processing."

As in May, the stock market showed no sign of worry that Mr. Wells and Dr. Gibbons's proposals could threaten the development or the profitability of Voisey's Bay. On October 23, Diamond Fields's shares had closed at $21.50 per share, having split 4:1 on September 21; after Mr. Wells's comments on October 24, they closed at $21.75, and on October 25, after Dr. Gibbons's "clarification," at $22.75.

Robyn Storer of CS First Boston's London office probably best captured the stock market's outlook at this time. On November 30, 1995, Robyn, who had been on Diamond Fields's trip to Voisey's Bay in June 1995, published a long and careful report on Voisey's Bay. Although she believed that Diamond Fields would eventually build its own smelter, she considered that, in its early years, Voisey's Bay would ship its production to a smelter owned by a third party, outside the province, and that the government would not block such shipments.

On November 27, 1995, the provincial government introduced Bill 43, the first of what it said would be two bills to amend the Mining and Mineral Rights Act. Bill 43 proposed a cap to the ten-year tax relief allowed in the amendments that the government had passed into law a year earlier, and allowed the government to impose a further tax — the "non-renewable resource development tax" — on big, unusually profitable operations.

On December 14, Ed Roberts, the Minister of Justice, revealed that the "non-renewable resource development tax" would be a "two-tier tax ... the first tier ... at a rate of 10% on the profits beyond a 20% rate of return and the second tier will apply if the project rate of return exceeds 30% in any given year. The tax rate on the second tier profits is a further 10%."

During the parliamentary debate on Bill 43, opposition Progressive Conservative member Alvin Hewlett reminded the Premier that businesses are shy about investing in jurisdictions where the rules of the game keep changing. Why, then, he asked, was the government proposing to change the rules of the mining game only a year after the last such change?

Premier Wells replied, "It is quite simple, Mr. Speaker. When the tax law was introduced a year or so ago ... the officials who advised us ... never contemplated a Voisey's Bay — a mine that rich. ... Mr. Speaker, no self-respecting government can see its laws ... continue to remain as they are if it results in an unfair treatment of the taxpayers of this Province. ... If ... we [say] wait until you discover something and then we will pounce, what kind of a message are we sending out?"

But that's "exactly what you are doing," cried another opposition member, Neil Windsor.

On December 18, 1995, Paul Dicks, Minister of Finance and Treasury Board, acknowledged that businesses were daunted by governments that changed tax regimes in an opportunistic fashion. For this reason, he and the rest of the government deemed it "appropriate to have a regime of general application to avoid uncertainty."

Nevertheless, there would need to be further changes in the rules. Despite what his colleague Mr. Roberts had announced on December 14, Mr. Dicks said that "The actual rates [of the non-renewable resource development tax] have not yet been determined," adding that the bill would allow the government to "impose what it believes to be ... appropriate incremental tax[es]." "Mr. Speaker," he concluded, "I expect that the mining industry will have some substantial views on this." He "would be interested in hearing what [the members of the opposition] have to say on the matter."

The Leader of the Opposition, Lynn Verge, responded that she was grateful that her party's pressure on the government, "for a more sane approach ... had been successful." And so, said Messrs. Hewlett and Windsor, were they. The leader of the New Democratic Party, the NDP, also blessed the bill.

On December 5, the government introduced Bill 46, which was the second bill to amend the Mining and Mineral Rights Act. On December 19, Rex Gibbons, Minister of Natural Resources, described Bill 46 to Newfoundland's House of Assembly as follows: "The amendments to the Mineral Act contained in this bill would permit the Lieutenant-Governor in Council[25] to require, if it deserved to do so, as a condition of a mining lease that a lessee complete ... smelting, processing or refining ... in the Province. ... The Lieutenant-Governor in Council shall not impose such a requirement where the lessee demonstrates that it would not be economically feasible to do so." He added, "We don't have to look any further than the closest province, Nova Scotia, and the next closest to that, New Brunswick, to see this same principle embedded in their legislation."

Alvin Hewlett was the first to debate Bill 46. He liked it, although he warned that "some large international company having widespread, worldwide holdings could buy up the entire [Voisey's Bay] project and sit on it for a period of time, given the fact that it may well have sufficient mineral properties elsewhere in the world to meet the needs of its other smelters."

Another Progressive Conservative, Alec Snow, recalled "the number of mistakes that we made in previous development[s]" that "cost this province untold billions of dollars." He surmised that the government was considering Argentia, on the island of Newfoundland, as the location for the future Voisey's Bay smelter.

"I know it is nice to be able to say that it will be good to have a smelter in Argentia; you can drive to work, even from St. John's." But, Mr. Snow implied, the construction of a smelter would require the addition of new capacity to the island's electric grid, so he asked, "Who is going to subsidize the electrical energy that will be consumed?"

Dr. Gibbons, Resource Minister, promised Mr. Snow that electricity for the smelter "will not be subsidized no matter where it is."

The NDP leader spoke in support of the bill. The first published criticism of Bills 43 and 46 came from outside Newfoundland — not, as Mr. Dicks had expected, from the mining industry, but from Julian Baldry who, as a mining analyst with the Bank of Montreal's investment arm, Nesbitt Burns, spoke on behalf of investors.

Mining analysts from competing firms spend a lot of time with each other, both at meetings with the management of mining companies, and on far-flung trips arranged by those companies in order to show off their mines, mills, and smelters. In the early days of her career, Liz had gone to the annual meeting of a mining company. As she looked around the room at analysts chatting with each other, analysts whom she had met one at a time, she exclaimed to Julian and me, "But ... but you fellows all know each other!" We laughed, and Julian replied, "Yes, and we're all good friends!"

The Swedish-Canadian mining company Boliden once put a group of analysts into corporate jets to visit its operations across Europe. On one leg, the stewardesses took out the guest book, which showed the plane's most recent charter had been to Aerosmith. Surprisingly, the interior of the plane bore no signs of excessive wear. Julian leafed further back in the book and was delighted to find the signature of the model, Naomi Campbell. "Golly," he said, beaming, "do you think that my family will be impressed when I tell them that my bum sat on the same toilet seat as Naomi Campbell's bum?"

Heads shook. A chorus of "No, Julian!"

Julian was a dedicated smoker, so dedicated that he once tried to light up during a tour of Falconbridge's nickel smelter in Sudbury, Ontario. "They grabbed my cigarette," he complained, "and hustled me through the dust and fumes and out the door, saying there was no smoking in the smelter! They might as well try to ban farting in a cowshed!"

On December 19, 1995, Julian and his associate Steve Butler published a comment on Bills 43 and 46 which, they said, reflected "discussions with both the Diamond Fields management and officials in the provincial civil service." It was, perhaps, from the latter that Baldry and Butler inferred that the proposed rates of the "non-renewable resource development tax" were to be based, not on 20% and 30% rates of return on 100% of the capital invested (as one might have inferred from Mr. Roberts's pronouncements of December 14), but on 110% of the capital invested. This would be slightly positive for Voisey's Bay because it would raise the level at which this tax — that Messrs. Baldry and Butler called the "Super-Tax" — kicked in. Nevertheless, Baldry and Butler calculated that the "Super-Tax" could increase the tax bill of a hypothetical Voisey's Bay operation by as much as $45 million per year. Although they described the tax as "punitive," they concluded that, because the tax would not take effect before the Voisey's Bay project had recovered most of its original investment, "the impact to NPV calculations is relatively small but not insignificant."

Despite evident support of Bill 43 by all parties in the House, Baldry and Butler hoped, "for Newfoundland's sake," that the final bill would be "a shadow of the current proposal." They surmised that Bill 46, the amendment to the Mineral Act that demanded local smelting where feasible, could be "in contravention of the interprovincial agreement signed by Newfoundland in 1994 and, on a wider scale, the terms of NAFTA and GATT." However, they conceded that the location of the smelter would "not change our investment opinion significantly."

In my own valuation models, I had been assuming that Voisey's Bay would send its output to a third party for custom smelting and refining. So did the analysts at, for example, First Marathon Securities and CRU International Limited. I think that we all believed that, if Voisey's Bay were to build its own smelter, what it lost on higher capital costs it would gain on lower operating costs and better recovery of cobalt. In other words, we believed that neither the location nor the ownership of the smelter was critical to the value of Voisey's.

On December 21, 1995, the Lieutenant-Governor of Newfoundland and Labrador signed Bill 46 into law.

On December 28, 1995, Clyde Wells resigned as Premier to pursue an employment opportunity he perceived at the Supreme Court of Newfoundland.

On January 17, 1996, Brian Tobin took the leadership of Newfoundland and Labrador's Liberal Party by acclamation. He then dissolved parliament. Bill 43, which Baldry and Butler had described as the "Super-Tax" bill, died on the order paper.

* * * * *

During the debates on Voisey's Bay, opposition member Hewlett identified three of the most important issues in the Great Smelter Debate, a debate which, for years to come, would define the relationship between the provincial government and Diamond Fields and its successor, Inco Limited.

Firstly, Mr. Hewlett remarked that "the mining community is out there saying you don't change the rules in the middle of the game." Secondly, he pointed out that Diamond Fields's commitment to a smelter was soft, as was that of its partner, Inco, because, as Diamond Fields's Cliff Carson had pointed out, the world already had more nickel smelters than it needed. Thirdly, Mr. Hewlett warned that, for every dollar that entered the provincial coffers from Voisey's Bay, the federal government could trim a dollar from its "equalization payments" — subsidies — to the province.

If the stock market cared about the developments in the Newfoundland House of Assembly, it did not care very much. On November 27, 1995, the day that the government introduced the "Super-Tax" bill, Bill 43, Diamond Fields's shares fell $0.25 to $26.625. When Bill 46 was introduced on December 5, they rose $0.50. Then, on December 14, when Mr. Roberts revealed the size of the "Super-Tax," they rose another $0.25. And on December 19, when Messrs. Baldry and Butler publicized the changes proposed in these two bills, they fell $0.75.

Clearly, at the end of 1995, investors were focusing on something more immediate than changes in mining laws. At the time, Diamond Fields's Cliff Carson told me that at least once a week they would hear from someone who wanted to buy the company or the ore body. I'm sure that he told other analysts the same thing. Would Diamond Fields soon become the object of a takeover battle?

CHAPTER 8

A BEAUTIFUL WOMAN IN A BAR

Right now, Diamond Fields is like a beautiful woman in a bar. There are a lot of rough-and-ready characters coming over to flirt.
— Edward Mercaldo, Executive Vice-President and Chief Financial Officer, Diamond Fields Resources Inc., quoted in *Maclean's Magazine*, May 22, 1995

INCO'S SHARE OF THE WORLD NICKEL MARKET
or: "why Inco was so keen to buy into Voisey's Bay"

Based on data provided by Inco Ltd. and on estimates by Raymond J. Goldie

Press release

February 9, 1996, Vancouver, B.C. — *Robert M. Friedland and Jean Raymond Boulle, Co-chairmen of Diamond Fields Resources Inc. (DFR) announced today that its board of directors has unanimously approved a merger proposal from Falconbridge Limited (Falconbridge) pursuant to which all of the common shares of DFR would be exchanged for a combination of cash and securities of Falconbridge.*

Press release

February 9, 1996, Toronto, Ontario — Falconbridge Limited (Falconbridge) announced today that Diamond Fields Resources Inc. (Diamond Fields) has accepted Falconbridge's proposal to merge Diamond Fields with Falconbridge. This transaction will result in Falconbridge becoming the operator and 75% owner of the Voisey's Bay nickel, copper, and cobalt project in Labrador, Canada. ... It is Falconbridge's intention to build a mine, mill, smelter, and refinery to support production of nickel metal from Voisey's Bay by 1999.

FAX
TO: Ray Goldie
Diamond Fields Resources Inc. (T-DFR) is pleased to invite you to a teleconference to discuss the recent merger proposal by Falconbridge Limited.
Date: Monday, February 12, 1996
Time: 4:15 p.m. Eastern Time
Call-in number: 212 346 6477
In attendance from Diamond Fields Resources will be:
Mr. Robert Friedland, Co-chairman and Director
Mr. Edward Mercaldo, Executive Vice-President and Chief Financial Officer
For further information, please contact Kalayra Angelyys.
** This call is open to the investment community and by invitation only **

At the morning meeting on February 13, 1996, I put my hand up. "I was on an analysts' conference call last night. Diamond Fields clarified its proposed merger with Falconbridge. Some of the more interesting points were: DFR's principals are prepared to make long-term commitments to the merged company. Messrs. Friedland, Boulle, and Mercaldo, who together own 25% of DFR's shares, have said that they will exchange their shares for Falconbridge paper, accepting no cash.

Messrs. Friedland and Boulle have also committed to keep at least half of their investment for at least two years.

"The next move would seem to be up to Inco. Remember, Inco owns 25% of the Voisey's Bay project. DFR has told Inco that Inco has until February 14 if it wishes to make a counter-offer. Inco's options are surprisingly restricted. Not only can Inco not buy DFR shares in the open market (because this action would be prohibited by its standstill agreement with DFR), Mr. Friedland reminded us that he holds the voting rights on the DFR shares held by Inco. This is weird. As it stands right now, Mr. Friedland will be voting Inco's shares in favour of a takeover bid by Inco's arch-rival, Falconbridge. Nevertheless, the February 14 deadline seems to be more metaphysical than real. There is nothing to stop Inco — or anyone else — making a counter-offer after that date, although DFR and Falcy hope to have their merger completed by April 30th."

"Do you think Inco *will* bid?"

"I do, Patricia, and then Falconbridge will probably make a higher bid. ... Look, I'd give odds of 55%, 35%, and 10% that the eventual acquirer will be, respectively, Falconbridge, Inco, or someone else. 'Someone else' is most likely to be Britain's RTZ; Australia's BHP seems to have lost interest.

"I suspect that Falcy has the edge because one of the biggest attractions of the deal offered to Diamond Fields by Falconbridge would be that it allows DFR's current management to continue to play an active role in the development of the Voisey's Bay deposits. Other potential bidders may not be willing to make such a provision."

"So, what should investors do?"

"The winner will have to issue a lot more shares. Now, I think we will see a spike in nickel prices beginning this year, so that nickel companies will soon enjoy their strongest earnings of the current business cycle. Voisey's won't be in production in time to take advantage of this spike. So the peak earnings per share of the winning company will be heavily diluted by all those extra shares.

"Not only that, the acquirer would have to pay the huge cost of bringing Voisey's Bay into production — perhaps $1.5 billion in Inco's case, $1.1 billion for Falconbridge."

"Why would Inco spend so much more?"

"I'm assuming Inco builds a nickel smelter and refinery, but that the Newfoundland government would allow Falconbridge to build just the smelter, from which smelted product would be shipped to the Falconbridge plant in Norway to be refined.

"In Falconbridge's case," I said, "these expenditures would come on top of the spending programs to which it has committed at two other big mining projects, Raglan and Collahuasi.

"So, investors should avoid investing in the eventual 'winner.' The best way to do this is to avoid the shares of both Falconbridge and Inco. DFR's shares closed last night at $38.25.[26] I'd still buy them on the basis that at least one more offer is likely."

The phone is ringing when I return to my office.

"Is Falcy offering too high a price, Ray?"

Even over the phone, I could almost smell Starbucks on Liz's breath.

"In a game like this, Liz, that's not the important question. The question really is, Does Inco — or another company — share the same assumptions as Falconbridge?"

"Why?"

"The winner's curse. The bidder that deserves to win should be the one which has the most realistic assessment of the value of the property under auction. However, provided it has enough money, the bidder that has the least appreciation of the property's shortcomings, and hence has the highest assessment of the property's value, will be the winner.

"The best example of an accursed winner I remember was Hudson's Bay Oil and Gas, which won an auction in 1981 to buy Cyprus Anvil Mining Corporation. Cyprus Anvil's main asset was a zinc-lead-silver mine in the Yukon. Less than a year after HBOG bought Cyprus Anvil, it had to shut the mine down to staunch its losses."

"So what are Voisey's shortcomings?"

"Just one, really — timing. Falcy thinks Voisey's can be in production by 1999. I think that the scolding trinity — government, natives and environmentalists — will delay start-up until sometime next century. So, even if my assumptions about tonnages, grades, costs, nickel prices, and so on were to be identical to Falconbridge's, their estimate of the Net Present Value of the project would be higher than mine, simply because the value of cash flow in the near future is greater than the value of cash flow in the more distant future. But, in a bidding war, my valuation doesn't matter. What matters is the value Inco would put on Voisey's. If they also think Voisey's will be in production by 1999, their valuation should be similar to Falcy's. So, if we assume that Falcy didn't initially bid the full value of what it thought the project was really worth, Inco should have room to make a counter-bid."

"*Does* Inco think a 1999 start-up is likely?"

"I've heard 1998."

"Thanks! We'll hang on!"

February 14 comes. Diamond Fields issues a press release announcing that "Inco has confirmed that it will not be submitting a counter-offer for Diamond Fields by 6:00 p.m. today." Accordingly, Diamond Fields and Falconbridge are to "execute an arrangement agreement" that would lead to the merger of the two companies. Diamond Fields's shares close the day at $37.75,[27] down $0.625 from where it closed the previous day.

The merger requires the approval of the shareholders of both companies. Accordingly, on March 11, 1996, Falconbridge's President and Chief Executive Officer Frank Pickard and Diamond Fields's Robert Friedland show up at a meeting for shareholders in Toronto, seeking their approval. Mr. Friedland speaks first. Even though my eyes are weak and my seat is halfway to the back of the auditorium, I can see his boyish face and his Falconbridge tie.

"We really mean this," he says. "This offer is not a stalking horse." He explains that Falconbridge has two natural advantages over any competing bidder: its ability to use a smelter in Newfoundland to treat ore from its proposed Raglan mine, along the coast of far northern Quebec, west of Labrador; and its ability to recover 80% of the cobalt at Voisey's vs. 40% for "a competitor."

Frank Pickard confirms that his company hopes to begin mining at Voisey's Bay in 1999, producing 115,000 tonnes of nickel per year, initially running the output of the mine through Falconbridge's existing smelter and refinery. In the first six or seven years, says Mr. Pickard, Voisey's Bay's cost per pound of nickel produced would be negative, a theme reiterated by Mr. Friedland in the question period: "Voisey's Bay can force its competitors to operate in an anaerobic environment."

I phone Rosie to see how she and her fellow Diamond Fields employees are faring. "Thanks for asking, Ray. We're kinda hoping that Falconbridge wins. Frank Pickard flew out to see us and assure us that Falconbridge would keep us all on the payroll after it takes us over."

"And Inco?"

"Invisible!"

March 26, 1996, evening

Finally. A counter-offer from Inco.

March 27, 1996, Morning Meeting

"How much better than Falconbridge's offer is Inco's offer, Ray?"

"Well, Patricia, Inco's offering a package of cash, common shares of Inco, preferred shares of Inco, something called 'targeted' or 'VBN' shares tied to the financial results of a future mine at Voisey's Bay and a diamond 'stub' — shares in an entity representing the DFR's original diamond business.

"Falconbridge had offered a package of cash, common shares of Falconbridge, shares called 'P' shares tied to Voisey's Bay's *exploration* results and the same diamond stub.

"If you use last night's closing share prices, and if you accept Inco's statement that those 'targeted shares' are worth $42.00 each, Inco's package is worth $41.20 per Diamond Fields share. I think the Falconbridge package is worth only $35.98 per share. It certainly *looks* as if the Inco package is worth more, but, to be sure, you'd have to know Inco's and Falcy's future share prices, Voisey's Bay's future financial results, and exploration results."

"Inco has committed itself to buying back its common shares in the open market," says Patricia. "They say that, over the next five years, they could afford to buy back approximately the number of common shares that they will have to issue in order to complete this deal. That should help support the price of Inco's common shares, Ray — but do you think they'll have the cash to do it?"

"Yes, I do, as long as the world's demand for nickel continues to grow at 7% a year!"

"Recommendations?"

"DFR closed last night at $36.375. Inco's offer seems to be worth $41.20. Hang on to DFR. It ain't over."

Later that day, Inco Chairman and Chief Executive Officer Mike Sopko holds a conference call for analysts. He reviews Inco's offer and Inco's plans for the development of Voisey's Bay: "Production of 270 million pounds [122,000 tonnes] of nickel per year and 200 million pounds [90,000 tonnes] of copper. ... Initial production could begin as soon as 1998, with full production attained by 2000." Diamond Fields's shares close that day at $39.50; up $3.125.

The next twist in the plot comes on April 2, 1996. Falconbridge amends its offer to acquire Diamond Fields, and adds a proposal to sell 25% of Voisey's Bay to Inco so that Voisey's would become a 50:50 joint venture of Falconbridge and Inco. The next day, Falconbridge's Chief Executive Officer Frank Pickard invites analysts to a conference call. He explains that he has recognized that investors had had a hard time comparing his company's bid with that of Inco, because it was difficult to figure out the values of either Falconbridge's proposed "P" shares (tied to the value of exploration at Voisey's Bay), or of Inco's proposed "targeted" or "VBN" shares (tied to the future cash flows from the Voisey's Bay mine).

"That's why," says Mr. Pickard, "we're making an offer with no smoke and mirrors." He outlines Falconbridge's new package: plain vanilla preferred shares, easy to value; cash, very easy to value; regular common shares. Their prices change every day, but you can look them up in the paper; and the diamond stub. Whatever that stub is worth, it's the same as in the Inco package. In total, about $38.00 per Diamond Fields share.

"Frank," asks one analyst, "Inco's offer is higher, so don't Diamond Fields's directors have a fiduciary responsibility to accept it?"

"We question that assumption, that the Inco offer is worth more than ours," replies Mr. Pickard. "Inco's package includes a quarter of a VBN share per Diamond Fields share. Inco *says* the VBN shares are worth $42.00 each, so a quarter of a share is worth $10.50. We think that a quarter of a VBN share is worth only $6.00. This means that our offer is worth *more* than Inco's."

The next day, Inco announces a coup. Diamond Fields's Board has agreed to accept a new bid from Inco. The new bid looks a lot like the old bid, but with enhancements to the "VBN" shares — the "targeted" shares tied to the financial performance of a future Voisey's Bay mine. These enhancements include a promise by Inco to spend $80 million in exploration of Diamond Fields's properties in Labrador, Norway, and Greenland,[28] representing $0.77 per VBN share, to be spent on exploration directed at improving the value of those shares. Inco also adds a stipulation that the dividend on the VBN shares would never be less than 80% of the dividend on the common shares. Assuming Inco does not change the dividend which it pays on its common shares, I estimate that this new provision adds $1.20 to the value of the VBN shares or $0.30 to the value of Inco's package per Diamond Fields share.

On April 4, Inco holds a telephone conference call. President Scott Hand reminds analysts that Voisey's Bay does not represent Inco's only potential for growth. The company is, he says, awaiting the results of studies of the feasibility of two other promising nickel projects — one in Brazil and the other at a property called Goro, in New Caledonia.

On April 23, 1996, I report to the morning meeting that I have prepared an elaborate valuation model for the Class VBN shares, and conclude that they are worth between $21.84 and $31.25 per share, not the $42.00 claimed by Inco. "Nevertheless," I add, "I bet that the takeover battle is over and that Inco has won. We're unlikely to see another bid from Falconbridge because Falcy's last bid signalled that it was uncomfortable about increasing its previous bid without the involvement of a partner, and Falconbridge is aware that Inco's management puts more value on having a dominant share of nickel markets than does Falcy. This outcome is bittersweet for Falconbridge's management. Bitter because Inco trumped them with what seems to have been an inferior offer. Sweet because Falcy pockets Cdn$101 million in fees, before expenses."

Before new securities are formally listed on exchanges, they often trade on an "if-, as-, and when-issued," or grey market basis. The Class VBN shares first trade on the grey market on April 24, 1996, closing at $38.25. They would reach their all-time high, $43.50, on August 21, the day Inco finally completed its takeover of Diamond Fields.

* * * * *

On May 15, a team of Texas lawyers issued a press release on behalf of an American mineral exploration company called Exdiam Corporation, saying that they had filed a lawsuit in Texas seeking settlement of a dispute between Exdiam and Diamond Fields. Exdiam alleged that Diamond Fields's Co-Chairman Jean-Raymond Boulle had improperly diverted diamond interests in Arkansas and Minnesota from Exdiam to Diamond Fields.[29] In public, Diamond Fields, assisted by Inco, requested that the court dismiss Exdiam's motion. In private, Diamond Fields, Inco, and Exdiam met to try to hammer out a deal that would allow Inco to take over Diamond Fields. On August 5, 1996, Inco announced in a press release that it had agreed to pay Exdiam US$25 million if it would just go away. On August 20, the court approved this transaction and, on August 21, Inco completed its acquisition of Diamond Fields in a transaction that Inco valued at $4.3 billion.[30]

Most of us in Toronto's financial community viewed Exdiam's lawsuit as opportunistic blackmail. Nevertheless, worries about the lawsuit had only a small effect on the price of the Class VBN shares because investors assumed, correctly, that any direct expenditures related to the suit would be borne by the holders of Inco's common shares and not by the holders of the Class VBN shares. As Newfoundland and Labrador's Mines Minister Rex Gibbons put it, the Texas lawsuit was "just a pimple on the back of an elephant."[31]

On August 23, Inco appointed Stewart Gendron as President of Voisey's Bay Nickel Company, a former subsidiary of Diamond Fields, which was now a wholly owned subsidiary of Inco Ltd. Four days later, Dr. Gendron announced the members of his new executive team, which was to develop Voisey's Bay from a base in St. John's:[32] Frank Armitage, Vice-President, Human Resources, who had a background in mining in Ontario; Herbert Clarke, Vice-President, Corporate Affairs, who had "initial responsibility to negotiate impact and benefit agreements with aboriginal groups" and had "more than two decades in the Newfoundland public service"; Derrick E. "Rick" Gill, Executive Vice-President, a former Executive Vice-President of Diamond Fields, who had a background in communications and advertising in Atlantic Canada; Gerald Marshall, Vice-President, Mining and Milling, who had worked his way up through Inco's ranks as a mine engineer; William Napier, Vice-President, Environment, Health and Safety, who had a background in environmental sciences related to mining; and Dr. Richard Stratton-Crawley, Vice-President, Smelting and Refining, a Cornishman with a background at Inco in mineral processing research.

CHAPTER 9

SELECTIVE DISCLOSURE

Canadian securities regulators today published a draft policy statement that provides guidance and best practices on corporate disclosure, and assists public companies in avoiding selective disclosure. ... The draft policy recommends public companies consider implementing the following best disclosure practices: ...
• Limit the number of people authorized to speak on behalf of the company to analysts, the media, and investors.
• Adopt an "open access" policy for analyst conference calls by permitting any interested party to listen by telephone and/or through a webcast.
— Press release, Ontario Securities Commission,
May 25, 2001

By designating its conference call on February 12, 1996 as "open to the investment community and by invitation only," Diamond Fields created a stir. In the February 19, 1996 edition of *The Globe and Mail*, reporter Karen Howlett commented that "Executives of Diamond Fields Resources ... [were] following a time-honoured tradition in this country in which public companies routinely hold invitation-only conference calls to flesh out information in news releases and provide an opportunity to question management. It's part of what John Bart, head of the Canadian Shareowners Association in Windsor, Ont. refers to as an unlevel playing field. Companies discriminate not only against individual shareholders but also smaller institutional investors by 'effectively shutting them out of this disclosure,' he said."

Within a few years, arguments like those of Mr. Bart had persuaded North America's securities commissions that all investors should have access to the same information at the same time.

Fortunately, technology had evolved so as to allow hundreds or thousands of people to participate in conference calls. The usual conference format became one where only professional analysts were permitted to pose questions. Everyone else joined the conference on a "listen-only basis." Few companies went to the lengths of Pan-American Silver Corp., Rosie Moore's employer after her stint at Diamond Fields. Pan-American allowed all interested parties to pose questions. At a call on November 9, 2001, the first question was from an individual shareholder who launched into a detailed exposition of the uses and husbandry of the quinchona tree. Pan-American's Chairman eventually interrupted, explaining that he knew nothing about quinchona, nor about its relevance to the production of silver, and that he would refer the question to Rosie.

CHAPTER 10

THE GOVERNMENT PREPARES TO CHALLENGE INCO'S CORPORATE POWER

"The current impasse is not rooted in the construction of a smelter refinery, but more so in an equalization program that stifles the province from moving forward," Peter Woodward, vice-president of operations, the Woodward Group of Companies, said Tuesday.

Revenues from Voisey's Bay are subject to clawback under the federal equalization agreement, which expires in 2004. ... "The smelter refinery is the province's way of deriving benefits through employment, which is not eligible for clawback."

— Pat Doyle, *The Telegram*, St. John's, November 29, 2000

[NDP Leader] Jack Harris: "What progress has been made in achieving a change in [the federal] equalization formulas ... as they will affect the revenues of the province for a project like Voisey's Bay?"

[Premier] Brian Tobin: "[It was] important for the country to take a look at the equalization formula and see if we can change that formula. ... We have in Canada a formula where you can have, basically, for every extra dollar earned, 75 or 80 cents clawed back. It is a problem, but it is not a matter that can be changed by the actions of one government or, for that matter, the federal government. It requires the agreement of all of the provinces of Canada. I can honestly tell the member opposite that governments of every political stripe ... have said no to changes because we have currently in this country an attitude that is based on: 'What's in it for me?'"

— *Hansard*, Newfoundland and Labrador House of Assembly, December 9, 1999

"Are you mad? Diamonds? In Labrador? Have you been taking Chuck Furey seriously again?"
— Hennessey, 1997, broadcast on CBC Radio St. John's, July 1994

"Resource development is primarily a political decision."
— John Gadsby, Gadsby Consulting Ltd., Vancouver B.C.; Prospectors and Developers Association of Toronto International Convention, Toronto, March 11, 2003

On March 27, 1996, Paul Shelley, a member of the opposition Progressive Conservatives, had risen in Newfoundland and Labrador's House of Assembly and asked the Minister of Mines and Energy, "In the last session of the House, the previous Administration introduced amendments to the Mineral Tax Act which have specific implications for Voisey's Bay. ... [Will] those amendments be brought back in this session?"

Dr. Gibbons responded, "We have to ... determine whether or not we want to go through a consultation process before we bring them back in."[33] The provincial Industry Minister, Chuck Furey, later added that the idea of imposing another layer of taxes on Voisey's Bay — the "Super-Tax" — was "very much alive."[34]

A year passed with no sign of proposals to amend the province's tax laws. On March 19, 1997, Mr. Shelley tried again. He asked the Minister of Mines and Energy, "With the legislation that is in this House, there is a ten-year tax break to Inco and Voisey's Bay. When does the Minister expect the legislation [to] be changed?"

Dr. Gibbons answered, "There is no ten-year tax break for Inco. Inco was told a year ago that there was no ten-year tax break for Inco. There will never be a ten-year tax break for Inco — never!" In fact, added Premier Tobin, "We are not going to negotiate [with Inco]; we are going to tell Inco what share we are going to take, and it is going to be a rather large share for the people of Newfoundland and Labrador."

Despite his intention to retroactively change the province's tax laws to the detriment of Inco, Dr. Gibbons evidently felt some affection for mining companies. He was a rarity — a Mines Minister with professional qualifications in mining. On April 4, 1997, after months of watching northern Labrador's nickel rush enrich his colleagues in the private sector, he resigned from Cabinet to join them.

On October 9, 1997, Chuck Furey, Dr. Gibbons's successor at what was by then known as the Ministry of Mines and Energy, visited Toronto. He brought with him Paul Dean, his Assistant Deputy Minister. I was one of a group of seven directors of the Prospectors and Developers Association of Canada that had come together at short notice. As we spread out around the Association's vast boardroom table, I recalled Mr. Furey's comments on the "Super-Tax" and asked him, "Minister, how do you respond to charges that uncertainty about the tax structure has driven exploration out of the province?" Mr. Furey, former chief of staff for Brian Tobin and every millimetre the telegenic politician (good hair, good teeth, cleft chin), replied that "The whole tax issue is being looked at now. I don't want a tax on windfall profits, and there will be consultation with the mining industry."

There the matter rested, and during the rest of Brian Tobin's tenure as premier, we heard no more about changes in mining taxes. The issue that came to define the relationship between Inco and Mr. Tobin's government was not taxes; it was whether or not the government would allow Inco to develop the Voisey's Bay mine without being required to build a nickel smelter and refinery in Newfoundland and Labrador.

The participants in this debate initially quarrelled over the development of the Voisey's Bay mine. Later, the debate over the smelter and refinery moved to centre stage.

As I watched the drama play out, I tried to learn about the subtexts. What was motivating the players? One of my first clues came from one of Premier Tobin's advisors, Bill Rowat, who pointed out that, "under Canada's ... equalization clawback arrangements ... a have-not province like Newfoundland would be no further ahead financially after the development of Voisey's Bay, since it would lose some federal financial support as its fiscal situation improved."[35]

Brian Lee Crowley, President of the Atlantic Institute for Market Studies in Halifax, Nova Scotia, explained equalization as follows:[36]

Equalization [is] a huge $10-billion federal program, the province of incomprehensible policy wonks and bureaucrats.

> ... Mr. Tobin made it his battle cry on his return to Ottawa. ... Equalization, despite its arcane language of "fiscal capacity" and "five-province standards," actually tries to do something very simple. Because some provinces are richer than others, they have a greater ability to pay for the services that are their responsibility under the Constitution. ...Enter equalization. While it does not make provincial revenues "equal" per capita across the country, it does transfer vast sums of money to the less well-off provinces. The average Atlantic province gets roughly 40% of its revenue from Ottawa, not from provincial taxpayers, the bulk of it in the form of equalization. ...
>
> Equalization works for provinces a bit like the welfare trap does for low-income people. As you move off welfare and into work, not only are your cash benefits withdrawn, but so are many other non-cash benefits, such as prescription drugs. On top of that, employment income is taxed. The result is that people at the lowest income levels are often materially better off on welfare than if they work. This traps people in dependence.
>
> Equalization can have analogous effects on provinces. ... when new money flows into the coffers of a province receiving equalization payments, the federal government, logically, reduces those payments. The "clawback" rate can vary from about 70% to 90%. ... The equalization clawback meant that virtually all of the tax revenues that the mine would generate would flow to Ottawa, not to the province that owns the resource.

When Chuck Furey visited the Prospectors and Developers Association of Canada in Toronto in October 1997, he had explained that he was there to ask for our help — our help in lobbying the federal government. He wanted the feds to maintain their equalization payments after tax revenues from Voisey's Bay had begun to flow into the provincial treasury. Although taken aback, we quickly came to the conclusion that such activity would stretch the Association's mandate of promoting Canada's mining exploration industry, and expressed our regrets. In this drama, we belonged in the audience, not on stage.

The Government Prepares to Challenge Inco's Corporate Power

As I sat in the audience, I realized that William Shakespeare could help me understand some of the subtexts that underlay the performances on stage.

CHAPTER 11

THE CALIBAN OF CANADA

The isle is full of noises, sounds and sweet airs, that give delight.
— *The Tempest*, William Shakespeare

June 30, 2001, Whangarei, New Zealand

I follow Aunt Betty down the steps, she, tall and slim, playing Sancho Panza to Uncle Bert's Don Quixote. I let Betty into the front passenger seat, then slip into the rear of their car. "Where are you taking us, Uncle Bert?"

"I have reservations at 'Reva's on the Waterfront,'" he says, backing down the driveway. "It's a new old place. They've been doing up the Town Basin, the waterfront, and Reva's is supposed to attract upmarket yachties."

We park and walk through the dark. Crunchy gravel, misty midwinter rain, salty mangrove swamp smell.

We continue onto a wooden deck and through a gingerbread-gabled door into Reva's. Victorian colonial architecture. A hostess who has just graduated from smile school. She settles Betty, Bert, and me by the window; outside, in the dark, we can make out a forest of yacht masts. As we tuck into a dish of antipasto brought by another graduate of smile school, Betty asks me how my book about Newfoundland is coming.

"Slow, slow, slow. The basic idea of the book is to show how, as a financial analyst, I tried to anticipate changes in the prices of shares related to the Voisey's Bay nickel deposit. To do that, I have to write not only about geological and financial stuff, I also have to explain how I tried to understand and then anticipate the moves of the major actors — mining companies, governments, and the people who live near the deposit in Labrador.

Another smile arrives, bearing plates. "Who was the vegetarian pasta?"

I raise my finger. "Mmm — looks yummy! And what are these?" I ask, pointing at the side of my plate.

"They're roast pumpkin seeds, sir. Enjoy!"

"Shall do!"

Betty tucks into her seafood pasta with obvious enjoyment. "So, Ray, what have you learned about the people involved in the project?"

"Well, let me ask you, how would you feel about the prospect of all of this" — I stretch out my arms, neatly intercepting a waiter bearing a plate of steamed mussels — "oops, sorry — of New Zealand giving up its nationhood to become another state of Australia?"

"Oh dear," says Bert. "We'd become impoverished and neglected, just like poor little Tasmania."

"OK! My reaction, too. Now, I remember hearing a radio interview with a lady from St. John's called Grace Sparkes, a Newfoundlander who fought against Newfoundland's absorption by Canada in the 1940s."

"Ah, right!"

"Ah, right!" is a New Zealand expression which means, "I have no idea what you're on about, but keep talking and perhaps you'll start making sense." So I keep talking.

"Near the end of the War, her husband, a Newfoundlander who had been educated in Ontario, had a quiet conversation with a couple of English officers who told him that the talk in London was that, once the war was over, Newfoundland was to become part of Canada. Mr. Sparkes, apparently, was horrified. I couldn't understand that. After all, he must have spent enough time in Canada to know that Canadians weren't ... weren't menacing wolves.[37] Then I tried to put myself in his shoes — I imagined that two Englishmen had just told me that New Zealand was about to be absorbed into Australia and found myself horrified as well."

Nods, over glasses of Australian shiraz.

"So, being a New Zealander helped you understand some of the motivations of today's Newfoundland government?"

"I think so. That and William Shakespeare."

Uncle Bert, former Principal of Whangarei Intermediate School, looks slightly surprised. "Shakespeare?"

"Well, what twigged me to it was that my all-time favourite band, Figgy Duff, a Newfoundland group, once recorded a song, 'Honour, riches.' The lyrics are from *The Tempest*."

"So you see the island in *The Tempest* as a metaphor for Newfoundland?"

"Maybe not just a metaphor, Uncle Bert. In Shakespeare's time, Newfoundland was a remote, misty, mysterious place. Maybe Newfoundland *was* the island in *The Tempest*!"

Uncle Bert begins to spread butter on a slice of bread. "I always had the impression it was Bermuda, or somewhere in the Caribbean."

"'This hard rock ... uninhabitable and almost inaccessible' sounds more like Newfoundland to me! But, more to the point, Caliban is a good metaphor for the way the Newfoundlander sees himself. Mocked by outsiders as they exploit him."

"Yes — it does sound like Tasmania!" concludes Uncle Bert.

"So the Caliban analogy made me realize that Newfoundlanders would likely support their government's insistence that whoever mines Voisey's Bay must also build a nickel smelter," I continue. "Their former premier, a fellow called Joey Smallwood, used to say that they were beggars, and 'beggars can't be choosers.' That mentality came from a history of being screwed by West Country English fish merchants, and that mentality led to Newfoundland giving away the shop to Reid Paper in order to get a railroad; it led to giving away most of the iron ore jobs in Labrador to Québec while Newfoundland got holes in the ground; it led to outsiders like Hydro-Québec, Alfred Valdmanis, J.C. Doyle, and John Shaheen walking away from the island rich and leaving behind half-baked, half-finished plants, empty dreams, and a growing sense of considerable embarrassment. One Newfoundland government even tried to find salvation in growing cucumbers! I got the impression that Newfoundlanders saw the mining company, Inco, as yet another outsider intent on scooping and running, leaving behind only an empty hole. Rape and run. Newfoundlanders seem to be determined not to be taken for fools again."

"Do you see this as New Zealand's economic history as well?" asks Betty.

"I do see some similarities, but I've found another part of Polynesia has taught me more."

"Where would that be?" asked Uncle Bert.

"Hawaii." Surprised faces. "Well, that's not so surprising. The Hawaiians are Polynesian just like the Maori here. Same people, same language."

Uncle Bert, who is part-Maori, chuckled. "Perhaps not *quite* the same language, Raymond. Remember, before Betty and I shifted to Sherwood Road, I lived on Kohe Street?"

"Up the hill."

"Up Parihaki. Well, I was once checking into a hotel in Hawaii, in Honolulu, and when the chap behind the counter read my address he burst out laughing. I asked him what was so funny, so he leaned over and whispered in my ear that, in Hawaiian, 'kohe' means," and Bert puts on his best American accent, "'a vagina!'" Sharp looks from the adjoining table as ours burst into raucous laughter.

Admonished, I continue. "Some of the similarities are that people have been living in both Newfoundland and Hawaii for a very long time, but most of them today are descended from those who arrived in the last 200 years. Both have had economies based on exploiting only one or two resources at a time — cod for Newfoundland, and sandalwood, then whaling, then sugar, then pineapples for Hawaii. Each place was dominated by less than a dozen interbred families of powerful merchants. Each had a monarchical tradition. Each had been profoundly shaped by American military occupation in World War II. And each was absorbed by larger, neighbouring countries under conditions that were and that remain controversial, even today."

"If this nickel deposit had been found in Hawaii, do you think the Hawaiian government would insist on construction of a smelter?" asks Betty.

"Umm ... I don't think so. There are also big *differences* between Hawaii and Newfoundland."

"No kidding."

"Not the least is that Hawaii is more prosperous than Newfoundland, thanks to federal subsidies of the sugar industry, much larger military spending, and a climate more conducive to tourism."

"Since you're talking about Hawaii," says Betty, "you should order the chocolate macadamia nut tart for dessert!"

"Done!" I say, and plunge back into my story. "Because of its prosperity, Hawaii has the luxury of being able to say 'no' to industries perceived as undesirable. So, to get back to your question about a smelter, Betty, smelters and refineries would probably be seen as not being compatible with Hawaii's biggest industry today, tourism.

"Another difference would be that Hawaii's merchant families evolved into multinational holding companies that have been adept at ensuring that the government, although traditionally Democrat, is, how shall we say, *aware* of the corporate point of view. In Newfoundland, however, Confederation with Canada enormously weakened the merchant families' hold on the economy. I suspect that the voices most commonly heard by Newfoundland's politicians are not corporate; they are those of Newfoundland's voters, and they want jobs.

"And yet another reason that voters have a stronger say in Newfoundland than Hawaii is that consensus is difficult to find in Hawaii. No ethnic group has a majority. But most Newfoundlanders are descended either from English West Country Protestants or from Catholics out of southeastern Ireland. They've developed a strong sense of what the Quebeckers call 'nous autres,' a sense of 'us-ness.' Newfoundlanders and Quebeckers would both line up in support of a leader whom they perceive to be battling outsiders on their behalf."

"Speaking of Irish," says Betty, "I recommend the 'Irish Fantasy Coffee!'"

CHAPTER 12

TOBIN VERSUS TORONTO

"Inco was sending out different messages ... and in this case [the issue of a smelter] they got caught ... the company's ability to communicate with people is just dreadful. I mean it is just awful."
— Peter Evans, resident of Nain, Labrador, to the Voisey's Bay Environmental Assessment Panel, September 17, 1998

"Newfoundland's a funny place. Everything seems to be going well then it blows up and you find yourself wondering why."
— Scott Hand, Chairman and CEO, Inco Ltd., musing to the Mineral Resource Analysts Group, Toronto, December 14, 2001

"But sometimes it is necessary to say no to an offer and walk away. ... In politics, the shareholders are the voters and taxpayers who put you in power, and politicians owe them the best deal possible, just as a company president owes the same to the shareholders."
— Brian Tobin, 2002

"I'd say probably the Voisey's Bay shag-up is the biggest [Newfoundland news story of 1998]."
— Former federal cabinet minister John Crosbie, St. John's *Telegram*, January 4, 1999

"In New York ... the f-word isn't even a word, it's a comma."
— American comedian Bill Lewis, quoted by Heather Mallick in *The Globe and Mail*, Toronto, April 10, 2004

From the outset, Inco and Mr. Tobin expressed their understanding of the requirement to build a smelter/refinery in terms that sounded similar, but that were, in fact, subtly different. In March 1996, just after Inco had bid for control of Diamond Fields, Inco's Chairman and CEO, Mike Sopko, made a courtesy call to Brian Tobin, who had been newly installed as premier. Mr. Tobin reported to the House of Assembly. "Today I have spoken with Mr. Mike Sopko of Inco, the President [sic] and Chief Executive Officer, and have confirmed ... [that] the only acceptable development plan for the government and for the people of Newfoundland and Labrador is one that sees a mine, a mine mill, a smelter and a refinery built in this province. ... I am delighted to report ... that Mr. Sopko has agreed fully to those terms and conditions."[38]

Dr. Sopko's recollection of his conversation with Mr. Tobin was that they had agreed that, by 1998, Voisey's Bay would begin to produce concentrate (feedstock for smelters) that would be sent out of the province to Inco's existing smelters. However, Inco would definitely build a smelter in Newfoundland or Labrador, and it should be up and running by 2000.[39]

The location of the smelter and refinery was of great interest to people of Newfoundland and Labrador. Paul Shelley suggested that, because "everybody in the Province has been promised a smelter ... one of the solutions ... [would be] to put the smelter on wheels!"[40]

It was fun to speculate about the location of the smelter and refinery, even though their whereabouts did not appear to be critical in determining the value of the Voisey's Bay project. They probably would not be at Voisey's Bay itself. There was no road out of Voisey's Bay, nor any prospect of one, and there was insufficient access to electricity. Moreover, Voisey's Bay is icebound in winter, which would make it difficult for Inco to efficiently serve the purchasers of its refined nickel and cobalt in a world of "just-in-time" inventories. Goose Bay, Labrador seemed a more likely choice because it could have access to cheap power from Churchill Falls. However, Goose Bay is also icebound in winter. It seemed most probable that the smelter and refinery would be on tidewater on the island of Newfoundland, but not on its iceberg-infested north coast. And it should be a "brownfield" site — one which had already been disturbed by industrialization — so as to avoid lengthy environmental permitting.

On March 11, 1996, the annual convention of the Prospectors and Developers Association of Canada features, as usual, several acres of tweed and beards. I buttonhole one tweedy, bearded gentleman,

Paul Dean from Placentia Bay in southeastern Newfoundland, who has just become Assistant Deputy Minister of Newfoundland and Labrador's new Mines and Energy department.

Mr. Dean explains that a key factor in the selection of a location for the smelter and refinery would be the availability of electricity. He tips Long Harbour on Placentia Bay as a likely site because it is the location of a former phosphorus plant that had available to it 100 megawatts from the island's grid. I recall that opposition member Mr. Alec Snow[41] had surmised that the government was considering Argentia, also on Placentia Bay, as the site for a smelter. Argentia is only 25 kilometres, as the fulmar flies, from Long Harbour — surely not too far to run a 100-megawatt extension cord.

November 28, 1996

"She's coming down tomorrow, Ray," is the word from our St. John's office.

Brokerage offices are the water coolers of the business world. Scarcely a week went by in 1996 without one of the stockbrokers at our St. John's office calling to find out what I was hearing in Toronto and to exchange gossip about exploration in Labrador.

"Wha?" I reply, brightly.

"The smelter site. Inco's going to announce the smelter site. My money's on Daniel's Harbour." Daniel's Harbour was the site of a zinc mine on the west coast of Newfoundland, recently closed by Teck Corporation.

"OK — I bet somewhere in Placentia Bay."

"Talk to you tomorrow!"

November 29, 1996

"Well, Ray, it was on the radio. Stewart Gendron — he's the President of Voisey's Bay Nickel — marched into a room at the Delta Hotel — apparently the place was packed — and announced ..."

"Yes?"

"... announced it was Argentia! The site of the old U.S. Navy Base. Um, what else ... construction to begin next summer ... smelting to begin in the year 2000. There you have it."

Later that day, Voisey's Bay Nickel's press release whirs out of our fax machine. Dr. Gendron is assertive: "The Company intends to build the smelter/refinery as quickly as possible ... Voisey's Bay Nickel Company anticipates ... [having] the smelter/refinery complex operational ... in the year 2000."

No "ifs," no "buts," no "maybes."

* * * * *

On December 2, 1996, Inco revised its estimate of the capital cost for the Voisey's Bay project from US$1.1 billion to US$1.4 billion.[42] Higher costs mean a lower Net Present Value, so, over the next two days, the price of Inco's Class VBN shares dropped from $36.50 to $35.00. Nevertheless, both the company and the government remained confident that there had been no slippage in the timing of the project.[43]

Permits to build the smelter/refinery in Argentia were to be in place by the end of summer 1997, with construction to begin in the fall. And the smelter/refinery was to be up and running in the year 2000. Not only were Inco and the government enthusiastic about Voisey's Bay's future, so was I. Once Inco had issued its VBN shares, I gave them a rating of "Accumulate," the same as my rating had been for the Diamond Fields shares which they effectively replaced.

By December 13, 1996, the price of the VBN shares, which had first traded at $38.25, had dropped to $32.50. Citing rising nickel prices and Voisey's Bay's great exploration potential, I boosted my rating to "Buy." However, by the spring of 1997, the slow pace of land claims had convinced me that Inco's management was giving false hope to investors (and probably misleading itself) by insisting that Voisey's Bay would be in production by 1999. Accordingly, on April 30, 1997, I changed my recommendation on the VBN shares, then trading at $29.35, from "Buy" to "Hold."

* * * * *

I was becoming increasingly worried about Voisey's Bay's timetable. To my concerns about the slow pace of land claims I added worries about the cleanup at Argentia, about Inco's negotiations with the provincial government and aboriginal groups, about the process of obtaining environmental permits for Voisey's Bay, and about the future of nickel markets. In each of these areas, I thought that investors were being too optimistic and, accordingly, were overpricing Inco's VBN shares. As a result, the VBN shares stayed off my "Buy" list.

Chatelaine magazine used to publish pictures of women before and after a beauty makeover. I hope to take some "before" and "after" photographs of the Argentia smelter site before and after a makeover directed by Inco.

It starts well. As I fly into St. John's from Toronto on a gloriously clear day in July 1997, I recognize the smelter site: a dun-coloured triangle pointing towards the dark green, wooded mainland to which it is connected by a narrow neck of land. On the east side of the neck are docks for the ferry to Nova Scotia. The most prominent feature of the triangle itself is a large grey cross, like a "Keep Out" sign. The cross is formed by the two former runways where Inco proposes to begin construction. I land and drive out to Argentia, now part of the amalgamated town of Placentia.

Argentia was named for a silver deposit mined sporadically and unprofitably in the nineteenth and early twentieth centuries. Until World War II, when the U.S. Navy moved in, the economy of the area had been largely dependent on fishing and the provision of transportation facilities, notably smuggling. Then, "on February 13, 1941, the American flag was raised in Argentia and the people felt like foreigners in their own community."[44] The Americans closed their base in 1994, leaving it in charge of watchmen, one of whom blocks my passage.

"No one but the government people are allowed here until it's all cleaned up," he explains.

"What about Inco? Isn't it planning to start building a smelter here in a few months?"

"Inco hasn't set foot here. Not till it's cleaned up."

"Any idea when that will be?"

"Maybe early next year."

Later, in St. John's, I meet Nancy Walsh, a lively CBC reporter whom I'd previously met by phone. Nancy had aired an interview with Mr. Emery Peters of the federal government's Public Works and Government Services, which had taken charge of the cleanup. Because the Americans had done some remediation before they left, Mr. Peters had not expected to find a big mess. So, his team was surprised to find copper, lead, PCBs, asbestos, extensive areas of sand, gravel, soil, and rocks soaked in oil and a garbage dump, as measured in North America's favourite unit of areal extent, "the size of five football fields."

Most of the oil seemed to be immobile — "we'll just leave it there and monitor it," said Mr. Peters. However, there was a plume of Bunker C oil moving towards the sea. Mr. Peters proposed to dig a trench to catch the plume as it oozed out.

The asbestos presented more of a challenge. Apparently, they couldn't just leave it there, and no other landfill in the province was able to accept it. So, said Mr. Peters, they would have to build a new landfill site on the spot, with dykes and liners and monitoring devices. This should be a boon for the town of Placentia, which could use it as an upmarket custom garbage dump.

Mr. Peters's team did consider moving the five football fields of garbage left by the Americans, but soon changed their minds when they realized that it could give off unpleasant substances such as hydrogen cyanide, a gas notorious as the active ingredient in America's gas chambers. Regrettably, the garbage dump is beside the ferry terminal and it is contaminating the harbour. The safest approach seems to be to cover it with something impermeable and hope for the best.

Mr. Peters was puzzled by a discovery at one of the Shag Ponds, at the south end of the base. The top 30 centimetres of the mud at the bottom of the pond — material which is known to geologists by the technical term "loonshit" — was intensely contaminated with lead. After much head-scratching, one of the team familiar with the practices of the U.S. Navy came up with the explanation: the Shag Ponds were the site of a skeet range, and the lead came from lead shot. The head-scratching continued: Now you know what it is, what do you do with it? Four years after my visit, even though the feds had temporarily drained one of the Shag Ponds in an attempt to figure out how to clean up the loonshit, "a final remediation plan for Shag Pond [had] not been selected."[45]

I return to Toronto to report that the site of the proposed smelter and refinery is unavailable for the foreseeable future, and that both Inco and the government are deluded if they truly believe that a smelter could be up and running by 2000.[46] I invoke the time value of money and reiterate that investors should not buy Inco's VBN shares.

A year after my attempted visit to the site of the future Inco smelter, the federal government announced that it had so far spent $12.3 million tidying up Argentia, that another $68.7 million of public money would be required to complete the job, and that it could take as long as ten years.[47]

In the federal House of Commons, the opposition Reform Party demanded to know why Canada did not force the Americans to pay for the cleanup. Public Works Minister Alfonso Gagliano replied that the External Affairs Department was negotiating with the Americans for a refund. However, because Canada and the U.S. were engaged in a dispute over salmon on their Pacific coasts, the U.S. Senate had refused to endorse any such payment.

* * * * *

Bill Rowat had been the federal government's Deputy Minister of Fisheries and Oceans, and had assisted Brian Tobin in the turbot dispute with Spain. In 1997, Premier Tobin borrowed him from the feds, and appointed him provincial Deputy Minister responsible for the Voisey's Bay project.[48] Why did Mr. Tobin need help from a federal operative? Mr. Rowat told a reporter that, because of equalization payments, "the federal government holds the financial key that could unlock negotiations leading to a settlement for Inco's multibillion-dollar Voisey's Bay nickel development." He added that he hoped "there [would] be a deal between [the federal government] and the province in the next few weeks on sharing revenue from Voisey's Bay. A revenue-adjustment deal ... would give the province more flexibility to strike financial arrangements with Inco."[49]

The summer of 1997 ended with no sign that the government had given construction permits to Inco. A St. John's man, James Brokenshire, formed the "Citizens' Mining Council of Newfoundland/Labrador," which he described as representing those who lived downwind from the proposed smelter in Argentia. Mr. Brokenshire feared that the Argentia smelter project had "a fast-tracked, behind-the-scenes bureaucratic process," and asked "the Federal Court [of Canada] to rule that the smelter construction should undergo the same public review process as is being given to the mine." The Canadian Environmental Defence Fund financed the legal action, which was filed in Toronto.[50]

I thought Mr. Brokenshire's group had a point — after all, the ground under the site was already brown, very brown — but the air blowing in from the ocean and over Argentia was as clean as the air over any greenfield site. I duly reported to our morning meeting that here was another possible speed bump in the way of the project.

I visited St. John's in late April 1998. The federal court in Toronto had not yet got around to hearing — and, Inco hoped, rejecting — the Citizens' Mining Council's application to have the smelter included in the environmental review of the proposed mine and mill.[51] At Fred's Records, I found the Council's Chairman, Jim Brokenshire. He invited me to coffee in a restaurant down Duckworth Street.

Jim's father had been a senior metallurgist with Inco and Jim himself used to work for Inco as a miner. If there had been a traumatic experience during that time, something which had encouraged him to make life difficult for Inco, he didn't reveal it, devoting our conversation to the Council's plans. He pointed out that there was a joint federal-provincial review of the proposed smelter/refinery and that it was up to the feds to decide whether or not to have public hearings. "If the Court should agree with our request to combine the review of the smelter/refinery with that of the mine and mill, well, for one thing, the Citizens' Mining Council would be eligible for intervenor funding."

"Which is?"

"The federal government gives money to people affected by the project so that they can make their views known to the review panel. Actually, we did get some intervenorship funding for the mine/mill hearings, so we'll make an appearance there."

"What are your main concerns about the smelter, Jim?"

"Originally it was air quality at Argentia. But now we've also become worried about the possibility of spills of sulphuric acid and fuel oil, and the province's reputation for a poor level of environmental monitoring."

* * * * *

In October 1996, Inco's CEO, Dr. Sopko, noting the slow pace of native land claims negotiations, pushed back his forecast for the start-up of Voisey's Bay from 1998 to the second half of 1999.[52] Perhaps no one had believed his original forecast, because the price of the VBN shares showed no discernable response. On September 19, 1997, despite Mr. Brokenshire's fears about a backroom deal, Dr. Sopko pushed his forecast back again, conceding that "initial production from the Voisey's Bay mine and mill facilities will be delayed by at least one year or until late 2000 at the earliest ... due to delays in [the] environmental review and approval of the mine and mill."[53]

This "confirms what I ... have been saying for months ... the company's start-up date was unrealistic,"[54] responded Premier Tobin. I wasn't at all sure that the premier had been saying any such thing,[55] but, if he had, no investors had been listening. Dr. Sopko's remarks shocked the market, and from September 18 to 23, Inco's VBN shares dropped by $5.60, to $20.30.

On September 25, 1997, Chris Flanagan of the St. John's *Evening Telegram*, who had seen my name mentioned in the press, called to tell me that, the previous day, he'd attended a press conference with Stewart Gendron, President of the Voisey's Bay Nickel Company. "So," said Chris, "I asked him about the timing of construction of the smelter at Argentia. He answered that 'there won't be a single thing moved on that site until we get all mine permits in place in Labrador.' You know, that's a new position for the company. Then Dr. Gendron took a shot at governments and at native groups, saying there'll be more delays if they don't ease up on their unrealistic expectations. I pointed out to him that Falconbridge's Raglan project is similar to Voisey's Bay, and that Falconbridge first consulted with the Inuit there around 1989. But Falcy wasn't able to sign a formal agreement with the Inuit until 1995, and Raglan should be in production in 1998, which would be nine years after the initial consultation. Even with its latest delay, Inco expects to be in production at Voisey's Bay just six years after it first bought into the project."

"Well, Dr. Gendron just said 'Voisey's Bay is different'; and, um, 'it's always envisioned to be pretty quick.'"

The next day, "three New York mining analysts dismissed the talk [by Dr. Gendron] as a negotiating strategy. Inco, they said, is under considerable pressure to bring Voisey's Bay into production as quickly as it can."[56]

If Inco's management was slow in recognizing how much control over Inco's future had shifted to government and special interest groups, my New York competitors were even slower. Even the government didn't fully appreciate the growing influence of special interest groups. Several members of the Prospectors and Developers Association of Canada who had had experience with opposition from environmental groups suggested to Mines Minister Chuck Furey, when he visited Toronto that October, that Inco and the provincial government establish a joint panel to carry out a limited review of the possible environmental effects of the proposed smelter/refinery.

"Your views are noted," he answered.

And that was the last we heard of that idea.

To an accountant, an asset has value only if it is able to produce cash or save money for its owner. And because Canadian accountants are required to be conservative, they are supposed to show an asset on a corporation's balance sheet at a value that is the lesser of what the corporation paid for it, and the value of the cash or the cash savings that it should be able to recover from the asset in the future.

When Inco bought Voisey's Bay, I suspect that the company's management used two arguments to justify, to its Board of Directors, the price it paid. Firstly, Inco would recoup its investment from the cash thrown off by operating the mine. Secondly, even if Inco were to buy the deposit and let it sit idle, it would have strategic value because Inco would have thereby prevented a competitor from entering the nickel business and gaining a share of the market by flooding the world with cheap nickel.

Accountants aren't supposed to consider the strategic value of assets. Thus, at the time of purchase, Inco's management and its accountants must have believed that they could justify the price paid for Voisey's Bay solely on the basis of the cash it would throw off — otherwise they would have immediately written down (reduced) the value of Voisey's Bay shown on Inco's books. They had not.

Writedowns can be big numbers. But they don't involve any immediate outlay of cash, and stock markets' reactions to them are often muted or may even be positive ("Ah, they've finally bit the bullet!").

By September 1997, a little more than a year after Inco had completed its purchase of Voisey's Bay, analysts began carping at the company, urging management to write down Voisey's Bay. In November 1997, Dr. Sopko "angrily refused" to consider a writedown,[57] and for more than four years thereafter he insisted that the rules of accounting did not allow a writedown.

Should Inco have obliged them? Let's look at what had changed since the purchase:

(i) Delays had pushed development further into the future. To an analyst, time is money and a delay represents a reduction in economic value. But, oddly, to a Canadian accountant, time has no value. A dollar today is worth the same as a dollar next year. I think that accountants prefer it this way because, if they were to value an asset on the discounted sum of its future cash flows, they would have to select an appropriate discount rate that would be, at best, an approximation. Accountants would rather be precisely wrong than approximately correct. So, a delay in development was not, in itself, a sufficient cause for a writedown.

(ii) In December 1996, Inco had increased its estimate of what it thought it would cost to bring Voisey's Bay into production. This increase would eat into the cash generated by the project and so reduce its value.

(iii) In 1997, Russia appeared to have increased its exports of scrap nickel to the West by 20,000 tonnes per year.[58] This added nearly 2% to the Western world's supply of nickel. At the same time, as we shall see in a later chapter, an economic crisis in Asia began to significantly reduce the world's demand for nickel. Higher supply and lower demand meant that, by the time of Inco's September 19, 1997 announcement, the price of nickel was US$2.93 per pound, down from $3.19 on August 21, 1996, when Inco completed its purchase of Diamond Fields Resources. Could a drop in nickel prices precipitate a writedown? Yes, but only if the weakness in nickel prices were to cause Inco to reduce its expectations of the average nickel price that would prevail during the life of the Voisey's Bay project.

Whenever the subject of Inco came up at meetings of the Mineral Resource Analysts Group, at least one of us would speculate that "the real reason" why Inco didn't take a writedown was that Inco's management wasn't anxious to say, in effect, "we paid too much." Newfoundland's Voisey's Bay negotiator, Bill Rowat, had his own views on Inco's reluctance to write down Voisey's.[59] Mr. Rowat said that Inco was arguing that, if it were to do what Brian Tobin wanted and build a smelter, its return on investment would be lousy. Now, said Mr. Rowat, Inco's return on investment in Voisey's Bay is defined as the income from Voisey's Bay divided by the value at which Voisey's Bay was recorded on Inco's books. Thus, by writing down the book value of Voisey's, Inco would increase the rate of return on investment and weaken its case against Mr. Tobin.

In the fall of 1997, I wasn't unremittingly gloomy about the prospects for Inco. There were some bright spots. I use a computer program called X-11, which was originally developed by Statistics Canada in 1959, to identify seasonal variations in stock prices. X-11 showed that there were seasonal patterns in the prices of big, liquid stocks, but that these patterns were not consistent from one year to the next.

At the end of November 1997, X-11 projected that Inco's common shares would bounce by 8% to 10% over the next three to four months. I pointed this out at the November 26 morning meeting, with Inco's shares at $24.90. But I thought it was a pretty risky 8% to 10% potential gain, because I was concerned that the deterioration in nickel markets might convince Inco's Board of Directors to cut the dividend. I polled our clients and found that most of them did not expect a cut in the dividend. So, if there were to be a cut, it would be a nasty surprise to the market. I also warned that a dividend cut would be bad news for Inco's Class VBN shares because of the "Friedland formula" — the stipulation that the dividend on the VBN shares would be at least 80% of the dividend on the common shares — which would allow Inco to cut the dividend on the VBN shares as well.

My forecast of the seasonal pattern in Inco's common shares was more prescient than my concerns about the likelihood of a cut in the dividend and its effect on Inco's share price. Inco's shares reached their high point for the year 1998 on March 10 at $28.90, despite having dipped $0.65 on February 11 when, as I feared, Inco announced that it had reduced its dividend.[60] The dividend cut proved to be a more unpleasant surprise for the holders of the VBN shares than for the holders of the common shares. The price of the VBN shares fell from $18.40 to $17.50 at the news, suggesting that income from dividends was more important to the holders of the Class VBN shares than to holders of Inco's common shares.

While the Asian crisis continued to pound nickel markets, Inco continued to talk with the provincial government behind the scenes. From time to time, Dr. Sopko would remark cryptically on the progress of these talks. When nickel prices had dropped to US$2.42 per pound, he warned analysts that "what was feasible at higher nickel prices is not feasible at today's prices," and he seemed to hint that he had become more open to the possibility of writing down Voisey's Bay.[61] And at the 1998 annual general meeting, he told shareholders that he still expected that the Voisey's Bay mine would begin production in late 2000, but, if Premier Tobin were to get too antagonistic, Inco had "alternative, very attractive projects." He paused and added, "I hope this isn't being broadcast live back to St. John's!"[62]

May 7, 1998

"Hello, Goldie. It's Chris Flanagan from the *Tely*."
  "Hello, Chris!"
  "Sorry I had to cancel lunch when you were in town last week."
  "That's OK. I hear it was in a good cause."
  "Yeah, well, I can't tell you who my alternate lunch partner was, but you'll probably figure it out. It wasn't Tobin, by the way."

Our salespeople once thought it a good idea to get me to do some of their work for them, so they sent me on the Xerox sales training course. And, says the Xerox sales training course, when in doubt, try an "open probe."

"Oh?"

"Tobin brought in Bill Rowat from Ottawa last year to talk to Inco about details like taxes, electricity costs at Argentia, and the size of the project. Rowat had been talking to Stu Gendron, the President of Voisey's Bay Nickel, here in town. But then, last week, Inco sent in the big gun — President Scott Hand — to talk to Rowat directly."

"I would say that Mr. Hand is a man with the reputation of doggedly pursuing what he wants and thinks he can get."

"Hmm. Looks like he and the government can hammer out some sort of deal by the end of June, something that will lead to a mining permit."

"Betcha it's July at the earliest, Chris!"

"Yeah, maybe you're right, these negotiations are slow."

"What has happened so far?"

"Well, Inco has presented documents showing that the project does not give an economic return on its investment in its currently proposed form: a mine, a mill, a smelter, and a refinery producing 270 million pounds [122,500 tonnes] of nickel per year. They've proposed several options, including making it smaller, and sending concentrates to be smelted in Ontario and Manitoba."

"Where Inco already has more smelting capacity than it can use."

"But the province rejected this argument, saying that the $4.3 billion Inco has paid for Voisey's can't be factored into the equation because it represents a strategic investment rather than a purchase based on market value."

"By a 'strategic investment,' you mean Inco bought it so they could stop someone else from having it?"

"Yes."

"So the province says it's like Inco bought a fence to keep out the neighbours' dogs, then complains that the fence doesn't earn any interest?"

"Something like that. And the province has brought in its own consultants who say Inco's calculations are flawed anyway. They think

Inco is trying to pull the wool over their eyes. But do you know the best part, Ray?"

"No?"

"I didn't even have to pay for lunch."

```
email
From: Chris Flanagan
Sent: Friday May 8, 1998
To: Ray Goldie
```

I'm off on a business trip to Europe, Goldie. I even know what I'm going to wear — a newly-acquired cotton shirt — and I've got the first line of a column written:

"I'm sitting in a plane/train/automobile/bus [drinking an ice-cold Harp/Kronenburg/can of Japanese coffee] ... on my way to London/Manchester/Oslo/Bergen ... sporting a $100 million shirt. It is denim blue and embroidered with "Diamond Fields Resources Inc." where the pocket should be.

The shirt is one of 20, which were acquired by Inco when it dished out $4.3 billion for the Voisey's Bay deposit — a deposit that analysts are now asking should be written down by about $1.4 to $1.6 billion U.S. — and subsequently given to me with no strings attached. The shirt, not the deposit.

The discount adds up to about $2 billion in Canadian funds, which must mean that, for its $4.3 billion, Inco received a nickel deposit worth about $2.3 billion and 20 really nice shirts.

You do the math. I'll keep the shirt.

Chris

So. Chris's lunch companion was suggesting that Inco would scale down the project. Smaller annual cash flows, but smaller upfront costs. Made sense. As nickel prices continued to drop, Inco had been cutting its expenditures on plant and equipment at its existing operations,[63] which would have made it a tad difficult to convince a bank that it was worthwhile to put money into a new nickel project. I fired up my computer to examine the implications of a smaller project and, on May 14, 1998, reported to our morning meeting.

It now seems likely that Inco and the government of Newfoundland and Labrador could have a deal sometime in July. A deal would probably include the following elements:

> *- Because nickel prices are low — currently around US$2.25 per pound — the mine plan would likely contemplate a production rate significantly lower than the original rate of 270 million pounds of nickel per year.*
> *- Inco would build a smelter at Argentia, with a capacity matching that of the mine. There's enough electricity in Newfoundland to run such a smelter, but maybe not enough to run a refinery as well. Perhaps the government will allow Inco to delay construction of a refinery.*
> *- Inco would face a tax structure similar to Newfoundland's current scheme, but with escalators to be applied during times of high nickel prices. (At least, that's what Paul Dean of the provincial government told me when I was in St. John's last month.)*

The first point is the most important. If Inco were to cut the size of the project from 270 million pounds of nickel per year to, say, 135 million pounds, it would reduce the Net Present Value of Inco's Class VBN shares from $25.10 per share to $19.35 per share. Higher than the current VBN share price of $16.00, but shares usually tend to trade at only about 70% of the market's perception of their NPV.[64] If their NPV was really only $19.38, the VBN shares should be trading at $19.38 times 0.70, or $13.57.

Inco's management has been telling us that they're still optimistic that the mine and mill could be in production by the end of 2000. I believe that this expectation will be disappointed because the environmental permitting process is so bloody slow and because, on May 11, CBC Radio in St. John's reported that talks between Inco and the Innu Nation were stalled.

With that, there are two reasons why I think that holders of the VBN shares will be disappointed: the project is likely to be both smaller and later than they expect. Reduce holdings.

Two weeks later, I am shocked as I go through the most recent production and inventory statistics and calculate that the Western world's demand for nickel dropped by 12% from the last quarter of 1997 to the first quarter of 1998. And Russia's Noril'sk is increasing its output of nickel by 8,000 tonnes per year, to help offset the revenues lost to lower prices![65] This is all terrible news for the Western world's nickel producers and, because it does not seem to have been fully appreciated by investors, I reiterate my negative views on the outlook for both Inco's common shares and its Class VBN shares.

July 14, 1998

Paul Dean is in Toronto for a day and a half of negotiating with Inco.
"Still no deal, huh, Paul?"
"Still no deal, Ray."
"Chris Flanagan wrote a story in *The Telegram* yesterday, saying Chuck Furey might allow as much as 25% of Voisey's ore to be smelted elsewhere. Could that be the deal maker?"
"Well, Ray, that was based on a misunderstanding. Mr. Flanagan asked Mr. Furey a hypothetical question. No, it's not being proposed by either party."
"Paul, last Thursday the VBN shares jumped 40 cents when *The Financial Post* quoted a negotiating document that suggested that you might let Inco begin mining and milling prior to completing a smelter and refinery in Newfoundland."
"Yes, that's left a pretty bad taste in our mouths, wondering who leaked it."
"And how about the environmental hearings for Voisey's Bay, Paul? They were supposed to begin this summer."
"I think you'll see them starting next month, Ray."

July 17, 1998

Before the market opens, I wander over to the trading desk.

"Donny — I've been wondering how the negotiations between Inco and Newfoundland have been going. I just checked the website for CBC St. John's and found out that, last night, Mr. Tobin said this."

I drop a printout on his desk.

> Based on the respective positions that have been put at the table over the last twenty-four hours in Toronto in the most recent negotiating session, there does not exist in my judgment and the judgment of the cabinet, the basis today for an agreement between Inco and Newfoundland and Labrador on the development of the Voisey's Bay mine. I will say further, that if there is not substantial movement ... very substantial movement by Inco on the issues that remain outstanding there will not be a development of the Voisey's Bay mine.

"And this morning, Donny, Mr. Tobin added that Newfoundland has to 'learn to say no.'"

"Is Tobin really that dedicated to forcing Inco to build a smelter?"

"I asked Nancy Walsh, my favourite St. John's CBC reporter, just that, Donny. She said that Mr. Tobin relies on polls, not principles. He's very heavy on polls. She obtained the results of some of them through the Freedom of Information law. Whatever he proposes, she said, you can be sure he has the polls behind him."

"Now, Ray, your experience has been — right? — that VBN investors outside Newfoundland, and that'd be most of them — usually don't bother to look at what gets published in St. John's?"

"Right."

"So this news from Tobin baby won't show up in the fucking VBN share price — which closed yesterday at ..." — he punches a few buttons and peers at one of the three screens facing him — "eleven spot fifty. Until people in Toronto find out about it, I don't think I have any holders who'd sell now, but I'll let my clients know. Thank you, Ray."

Donny is right. The VBN shares drop only marginally that day but a week later — after a Toronto newspaper reports that Premier Tobin had notified Dr. Sopko that further discussion are "pointless"[66] — they drop 13%, to $9.90.

On July 27, 1998, Inco holds two conference calls — one for analysts and one for journalists — to review its most recent results. I call Chris Flanagan to compare notes on the question-and-answer periods of our respective calls.

"Ray, before our call, I'd spoken with Bill Rowat. He said that Inco argued that, because nickel prices had fallen so much, Inco's only firm proposal would be to 'scoop and run': mine just the Ovoid and ship raw concentrate out of the province to be smelted and refined in Ontario and Manitoba. I'm sure you saw that in Inco's press release today; they confirmed that stance."

"In *our* conference call, Chris, Mr. Hand said that he had proposed a compromise — his '55% solution' — a tentative concept for a mine, a mill and a $700 million smelter at Argentia, which would smelt 55% of the ore from Labrador, but refine none of it. And it came with a major caveat: federal and provincial tax breaks and infrastructural assistance. The government rejected this proposal, and cut off talks. In response, Mr. Hand said he would cease procurement in Newfoundland and Labrador and move to emphasize development of Inco's Goro nickel project in New Caledonia. And he sounded pretty enthusiastic about the productivity improvements that Inco has achieved at its existing operations. Reading between the lines, Chris, I think that Inco probably wouldn't mind if the current standoff was to lead to several years' delay in developing Voisey's. Its operations would become more cost-effective, so that Inco could better reap the benefits of the higher nickel and cobalt prices that would result from Voisey's absence from the market."

"He mentioned the '55% solution' in our call, too."

"Any response from Mr. Tobin?"

"Oh yes! He's on the road, but I tracked him down. He said 'our bottom line has not changed, no smelter/refinery, no mine/mill.'"

And Inco's Class VBN shares end the week down again, at $9.05.

July 31, 1998, Morning Meeting

"More on Voisey's Bay," I begin.

"First point: The joint Federal-Provincial Panel charged with reviewing the environmental aspects of the proposed Voisey's Bay mine and mill has published its schedule of hearings. They'll begin in September.

"Second point: Inco's President Scott Hand says Inco is continuing to talk informally and confidentially to the province.[67] But Premier Tobin doesn't appear to be listening. He has assigned the government's chief negotiator, Bill Rowat, to negotiate with Quebec, on behalf of Newfoundland, with respect to the proposed Lower Churchill power project.[68] I think Mr. Rowat still has the Voisey's Bay file, but the message seems to be that he won't be spending much time on it.

"Mr. Tobin appears to have broad support for his tough stand against Inco. The Mayor of the municipality and the Chairman of the Regional Economic Development Board where the smelter and refinery are to be built, the Labrador North and the Newfoundland and Labrador Chambers of Commerce, and the leader of the provincial opposition all seem to believe Mr. Tobin's stance to be appropriate."[69]

"And what's Inco saying?" Patricia is using her pen to outline neat circles in the air over her pad.

"Mr. Hand says he wants Newfoundlanders to understand that by making proposals such as his '55% solution,' Inco isn't going back on its word. He says Inco made a commitment in 1996 to smelt and refine ore in the province to the extent that it was economically and technologically feasible. But nickel was US$3.50 a pound then and it's $2.00 now.

"As for the government's claim that, even so, the smelter/refinery would still be economic, Mr. Hand says, 'they question, I guess, our [estimates of] costs. ... The only point I would make is, you know, we've been in this business for 100 years, we build smelters, we build refineries ... I don't know what they've done in terms of building real-time facilities.'"

"Still a 'Reduce' recommendation on the VBN shares?"

"Still a 'Reduce.'"

The following month, August 1998, Mr. Tobin extended Bill Rowat's contract to act as Voisey's Bay negotiator for another year. Mr. Tobin told Mr. Rowat that Voisey's Bay probably wouldn't keep him busy, and that his tenure would be reviewed "informally after every four to six months." When Mr. Rowat revealed these arrangements to the press on August 20,[70] stock traders realized that an agreement on the development of Voisey's Bay was probably years away. The price of Inco's Class VBN shares dropped $0.55 that day, closing at $7.75.

September 16, 1998

"Well, just for a change," I tell the morning meeting, "I have a comment on Inco from *The Sudbury Star*.

"Inco's Chairman, Mike Sopko, told the *Star* that 'if Inco acquiesced to the Newfoundland government's demands for a smelter/refinery complex, the company would not be able to secure financing for Voisey's Bay.'

"This is interesting. My banker friends have been telling me that, last spring, they advised Inco that they no longer believed that they could finance the Voisey's Bay project as then contemplated — a mine, mill, smelter, and refinery — if Inco were to proceed without a partner. Dr. Sopko has, in effect, confirmed that rumour.

"However, he did effectively deny another one — the rumour that Inco was considering bringing in Falconbridge as a partner.[71] Because of the 'messy situation' at Voisey's, said Dr. Sopko, 'there has been no other interest in Voisey's Bay from other industry players.'"

"Now, Dr. Sopko used the word 'messy.' I'd use the word 'nasty.' The nastiness increased yesterday as Premier Harris of Ontario and Premier Tobin hurled insults at each other — of course, Ontario would lose jobs if Inco were to construct a smelter/refinery in Newfoundland. I think that the most likely outcome now is that Voisey's sits in the ground for another five to ten years."

Bill Rowat visits Toronto on September 28, 1998, accompanied by Bruce Hollett, a sixteen-year veteran of the provincial government. In a presentation to the Mineral Resource Analysts Group, Mr. Hollett complains that Inco's only motivation is to get its costs of producing nickel below US$2.00 per pound, and that it plans to do so by mining out the Ovoid over five or six years, then leaving.

"The province has been flexible," declares Mr. Hollett. "Inco objected to the cost of electricity and we indicated we could be flexible. Inco objected to the proposed 'Super-Tax' and we proposed a revised internationally competitive taxation scheme ..."

"What was that scheme?" Harry, one of the analysts, interjects.

"It's confidential. We yielded to Inco by not requiring them to build a copper smelter, and we fast-tracked for them the native land claims process. The province is open to creative solutions, but a small, government-assisted smelter in Argentia will not suffice."

"But, Bruce, how can you force Inco to engage in a project which its bankers won't finance?" asks Harry.

"If the company is in severe financial difficulties and can't finance a deal, then we'll wait too, leaving the ore in the ground. Or have Inco bring in a partner. There are other companies who want to be that partner. Like Falconbridge. Falconbridge has approached us."

"Well, Inco does say it has other, more attractive projects."

"Really? Their Goro project in New Caledonia isn't even at the pilot plant stage. Expand their operations in Indonesia? Indonesia is unstable. Expand their operations in Ontario and Manitoba? Their costs are too high."

"We've heard that you question Inco's valuation of the project."

"We certainly do. The capital costs they put on the table rose 50% during negotiations, and the figures now proposed are 10% to 25% too high. Their analysis was confused and they made elementary mistakes; for example, in the manner in which they adjusted figures for inflation.

"Inco's proposed production rate of 270 million pounds per year was never realistic — not even at the time of acquisition. Even 220 million pounds [100,000 tonnes] is probably unattainable. But it's hard to tell. Inco has conducted its drilling so as to make it impossible for us to tell what its reserves at Voisey's really are."

"How are the land claims going?"

"They're close to settlement," replies Mr. Hollett. "Just waiting for Inco."

"How long could you and Inco be at loggerheads?"

"Inco has a five-year licence to do exploration, dating back to when Diamond Fields staked the claims in 1994. You can get three five-year rollovers — that is, another fifteen years — essentially automatically, taking you to 2014. After that, if there were still no development and the mines minister had declined to convert the exploration licence to a mining licence, it would expire. Inco could contest that in court. And they'd lose."

Bill Rowat adds, "But expropriation has never been raised as a topic at meetings with Inco. I'm uncomfortable with the idea myself, having been involved in Pearson Airport negotiations."

Earlier that day, Inco's management had made a presentation in the same room to the same group. It was as impressive and authoritative as that of the province. President Scott Hand said that, although he had been sincere in his intent in 1996 to build a smelter/refinery "based on what we knew then," the nickel business had changed. The Russians had stepped up their output by 30%, big new hydrometallurgical[72] projects were coming on stream in Australia and existing producers were expanding. Thus, it would no longer be in the shareholders' interests for Inco to proceed with construction of a smelter/refinery in Newfoundland. I asked if it would make sense for Inco to follow the lead of the big new projects in Australia and build a hydrometallurgical plant at Argentia. Mr. Hand replied that hydromet would be "a long shot" for treating Voisey's Bay's ores, and that a suitable "hydromet" process would be at least ten years from commercial development.

Both sides in the debate left Toronto's mining analysts with the impression that each side was prepared to wait, and wait a long time, rather than commence development of Voisey's Bay under the terms proposed by its opponent.

The next day, I repeat to the morning meeting that the most likely outcome is that Voisey's Bay stays undeveloped for another five to ten years. I rashly publish this prognostication and soon find myself enmeshed in several bets involving bottles of single malt whisky as to whether or not Voisey's Bay will be in commercial production by 2008.

That week, the price of Inco's VBN shares drops from $7.25 to $6.00.

* * * * *

On October 16, 1998, Franco-Nevada Mining Corporation buys 6.3% of Inco's Class VBN shares for $50 million. Because the VBN shares represent 25% of the free cash flows of the Voisey's Bay project, this transaction implies that the entire project was worth only $50 million divided by 6.3%, divided by 25%, or $3,170 million dollars. Or actually a little less. The "Friedland formula" stipulated that, until 2006, or until cash began to flow from Voisey's, whichever came first, Inco would pay a dividend on the Class VBN shares equal to 80% of the amount, per share, it paid on its common shares. Hence, the cash flowing to an owner of the VBN shares would be greater than that just from Voisey's alone.

Shortly after the transaction, I phone David Harquail of Franco-Nevada.

"Ray, I know that you guess that the project won't start up before 2008," he says. "But we're betting on 2004 for the start-up of a project smaller than previously planned. We can afford to wait. The VBN shares have declined so much that their yield [the dividend divided by the share price] is effectively 3% on a pre-tax basis. That's not far off what government treasury bills were paying us. We also got a board seat and, who knows, some chances to cash out before Voisey's goes into production if there are any corporate developments at Inco. I'd say, for a long-term investor, the ratio of risk to reward is pretty good."

"David, Chris Flanagan at the St. John's *Telegram* wrote a piece saying that, just before you bought your shares, Robert Friedland quietly visited St. John's to determine whether Brian Tobin was serious in saying he wouldn't allow a Voisey's Bay project that did not include a smelter/refinery at Argentia."[73]

"We bought our VBN shares from three parties, Ray, one of whom was Mr. Friedland."

"He came, he heard, he sold!"

October 21, 1998

I'm back in St. John's. The only other customer in the restaurant waves at me.

"Since we're both dining alone, why don't you join me?"

I carry over my Guinness and club sandwich. My new companion is a pleasant chap, a dentist from Halifax. He tells me he is in town on business, and asks what I am doing in St. John's.

"I'm here to listen to the environmental hearings for Voisey's Bay at the Hotel Newfoundland."

"The 'Voisey's Bay' ... uh? What's 'Voisey's Bay'?"

"It's a proposed nickel mine in Labrador. It's not a big thing outside Newfoundland. I live in Toronto, but I know about it because I follow the mining business. The government and the mining company are arguing about whether the company should have to build a smelter in Newfoundland."

"And I've never heard of it. You sure it's a big issue down here?"

"Tell you what. Ask our waitress."

He calls over our animated, twenty-something server and asks her if she has heard of Voisey's Bay.

"Oh my dear, I certainly have and I tell you there's not much I agree with Brian Tobin on, but I'm with him all the way on that one. No smelter, no mine!"

Meanwhile, at the other end of the province, the inhabitants of the iron-mining town of Labrador City are also very well aware of Mr. Tobin's stance. In fact, they believe that Mines Minister Furey should treat the Iron Ore Company of Canada in a fashion consistent with Mr. Tobin's treatment of Inco. The I.O.C. plans to export raw iron ore from Labrador to be processed into pellets in Quebec. In October 1998, Mr. Furey reluctantly decides to allow the Iron Ore Company of Canada to proceed, arguing that it would have been uneconomic for the company to have built a pelletizing plant in Labrador. Residents of Labrador City protest, and, on November 15, 700 vehicles meander through the town, their occupants demanding that the provincial government block the export of raw iron ore. Premier Tobin explains his Minister's apparent inconsistency: I.O.C.'s right to ship ore out of Labrador was granted in the 1930s and could not be reversed. He adds that the government would grant no such allowances in the future.[74]

The government's embarrassment at having to let I.O.C. ship unprocessed ore out of the province seems to stiffen its resolve to stand up to Inco. Premier Tobin sends a team of economists over to Labrador to have a little chat with the Voisey's Bay Environmental

Assessment Panel. They show the Panel some new analyses which justify their view that the government should stand firm and insist that Inco build a smelter and refinery in the province. Inco's response is equally stubborn: "a smelter/refinery is not economically viable."[75]

November 17, 1998

"Goldie?" asks Patricia, as she taps the end of her pen on the screen. "This news item, 'Newfoundland Government introduces amendments to Mineral Act'[76] ... it's, what, the third time they've retroactively changed the rules of the game for Voisey's Bay?"

"Let me look. 'The key aspect of this bill,' blah blah blah, 'will set out the conditions under which a mining lease is granted, and the requirements for further processing of mineral resources.'"

"OK," says Patricia, "they've already said that Inco has to build a smelter and refinery in the province. What do they want now?"

"Hmm ... it looks as if they don't want anything more. They're just 'reaffirming their right to order further processing of minerals' in Newfoundland so there won't be any 'lack of certainty.' I'll bet you, Patricia, that the premier is responding to those Labradorians who say he sold them out when he let I.O.C. ship unprocessed minerals out of the province to be processed. Hmm. Just so you don't miss the point, here's the Mines Minister, Chuck Furey, saying 'it's retroactive to 1993 to capture Voisey's Bay.'"

"Goldie, you're going to win your bet that Voisey's won't be in production before 2008, aren't you?"

"Yup. Now, do you have any clients who still own the VBN's?"

A few days later, I found another reason to believe that Voisey's wouldn't be in production for many years. Canada's Federal Court of Appeal upheld a ruling on "The Sunpine case,"[77] which was a precedent for the manner in which applications for environmental permitting should be considered. The "Sunpine" judge had found that federal departments broke their own law by granting a permit for a bridge without considering the impact of the logging road to which it provided access. I recalled that the Citizens' Mining Council's application to have the Voisey's Bay smelter, refinery, and transportation facilities considered as part of the same package as the mine and mill was still awaited a ruling, and I speculated that Sunpine might influence that ruling in the Council's favour.

At the beginning of December 1998, Scott Hand considered the prospects for Voisey's Bay. He saw nickel prices of US$1.85 per pound, a stubborn government, an environmental permitting process that looked as if it could be derailed by legal challenges, and the Class VBN shares trading at only $8.00, far below their all-time high of $43.50 in August 1996.

"Why would anyone want to get involved in Voisey's Bay under the current circumstances?" Why not sit back and wait? he asked.[78]

Mr. Tobin was listening. He decided to make it clear to Inco that there was no point in sitting, waiting, and hoping he'd change his mind. First, he gave his players new roles, moving Chuck Furey to the Ministry of Tourism and appointing Roger Grimes as Minister of Mines and Energy.[79] A week later, under murky circumstances, he fired Bill Rowat and gave Bruce Hollett the former's responsibilities for Voisey's Bay.[80]

Then, on January 18, 1999, Mr. Tobin called an election for February 9. The principal purpose of the election, he said, was to give himself a mandate to continue to take a tough stance with Inco. It was not a controversial issue. The main opposition party said that, if it were to form the government, it would "require that 100% of Voisey's Bay nickel be fully smelted and refined" in Newfoundland and Labrador.[81]

Mr. Tobin easily won his election and, on February 15, announced that he had reappointed Roger Grimes as Minister of Mines and Energy. The next day, the government's Speech from the Throne declared, "A loud and clear message has been sent to Inco by the people of Newfoundland and Labrador: There will be no mine at Voisey's Bay unless the ore is processed in this province. That is the choice. It is Inco's to make. My Government's position — the position of the people of Newfoundland and Labrador — will not waver."

I wondered if Roger Grimes would be more successful than Chuck Furey in reaching an agreement with Inco. Before he entered politics, Mr. Grimes had been a science teacher, so he should have had a sound basis for understanding technical issues such as the merits of hydromet versus pyromet. I met him at a reception in Dublin Castle,[82] a trim man with a trim moustache. I could imagine him in a tweed jacket patiently guiding students in the use of the pipette. Although he had been a teacher, the earthy patterns of Newfoundland speech sometimes slipped from his mouth. He could charm a group of Irish mining executives by referring to "me arse pocket," and he could tell New York financiers a story that included the word "fuck."[83]

Inco did return to the table, but not because of Mr. Grimes. At the end of April 1999, with the price of nickel back up to US$2.35 per pound, having touched bottom at $1.69 in December, Inco conceded that it had resumed talks with the government.[84] Nevertheless, the company denied that it was softening in its refusal to build a smelter and refinery.[85] And, despite my continued negative recommendations, the price of the Class VBN shares moved up with the price of nickel, reaching $13.00 in late April.

In the months that followed, trying to keep abreast of Voisey's Bay was like trying to catch shadows. On May 19, 1999, Nancy Walsh called from CBC Radio in St. John's.

"Ray, last night, Mines Minister Grimes told us that, within four to six weeks, he expected Inco to submit a new proposal for development of Voisey's Bay. He added that it had better provide for 'some' smelting in the province. I talked with him on today's morning show, and he said that the smelter/refinery that Inco originally proposed was too big — it would've flooded the market with nickel. Although he conceded that he didn't have any idea of what would be in the new proposal, he said that he is expecting Inco to propose a smaller plant. Grimes also said that he won't enforce Inco's earlier commitment to build it in Placentia."

"Thanks, Nancy. 'Four to six weeks,' eh? Bet it's more like two or three months, given how bloody slow these negotiations have been so far!"

Nancy's reference to only "some" smelting in the province sounded like a major concession on the part of the government. Intrigued, I called Sandra Scott at Inco.

Sandra has a professional demeanour, a ready smile, and is so dauntingly well-organized that she has won awards for the quality of her work in investor relations. Regrettably, she must occasionally endure respectful abuse from her colleagues. For example, when she injured an ankle, Scott Hand attributed it to "kicking executives around." Others have nicknamed her "Attila the Hen." Nonetheless, all admire the discipline she has brought to Inco's investor relations department. I asked Sandra if she had any response to Mr. Grimes's comments.

"We don't comment on speculation, Ray. But the Minister's comment is accurate. Mr. Grimes does not have any idea of what will be in our new proposal!"

It took the market several days to respond to the prospect of a deal between the government and Inco. Inco's VBN shares, which had been drifting down again, hardly moved on May 19 but, on May 20, jumped $0.90, closing at $12.90.

Nancy called me back on May 28. "There's been a big shift in the province's stand on Voisey's Bay," she said. "On CBC TV the night before last, Minister Grimes reminded us that the Premier had said, 'If there's no smelting and refining there won't be a mine.' Grimes added, 'Now, did that mean every single spoonful of nickel concentrate that comes out of Labrador must be absolutely smelted in Newfoundland and Labrador? It may or it may not.' So, of course, yesterday there was an unholy stink in the legislature as the Opposition attacked the government for backing down on its commitment to smelting and refining. And there was something else. Do you know what 'hydromet' is, Ray?"

"It's when you use a giant pressure cooker as a way of extracting metals from concentrates."

"Well, Mr. Grimes wants Inco to look at using hydromet for the Voisey's Bay smelter/refinery."

"It would surprise me if Inco agreed, Nancy," I said, and recounted Scott Hand's dismissal of hydromet the previous September.

"Better be prepared to be surprised, Ray!"

On June 1, Nancy phoned again. "Tobin's really insistent on this hydromet. He just told me that he'd told Inco that they should form a partnership with Sherritt International to develop hydrometallurgical technologies for extracting nickel."

Mr. Grimes's deadline passed. No announcements, no new proposal from Inco, no deal. "We are waiting for Inco," said Mr. Grimes.[86] No, said Inco, we're the ones who are waiting. We're waiting for both the federal and provincial governments.[87]

Other analysts began to share my views about Voisey's Bay's prospects.[88]

September 13, 1999

"Have you noticed the price of nickel today, Goldie?"

"Hi, Chris!" Chris Flanagan. "Chris, it's — um — around $3.20 a pound. Doing well. Asia's rebounding and the new Aussie nickel projects aren't producing as much nickel as their owners had hoped."

"Yes — so, you realize that nickel's now back above where it was when Inco committed to building a smelter and refinery at Argentia?"

"Hey, you're right! Any sign Inco and the government are talking?"

"Friend of mine works out at the airport. Says he's seen Inco's jet parked there a couple of times in the past few weeks."

On Saturday, October 23, Premier Tobin said that he was once again expecting "a phone call [from Inco] sometime in the weeks ahead."[89] The following Monday, while the markets were open, Scott Hand confirmed that he expected that Inco would soon submit a formal proposal to the provincial government. Assuming that the province agreed by the end of 1999, said Mr. Hand, the company would be in a position to commence construction at Voisey's Bay "when the ice moves out in June 2000."[90]

Shortly after Mr. Hand's announcement, my phone rang. "Hello, Ray, it's Pat Doyle at *The Telegram* in St John's. Chris Flanagan used to talk to you before he moved on to his new job."

"Yes, Pat, I'll miss him."

"Can I talk to you?"

"Sure!"

"I think you were one of the analysts who listened to Inco's conference call just now."

"Right."

"If the government were to accept Mr. Hand's proposal, that would lead to production starting in late 2003, wouldn't it?"

"Right."

"What do you think?"

"Well, Mr. Hand also talked about last week's official opening of the pilot plant for its Goro project in New Caledonia. I'm not sure Inco has the financial wherewithal to proceed with both projects at the same time. And Inco still has to reach agreements with the aboriginal groups at Voisey's. My sense is that, if it comes to a choice, Voisey's

Bay, not Goro, will be put on the back burner. I don't believe we'll see production before *2008*."

Inco's Class VBN shares rose $0.10 to $11.60 that Monday, and another $0.50 the next day.

On November 15, 1999, Premier Tobin had lunch with the Canadian Society of New York. He told the audience, assembled from Wall Street, that Inco had broken off negotiating with him when the price of nickel dropped to about US$1.87 per pound. "We didn't hear boo from those guys. I spent the whole summer improving my golf game." But with nickel at $3.70, Inco now seemed eager to return to the bargaining table, he said. Mr. Tobin then confided that he, Tobin, had "a Wall Street mentality. ... Inco ... had this notion that ... if they paid too much [for Voisey's Bay] it wasn't a problem, because the people of Newfoundland and Labrador would take nothing in the way of royalties to help them get over their problem. ... I've had real trouble explaining that right-wing view to my left-wing friends at Inco."

Having thus created the impression that the critical area of disagreement between the government and Inco was the nature of the tax and royalty regime to be imposed at Voisey's Bay, Mr. Tobin went on to boast that Inco had made an about-face on the smelter issue, and had "proposed a project which would see concentrate processed in the province."[91]

The parties who were actually doing the negotiating seemed to have been caught unawares by Mr. Tobin's remarks. Reporters couldn't find Minister Grimes, and Inco's Sandra Scott issued a press release that noted, in a tone which I inferred to be somewhere between bemused and indignant, that there were negotiations, that they were continuing, and that they were confidential.

In the House of Assembly the next day, the Leader of the Opposition, Ed Byrne, pressed the premier. "What has Inco proposed? A full smelter/refinery? Yes or no?"

The Premier replied, "Mr. Speaker, the Leader of the Opposition is misrepresenting what I was doing in New York. ... I was down talking about the good news associated with the economy of Newfoundland and Labrador. ... The fact is the Province of Newfoundland and Labrador is growing. It is doing well because of sound fiscal management and good negotiations, and that will not change no matter what kind of temper tantrum the Leader of the Opposition is having."

Bay Street responded uncertainly. Did Mr. Tobin expostulate prematurely in New York? If not, were his comments good news — development of Voisey's Bay would be sooner rather than later? Or were they bad news — development would be more expensive? Inco's VBN shares jumped $0.70 to $12.65 on November 15, another $1.05 on November 16, then fell $1.65 over the next three days.

On November 23, 1999, Minister Grimes flew to Toronto for what he termed "exploratory" discussions with Inco. The next day, in the minister's absence, Ed Byrne asked Chuck Furey what was in Inco's proposal. Mr. Furey replied, "Mr. Speaker, first of all let me correct the underlying premise of the question that the Leader of the Opposition put forward. He assumes there is a proposal. There is no proposal. There is no formal proposal presented by Inco to the government."

Mr. Byrne tried again. "Mr. Speaker. ... The premise I am starting from is the very premise that the Premier talked about himself. He chose to talk about it in Wall Street ... the premise I am starting with is based upon information provided by the Premier."

Nevertheless, replied Mr. Furey, Mr. Byrne's "premise remains incorrect. He is building his questions on a very faulty, very foolish foundation. ... I say to [Mr. Byrne]: Stop getting hyper."

Mr. Grimes returned to St. John's and said that Inco was "seeking to finalize" a proposal for a twenty-five-to-thirty-year project which would include a hydrometallurgical smelter/refinery.[92] "There are other hydrometallurgic [sic] processes active today in the world," he said, "but ... we are talking about the first time ever for nickel from a sulphide ore, which is what Inco is looking at proposing for Newfoundland and Labrador."[93] He added that "Inco knows the province's ten-year tax holiday for new companies does not apply to them."[94]

Inco's VBN shares rose $0.80 that day, closing at $13.95. I wondered why Inco would have changed its corporate mind about hydromet. Only fourteen months earlier, Inco had dismissed hydrometallurgical treatment of Voisey's Bay ores as "a long shot." Now, if Mr. Grimes was correct, Inco was prepared to invest what would be hundreds of millions of dollars in developing and constructing a hydrometallurgical plant. And it would do this when it already had excess smelting and refining capacity in Ontario and Manitoba. I concluded that Inco had decided that an investment in hydromet would be an insurance policy: If the company didn't develop a hydromet process for treating ores of the type found at Voisey's Bay, someone else might. And that someone else might just find that hydromet was so cheap and so efficient that it could drive Inco's existing smelting and refining operations out of business.

A second reason for Inco's changed attitude to hydromet was probably that the company had reluctantly realized that there were probably no economic quantities of precious metals at Voisey's Bay. With no precious metals, Inco would not need to face the expense of figuring out how to modify a hydromet plant so that it could recover precious metals as well as nickel, copper, and cobalt.

Although Mr. Grimes's remarks cheered investors, they worried opposition politicians, who asked Mr. Grimes if he would "accept a proposal that does not contain a guarantee from Inco that all ore will be processed in this province?"[95]

"I am a very simple, basic person," replied Mr. Grimes, "and I don't mind saying that maybe my limitations in being simple keep me from the torment of trying to wonder about what might happen sometime in the future. I am quite willing to wait until we get a proposal so we can analyze it, see if it is in the best interest of Newfoundland and Labrador. ... Maybe I am stunned,[96] Mr. Speaker, but I am stunned enough to wait instead of trying to guess what might happen next week or the week after."

But the Opposition feared that the mainlanders would put one over on Mr. Grimes. Mr. Ed Byrne asked if Inco's proposed "hydrometallurgic plant, test plant, or pilot plant. ... Will that be built here or will it [as was the case with Inco's pilot plant at Goro, New Caledonia] be built elsewhere and assembled here?"

Mr. Grimes replied, "The government [will] try to secure full and fair benefits for Newfoundland and Labrador with respect to Inco ... full and fair benefits in all its aspects means: if something can be done here, it should be done here."

"There are many great Newfoundland expressions that aptly describe people," said Mr. Byrne, "and my grandmother had one of them that aptly describes the minister. This minister has enough lip for three rows of teeth."[97]

Messrs. Tobin and Grimes left St. John's on December 2 to meet with Inco in Toronto the next day. As *CBC Newsworld* commented, "Brian Tobin doesn't make a habit of attending routine discussions ... the two sides could have the basis for a deal this weekend."

Back home on December 6, Mr. Grimes said, "We do not have a formal proposal from Inco, we do not have the basis for a return to formal negotiations."[98]

"I wouldn't bet your mortgage on ... [a deal] anytime soon," added Mr. Tobin.[99]

The opposition parties continued to worry that the government might leave loopholes in any deal with Inco. They asked when the government would act so as to disqualify Voisey's Bay from the ten-year tax break that was still on the books.[100] Mines Minister Grimes replied that there would not be a tax holiday, "whether or not the law would change or whether or not there will be a special contract arrangement with Inco; if we ever have an arrangement with them, it will be determined at the time. It has always been known. They understand that."

Next, the Opposition wanted to know, "What royalty regime[101] will apply to the peoples' ore deposit in Voisey's Bay, Labrador?"

"There has been no determination as to a royalty regime," answered Mr. Tobin.

The following week, on December 15, 1999, Inco's management meets over lunch with the Mineral Resources Analysts Group in Toronto. President Scott Hand confirms that Inco is considering developing a hydrometallurgical process to treat Voisey's Bay ore. Chairman Mike Sopko, himself a metallurgist, contrasts hydromet with the traditional pyrometallurgical techniques that Inco had previously considered. Dr. Sopko believes that, per tonne of nickel produced, hydromet would have capital costs that were 35% to 40% lower, and operating costs 30% lower. Hydromet should also recover 96% of the cobalt in the ore, versus 40% to 50% for pyromet. It should use less electricity than pyromet and it should be easier to qualify for environmental permits.

I ask Dr. Sopko if his new-found comfort with hydromet comes, in part, from the company's failure to find any precious metals at Voisey's. He concedes that it does.

"How long would it take you to develop a hydromet process?" I ask. "Five to seven years?"

"That's reasonable."

"Do you have a name for the process?"

"No, not yet."

"How about 'The Tobinator'?"

"We'll keep that suggestion in mind, Ray." Even though he is smiling, his eyes carry his characteristic, slightly perplexed look.

Harry's turn. "Scott, to begin production by late 2003, you said you need to begin construction next June. To do that, how soon would you have to have a deal?"

"Early next year, Harry."

"January?"

"Early," says Mr. Hand, wagging his finger.

"And remember," adds Dr. Sopko, whose surname is Slovakian, "that some of us are on an Eastern Orthodox New Year!"

On January 6, 2000, *The National Post* reported that Dr. Sopko had sent a written proposal to Premier Tobin in mid-December outlining a twenty-five-to-thirty-year project that included a hydrometallurgical smelter/refinery. Minister Grimes told the *Post* that he was "now trying to formalize a written response" that reflected the government's desire for guarantees should the hydromet process not work. The next week to ten days, he said, "will determine whether ... we decide to abandon the project for the foreseeable future."

The next day, while Mr. Tobin and Mr. Grimes laboured on a reply to Inco, Mr. Grimes's communications director protested that his boss's words had been taken out of context. Even if there was no agreement in the next few days and, as a result, Inco was to miss the 2000 construction season, he said, "the project will not be shelved."[102]

Less than a week later, however, on Tuesday evening, January 11, 2000, Inco issued a press release that said that it had not been able to reach agreement with the government. "As a result, the Company will not be in a position to commence construction of a mining and milling operation at Voisey's Bay this year."

In a conference call to discuss the press release, Inco said that it had proposed the expenditure of $845 million on a mine, mill, and exploration, and $180 million to investigate hydrometallurgical processing of Voisey's Bay ores. The latter program would have included building a pilot plant in Newfoundland and Labrador. However, the province had responded that it would require Inco to guarantee that it would build a full hydrometallurgical facility within a specific time frame, "even if such a facility would make the project uneconomic." This was, said Inco, the "key factor in not being able to reach an agreement." Nevertheless, the company said, there was no reason for the company to write down its investment in Voisey's Bay,[103] and Inco would continue to do research on developing hydrometallurgical technology to treat Voisey's Bay ores, and it would continue exploration in Labrador. Oh, and by the way, that Goro project in New Caledonia was looking really good.

Premier Tobin also issued a press release, confirming that he would "not agree to less than ... a commitment to full processing in the province," adding that Inco's proposal had "more escape clauses than there are off-ramps on [Highway] 401."[104] He wished Inco well with its research into hydrometallurgical processes, commenting that "Hydrometallurgy ... may take several years to prove up. From our perspective, it's worth waiting a year or two." Oh, and by the way, "our province is growing economically without Voisey's Bay."

In the week before Inco announced the failure of its negotiations with the government, the price of the Class VBN shares had hovered around $12.40. On Monday, January 10, 2000, it dropped to $11.60. On Tuesday, January 11, in the hours leading up to Inco's announcement, the price of Inco's Class VBN shares dropped $1.10 to close at $10.50, with 107,440 shares changing hands. The markets closed at 4:00 p.m. At 4:12 p.m. on Tuesday, January 11, Inco issued its press release announcing the failure of the Voisey's Bay talks. The next day, the shares dropped again, and ended the week at $8.00. On January 13, *The Globe and Mail* suggested that the Toronto Stock Exchange was looking into the possibility that there was a leak. Perhaps there was, but the Exchange refused to comment and the story faded from memory.

The leader of the third party in Newfoundland and Labrador's House of Assembly, the NDP, responded mildly to the collapse of negotiations. "I can't criticize the government for being firm." However, the PC Opposition party credited itself and "public pressure" for the government's refusal to accept Inco's proposal, adding, "the government's own polls clearly showed them that people will not tolerate ore leaving Newfoundland and Labrador for processing."[105] In fact, said the PCs, the government should take an even harder line with Inco, and impose a "fallow field" tax of $10,000 for every day Voisey's Bay sat undeveloped.[106]

Under attack, Premier Tobin changed the players again. On January 13, 2000, he moved Roger Grimes to the Health and Community Services portfolio. Paul Dicks, formerly Minister of Finance, replaced Mr. Grimes at Mines and Energy. The PC Opposition party said that the move reflected "the sharp and significant difference of opinion ... on the Voisey's Bay file" between the Premier and Mr. Grimes,[107] and that St. John's was rife with rumours that Mr. Tobin believed that Mr. Grimes had become too sympathetic to Inco.[108]

The new Mines Minister, Mr. Dicks, had the reputation of being a smart, tart-tongued lawyer. And he certainly had a tough attitude towards Inco. In November 1999, he had said, "I'm surprised [Inco's] Board of Directors [hasn't given management] the heave-ho," adding, indefensibly, "[the] problem with Inco is, they haven't developed a mine in the civilized world in fifty or sixty years."[109] He assured Newfoundlanders and Labradorians that he would not give in to critics who wanted him to accede to Inco's demands.[110]

On January 27, 2000, Pat Doyle of the St. John's *Telegram* called to ask my views on Premier Tobin's insistence that Inco give him an ironclad guarantee that Voisey's Bay ore would be fully processed in the province. "Inco won't give him one," said Pat. "Who do you think is right?"

"Pat, the Premier was probably doing the right thing, on behalf of his constituency, to ask for a guarantee. Yet Inco was clearly justified in refusing to give one."

"Why do you think Inco was right to refuse?"

"It now looks as if the most economic smelter/refinery you could build in Newfoundland would be a hydromet plant. But the biggest of the new hydromet plants in Australia, Murrin Murrin, which has an official capacity of 45,000 tonnes per year, seems to have produced less than 1,500 tonnes of refined nickel in 1999.[111] Now, even though I think hydromet probably will work well on Voisey's ores, I also think you'd be crazy to give an absolute guarantee of it!"

A few weeks later, Nancy Walsh calls.[112]

"Ray, I see that Inco announced today that it was investing $70 million to extend the life of its Birchtree nickel mine in Manitoba."

"Yeah, what's interesting about that, Nancy, is that Inco is demonstrating that Mr. Tobin has a point when he insists on a smelter in Newfoundland."

"How so?"

"Well, Inco has a smelter in Manitoba. It's hungry and Inco wants to keep it fed. If the smelter hadn't been there, I suspect that Inco would've just shut down the Birchtree mine. You saw the same thing with Cominco in British Columbia. Cominco had a big zinc-lead smelter that was fed by Sullivan, a big zinc-lead mine. When management realized that Sullivan was running out of ore, it went and found a new mine, Red Dog, to keep the smelter running. I think Brian Tobin realizes that if you put a smelter in Newfoundland it will stimulate Inco to look for new mines to keep the smelter running long after Voisey's Bay is exhausted."

Justifiable or not, Mr. Tobin's stance was not as popular in Toronto as it was in St. John's. Ontario's premier, Mike Harris, eyeing the jobs his province would have gained had Mr. Tobin allowed Inco to smelt and refine Voisey's concentrates in Sudbury, professed himself to be "shocked" by Mr. Tobin's handling of negotiations.[113] And Seymour Schulich, Chairman of Toronto-based Franco-Nevada Mining Corporation, claimed outrage at the actions of the Government of Newfoundland and Labrador which, he said, was "currently the biggest sinkhole in the country." "It appears as though beggars can be choosers in Canada," continued Mr. Schulich, so "the Prime Minister should pull [Tobin's] chain and he will heel. The man is working against the interests of his province and our country."[114] (And against those of Franco-Nevada, whose interests lay in maintaining Inco's corporate power because Franco was by then the largest holder of Inco's Class VBN shares.)

Mr. Tobin replied in equally overstated terms. "To refer to me, the Premier, as some kind of dog ... [demonstrates] a level of arrogance and condescension that is without equal in the twenty years I've been in politics."[115]

Mr. Schulich's turn. He revealed that he had lashed out at the Premier because the Premier had once called him a "raving asshole." "He's pretty good at dishing it out," said Mr. Schulich, "but ain't too good at taking it!" And, he went on, Mr. Tobin is inconsistent. "It's impossible to make a deal with this guy. Why not say 'Not a drop of oil is leaving the Grand Banks unless it's refined in Newfoundland'?"[116]

"'A raving asshole'?" replied Mr. Tobin. No, he had called Mr. Schulich "an arrogant and pompous asshole."[117]

I could imagine Inco's management responding to this exchange with emotions ranging from *schadenfreude* to mild horror. Nevertheless, Mr. Schulich felt a need to continue. He claimed that Newfoundland had become a pariah "when it comes to attracting private investment capital," and recommended that Newfoundland's Cabinet take a trip to New Caledonia to see Inco's Goro project. "Voisey's Bay offers nine months of deep Arctic climate, with icebergs floating by a hostile coast year-round. [New Caledonia's] climate is tropical, offering year-round ease of exploration ... the competition is very real! ... Premier Tobin's alternative — to let the ore rot in the ground — displays an unprecedented level of ignorance about mineral deposits."[118]

Mr. Tobin had the last word. "Commentary designed to insult the intelligence and character of the entire province of Newfoundland and Labrador," he said, "does little to advance [Mr. Schulich's] case."[119]

By now the world should have realized that Mr. Tobin's oratorical style often encompassed that which he wished were true rather than that which was true. Yet one more Torontonian felt the need to chastise the Premier for having been "deluded by his own public exaggeration." Mr. Tobin had told the Canadian Club in Ottawa[120] that Voisey's Bay was too important to remain undeveloped. After all, he pointed out, "it's the richest nickel, copper, and cobalt deposit on the planet."

Enter Emeritus Professor Tony Naldrett of the University of Toronto.[121] At current metal prices, Tony objected, the deposits at Noril'sk, Russia, were worth as much per tonne and twenty times as much in total as the total reserves and resources at Voisey's Bay.

Falconbridge's new Raglan mine was worth about the same per tonne as Voisey's Bay's sweet spot, the Ovoid, and the copper-platinum-palladium-gold veins in some of Inco and Falconbridge's Sudbury deposits were worth, in aggregate, 5.4 times as much per tonne as the Ovoid.

As far as I know, Mr. Tobin did not respond.

* * * * *

By early February 2000, the price of nickel had climbed to US$4.45 per pound, which was 80 cents above its level when Inco and the government had parted company on January 11, 2000.

Brian Tobin boasted that soaring nickel prices would bring Inco crawling back to the table. "Mike Sopko knows my number and he can call me. ... I think it is conceivable that this deal could be done in months," although, in a rare moment of public self-doubt, he added, "I'm like [a] little guy in [a] little boat. I'm not sure whether I am sinking or surfing."[122]

Alarmed by Mr. Tobin's and Mr. Dicks's tough stance and outrageous remarks, "an Inco spokesman" told the world, from behind a mask of anonymity, that Mr. Tobin was wrong to have claimed that the company had once promised to build a refinery and smelter. According to the spokesman, Inco had, in fact, said "that it would build a smelter if it was 'environmentally and economically feasible.' There was no firm promise."

What had changed was that Inco now expected a "flood" of nickel from Australia's new, low-cost hydromet plants[123] — despite the evidence that so far these plants had produced scarcely a trickle of nickel. So, instead of crawling back to the table, Inco announced on February 18 that its Newfoundland subsidiary, Voisey's Bay Nickel Company, was going into hibernation, reducing its staff from twenty-three to three.

March 8, 2000

I bump into Harry at the Prospectors and Developers Convention in Toronto.

"Hey, Harry, when I left the reception at the Newfoundland government suite last night, you were deep in conversation with Mines Minister Dicks. How did it go?"

"Oh, I don't know, Ray, too much alcohol I guess. I was advocating Seymour Schulich's point of view on Voisey's Bay and I nearly came to blows with the arrogant so-and-so."

Mr. Dicks's account of his near-altercation is much milder. "Inco has done a good job of swaying people to their point of view ... many people ... aren't sold on Newfoundland's position [but] they're willing to listen."[124]

During the convention, Inco announces that it has made a big, rich nickel discovery at Kelly Lake, Sudbury.[125] A phone call from Nancy Walsh catches me in my office as I drop off some of the maps, charts, and scribbled notes that I have been accumulating.

"Ray, could I quote you as saying Inco's announcement is a 'poke in the eye for Newfoundland'?"

"No, you may not, Nancy! Hey, you know what? Inco's shares actually went down when the news of Kelly Lake came out; maybe it's because discovering more nickel in the world is bad for nickel prices, and in that sense it's seen as bad for Inco."

"But do you think that Inco wants to convince its shareholders that it can survive without Voisey's Bay?"

"Hmm, that's fair. And it wants to remind Premier Tobin that Inco does not need a smelter in Newfoundland."

At our morning meeting on April 6, 2000, I comment on a news item that Inco is to buy 6,000 tonnes per year of nickel contained in concentrates, and run it through its smelters in Manitoba and Sudbury.

"Why would they do that, Ray?" asks Patricia.

"I can think of three reasons. One is that it's cheaper, per pound of nickel produced, to run a smelter flat out, and Inco doesn't have enough feedstock from its own mines to run its smelters flat out. A second would be that Inco currently buys about 75,000 tonnes of nickel on the open market every year, and — or so they claim — they resell it for about the same price. Actually, I suspect they make a little money on it. This new deal gives it a way of purchasing nickel and making a little more money on it. And thirdly, it sends a message to Newfoundland that Inco already suffers from a surplus of smelters and a shortage of feed for them."

In June 2000, Brian Tobin, Scott Hand, and Stewart Gendron all showed up at the "Voisey's Bay and Beyond" mining conference and trade show in Labrador. Surely, speculated the media, this was more than coincidence — surely they planned some backroom talks?[126] "Ha!" I thought. "Just journalists seizing any scrap of evidence on which to build a story." A few months later, I wasn't so sure.

On Friday, September 8, the secretary of Assistant Deputy Mines Minister Paul Dean leaves me a phone message to let me know that Mr. Dean will be in Toronto the following week, and invites me to reply by email. I trot over to the sales desk and ask if anyone has clients who might be interested in meeting Mr. Dean. They think there are, so I send back an email, offering to arrange meetings.

On Monday morning, I find a reply.

```
Mr. Goldie,
I spoke with Paul this morning. His schedule for
the next days is very busy and therefore he will
not be available to meet with holders of the VBN
shares.
```

A few minutes later, Patricia, who is one of the salespersons who had just been stood up by Mr. Dean, comes into my office waving a copy of that morning's *Globe and Mail*.

"Ray — do you think this story by Jacquie McNish has anything to do with your friend from the Newfoundland government?"

I read Ms. McNish's article. "'Sources familiar with the talks said executives with Inco ... contacted Newfoundland officials earlier this month to explore the possibility of reviving negotiations,' and, 'sources familiar with the discussions said it is unlikely formal negotiations will start until mid-October,' and, '"the company is sounding very conciliatory,"' said Heidi Bonnell, a spokeswoman for Newfoundland Premier Brian Tobin,' and, 'now Inco is knocking on Newfoundland's door again, sources said, because spot nickel prices have risen to $3.94 (U.S.) a pound.'"

Patricia stands, arms folded, one pencilled eyebrow raised.

"Gosh, I don't know, Patricia. I can't figure it out. Why would Paul Dean's secretary want me to know that her boss would be in town this week, then tell me he would be too busy to see anyone?

And this bit about nickel prices is nonsense," I say, stabbing the paper. "Three dollars and ninety-four cents is more than 50 cents lower than it was when Inco shut down most of its Newfoundland operations back in February. I have an uncomfortable feeling that the government wanted to use Ms. McNish and me to disseminate the rumour that Inco and the government were talking again. But why?"

As we'll see in a later chapter, the call from Paul Dean's secretary to me had come only two days after Inco had announced that it would attempt to buy back all of its Class VBN shares. If the government and Inco were to have restarted their negotiations just after Inco had made that announcement, Inco would have run the risk of creating a material change in the affairs of the company. This, in turn, would have required refiling of the documents needed to consummate the buyback, more legal expenses, delays, etc., etc. And the mere prospect of further talks would likely have made the holders of the Class VBN shares more intransigent and less likely to accept Inco's buyback offer. Is that what the government wanted?

I was even more puzzled, bemused, and suspicious that mischief was afoot when, later that day, Premier Tobin "downplayed reports that the two sides were set to resume talks,"[127] and the next day, when Mines Minister Dicks felt compelled to state that "no talks have taken place since January of this year and no new talks are scheduled."[128] And, when an anonymous "former well-known Wall Street mining and metals analyst" recommended that the holders of the Class VBN shares refuse to tender them to Inco,[129] Paul Dean called to ask if I knew his identity.

After spending most of the summer sulking below $7.00, the price of the Class VBN shares jumped to $9.00 in early August 2000. In a later chapter, we shall examine the rumours that swirled around this event; here we shall be concerned with only one of those rumours. I first heard it from Liz, on August 11.

"Ray, I've heard that Tobin will be stepping down to go to the federal level of politics. That's why the VBN share price is up. People feel that, obviously, a deal could be done more quickly between Inco and a new premier." I bounced the idea off Margaret Butt, a St. John's businesswoman, whom Richard Garnett and I had met after our presentation in St. John's in 1995.

"Ray," said Margaret, "the talk here is that Mr. Tobin has looked at his polls and doesn't think he could defeat either of the two leading candidates to replace Ed Byrne as leader of the PC Party — Vic Young, of Fishery Products International, or Danny Williams, the cable guy."

I called another friend in Newfoundland. "True, no talks between Inco and the government since January. But there could be truth to the Tobin rumour. He's spent a lot of money on roads and hockey arenas on the west coast, so he's very popular there, but he's in deep trouble 'east of the overpass,'[130] even on his Voisey's Bay policy. And his recent plan to disperse civil servants across the province played very badly in St. John's. He's also being hurt by the continued decline in population everywhere but St. John's — a previous administration changed the number of seats in the House of Assembly to allow for this. Dicks? Smartest man in the House, but not liked for his perceived arrogance and love of the ladies. Don't count out Roger Grimes, Ray."

And another friend: "I know Tobin well and I know Sopko. Sopko's told me he'll never sign a deal with Tobin."

On October 16, 2000, the Tobin era ended. Brian Tobin announced his resignation as Premier of Newfoundland and Labrador[131] and returned to federal politics and a cabinet post.

The people of Newfoundland and Labrador appeared to believe that Mr. Tobin would be best remembered for having appropriated to the government powers which were once thought to belong to corporations. In an admittedly unscientific survey, 46% of voters thought that "holding out on Voisey's Bay" ... "was Brian Tobin's best legacy as Premier."[132]

In Toronto, columnist Diane Francis wrote on behalf of those who mourned the erosion of corporations' power to decide where and how to invest their money. Her epitaph to Mr. Tobin's tenure as premier was: "He completely and irrationally [squandered] a chance to develop the gigantic Voisey's Bay nickel ore body in Newfoundland [sic]."[133]

And Mr. Tobin's last volley in this sad war of words between Tobin and Toronto? Let him tell the story:

"A day or two later, I received a personal telephone call from Diane Francis. 'I have been told,' she said in a voice as cold as any

January wind that ever roared through Labrador, 'that you told Seymour Schulich I was a bitch. Is that right?'

"'No, that is *not* right,' I replied. 'I did not say you were a bitch.' I paused long enough for the words to sink in, then added, 'I said you were a pompous bitch.'"[134]

CHAPTER 13

BURNING INCO'S BIRD

Hey ... what about the Light and Power Company raisin' their rates? Wouldn't that burn your bird? Those bloodsuckers!
— Broadcast on CBC Radio, St. John's, March, 1996
(Hennessey, 1997)

January 15, 1997; Toronto

I settle into a subway seat and pull out a *Financial Post* article which Patricia has highlighted for me.[135] The article begins by pointing out that Newfoundland and Labrador Hydro Electric Corp. had an agreement in principle to supply Inco with 200 megawatts of electricity once Inco's smelter began production in Argentia in 2000. "But [Hydro] doesn't have the power. ... [O]f central importance is how much of the capital and operating costs Inco will agree to."

Uh oh. I've been assuming that Inco would pay standard industrial rates for its electricity, about 3.7 cents per kilowatt-hour. Now it looks as if Inco is going to have to pay a premium to bring new capacity on stream. I spend the rest of the subway ride feeling slightly remiss that I'd overlooked this possibility.

A year and a half later, I recounted this feeling to Newfoundland's Voisey's Bay negotiator, Bill Rowat, when he visited Toronto.

"Well, you weren't the only one who *assumed* that the electricity costs at Argentia would be at standard industrial rates," he said. "Inco's people have told us that, when they did their 'due diligence' — background research — as they looked into the merits of taking over Diamond Fields, they assumed that they would pay standard industrial rates. We just listened and didn't say anything, and they never asked! After Inco took over the Voisey's Bay project, we told them they would have to pay around 8 cents because we'd have to build new generating capacity and we didn't want to have the existing power consumers of Newfoundland pay a premium in order to subsidize Inco."

But back to January 15, 1997. As I trudge out of the subway station and through the snow on Dupont Street, I decide that I should take a look at Newfoundland's power situation so that, when there are further developments, I'd be prepared.

The first thing I do when I get home is to check my *Atlas of Newfoundland and Labrador*.[136] The island of Newfoundland has the capacity to generate about 1,450 megawatts of electricity, and it has no connection with the massive power projects in Labrador. That means that the 200 megawatts that Inco would need to run a smelter would be equivalent to about 14% of the island's capacity. Hmm. It's not surprising that Hydro would have to add to its capacity if Inco were to construct the smelter that it has promised to the government.

On July 25, my preparation pays off. I read in that morning's St. John's *Evening Telegram*[137] that Newfoundland and Labrador's Mines and Energy Minister has confirmed that his government will force Inco to pay the full cost of new power-generating facilities. Thus, Inco would have to pay 6 to 8 cents per kilowatt-hour versus the industrial price of 3.7 cents per kilowatt-hour. "That minor detail," said the *Tely*, "will add several million dollars to a smelter's operating costs."

In fact, my calculations show that every one-cent increment would add $17 million a year to the cost of operating a 200-megawatt plant if you ran it flat out all the time. I presume that Inco would incur these extra costs until the cost of the new power-generating plant had been paid off.

I point this out at our morning meeting, and also observe that Newfoundland's existing electrical grid is unreliable. For example, the Come By Chance oil refinery, located near the site of Inco's proposed smelter, is claiming that Newfoundland and Labrador Hydro has failed to provide a steady supply of electricity, and it is suing Hydro for over $20 million.[138, 139]

Inco would need, I continue, approximately 200 megawatts of power to operate its proposed smelter/refinery at Argentia. It has two options other than buying electricity from Newfoundland and Labrador Hydro — to build its own generator, or to use a third party.

"Ray, what's the difference between a kilowatt-hour and a megawatt?" asks Patricia.

"The analogy that my old physics teacher, Ralph Miller, used to use was that electricity was like water in a hose. Kilowatts and megawatts measure the rate at which water is coming out of the end of the hose. A kilowatt-hour would be the amount of water that comes out of a one-kilowatt hose in an hour. A megawatt is 1,000 kilowatts and a megawatt-hour is 1,000 kilowatt-hours. To give some perspective, a kilowatt would light ten 100-watt light bulbs and, at standard Newfoundland industrial rates, every hour that they were lit would cost you 3.7 cents."

"And what would be the cost of building a new generating plant?"

"For a hydro plant, about $3 million to $4 million for each megawatt that the plant was capable of producing; and for a coal or oil-fired plant, maybe only $1 million per megawatt. But a hydro plant costs almost nothing to run whereas, for a coal or oil plant, you'd still have to buy the coal or oil."

"Which would be more likely — hydro, coal, or oil?"

"Patricia, for Newfoundland and Labrador Hydro, the easiest thing to do would probably be to expand their Holyrood station, which is located between St. John's and Argentia and which is oil-fired."

"And a third party supplier?"

"Well, Premier Tobin suggests it could come from Nova Scotia, via a 145-kilometre undersea cable."[140]

"Let's wrap it up here, Ray," interrupts the head of institutional sales, chairing the meeting. "Can you tell us your conclusion?"

"OK — the Voisey's Bay project is likely to come on stream later than Inco's projected 1999 start-up. It now also seems likely that costs will be higher than previously thought."

Three weeks later, the province's Mines and Energy Minister, Chuck Furey, appointed an engineer to review fifteen proposals — including one from Newfoundland and Labrador Hydro — to supply 200 megawatts for the Voisey's Bay smelter/refinery at Argentia.[141] By November, however, the government had become frustrated by the lack of progress towards construction of the smelter/refinery, and it called off the review.[142]

On August 31, 1998, Premier Tobin announced a comprehensive review of the province's electricity policy. He was still keen on undersea cables, and said that the government would look at the possibility of an 800-megawatt transmission line from Labrador to Newfoundland under the Strait of Belle Isle.

The following year, Mr. Tobin expanded his hopes and dreams for the Strait of Belle Isle to encompass a vehicular tunnel (which, presumably, could house a transmission line as well as a road) between Newfoundland and Labrador.[143] He noted that such a project would require the financial support of the federal government, which was odd because the federal government had already ruled out his earlier, more modest proposal to link Labrador and Newfoundland with only a transmission line.[144]

I imagined that Mr. Tobin planned to lobby his former colleagues in Ottawa to change their minds. But if he did, it had no effect. Mr. Tobin's government eventually conceded that "We don't see an economic case for building [a transmission line from Labrador to Newfoundland] unless someone can find in the vicinity of $1 billion or $2 billion to subsidize it,"[145] and that the federal government seemed unwilling to be that someone.

Which left open the question: Where would Inco find the electricity for its Argentia operations?

CHAPTER 14

A COPPER SMELTER, TOO?

Copper for the craftsman cunning at his trade.
— Cold Iron, Rudyard Kipling

It was a good thing that the government was insisting that Inco build a nickel smelter/refinery, said opposition member Paul Shelley in Newfoundland and Labrador's House of Assembly. But why not also require Inco to build a smelter to treat the copper concentrates that would be produced at Voisey's Bay?

"In my own department," replied Rex Gibbons, the Minister of Mines and Energy, "we are continuing our assessment of the copper."[146]

Premier Tobin acknowledged that his government had hired a consulting firm, Hatch Associates, to look into the feasibility of a copper smelter.[147] However, Hatch Associates had advised him that "there is not sufficient copper in the current plan put forward by Voisey's Bay Nickel to warrant a copper smelter and refinery. The Voisey's Bay project, as now constituted, is going to produce somewhere between 55,000 and 65,000 tonnes of copper annually. Most copper smelters around the world require in excess of about 150,000 tonnes annually ... there is [also] a problem with the nickel contamination in the copper concentrate."

Hatch Associates' advice represented an application of the theory of "economies of scale" — the view that, if one were to decrease the size of a plant by X per cent, the costs of building it and operating it would fall by less than X per cent. One rule of thumb is that the cost of building a plant is proportional to its planned rate of output, raised to the power of a number between 0.3 and 0.7.[148] Let's assume that the number is 0.5. A theoretical 60,000 tonnes per year Voisey's Bay smelter would produce 60,000 ÷ 150,000 or 40% as much copper as

Hatch Associates' 150,000 tonnes per year smelter, but it would cost (60,000 ÷ 150,000) to the power of 0.5, or 63% as much. Thus, to build a 60,000 tonne per year smelter would cost 63%/40%, or 158% more, per tonne of annual copper production, than a 150,000 tonnes smelter.

Mr. Tobin's last comment revealed a shortcoming of making decisions based only on consideration of economies of scale. His reference to a "problem with the nickel contamination in the copper concentrate" suggests that Hatch Associates believed that Inco's mill at Voisey's Bay would not be able to effect a clean separation of nickel minerals from copper minerals. Thus, the copper concentrates produced by Voisey's Bay mill would be rich in nickel. Nickel-rich copper concentrates are notorious for causing problems in stand-alone copper smelters, which are accordingly reluctant to accept copper concentrates that contain more than 0.4% nickel. In fact, nickel's name is an abbreviation of a name given to it by early metallurgists: *kupfernickel* — "devil's copper." Although it would be possible for Inco to design a mill that minimized the amount of nickel picked up by the copper concentrate, the devil of it is that it would be at the cost of losing more *copper* to the *nickel* concentrate.

Hatch Associates was probably considering dilution as a solution: to spread Voisey's copper concentrates among many custom copper smelters, each of whom could blend nickel-rich Voisey's concentrates with nickel-poor concentrates from other mines. Even so, custom smelters would be likely to charge Inco penalties to cover their costs of dealing with the errant nickel.

Had the province been a little craftier, it could have asked Hatch Associates to consider not a stand-alone copper smelter, but a copper treatment facility as an integral part of an Argentia metallurgical complex. On this basis, Inco could have designed the mill at Voisey's Bay to reduce the amount of nickel picked up by the copper concentrate, at the expense of having more *copper* in the *nickel* concentrate. The company would then more readily find buyers for Voisey's Bay copper concentrates. As for the copper-rich nickel concentrates, Inco could ship them to Argentia, where it would separate the two metals during the smelting process.

A more extreme version of this idea would be for Inco not to bother separating nickel minerals from copper minerals at its Voisey's

Bay mill. After all, this is what Inco does at Sudbury, where nickel and copper are not separated until they reach the smelter. Hatch Associates might have found that the diseconomies of scale of a similar arrangement between Voisey's Bay and Argentia might be offset by Argentia's ability to treat both copper and nickel without losses or penalties, and by the reduced costs of a simpler milling process at Voisey's Bay.

The Leader of the Opposition, Loyola Sullivan, was suspicious that the government had instructed Hatch to find that it would not be feasible to build a copper smelter.

"Why is this government continuing to use every means possible to paint a negative picture for the possibility of a copper smelter?"[149] he asked, speculating that "it's quite possible the copper is already spoken for. ... Tobin has probably sold out already."[150]

Although Mr. Sullivan's statement made no sense, it did have the merit of demonstrating that Mr. Tobin was under political pressure to adopt a harder line with Inco.

On September 19, 1997, new Mines Minister Chuck Furey released the long-awaited results of Hatch Associates' $45,000 study of the viability of a copper smelter. The study confirmed the conclusions signalled by Mr. Tobin in April, although noting that the nickel smelter/refinery should also treat 20% of Voisey's Bay's output of copper,[151] likely as a response to the "contamination" issue.

But one fifth of a copper smelter was not enough for Newfoundland's challengers of corporate power. Al Chislett, one of the two prospectors who had discovered the Voisey's Bay deposit, launched a new political party to push for a Voisey's Bay copper smelter in the province.[152] The party died, but the idea lived a little longer. At the end of 1999, just as the provincial government seemed to be ready to do a deal with Inco, the parliamentary opposition demanded that the government force Inco to treat copper concentrates from Voisey's Bay in the province.[153]

The provincial government's final stance on the issue of a copper smelter emerged in June 2002, when the government announced that it had reached a deal with Inco on the development of Voisey's Bay. The government and Inco agreed to a plan which included two elements. At Voisey's Bay, Inco would build a mill that produced two products: copper concentrates and nickel concentrates. In order to minimize the nickel content of the copper concentrates, the nickel concentrates would necessarily be rich in copper. In Argentia, Inco planned to build a hydrometallurgical nickel smelter. One of the functions of this facility would be to remove the copper from the nickel concentrates, yielding a nickel-free intermediate product. That product, along with the copper concentrates produced directly at the Voisey's Bay mill, would be shipped for further treatment at custom copper smelters and refineries beyond the borders of the Province of Newfoundland and Labrador.

CHAPTER 15

STEP ONE OF THE ENVIRONMENTAL ASSESSMENT OF VOISEY'S BAY

What do you come in here for?
— John Iglo, Nain, Labrador, to the Voisey's Bay
Environmental Assessment Panel

Inco bought Diamond Fields Resources on August 21, 1996. A month later, Inco's wholly owned subsidiary, Voisey's Bay Nickel Company, submitted the Voisey's Bay mine and mill project to the Federal Department of Fisheries and Oceans for environmental review. The federal government consulted with the government of Newfoundland and Labrador and the presidents of the Labrador Inuit Association and of the Innu Nation.

On November 22, 1996, these four parties agreed to, and on January 31, 1997, signed a Memorandum of Understanding (MOU) to establish a Panel to review the proposed mine and mill. The transcriptions of the Panel's hearings eventually comprised a pile of paper over 40 centimetres thick.[154]

Lesley Griffiths, chairman of the Panel, began the review at a public meeting in Nain, Labrador, on April 16, 1997. Ms. Griffiths outlined the purpose of the review as follows:

> "The final product will be a report written by us. ... There are five main steps in the process leading up to this report.
> "The first step is ... [through] public meetings ... to identify or scope out all of the issues and concerns that must be addressed."

Then, she said:

"The Panel prepares instructions that go to ... Voisey's Bay Nickel Company telling them what information they need to provide. ... We are committed to producing these instructions by June the first [1997].

The second step is that the company will produce ... an Environmental Impact Statement. ... We do not know exactly when.

In the third step ... there will be a period of seventy-five days in which the public can comment on ... the Environmental Impact Statement. ... The Panel then has thirty days to decide, based on its own review and the public comments, whether to proceed to public hearings or to ask the company to provide additional information.

The fourth step is a second round of public meetings. ... We will announce a schedule with a minimum of thirty days' notice.

The final step is when ... the Panel writes its report and submits it [to the federal and provincial governments.] We have ninety days to complete and submit our report.

For the next six weeks, Ms. Griffiths, her panel, and observers from Inco hopscotched across the province, trying to hear the concerns of the people who would be most affected by the project. Those people could be hard to find.

Joanna Lampe, a resident of Nain, told the Panel, "When I came in yesterday, I thought I was walking into a mining convention. There were more people from outside than there were residents in Nain. ... Very few [Nain] people have come out."

And even when the Panel found them, they could be obtuse. John Iglo of Nain asked, "What do you come in here for? I don't come in your land and ask you for nothing. ... I never see you before."

The Panel condensed the minutes of its meetings into a set of guidelines which it published on June 20, 1997, three weeks behind schedule. Inco took these guidelines and began the second step of the process, the preparation of an Environmental Impact Statement (E.I.S.).

Everything was following the plan which Ms. Griffiths had laid out. However, Labrador's native groups were growing increasingly frustrated with the slow pace of progress of their land claims negotiations with the provincial government and, in September 1997, checked the Voisey's Bay project with a stunning blow.

CHAPTER 16

LOST VISIONS, FORGOTTEN DREAMS

The North Atlantic region is the most sensitive region on earth to climate oscillations.
 — Lacasse and van den Bogaard, 2002

Scratch two archaeologists, you get three opinions.
 — David Yesner, University of Anchorage, Alaska, professor, speculating on whether changes in the tools left by ancient native people imply changes in the people who made them.
Anchorage Daily News, July 12, 2004

Every December, the sales department treats its clients — managers of pension funds and mutual funds — to a form of dinner theatre. The salesmen and the clients eat while we, the research analysts, stand up and talk about our stock picks for the coming year. In December 2000, fresh from our performances in Toronto, analysts and salesmen shamble into a party bus, with shag on the ceiling and lights on the floor, and embark on an alcohol-enriched trip to Montreal. The next evening, after two performances within the dark-panelled walls of the University Club, we sink, sodden and weary, into the leather seats on the bus.

"So where did you disappear to this afternoon, Ray?"

"Just down the street, the McCord Museum has an exhibition on what they call 'Palaeo-Eskimos,'[155] the first people to occupy the Canadian Arctic. Arrowheads, knives, carvings, masks."

"Any particular reason for going?"

"You know I'm writing a book on Voisey's Bay?"

Patricia nods.

"For background, I've been reading the minutes of the panel that carried out the environmental assessment of Voisey's Bay, I've been reading about the history of Labrador,[156] and I've been reading a book on how the Alaskans resolved their native land claims issues.[157] This stuff raised some real questions. The exhibition didn't give me any answers, but it helped me to clarify what the questions were."

"And what are they, Ray?"

"Well, who were the first occupants of Voisey's Bay? Are they the same people as the people there now? And what claims should they have to the land and to Inco's ore body?"

"*Are* they the same people?"

"Well, as I understand archaeology — and I'm a geologist, not an archaeologist — as I understand archaeology, one of the big problems is that it's bloody difficult to identify people from what they leave behind. For example, we have tools, weapons, body decorations, and even skeletons of the people who inhabited the island of Newfoundland three or four thousand years ago, yet archaeologists can't tell if those people were the ancestors of Beothuk Indians who lived in Newfoundland until they were killed off in the nineteenth century, or of the Mi'kmaq Indians who live there today. Or both. Or neither."

"Can't they tell from artistic styles of carving, that sort of thing?"

"Cultural traits, yeah. So if an archaeologist of the future were to find a music video in a midden in central Africa, should she conclude that the people who lived there looked like and sounded like Britney Spears?"

"Goldie ..."

"OK, but cultural traits may be as important as genes. Who today should have the greater claim to land at Voisey's Bay: someone who is a full-blooded descendant of the first occupants of Voisey's Bay, but is now living, say, in Québec or St. John's, or someone who lives in Voisey's Bay in traditional native style, but is descended mostly from European settlers?"

"Somewhat academic, surely?"

"No, it's not, Patricia! This exhibition shows that the earliest inhabitants of northern coastal Labrador, the 'Palaeo-Eskimos,' vanished from the archaeological record between 1200 and 1500 AD. And you know who else lived there and also seems to have disappeared around the same time?"

"No ..."

"*Our* ancestors. Well, sort of. The Vikings."

"And why did they and the 'Palaeo-Eskimos' both vanish?"

I shrug.

A pothole in Highway 401, a groan from a salesman trying to sleep in a bunk.

"No one seems to be sure. But part of the story seems to be the weather. You know how, in the past coupla decades, the world's climate has got warmer?"

"Doesn't everyone, Ray?"

"Well, it may be that this warming trend has just brought us back to the normal state of affairs. Around 1000 AD, it was warm enough for the Vikings to make their way to Greenland, Labrador, and Newfoundland. But, over the next few centuries, the weather became a lot colder. Cold enough to make people move.

"In western Canada, Indians from the Lake Athabasca area moved south and became the ancestors of people like the Navajo. In the Canadian Arctic, the Inuit began to move south to Labrador. In Greenland, and perhaps Labrador, some of the Vikings went back to Iceland. And, in the highlands of the interior of Labrador, some of the Innu — Indians — began to move down towards the coast. Did the Inuit and Innu chase away the Palaeo-Eskimos and the Vikings who were left? Kill them? Absorb them by interbreeding?"

"Probably all three," says Patricia.

"I've no idea, but Lynne Fitzhugh, who wrote the book I read on the history of Labrador, thinks that the Inuit absorbed some of the Vikings' cultural traits, if not their genes. She says that's where the 'vik' comes from in Inuit place names like 'Makkovik.'"

"So, if Europeans — Vikings — were in Labrador before the Inuit, don't Europeans have aboriginal rights in Labrador?"

I don't know how to answer that question, so I continue with my impressions of Voisey's Bay's history. "Global cooling may also have sent codfish west across the Atlantic, with European fishermen — Basques, for example — following them. So, sometime in the mid-1500s, as the Inuit continued to move south, they started bumping into this second wave of Europeans. They didn't get on very well with each other, the Inuit and the second wave of Europeans. In fact, the Inuits' reputation for violence kept Europeans away from northern Labrador, away from Voisey's Bay, until the mid-1700s. But by then, the Inuit had become dependent on booty captured from the Europeans — especially boats and iron. So, in the late 1700s, it was safe enough for Moravian missionaries, Protestants, to establish stations along the coast of northern Labrador.

"There wasn't a station at Voisey's Bay, but there were stations to the south and to the north; the closest to Voisey's Bay was to the north, at Nain. The Moravians ministered to the Inuit and tried to keep them separate from other European settlers, whom the Moravians saw as dissolute. But, by the mid-1800s, the Moravians were allowing intermarriage, and the settler communities and the mission communities began to merge. Amos Voisey, for example, the chap who gave his name to Voisey's Bay, was a cabin boy from Plymouth, England, who married an Inuit woman.

"Up until the early twentieth century, there were epidemics, the last of which were of syphilis and of influenza. Mixed-blood people survived them better than pure-blooded Inuit. So, today, the people whose cultural traits are Inuit have genes which are a fair old mixture of Inuit and European."

"And Innu genes, too?"

"I'm sure, but the Moravians tried to keep the Innu away. After all, they were Catholics!"

"Ah! But how about the Innu's own land claims at Voisey's Bay?"

"Hmm. They had less interaction with literate people, so the story is murkier. The Innu originated in the highland area that straddles what is now the border between Quebec and Labrador. From about the year 1300, as it got colder, they began making seasonal visits to the coast, to places like Reid Brook, at Voisey's Bay, for fish and wood."

"When did the seasonal become permanent? Davis Inlet — all those stories about substance abuse and fetal alcohol syndrome — that's Innu, and on the coast, isn't it?"

"Yes, it's Innu and yes, it's on the coast, and I think it's the *only* Innu village on the coast. It's been there less than fifty years! Its Innu name means 'Place of the Boss.' The church and the government settled the Innu there in the 1960s."

"So you're saying the Innu have no aboriginal claim to any of the Labrador coast because they settled there only recently?"

"I guess I'm really asking a question: What is the basis for an aboriginal land claim? If it's traditional use of land, not necessarily permanent settlement, it's hard to distinguish the claims of the Innu and Inuit since they both probably began to frequent the Labrador coast around the same time, 1300 or so.

"And, just as with the Inuit, you have the question: Who, today, are the Innu?"

Patricia arches an eyebrow that shows signs that she had been hungover when she penciled it.

"In her book, Lynne Fitzhugh quoted an anthropologist who had traced the Rich family of Davis Inlet back to the union of a Scotsman — or maybe a Scots-Cree — and an Ungava Inuit woman. The anthropologist added that the family had become 'completely Indianized.' So, again I wonder, which should count more in land claims: cultural traits or genes?"

"Well, Ray, you mentioned native land claims in Alaska. Did the Alaskan experience answer that question?"

"It did, though I'm not sure I'm happy with the answer. All U.S. citizens with at least one-quarter Alaskan native blood are Alaska natives. I suspect that I prefer one of the ways the New Zealand government answers the question, Who is a Maori? In New Zealand, there are two electoral rolls, Maori and general. To be included on the Maori roll, the only requirement is that you be willing to declare yourself to be a New Zealand Maori."

"OK, so you have an Inuit person and a person of European descent living in Nain, and an Innu from Davis Inlet, all three willing to declare themselves to be Labradorian natives. How do you allocate their claims to Voisey's Bay?"

"Actually, the question's even more complicated than that. How do you allocate the claims of an Innu from Davis Inlet and an Innu from Sheshatshiu? The Innu have been arguing this among themselves, with the Davis Inlet Innu saying it should be a 60:40 split in favour of Davis Inlet because Davis Inlet is closer to Voisey's Bay, and the Sheshatshiu Innu are saying it should be a 60:40 split in favour of *Sheshatshiu* because there are more people in Sheshatshiu."[158]

"That's not an answer, Goldie."

"Well, I really like the Alaskan approach to native land claims because of the way it addresses questions like these. In Alaska, no person directly owns native lands — corporations do. For each region of Alaska, there's a corporation that owns the native land. And the shareholders of each corporation are the native people who live there — *regardless* of their race. So Cominco's[159] Red Dog mine, for example, in northwestern Alaska, is mostly on land owned by NANA — Northwest Alaska Native Association Regional Corporation — and NANA and Cominco can deal with each other corporation to corporation. A 'Northeast Labrador Native Association Regional Corporation' would have Innu *and* Inuit shareholders. More importantly, it would have Metis shareholders — people with mixed Innu, Inuit, Mi'kmaq, and European blood, and equally mixed cultural affinities. And why not? The Metis say that there are more of them than there are members of either the Innu Nation of the L.I.A.[160] The Metis are not recognized as natives by the provincial government, and that worries me. It might come back and hurt Inco one day. It sure would clarify matters if there were to be Alaskan-style corporations in Labrador, but it ain't going to happen. Divide and conquer. And the Alaskan model wouldn't solve the other big issue."

"What's that?"

"Just because white men drew a line and said 'this side is Quebec and this side is Labrador,' does that mean that the nomads who, when the line was drawn, were on the west side have no claim to what they say are traditional lands on the east side?"[161]

"I don't know, Ray, but I'm going to lie down and try to sleep. At the rate we're going, we won't be in Toronto until 1 a.m."

"Sweet dreams!"

CHAPTER 17

JUDGE MARSHALL IMPEDES THE "IMPETUOUS AND HEEDLESS PACE OF MAN"

I'm not going to say we're going to be able to stand in the way of a billion-dollar development.
— Peter Penashue, President, Innu Nation; comment to *Reuters*, March 29, 1996

[The] just over 1,200 people [who] presently live in Nain ... have got the attitude that [Voisey's Bay] is too big ... they are not going to stop it anyway.
— Nain Mayor Rex Holwell to the Environmental Assessment Panel, Nain, Labrador, April 16, 1997

Everyone has said they're for Voisey's Bay. ... We're not out to stop it.
— Makkovik Mayor Wayne Broomfield to the Environmental Assessment Panel, Goose Bay, Labrador, October 3, 1998

The majority of the people ... that I've been talking to ... are pretty well opposed to [Voisey's Bay].
— Edward Aggek, local resident, to the Environmental Assessment Panel in Hopedale, Labrador, October 28, 1998

One of the more humbling aspects of a mining analyst's job is that it makes one realize the difficulty of understanding the motivations of people whose lives are very different from one's own.

In 1988, I went to the island of Bougainville in Papua New Guinea to see where Uncle Bert had served at the end of World War II and to visit the giant Panguna copper mine in the company of a group of geologists. Although my employer had paid my way, and although our group was allowed to wander the open pit, I failed to pick up the most important issue for an investor. The only major problem I observed at Panguna was that the mine's effluents were making a good deal more mess than was acknowledged by the mine's operator, Bougainville Copper Limited. I came away thinking that the shares of Bougainville Copper represented a good investment.

Only six months later, the mine was shut down by the armed uprising of separatist landowners. I had had no inkling of their dissatisfaction, nor did any of the mine employees — mostly expatriates — indicate that they were aware of it. (I admit that Bert had warned me that the locals could be non-communicative. His sharpest memory of Bougainville was of "Silent Jack," whose favourite pastime was stalking and spearing unwary Japanese.)

In Labrador, before the discovery of Voisey's Bay, negotiations over native land claims had been proceeding in a desultory fashion. In July 1996, just as Inco was attempting to complete its takeover of Diamond Fields Resources, the Labrador Inuit Association signed an agreement with the federal and provincial governments. The agreement outlined the process by which the three parties expected to achieve a land claims treaty.

The Innu also wanted a deal. In 1993, a video depicting the despair of the young Innu of Davis Inlet, Labrador, came to the attention of the international media. Peter Penashue, President of the Innu Nation, found himself thrust into the spotlight.[162] He used his new-found celebrity to lobby Premier Clyde Wells who, by May 15, 1995, told the Newfoundland and Labrador House of Assembly that he had agreed to "a speeded-up process for land claims with the Innu."

Ten months later, on March 29, 1996, the new premier, Brian Tobin, the federal Minister of Indian Affairs and Northern Development, Ron Irwin, and Mr. Penashue signed an agreement similar to the one signed with the L.I.A. the previous year. They committed themselves to achieving a final treaty within five years.

In the months that followed, the Inuit became increasingly frustrated by the slow pace of land claims negotiations. In July 1996, William Barbour of the L.I.A. became concerned that his association and the government would miss their target date, March 31, 1997, for the completion of the next step, an agreement-in-principle. He threatened legal action to stop the development of Voisey's Bay[163] if the land claims negotiations did not make better progress. Inco took note. As we have seen, on October 28, 1996, Dr. Sopko announced that he had pushed back his forecast for the start-up of Voisey's Bay from 1998 to the second half of 1999.

The L.I.A.'s chief negotiator, Toby Anderson, reminded the world that, if there were no progress, he would take legal action, and he made it clear that his idea of "progress" was for the provincial government to guarantee that the L.I.A. would receive a share of the royalties from Voisey's.[164]

April 30, 1997, Morning Meeting

"I'm downgrading my recommendation on Inco's Class VBN shares from a 'Buy' to a 'Hold.'"

"Why, Ray? Weren't you telling us last week that Inco's exploration people now think that the prospective rocks at Voisey's Bay, er ..."

"Troctolites."

"... troctolites, are four times more extensive than they previously thought?"

"Yeah, Patricia, but I think we're now at the point where investors are becoming less interested in exploration, and more interested in seeing some signs of development. The native land claims negotiations have been going so slowly that I thought everyone now realized that Voisey's Bay couldn't begin production before 2000. But only last week, Inco was still insisting that 1999 is the most likely date for start-up.[165] I wonder if the company is really fully aware of what's going on. Should the sluggishness of the land claims negotiations force a delay, investors in the VBN shares are going to be disappointed."

"But Ray, how can 'sluggishness' force a delay? For almost a year now, the natives have been threatening to ask for a court injunction to stop development. Their lawyers must have advised them that they have no legal basis on which to request an injunction, or else we'd have seen one by now."

"Patricia, I don't know the mechanism by which they could block development. If it's not a legal action, it'll be something like lying down in front of bulldozers. But there's so much frustration, I really worry that they'll slow or stop the project one way or another.

July 15, 1997, Morning Meeting

"Last week the L.I.A. — Inuit — petitioned a Newfoundland court to deny Inco a permit to build a road and airstrip to support exploration at Voisey's Bay. The Innu joined them, and the Inuit from just across the border in Quebec tried to join them. Guess the Innu and the Quebec Inuit wanted to make the point that they had claims on Voisey's Bay, too. The St. John's papers say the court should make a decision by the 18th."

"What's the basis for the petition, Ray?"

"Patricia, Inco is preparing an Environmental Impact Statement as part of the process of obtaining a permit to begin development at Voisey's Bay. The L.I.A. says that it's a waste of a perfectly good environmental permitting process not to use it to assess the road and airstrip."

"Well, a road and airstrip *do* sound more like part of a mining project than part of an exploration project."

"To avoid environmental damage, Inco has been continuing Diamond Fields's practice of supporting exploration work entirely by helicopter. Inco argues that this is a terribly dangerous way of doing things[166] — not to mention expensive — and they really need an airstrip and road to continue safely. The usual practice in the rest of Canada is that any infrastructure needed to support exploration is exempted from the full environmental assessment applied to a mining project."

The chair of the meeting interrupted sharply. "Can we move on? We have several more analysts to hear from before the market opens."

"OK then — I still think that Voisey's Bay's schedule is likely to slip beyond the 1999 start-up date projected by Inco. Until this has been recognized by the market, I'd be in no hurry to buy Inco's VBN shares."

Monday, July 21, 1997, Morning Meeting

"On Friday, Judge Raymond Halley of the Supreme Court of Newfoundland dismissed the native groups' bid to stop Inco building a road and airstrip at Voisey's Bay. A millisecond later, the province gave Inco a permit to go ahead. But the market must've been expecting that, because the VBN shares didn't go up on the news. Actually, they dropped a bit, from $26.00 to $25.55."

"Well, Ray, the market's always looking ahead to the next piece of news. Could be it's now anticipating that the L.I.A. and the Innu Nation will appeal the decision."

"Could be."

Monday August 15, 1997, Morning Meeting

"Ray, you had something to say on Voisey's?"

"Yeah — this is all from the St. John's *Telegram*. The L.I.A. *did* appeal Justice Halley's decision and, again, the Innu Nation joined them. The L.I.A. has also asked the Court of Appeal for an injunction to stop construction until the judges have made their decision on the appeal. Both native groups have been threatening that, if they don't get that injunction, they'll show up at Inco's dock to physically stop Inco from unloading equipment. So far, though, neither they nor the judges have actually got around to doing anything."

"How's the construction going?"

"Inco has now completed nearly a kilometre of road, just over 10 kilometres to go."

On August 19, I noted that Al Chislett's and Chris Verbiski's company, Archean Resources, had further complicated Inco's attempts to build a road at Voisey's Bay. Archean alleged that it retained quarrying rights on the ground, which it had claimed on behalf of Diamond Fields Resources, so Archean had filed a lawsuit demanding compensation for the sand and gravel that Inco was mining.[167]

On August 21, 1997, I reported that more than fifty members of the Innu Nation and the L.I.A. pitched tents in front of bulldozers and on a gravel quarry. Had they stayed, Inco would not have been able to complete the road and airstrip before freeze-up. But they didn't have to stay. On August 28, Inco announced that the Court of Appeal had granted the natives' request for an injunction to stop work.

Curiously, the VBN stock price hardly moved after this announcement. It also failed to move when, for the first time, a reference to the court case appeared in the U.S. press.[168] But the share price did drop, and it dropped by about $3.00 when Mike Sopko announced[169] that, because of what was happening in court, production from Voisey's would be delayed by at least a year. The price dropped another $3.00 or so after the judges at the Court of Appeal announced, on September 22, that they had ruled in favour of the natives.

On October 8, 1997, after Chuck Furey, Newfoundland and Labrador's Mines Minister, had appealed to the Prospectors and Developers Association of Canada to help Newfoundland in its battle with equalization payments, he took me aside. What, Mr. Furey asked, did I think of 'the Marshall decision'?

"Pardon me?"

"The decision of Judge Marshall and his two colleagues at the Court of Appeal last month against us and against Inco. It certainly affected the future of the Voisey's Bay project, so I thought you financial people would have a view."

"I'm afraid I haven't read it."

"You should, Ray. It's disturbing. It creates a legal precedent across Canada for a much broader interpretation of environmental laws than had previously been applied to mining companies. Hard to believe that Justice Marshall used to be our Mines Minister! He and the other two judges revoked the permit that the government had given to Inco, saying that we had no right to grant it, that Judge Halley was wrong to have ruled in our favour, and that the road and airstrip had to pass the environmental review of the mine and mill. Their decision cited Rachel Carson more than legal precedents."

So I curled up on the sofa at home and read the decision.[170] The score was Rachel Carson: 1 citation (a warning of the dangers of the "impetuous and heedless pace of man"); legal precedents: 5.

The judges observed that Judge Halley believed that the government of Newfoundland and Labrador should not require Inco to submit its road and airstrip to a full environmental review because the purpose of the road and airstrip was — initially, at any rate — to support exploration, not mining. However, Judge Marshall and his colleagues, Judges Derek Green and Geoffrey O.L. Steele, pointed out that the environmental review of Voisey's Bay was supposed to encompass mining, milling, and "associated activities." By excluding associated activities such as exploration, Judge Halley had erred. He had made the mistake of "emphasizing purpose rather than impact."

Judge Marshall's conclusions seemed sound to me. Were I a goose, sitting on my nest, I would not be reassured if someone from Inco were to tell me that the airstrip it was constructing next to my nest was an "exploration airstrip" rather than a "production airstrip."

I began to wonder: might another judge rule that a smelter and refinery could also be regarded as "associated activities," and therefore rule in favour of the Citizens' Mining Council of Newfoundland and Labrador's plea to have the smelter and refinery included in the environment assessment of Voisey's Bay?

And I reflected on an irony of the ruling. The Inuit and Innu had wished to punish the Government of Newfoundland and Labrador for dragging its heels on land claims negotiations. The result was a legal ruling that was likely to slow the permitting process for Voisey's Bay. In turn, this would remove the provincial government's incentive to come to an early resolution of land claims.

CHAPTER 18

WOMAN OF LABRADOR

Daughter of Labrador
Those days are here no more
Wonder if your baby will ever understand
The hardships that you endured
When everyone you knew was poor
Sharing everything you had
And living off the land.
— *"Woman of Labrador"* © Andy Vine
SOCAN registered. All rights reserved.

I used to live at Emish, Voisey's Bay. ... My father was the first one to pass away and that is where he is buried, where they are going to do the mining. The white people want to dig out my father's grave.
— Monique Rich, mother of Katie Rich, through an interpreter, to the Environmental Assessment Panel, Davis Inlet, Labrador, April 19, 1997

At this time, the only economically viable project to which the company could commit would be a mine, mill, and related infrastructure in Labrador, based on the Ovoid's reserves with the intermediate nickel product [concentrate] to be processed [in Ontario or Manitoba]. As the Company is able to prove up additional reserves beyond the Ovoid, then it would evaluate which further processing facilities in [Newfoundland and Labrador] ... could be supported on an economic basis.
— Voisey's Bay Update, Inco press release, July 27, 1998

Because of this [apparent change in the] terms of the project ... we don't know what we're assessing here. ... I want to use an analogy. ... Is it an outhouse or a full water and sewer treatment plant?
— Todd Russell, Labrador Metis Nation, questioning the scale of the Voisey's Bay project before the Environmental Assessment Panel, Goose Bay, September 11, 1998

The operation was a success but the patient died. ... Expectations grew faster than resources.
— Bevin LeDrew, LeDrew and Napier (2000)

On December 16, 1997, after six months of preparation, Inco submitted its Environmental Impact Statement to the Canadian Environmental Assessment Agency. On April 1, 1998, the federal Minister of the Environment, daunted by the size of Inco's submission, extended the period allowed for public review from seventy-five to 105 days.

The Panel considered the public's federally funded responses and decided that Inco's statement had not adequately responded to the Panel's guidelines. So Inco went back around the loop, rewrote its Environmental Impact Statement, resubmitted it, and waited through another forty-five days of public review. The provincial government, the Labrador Inuit Association, and the Innu Nation, all claiming that Inco's July 27 press release (quoted above) constituted a change in Inco's plans for Voisey's Bay, asked the Panel to suspend public hearings until Inco had clearly stated the scope of its proposals for the development of Voisey's Bay.

But the federal government said to the Panel: don't listen to these people, go ahead; after all, we're the ones paying you.[171] And there had been no word from the court that was hearing the application by the Citizens' Mining Council of St. John's to shut down the environmental assessment. So, on September 9, 1998, almost two years after Inco had applied for an environmental review of the Voisey's Bay project, the second round of public meetings began. Chairman Lesley Griffiths called them "the most important stage in the Environmental Assessment process."

As the hearings opened in Goose Bay, Labrador, Chairman Griffiths was frustrated. The plane carrying representatives of the L.I.A. and the Innu Nation was late.

"I was thinking this morning," said Ms. Griffiths, "that we had some leeway and could carry on early this evening if necessary. I discovered it's Bingo Night. I guess every night is Bingo Night."

Stuart Gendron, President of Inco's subsidiary, Voisey's Bay Nickel Company (V.B.N.C.), was also frustrated. The Panel had complained to him that V.B.N.C. had applied for permission to build a mill, open-pit mine, and underground mine and operate them over twenty-five years, yet it had presented a schedule of activities for only the first twelve years. Dr. Gendron pointed out that, in order to give a schedule for years thirteen to twenty-five, his company needed to carry out a program of underground exploration and evaluation. However, thanks to the Marshall decision, V.B.N.C. couldn't begin such a program until the whole project had cleared the environmental assessment process.

And Daniel Ashini, Vice-President of the Innu Nation, gave every appearance of being *very* frustrated, and not only because his plane had been late. Perhaps he had sensed that Inco had entered the environmental assessment process with the view that native people shouldn't be very concerned about the project because the Voisey's Bay deposit was on a peninsula and, hence, according to Inco's way of thinking, must have been off traditional native migration paths.[172] He told the Panel that a woman from Sheshatshiu had told him "We don't have to accept dirty money," and that a man from Utshimassit had told him that "the mining developments will destroy ... all the living creatures that live from the land." And now, because Inco would no longer make plans beyond Year 12, he argued, the company was no longer committed to the project as described in the Memorandum of Understanding that the Innu Nation, the L.I.A., and the two governments had signed in January 1997. Perhaps there will be production only from the Ovoid, he said, which would mean a project life of a mere seven years — quite unsatisfactory for Innu seeking jobs.

Bill Rowat, representing the province, joined the attack on Inco. According to Mr. Rowat, when Inco presented its Environmental Impact Statement in December 1997, Inco said that "'the two underground deposits ... will be mined,' not 'may be mined,' not 'could be mined if the price is right' ... 'will be mined.'" But, on July 27, 1998, said Mr. Rowat, Inco backed away from what had seemed like an unconditional guarantee. The company issued a press release which, "for the first time introduced ... [the idea that, partway through the life of the project, there would be] a critical go or no-go decision to be taken to proceed with the underground development."

"I'm sure that whoever wrote that ... press release is probably looking for a job right now," speculated one of the Panel.[173]

"Has Inco changed its corporate strategy?" continued Mr. Rowat. "Yes." He then speculated that among the reasons for the apparent change in strategy were pressure from financial analysts, political instability in Indonesia, where Inco had a nickel mine, and low nickel prices.[174]

Mr. Ashini agreed with Mr. Rowat that there had been a significant change in the project. In fact, he asked the Panel to rule that there had been change so significant that the parties to the Memorandum of Understanding, which had established the Panel, should renegotiate their agreement.

"This is news to us," said Inco's legal counsel.

"We just got notice of this motion," said the L.I.A.'s legal counsel.

Inco[175] assured the Panel that "the project has not changed. Some people are suggesting that we're interested only in mining the Ovoid. That's simply not correct. ... We have a phased approach."

Chairman Griffiths decided to continue with the session while she sought advice on Mr. Ashini's request. Inco's George Greer added that he and his colleagues had "put our heads together and [come] up with ... the worst possible scenario we could see up at the Voisey's Bay site," and had concluded that the life of the project would be at least 22 years. It had better be, warned Paul Dean, Assistant Deputy Minister for the provincial Mines Branch.[176] "The company must obtain a mining lease authorized by the Minister of Mines and Energy [and] the Department ... will not issue a mining lease until the Environmental Assessment Panel has submitted its report. ... Any proposal for mining only the higher grade Ovoid open pit should be rejected."

On September 11, the Panel decided that there had not been "a significant change to the undertaking so as to require the Panel to inform the ... parties to the Memorandum of Understanding."

So the hearings continued, to the disappointment of the province, the Inuit, the Innu ... and of *Telegram* reporter Chris Flanagan, who was frustrated that he was stuck in Goose Bay and gagged by the Panel's ruling that journalists could not ask questions.

Local Labradorians continued to attack Inco. They believed that they had ample justification. One of them[177] said, "I sort of feel like I'm a bumblebee in a nudist colony. I know what I'm supposed to do but I don't know where to begin."

The Labradorians recalled contamination left behind by other mining operations in the province, notably the Kitts and Michelin test uranium mines in Labrador and the Hope Brook gold mine in Newfoundland. They told the Panel that the Voisey's Bay Nickel Company's ban on hunting at the project site was a violation of "aboriginal rights to harvest."

And they said they were "burnt and pissed off pretty badly," having "lost a lot of sleep" over proposals by NDT Ventures, the junior exploration company which had sponsored Professor Morton's visits to Toronto and New York, to drill within the town of Nain.

* * * * *

In the late 1960s, Macmillan of Canada began to publish a series of books about travels in Canada's provinces and territories. Harold Horwood wrote the Newfoundland and Labrador volume, entitled simply *Newfoundland*, which was published in 1969. In his book, Mr. Horwood recounted a visit to Davis Inlet, Labrador, to meet the Naskapi Indian chief, Joe Riche, his son, Ben, and the children whom Mr. Horwood saw as the future leaders of the Naskapi, Ben's sons and nephews.

By 1998, Davis Inlet had become Utshimassit, the Naskapi called themselves Innu, and the Riches spelt their name "Rich." But the Rich family had retained their leadership of the community. The most prominent opponent of Inco when it arrived in Labrador, the President of the Innu Nation, was neither a son nor a nephew. Her name was Katie Rich.

Inco had anticipated criticism from the Labradorians at the Panel hearings. Herb Clarke, Voisey's Bay Nickel Company's Vice-President, Corporate Affairs, told the Panel, "in order to give the

Innu and Inuit a first-hand view of an open-pit mine," Inco had taken some of them to see Cominco's Red Dog zinc mine in Alaska. Inco had also arranged meetings with Inuit of the Northwest Alaska Native Association, the native corporation that was Cominco's partner at Red Dog, and visits to Inco's operations at Sudbury, Ontario, and Falconbridge's Raglan mine in far northern Quebec.

The Labradorians' response? Of her visit to Sudbury, Katie Rich said, "The first thing I noticed was the [Super] stack and the smoke coming out of it. ... It scares me."

David Nuke of the Innu Nation told the Panel that "Cominco is very good to the Inuit. ... They weren't treated like second-class citizens. ... They're treated differently than we're treated at Voisey's Bay. Cominco is not Inco, and that's the sad part."

For Ms. Rich, the deciding factor was that Inco had reportedly constructed a building over her grandfather's grave at Voisey's Bay. "Inco will never mine Voisey's," she vowed.[178]

CHAPTER 19

PRAGMATISTS, FINGER POINTERS, TRICKSTERS, AND THE BIG CLUMSY GUY

You go outside and raise your head
Watch the northern lights go dancing
High over the sea.
— *Woman of Labrador*, Andy Vine, SOCAN registered

"Thanks for inviting me to dinner, Goldie. I'm glad you came here for the Voisey's Bay hearings."

Margaret Butt, whom I had met in St. John's in 1995, has figured out that I enjoy spicy food and has chosen a Mexican restaurant for a late supper.

"Well, now that I have bet five bottles of single malt whisky on Voisey's not starting production before 2008, I have to look after my interests!"

"This is a treat. We don't get many visitors in October."

"Even so, the Winterholme — Ruby and Dick Cook's place, where I'm staying — is as crowded as in summer."

"Why's that?"

"Because it's a 'heritage home.' They're using it as the set for a movie — *The Divine Ryans*. Place is full of lights and cables. The most startling thing happened yesterday. There was a series of thuds — seems one of the technicians slid off the roof and hurt himself really badly."

"Oh yes, I heard about that. He could be in hospital for months."

"Of course, I forgot, everyone in St. John's knows everyone else."

Margaret smiles wryly. "There's some truth to that! Anyway, I hope the hearings weren't quite so dramatic."

"Not quite ... are you going to eat that jalapeno? I'll have it if you won't. ... The best drama was from Andy Jones. He's that actor fellow ..."

"Oh, what's Andy up to now? He hasn't had a gig in a while, so he shows up at government hearings?"

I realize that Andy Jones might be a customer of Margaret's pharmacy, or that she had probably been to school with someone who was a close relation of his. Or both.

"He presented himself as a NATO pilot, Hansfeld Horseflesh. In his best German accent he explained that he knew Labrador well because he was accustomed to flying over it at 1,000 kilometres per hour, 30 feet above the ground. Then he managed to compare Newfoundland's government with Hitler, and he described Robert Friedland as a man who confiscated land from the natives, kicked the constitution of Canada in the *cojones*, and walked away with $600 million."

"I wonder if that crowd up at the university put him up to it?"

"I don't think so. I spoke to him afterwards and he said it was his own idea because he was concerned that rural Newfoundland culture and aboriginal culture were slowly dying and no one seemed to care. There *were* some university people there, speaking on behalf of Jim Brokenshire's group, the Citizen's Mining Council of Newfoundland and Labrador. Jim's group's main recommendation is to stop the whole environmental assessment process as the Panel hearings aren't really the best forum for that point of view ... you know, telling a bunch of people that they should quit what they've been doing for the past few months and start over. It's not going to get you very far. In fact, the Chairman took them to task when they alleged that all the participants in the hearings, except Inco, wanted the hearings stopped."

"And Jim's still waiting to hear from Federal Court?"

"Yeah, his group asked the Court to rule that the mine and mill and the smelter and refinery should all be included in one big environmental assessment, so the whole process should start over."

"In my MBA program, they kept harping on the time value of money, so I know that a delay like that would be bad news for investors. Do you think it's likely?"

"A delay? My bet is that the courts will rule against Jim's group. Anyway, I don't think the environmental assessment process will be the bottleneck. I must admit, though, Inco had been telling people that the Panel would give its final approval to Inco before the end of the year,[179] but Inco now seems to think it'll be early next year. Even so, the bottleneck will be getting Inco, the government, and the native groups all to agree." I pause. "There *was* one piece of bad news for investors in today's presentations."

"You're going to have to tell me, Goldie, I can't guess."

"A fellow from a local association of trade unions requested that, in the interests of labour peace during construction at Voisey's Bay, Inco adopt what he quite frankly called 'featherbedding,' by which he meant doubling-up on some jobs as a training program. When the Panel asked if featherbedding is expensive, he replied 'Oh, yes!'"

I begin to wriggle in my seat.

"Are you all right, Goldie?"

"Oh yes. I just have a numb bum. Those hotel room chairs are about as comfortable as a Presbyterian pew. The Panel members have been at it for weeks. Must have brass arses."

"Probably better padded than yours, anyway. Have another dollop of sour cream."

"No thanks, Margaret. But I will look at the dessert menu. Wonder if they have helados?"

"Goldie, last year you told me that when you came to the hearings you'd be cheering for the good guys. Have you decided yet who the good guys are?"

"Margaret, I guess I was being too simplistic. Rather than good guys/bad guys, I'm starting to see them as pragmatists, finger pointers, and tricksters. The pragmatists are the Inuit. The finger pointers, who blame the whites for their problems and defend a lifestyle which they designate as traditional, but which has incorporated some unpleasant aspects of the modern world, are the Innu. And the tricksters are some of the people with the government of Newfoundland and Labrador. Their motivations may be sound, but they're not above fabricating stories and tricks to further their ends."

"And Inco?"

"Inco is coming across as the big guy who keeps stumbling into the furniture."

"How's that?"

"For example, the CEO, Mike Sopko, pronounced Newfoundland as 'NewFOUNDland,' long after the company had bought into Voisey's Bay."

Margaret winces. Newfoundlanders are sensitive about mispronunciation of the name of their home.

"And today's episode with Janet Holmgren was telling. Janet Holmgren is a Metis from Uranium City in Saskatchewan. She gave an impressive presentation on how native groups had built mutually beneficial relationships with uranium mining companies in northern Saskatchewan. When she suggested that a similar approach might work at Voisey's, one of the Innu Nation fellows, big burly chap with a ponytail, stormed up to the front and bellowed, 'I'd like to know how you got here!' It turned out that Ms. Holmgren was not aware who had paid for her trip to Newfoundland."

"And who had, Goldie?"

"Well, finally an Inco spokesman said that her visit had been arranged by a consulting firm, acting on behalf of Inco. This gave the impression that Inco had covertly set up Ms. Holmgren. I think it would have been much more effective for Inco to have introduced her as their guest who had a good story to tell."

"Any other furniture that Inco's bumped into?"

"I remember spring last year, during a conference call with analysts, Mike Sopko was making optimistic noises about the provincial government's land claims negotiations with the Inuit. Dr. Sopko said he looked forward to a settlement within the next few weeks — this was a couple of days after CBC Radio in St. John's had announced[180] that the two sides had walked out of talks and were likely to stay out until the end of summer. Obviously, Inco's senior people in Toronto didn't have very good lines of communication with their own office here in St. John's. And another area where Inco lost ground today ..."

"Goldie, you're going a hundred miles an hour."

"... was that two environmentalists said that Inco would be releasing 'a few hundred million tonnes of toxic tailings' into the ocean at the Goro project in New Caledonia. Toxic or not, Inco's plans are to keep all their tailings on land. The chairman of the Panel gave the Inco people the chance to respond, but they passed."

"Are there many environmental groups there?"

"No. And one of the things that surprised me as I was reading the transcripts of the hearings in Labrador was that national and international environmental groups had so little presence. In Labrador, the Panel's concerns about the environment tended to be linked to the aboriginals' traditional use of land. There was a presentation today from a coalition of Toronto environmental and aboriginal rights groups, and their focus was on how to be nice to the Innu, not on saving whales or endangered arthropods. ... *¿Cerveza más?*"

"No, thanks. I have to get up early tomorrow. I'm working on some ideas to expand the business."

"Good for you, put your Queen's MBA to use! If you're really looking for a business venture, I've got an idea for you."

"What's that?"

"Well, there must be half a dozen Mexican restaurants in St. John's."

Margaret closes her eyes and begins counting on graceful fingers. "Yes, about that."

"And no Thai restaurants, right?"

"Right."

"You'd clean up."

CHAPTER 20

IMPACT BENEFIT AGREEMENTS TO THE END OF THE TOBIN ERA

When I go to Emos [Voisey's Bay] again, later on, me and my friends, we will go partridge hunting there later on snowmobiles. ... You are the white people ... you should all go home. I think you should all go home. You are white people. You serve us no purpose.
— Davis Inlet resident Lloyd Rich to Voisey's Bay Environmental Assessment Panel, April 20, 1997

Last year, the Innu of Sheshatshiu and Davis Inlet set up a task force to survey their people ... and ask them what they thought about this mineral bonanza. ... In Sheshatshiu ... more than half the people opposed any mining development at Voisey's Bay. At Davis Inlet ... the opposition is almost unanimous. ... In a few cases the Innu are worried about what the outsiders will do to them. ... Most of all, most painfully, they are worried about what they will do to themselves — alcoholism, child neglect, abuse, family violence, suicide.
— John Gray, *The Globe and Mail*, Toronto, April 1, 1997

Our plan is to continue negotiating the Impact Benefit Agreements as quickly as possible so that by the time that we get to the point where we are ready to start construction we do have agreement in place.
— George Greer, Manager of Mine Development, Voisey's Bay Nickel Company, to the Voisey's Bay Environmental Assessment Panel, Rigolet, Labrador, October 5, 1998

On October 31, 1998, John Mameanskum told the Environmental Assessment Panel that he was disappointed.[181] Mr. Mameanskum was

Director General of the Naskapi Band, a group of Innu who lived in Quebec near Schefferville.

"The Band made a submission to this Panel's scoping sessions in May 1997," he said. "Our submission argued that the Quebec Naskapis must be recognized as an affected group. ... Regrettably ... we were never given any opportunity for input by Voisey's Bay Nickel. ... You can imagine our surprise by the claim in [Voisey's Bay Nickel's] Environmental Impact Statement ... that the Naskapi Band of Quebec was 'contacted in writing [by Voisey's Bay Nickel] during September 1997 and ... as of October 31, 1997, no response was received.' Contrary to this claim, the Naskapi Band of Quebec was never contacted by Voisey's Bay Nickel Company."

Nor, it seems, did V.B.N.C contact two other groups of natives, the Quebec Inuit and the Labrador Metis, who also claimed interests in Voisey's Bay.

"Why not?" wondered Todd Russell of the Labrador Metis Nation.[182] "What is the premise under which [Voisey's Bay Nickel] will enter into a negotiation process with one group of aboriginal people?"

Frank Armitage, Voisey's Bay Nickel's Vice-President of Human Resources, replied,[183] "The guide that we took for our lead was based on the fact that land claims were under way, but recognized by both the federal and provincial governments."

Only two groups met Mr. Armitage's criteria: the Labrador Inuit Association and the Innu Nation. Unfortunately, as Mr. Armitage said,[184] "the mine/mill is located in an area which is subject to overlapping land claims from the Labrador Inuit Association and the Innu Nation," which made it difficult for V.B.N.C. to decide how to share benefits between the two groups.

A member of the Labrador Inuit Association, Daniel Ashini of the Innu Nation, conceded the problem. "There's certainly been discussions on the part of the Labrador Inuit Association and the Innu Nation [with each other] ... but it's unfortunate to report there is no resolution." Just resentment.

"I wish that Inuit people can get the free stuff like Innu people," complained Richard Haye of Nain.[185] "Like building a new [town]; they get that free from the government."

Inco began to negotiate Impact Benefit Agreements with the L.I.A. in the fall of 1995[186] and with the Innu Nation sometime in late 1995[187] or in January 1996.[188]

When the L.I.A. and Inco began negotiating, both believed that they could reach a deal by April 30, 1996. However, by March 31, 1998, there was still no deal in sight. Both sides had left the negotiating table. Although the progress of the talks was supposed to be confidential, Ches Andersen of the L.I.A. complained[189] that "there is not even an agreed process for the continuation of the Inuit Impact Benefits negotiations at this time."

Voisey's Bay Nickel's Gerry Marshall blamed the Inuit for the failure of the talks because the Inuit wanted Inco to promise "measures beyond which a private sector company [cannot] be reasonably expected to do." Adding that the Inuit wanted too much money, he asked the Panel to recommend that "development can proceed in advance of land claims agreements."

"Don't put the blame on us!" responded Mr. Andersen. "Compare us with the Innu Nation," he said. Initially, the Innu wouldn't even talk to Inco until they had completed a land claim with the government. The L.I.A., however, had been much more flexible.

"[We tried] to negotiate, in the absence of a land claim, an Impact Benefits Agreement with the company at the same time we were out there negotiating with the governments on a land claims agreement," said Mr. Andersen. "[But] the L.I.A. has learned the hard way from painful experiences with [Voisey's Bay Nickel Company] that commitments must be spelled out in writing and with precision. For L.I.A., a commitment is an obligation."

In an apparent reference to Inco's press release of July 27, 1998,[190] he complained that "for V.B.N.C., a commitment appears to be an expression of willingness if certain conditions do not materialize." He concluded that "the proposed project cannot proceed without Inuit consent."

Mr. Andersen's colleague, Isabel Pain, a negotiator for the L.I.A., believed that the L.I.A. had been too flexible in the past, adding that "before the Inuit will consent to the project ... [there must be] a land claims agreement in principle ... in addition, there must be an Impact Benefits Agreement between L.I.A. and V.B.N.C."

Impact Benefit Agreements to the End of the Tobin Era

By the following February, Ms. Pain's opinion seemed to have become the official view of the Labrador Inuit Association. "Labrador Inuit leaders have changed their minds and now say they won't allow Voisey's Bay work to proceed until they have a final land claims deal in place. ... The L.I.A.'s claims director, Toby Anderson, said 'the L.I.A. changed its position because the agreement-in-principle [with the provincial government over land claims] would not settle rights in the Voisey's Bay project area.'"[191]

I inferred from the Panel hearings that Inco's talks with the Innu were also going badly. The following exchange at the Panel hearings in Davis Inlet, on April 19, 1997, illustrates how poorly the two groups were communicating.

Katie Rich, Innu Nation: "I would like to have Herb Clarke apologize to the women."

Herb Clarke, Voisey's Bay Nickel Company: "There must have been some serious misunderstanding and I don't understand the charge that was made."

As does this comment, April 20, 1997:

David Nui, Innu Nation: "When we hear V.B.N.C or Inco making promises about what they're going to do to protect our environment and share the wealth with the Innu and the Inuit, it's pretty hard to believe them."

Inco eventually confirmed that its talks with the Innu had run into problems. The company complained that the Innu's demands were "unrealistic"[192] and, on a per capita basis, were "at least fifty times higher than a recently completed agreement for a major mining project."[193] The Innu retorted that "If you [Inco] can't get reasonable talks in an honourable way, this is a clear warning, you're going to lose ... money."[194]

Somehow, the threats and complaints subsided and, by November 3, 1998, Inco and the Innu were co-operating to the extent that they were able to make a joint presentation to the Environmental Assessment Panel. However, Daniel Ashini of the Innu Nation commented to the Environmental Assessment Panel that "there remains a lot of work to be done if the Innu and the company are to come to a fair agreement," and, indeed, the talks seemed to grind to a halt in the months that followed.

In August 1999, Inco announced that the two sides had resumed negotiations. Inco also announced that it had renewed discussions with both the L.I.A. and the Innu Nation, and said that its objective in both sets of talks was to reach Impact Benefit Agreements by late 1999.

Inco reported that "at the request of the two aboriginal groups, the federal court had agreed to [suspend the L.I.A. and Innu Nation's court actions] ... until the end of November 1999, pending the outcome of the [I.B.A. negotiations].[195]

The talks between Inco and the two native groups continued to be confidential, but I was able to get some idea of the topics under discussion by noting the questions that had been raised before the Environmental Assessment Panel:

- **Land claims** – Did they need to be settled before Inco could begin construction at Voisey's Bay?
- **Hunting** – Is Voisey's Bay Nickel's ban on hunting by its employees on-site "a violation of aboriginal rights to harvest?"[196] And was the project a threat to wildlife?

  Paul Nochasak, Jr. told the Panel[197] that "since the discovery of minerals at Voisey's Bay, there has been a reduction of seals, different species of fish, etc."

  "I don't think so," retorted his neighbour, Jerry Tuglavina. "I don't think so, because I work up there ... I think Paul, you know, don't know what he's talking here."
- **Fishing** – Was the project a threat to the local freshwater fishery, where locals had been catching 10,000 char each year?[198]

  The company said that it had, "where possible, attempted [to reduce] any intrusion of project features into ... Reid Brook. This is quite a challenge, of course, because the ore body is already located in the Reid Brook watershed."[199]
- **Scheduling** – How long a project life was Inco prepared to guarantee? Inco proposed that employees work two weeks on-

site, then return home for two weeks. Would this allow people to retain their traditional culture? Or should Inco accede to the request of Joachim Nui[200] of the Innu Nation that "Innu people should be allowed to come and go from the site when they like"?

- **Education, training, and jobs** — 37% of V.B.N.C.'s initial workforce on-site was Inuit or Innu.[201] Was this a satisfactory proportion? What preference should aboriginals be given over non-aboriginals; locals over other Labradorians; Labradorians over Newfoundlanders; Newfoundlanders and Labradorians over other Canadians?
- **Sharing revenues** — Expressing concerns that more money would make the Innu drink more, fight more, and put each other down more, Paul Rich, Chief of the Band Council, concluded,[202] "So, when you look at it, money is not the answer here."
- **Contracting** — Did Inco seriously want to encourage natives to be entrepreneurs? The Labrador Inuit Development Corporation complained[203] that Inco had cancelled, with only twenty-four hours' notice, a catering contract despite the "considerable time and money" the Inuit had invested in the venture.
- **Year-round shipping** — The principal product of the mine was to be a nickel concentrate. Would it be toxic? Would it be dangerous?

"You can't store this stuff ... for more than two months," said V.B.N.C.'s Bevin LeDrew.

As Voisey's Bay Nickel's metallurgist, Ric Stratton-Crawley, explained,[204] "Drying causes elemental sulphur to form on the surface of the nickel concentrate, which is a fire hazard. ... But it's not as dangerous as the nickel concentrate from Falconbridge's Raglan operations in Quebec. Their concentrate ... is very, very different from our concentrate — it spontaneously catches fire; ours doesn't."

Nevertheless, Inco appeared to be very anxious to ship product throughout the year. But year-round shipping was a particular concern of the Inuit, who were worried that icebreakers would disturb snowmobile travel to their traditional winter hunting and fishing grounds on the ice at the margin of the sea. In the early 1980s, hunters from Rigolet, Labrador had lost their snowmobiles when they attempted to stop a vessel on an experimental icebreaking voyage.[205]

- **Government issues** — Could Inco deduct payments to native groups from its taxable income? And would governments reduce their subsidies to native groups, saying, "Well, now you don't need as much money from us, because you're getting money from Inco"?

By early 2000, Inco had agreements "more or less in place" with the Labrador Inuit Association and the Innu Nation regarding environmental concerns, revenue sharing, jobs, and contracting.[206]

In April 2000, alarmed that Inco seemed to be regaining control over its future in Labrador, challengers of corporate power[207] brought two Indonesians to Canada, two people who lived near Inco's mine in Indonesia. In Davis Inlet, Labrador, they warned the Innu that Inco had yet to compensate villagers near that mine.[208] During the question period at Inco's Annual General Meeting in Toronto, they cast doubt on the company's motives at Voisey's Bay. And, at the University of Toronto, they called on Canadians to protect indigenous rights and the environment from Inco, at home and overseas.

CHAPTER 21

NATIVE LAND CLAIMS TO THE END OF THE TOBIN ERA

On current use of land and resources for traditional purposes by Aboriginal persons: ... it occurs to me ... that we have a very substantial amount of evidence in that regard from the Labrador Inuit Association. We actually have very little specific evidence from the Innu.
— Dr. Peter Usher of the Voisey's Bay Environmental Assessment Panel, to the Panel, October 31, 1998

While Labrador's native groups negotiated Impact Benefit Agreements with Inco, they were also negotiating land claims with the federal and provincial governments.

Greg Gauld of the Federal Government outlined these negotiations as follows:[209] "The Government of Canada has entered into three comprehensive claims negotiations in Labrador. The Labrador Inuit Association and the Innu Nation are each actively negotiating their claims with both the Government of Canada and the Government of Newfoundland and Labrador. The third claim by the Inuit of northern Quebec has been accepted by the Government of Canada for negotiation of federal interests only. ... There are several other claim applications. ... [One] is from the Labrador Metis Association. ... The land [in Labrador] is provincial Crown land with very minor exceptions and we're not really involved in negotiating the land aspect in any case."

How did the government propose to handle overlapping claims? According to Mr. Gauld, "overlaps are generally ... negotiated between or among the aboriginal groups ... we are not party to these agreements." He also noted that land claims discussions were "highly confidential" and that "they typically take many years."

Presumably, much of the native groups' case for land claims settlement would rest on traditional patterns of land use. It surprised me, as I read the minutes of the hearings of the Environmental Assessment Panel, the extent to which both the Inuit and the Innu considered snowmobiles to be part of their "traditional" patterns.

The Inuit had filed their first land claims in 1976.[210] It wasn't until November 1990 that the Inuit and the two levels of government set up a framework for negotiating these claims, with a view to completing an agreement by July 31, 1996.

On July 9, 1996, with no deal in sight, the three parties agreed to continue and to accelerate the land claims negotiations, setting March 31, 1997 as a new target date for an agreement-in-principle.

However, by January 1997, the Inuit's frustration had reached the point where they threatened to go to court to force the provincial government to guarantee that, agreement or no agreement, they would receive a share of Voisey's Bay mining royalties.[211] Negotiations missed the March 31 target date, and, on April 16, 1997, the province's chief negotiator called for "an indefinite recess."[212] To William Barbour, President of the Labrador Inuit Association, the situation was outrageous. "We ... the Labrador Inuit, Sikunuit, the People of the Sea Ice ... remain the only Inuit in Canada without treaty rights in their homeland."[213] He threatened legal action. Yet negotiations resumed only after the *province* threatened to take the *Inuit* to court.[214]

By October 1997, the government and the L.I.A. had hammered together "a substantive framework for the final phase of agreement-in-principle negotiations." But the Inuit warned that they would require a full agreement-in-principle before they would consent to the Voisey's Bay project."[215]

Although the Inuit believed that they and the government had produced only an agreement-in-principle to reach an agreement-in-principle, the provincial government trumpeted, on October 3, 1997, that it, the feds, and the L.I.A. had reached a full "land claims agreement."

On November 5, 1997, the provincial government released details of this supposed agreement. The Inuit were to receive surface title to 6,100 square miles — which did not include Voisey's Bay — and "priority rights" to gather food in a much larger area. At Voisey's Bay, the Inuit were to receive 3% of the province's resource royalties. Then everything went very quiet.

More than a year later, the provincial government once again took out the trumpets and blew them to herald the news that the federal and provincial governments had achieved a tentative agreement-in-principle on the Inuit's land claims.[216] "The next step will be approval for initialling," said the government. "That is expected early in 1999. ... [the next and] final stage of land claims negotiations is anticipated to last from twelve to eighteen months."

But the two governments and the L.I.A. continued to bicker behind the scenes and did not initial the Labrador Inuit land claims agreement-in-principle until May 10, 1999.

"This day has been a long time coming for all of us," exclaimed Premier Tobin. "I look forward to the ceremony a year or so from now that will celebrate the culmination of this process."

Even so, there was still no agreement on the Inuit land and resource rights which would apply within the Voisey's Bay project area.

On July 26, 1999, the rank-and-file members of the L.I.A voted on ratifying this deal, and 84% of those who voted, voted in favour. But what they voted on wasn't a "final" deal. Both the provincial government and the President of the L.I.A. conceded that there must be another round of negotiations before there was a final "final" deal.[217, 218]

"Once ratified, the agreement-in-principle becomes the basis for negotiation of a final agreement." In order to ratify this final "final" deal, the L.I.A. would need a majority of eligible voters to vote in favour.[219] This looked as if it could be a challenge. The July 26, 1999 vote would not have passed such a test.

The federal and provincial governments' land claims negotiations with the Innu Nation began later than those of the L.I.A. However, by late 1998, the provincial government believed that "an agreement-in-principle with the Innu [was] attainable within the time frame that would be conducive to the development of this project realistically," because the parties involved had "collectively committed, at the most senior levels, to work harder and faster, to work on ways of speeding up the process."[220]

Nevertheless, over the next twelve months, Premier Tobin would periodically pop up and complain that the Innu were being difficult. First he said that he was "puzzled about the motives of the Innu Nation."[221] Later he complained that, in dealing with the Innu Nation, he'd "seen frequent changes in leadership ... and abrupt changes in the posture and position ... [of] the Innu Nation."[222] Eventually he concluded that "we have to be honest and acknowledge that it is difficult, if not on some occasions impossible, for the leadership of the Innu Nation to undertake the difficult, complex, and vitally important question of land claims."[223] "A crisis now exists in the Innu community," he added. "In the space of a few months, three suicides and other deaths have occurred." Mr. Tobin called on "the federal government to fulfill its full constitutional and fiduciary responsibilities to the Innu people of Labrador by giving them full First Nations status as defined by the Indian Act."

This was a smart, if belated move by Mr. Tobin. First Nations status would shift the costs of welfare payments for the Innu from the provincial to the federal government. The Innu Nation's President, Peter Penashue, welcomed the proposal because it would oblige the R.C.M.P. to enforce the Innu's own bylaws banning alcohol and other abused substances.[224]

Three weeks later, the provincial government and the Innu Nation announced[225] that they and the federal government had reached a tentative deal on First Nations equivalency for the Innu.

* * * * *

While the L.I.A and Innu Nation drove down the potholed and poorly marked roads that led to land claims deals, many aboriginals felt that they had been left behind.

"The majority of the people here," a native of Cartwright, Labrador, told the Environmental Assessment Panel,[226] "are mixed-race aboriginal people ... I'm Mi'kmac ... also part Inuk and Innu. ... We're sick of getting pushed around by the associations that say they represent the Innu and Inuit."

Todd Russell of the Labrador Metis Association took these concerns to their logical conclusion. He told the Panel[227] that his association had land claims. Voisey's Bay was included in these claims, but was a "secondary" part, overlapping with the claims of the L.I.A. and the Innu Nation. Mr. Russell returned to the Panel the following year[228] with a bolder name for his organization — it was now the "Labrador Metis Nation" — and a higher level of frustration.

"[We are] the largest aboriginal group in Labrador ... our claim was submitted [to the federal Office of Native Claims] back in 1991, 1992 ... there was a draft response by Justice this past spring, which ... denied the rights and interests of Metis in south and central Labrador. ... Where do our rights and interests lie?"

Yet another aboriginal group claimed interests in Voisey's Bay. The Inuit of Nunavik — far northern Quebec — had a "federally validated claim to certain sections of northern Labrador," stated Zebedee Nungak of Makivik Corporation.[229] "Unfortunately, that claim has not moved an inch due to the Government of Newfoundland and Labrador's refusal to recognize [our claim]," even though the federal government had encouraged the Nunavik Inuit "to pursue an overlap agreement with the Labrador Inuit."

It would have made sense for the feds to encourage the Nunavik Inuit in whatever ventures took their fancy. If Quebec were ever to show signs that it was about to declare itself independent of the rest of Canada, it could help the federal cause if the federal government were to have friends among Quebec's native groups, especially in areas where natives constituted the majority of the population.

However, the L.I.A. did not welcome the Nunavik Inuit's interest in Labrador. In May 1996, the L.I.A. passed a resolution denying the Nunavik Inuit's claims. And, in July 1997, the Innu Nation asked Justice Halley to disallow the Nunavik Inuit's application to join the L.I.A. and the Innu Nation in attempting to halt Inco's construction of a road and airstrip at Voisey's Bay.

Nunavik's Inuit struck back. They asked for a federal court review of the L.I.A.'s land claims agreement-in-principle,[230] claiming that it infringed on their rights.

In August 1998, a federal court provided support for the Quebec Inuit's claims.[231] But the federal government did nothing. So, in October 1999, the Nunavik Inuit filed suit against the federal environment minister, David Anderson, claiming that he had not protected their rights in land claims negotiations.[232]

The Innu or Naskapi of Quebec were the fifth native group to claim an interest in Voisey's Bay. They, too, felt frustrated, because they had been excluded from making decisions about Voisey's Bay.

They told the Environmental Assessment Panel,[233] "We do want to have a say in what is being developed ... in Voisey's Bay ... we do have aboriginal land rights, title, or interest in this region," because "Voisey's Bay is Innu land," and archeological work had "proven ... that the Innu have occupied this territory for at least 5,000 years. ... [We] and the Davis Inlet Band were, way back, one group."

Schefferville's Innu Band Chief Taddé Andre began to explain that the development of Voisey's Bay was an opportunity to make restitution for the promises that the government of Quebec had made, but the record stopped at this point. The Panel's reporter noted that there was no translation because Mr. Andre's Montagnais dialect and that of Labrador's Innu were mutually unintelligible.

Thus, by October 2000, the end of Brian Tobin's term as premier, here's how the land claims stood:

The provincial government and the L.I.A. were negotiating the selection of land to be included in a final "final" agreement. The province had, however, despaired of reaching a deal with the Innu Nation and had turned these problem children over to the care and attention of the Federal Government. And Labrador's Metis and the Inuit and Innu of that portion of Quebec adjacent to Labrador all believed that the government of Newfoundland and Labrador had unfairly denied their land claims in Labrador.

Nain, Labrador, in August 1970 (top) showing the *Prince Andrew* leaving port; and in June, 1995 (bottom).

Top: On the dock at Nain, August 1970.
Bottom: Sled dogs "sweltering in the 10 degree Celsius heat," August 1970.

Top: Coastal Labrador, south of Nain, June 1995. Treed valleys and steep-sided hills whose flat tops lie above the treeline.

Bottom: Kennco Explorations's crew, the first geological party to explore coastal Labrador for base-metal sulphide deposits hosted by mafic intrusions.* Seated, David McAuslan. Standing, from left, unidentified helicopter mechanic, Raymond Goldie, Tom Webster, David Barr. The shadow is of the helicopter pilot, Fred Wagner, who took the picture. Village Bay, Kiglapait Mountains, Labrador, August 1970.

* The Voisey's Bay deposits are of this type.

Top: Universal Helicopters's Bell 47-G2 helicopter, chartered by Kennco. From left to right: Raymond Goldie, David McAuslan and pilot Fred Wagner. Village Bay, Kiglapait Moutains, Labrador, August 1970.
Bottom: Kennco's camp on Village Bay, Kiglapait Mountains, Labrador, August 1970. Photo courtesy of David Barr.

Top: Ice, Village Bay, Kiglapait Mountains, Labrador, August 1970.
Bottom: Nain resident with her sick baby, flying to Goose Bay, Labrador, in a Twin Otter chartered by Kennco, August 1970.

Top: Eastern Provincial Airways Otter, Goose Bay, Labrador, preparing for flight to Kiglapait, August 2, 1970. Photo courtesy of David Barr.

Bottom: David Barr, the geologist who initiated Kennco's program of exploration for base-metal sulphide deposits hosted by mafic intrusions in coastal Labrador, Village Bay, Kiglapait Mountains, Labrador, August 1970.

Top: (See captions in photo.) Voisey's Bay, Labrador, June 1995.
Bottom: Diamond Fields's geologist Rosie Moore on the discovery outcrop, at the east end of Discovery Hill; June 1995.

Top and bottom: Archean Resources/Diamond Fields's Voisey's Bay camp, June 1995.

Top: Innu workers in Archean Resources/Diamond Fields's Voisey's Bay camp, June 1995.
Bottom: University of Toronto Emeritus Professor Anthony Naldrett discusses drill core samples in the coreshack of Archean Resources/Diamond Fields's camp, June 1995.

William Andersen, President of the Labrador Inuit Association (top) and Peter Penashue, President of the Innu Nation (bottom) at Voisey's Bay, August 2004. Both gentlemen are wearing the reflective safety vests required of visitors.

Top: Looking west across the Ovoid at Voisey's Bay. At the time the photo was taken, Inco was stripping soil and glacial debris from above the Ovoid, which lies in the top left-hand portion of the light-coloured area. Light-coloured areas closer to the camera are dedicated to the storage of this soil and glacial debris, August 2004.

Bottom: Heather White, Voisey's Bay's Chief Mine Engineer and visiting analysts observe stripping operations on the Ovoid. This view is from beside the road which can be seen in the upper left of the top photo, August 2004.

Top: Heather White, Voisey's Bay Chief Mine Engineer, standing before the Ovoid and explaining the mine plan to visiting analysts, August 2004.

Bottom: Voisey's Bay mill, between Discovery Hill and Camp Lake, under construction in August 2004. The purpose of the mill is to crush and grind ore and to separate from it, in the form of concentrates, the minerals rich in nickel, copper, and cobalt. Concentrates are the final product of the operations at Voisey's Bay.

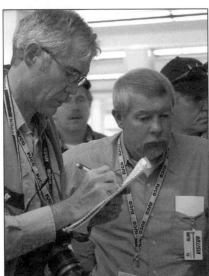

(Top) Voisey's Bay's Dan Lee (right centre in vest) describes drill core from Voisey's Bay, while (bottom left) analysts David Davidson (right) and Raymond Goldie (left) look on. (Bottom right) Inco President Peter Jones. Voisey's Bay, August 2004.

Top: End of a dream. This is a notice posted at Preston Resources' Bulong plant, Western Australia. Bulong was one of the three Australian nickel laterite projects which came on stream before Voisey's Bay and which all disappointed those who had invested in them. Bottom: Voisey's Bay's finished product — a drum of refined nickel.

CHAPTER 22

1997: CRISIS? WHAT CRISIS?

It is dangerous to be right when the government is wrong.
— Voltaire

It's not a good idea to burn bridges on Bay Street. Your assistant today may be your client tomorrow and your boss next week. One of my on-again, off-again colleagues is Ed Pennock, a silver-tongued salesman with a shock of brown hair that belies his many years on the Street. Not only is Ed good at persuading people to buy or sell securities, he is also good at persuading them to come and work for him. This accounts for my having joined Deutsche Bank's investment arm, which was then called Deutsche Morgan Grenfell, in Toronto in late 1996.

Early the following year, Ed phoned Deutsche's New York office for permission to take part in a peculiarly Canadian type of trade known as a "bought deal."

"How much of the deal would we have, Ed?"

"Fifteen per cent."

"For a firm as prestigious as ours, that's not enough. Wouldn't look good. Don't do it, Ed."

After Ed had ignored these instructions, closed the deal, and posted a $600,000 profit, he had another call from New York.

"Ed, this won't happen again."

"Oh, it might!"

Two months later, on his way out the door, he mused, "You know, I think I made them just enough money on that deal to cover my severance!" Then he was gone.

His departure left me confused. Who was my supervisor? Was it the Head of Toronto Research, the avuncular forest products specialist Robbie Duncan? Was it the man Upstairs, the suave cell-phone that walked like a man? Was it Wiktor Bielski, Head of Global Mining Research in London, whose appearance suggested the leader of a group of well-armed, well-fed partisans, but whose accent and attitude were strictly Surrey? Or was it the inscrutable Fraser Phillips, who looked like a grown-up Harry Potter? Fraser's arrival in the office next to mine had been heralded by a memorandum that explained that his duties would be to share coverage of base metal mining stocks with me, but he had lately begun to insist on checking and signing my expense account before sending it Upstairs. Or was my supervisor one of the "seagulls" who would fly in from New York for a day, never to be heard from again?

* * * * *

In the first half of the 1990s, the Western world's demand for nickel grew at a ferocious 7% per annum. I attributed much of this growth to the emergence of the economies of East Asia, and I began to think that we were seeing a repetition of the period 1955 to 1974. Back then, industrial production in the Western world had grown at 5.7% per year, more than double the rate of the following fifteen years, 1975–1990. Ah, the good old days were back — that's why I shared the views of Inco and Falconbridge and Diamond Fields's Cliff Carson, who all believed that the world would soon need all the nickel that Voisey's Bay could produce.

By the summer of 1997, my faith in this forecast was starting to shake. We had still not seen the spike in nickel prices, which I had confidently forecast in St. John's in June 1995. I initially attributed this to a surge in Russia's exports of nickel-rich stainless steel scrap, which had reduced, by about 2%, the Western world's need for virgin nickel. But in August, I watched nickel prices decline, even though Falconbridge's Sudbury operations had gone on strike, removing about 4.5% of the Western world's supply of nickel. This told me something. It told me to go and talk to Robbie Duncan, Head of Toronto Research.

"So, Robbie, the fact that nickel prices dropped when Falconbridge went on strike suggests that something's wrong with demand."

1997: Crisis? What Crisis?

Robbie, whose face looks as though he had slept in it, smiles and tosses a fax across his desk. "One of the great things about working for this firm is that it gives you access to research from around the globe. This is from a Deutsche Morgan forest products analyst in Singapore. So far this year, the currencies of the "Tiger" economies — Taiwan, South Korea, Singapore, Malaysia, Indonesia, and Thailand — have dropped between 5% and 25% against the U.S. dollar. Our man in Singapore thinks that these declines are symptoms of a significant economic slowdown."

I return to my office in search of more numbers. Unfortunately, the agencies which report supply and demand for nickel do so only every three months. Quarterly figures are a blunt weapon in the fight to find truth, so I look at a sharper set of numbers: monthly figures for consumption of aluminum, copper, and zinc in the Western world.[234] I define consumption as, in any one month, production plus net imports from the former East Bloc, minus any increase in stockpiles held by producers and metal exchanges, and adjust the result for seasonal variations. I then calculate an index based on month-to-month unweighted average changes in consumption of each metal. For example, if I were to set the index at 100.00 and, in the following month, consumption of aluminum, copper, and zinc were to rise, respectively, 1%, 2%, and 4%, the index would rise from 100.00 to 102.33, 2.33% being the average of 1%, 2%, and 4%.

I call this index the "Index of Global Consumption of Base Metals," or "Paasche," after Hermann Paasche, a nineteenth-century German politician and professor of economics who devised this type of index. Because aluminum, copper, and zinc are all used widely in the economy, Paasche is a good indicator of the world's consumption of stuff (as opposed to intangible items like services and software) and is more timely than formal economic statistics. In fact, preliminary metal consumption data for any one month are usually available about six weeks after the end of that month.

"Paasche" shows me that the Asian crisis began, unnoticed at the time, in the second quarter of 1996. From 1991 to the second quarter of 1996, consumption of metals had grown at an average of 5.5% per annum. Since the second quarter of 1996, however, it has grown at only 2.8% per annum. I call the marketing departments of some of the big Canadian mining companies. Yes, they've noticed a slowdown, and yes, it is most evident among their clients in Asia.

I take a closer look at my numbers and estimate that Asia, excluding Japan and China, accounts for only 15% to 20% of the Western world's metal consumption. However, this area has accounted for about 2 points of the 5.5% per annum *growth* in consumption. Furthermore, China's net imports from the West appear to account for another point of this growth. I prepare a report which concludes that "the slowdowns in the 'Tiger' economies resulted in sharply lower values for the local currencies. Because base metals and their downstream products are denominated in U.S. dollars, these goods have become more expensive in local currency terms. As a result, we do not foresee any early recovery in the Tigers' demand for base metals. Accordingly, we expect growth in the Western world's demand for base metals [aluminum, copper, and zinc] to continue at its current rate of 2.8% for the foreseeable future," and that "the world's demand for nickel would grow at 3.5% per annum."[235] Hence, I forecast that "nickel prices will remain weak for, at least, the rest of this year."

Deutsche's quantitative analyst Chris Dutton and I put together a draft report. On August 21, I drop a copy on Fraser Phillips's desk and, just in case Wiktor Bielski really is my supervisor, fax a copy to him in London. Robbie and I decide that we'll wait a week and, if no one has raised any objections, we'd go to print.

* * * * *

On the morning of August 26, 1997, I am astonished as Wiktor strides into my office. "Ray, I've come to shut you down. You're doing your numbers wrong. There *is* no crisis in Asia."

CHAPTER 23

WHAT DID THE BIGGEST BUSINESS STORY OF 1998 HAVE IN COMMON WITH A BELLY DANCER?

Nickel: Our earlier expectation that a very tight market could unfold in 1998 with prices spiking well above 400c[U.S.]/lb have now faded. [Because of] the emergence of what could be a year-long recession in Korea and the "Little Tigers," coupled with a continued high level of East Bloc exports ... for 1998 we project [prices of] 270 — 280 c/lb. ... By year-end 1999 the market could be below 250c/lb.

With the launch of the giant Voisey's Bay mine early in the next decade, there is no light at the end of the tunnel.

— Metals Analysis and Outlook, Exton, PA, December 1997

In the late 1990s, the Program Chairman of the Mineral Resource Analysts Group was Terence S. Ortslan, a jovial, curly-haired, part-time instructor at McGill University and a full-time mining analyst. He frequently shuttled between Toronto, the mining finance centre of North America, and his home in Montreal, and he often attended meetings via telephone. Once, while he was an employee of a brokerage firm known as "B.B.N." — the former Brown, Baldwin, and Nisker — he had trouble registering for a conference call hosted by Falconbridge Limited. The operator of the call asked for his name and affiliation.

"Terry Ortslan, B.B.N."
"How do you spell that please, sir?"
"O – R – T – S – L – A – N."
"No, no, the name of your affiliation?"
"B.B.N."

"Yes and how do you spell that, please?"

"B – B – N."

"Could you spell that please?"

"(Sigh) OK – B as in Bob, B as in Bob, N as in Norman."

"Thank you, sir."

Which is why, when it was Terry's turn to ask a question – and Terry always asks a question – the operator introduced him as "Terry Ortslan of Bob, Bob, and Norman Limited."

Terry's tenure with B.B.N. didn't last. Having already worked at least once for just about every dealer on the street, he decided it was time to set up his own shop. He named his new firm after himself – "T.S.O. and Associates" – thereby continuing to confuse conference-call operators. On an Inco call, the operator introduced him as "Terry Ortslan of Tso and Associates," and on a Freeport-McMoran Copper & Gold call he became "Terry Ortslan of T.S. Owen Associates."

Terry has the reputation both of ubiquity and of the ability to surprise. His sister was a travel agent, and I suspect that Terry was her best client. My competitor and fellow analyst, Harry, swears that, while sheltering from a torrential downpour in a shack somewhere in the rainforests of Guyana, he looked up to find "T. Ortslan" inscribed on a beam. And Terry's last-minute appearance at a tour of Falconbridge's nickel refinery in Kristiansand, Norway, without his having been sighted on any of the flights into Kristiansand, provoked rumours of a parachute.

Terry organized the Mineral Resource Analysts Group's Christmas dinner in December 1998. It lasted almost four hours, and brought analysts together with our counterparts in the metals and mining industry. One after another, the industry representatives stood up to outline their prognostications for the prices of gold, silver, diamonds, copper, nickel, lead, zinc ... and aluminum. The aluminum forecast concealed Terry's surprise of the day: a sample of his Armenian heritage. The aluminum presenter, Roger Scott-Taggart of Alcan, was to retire early the following year. To help him celebrate, Terry had persuaded a belly dancer to burst into the room, embrace a surprised Mr. Scott-Taggart, and perform for the Group. Roger joined in.

Then came the most significant part of the meeting: the Ortslan prize for the best metal price forecast made the previous year. At the 1997 dinner, Terry had asked everyone present – analysts and industry representatives alike – to forecast metal prices for December 1998. (Of course, I'm sure I would have won had I been there in December 1997 but, to my great regret, I had been on my way to the South Pacific.)

Everyone's forecast missed by miles. Even the winner's average error was huge — something over 70% (Terry wasn't very precise on this point) — and the most notable failure of everyone was an inability to forecast the decline in the price of nickel, which had been at around US$2.75 per pound in December 1997, but was around $1.70 as the belly dancer performed.

A week earlier, Jim Pirie had presided over a similar shambles at the Christmas lunch of The September Club. This was an investment club composed of twenty-five people, all connected with the mining industry. The average error in the commodity price forecasts made by members of the Club only nine months earlier had been 24%. Again, nickel was the stumbling block: every nickel price forecast had proven to be too optimistic. The Brian Tobin Memorial bottle of Ontario wine for excellence in nickel price forecasting was awarded to a gentleman whose prediction had been "only" 27% too high.

On December 22, 1998, Eric Reguly of Toronto's *Globe and Mail* decreed that the top business story of 1998 had been the unexpected plunge in commodity prices. In fact, he wrote, the surprising weakness in the price of nickel was the real reason why Inco had failed to reach agreements to turn the Voisey's Bay deposit into a mine. "Politics ... officially took the blame, but you can bet both sides would have found a solution if nickel prices were high enough to turn Voisey's Bay into a cash machine."

Although Mr. Reguly overstated the case, the collapse in nickel prices in 1998 clearly was a surprise to all the players in the Voisey's Bay drama, and it did temper the enthusiasm of some of those players, notably Inco and its bankers. I had been painfully aware of the tempered enthusiasm of one banker — Deutsche Morgan Grenfell. On February 23, 1998, Robbie Duncan and I, and 22 other people, had been invited to a meeting Upstairs. We learned that, because of the unexpected financial crisis in Asia we — and thousands of other Deutsche Morgan Grenfell employees around the world — were being terminated.

Why *was* the collapse in commodity prices in 1998 such a surprise? The most popular ways of forecasting the prices of commodities are technical analysis and fundamental analysis. Technical analysis relies on finding patterns in historical price charts, and using those patterns to forecast future prices. Fundamental analysis considers the relationships between the supply of a commodity, the demand for a commodity, and the price of that commodity. By projecting supply and demand into the future, you are supposed to be able to forecast prices.

They teach fundamental analysis in economics courses at school. The folks who write economics textbooks have a fondness for widgets, and go to great lengths to explain how the price of widgets is determined by the intersection of two lines on a graph. One of the lines represents the tendency of purchasers of widgets to restrict their buying when prices are high, but to buy more when prices are low. The other line shows that suppliers of widgets will produce fewer widgets when their price falls. If the price were to fall below the cost of producing them, producers would stop making them. Otherwise they would lose money. The price is supposed to settle out at the level at which supply and demand are equal: widgets are purchased as fast as they are produced — and no faster. According to this analysis, it is the cost of producing widgets which ultimately determines their price.

I used to argue with this approach, saying that there were no such things as widgets. However, around the end of 1998, Guinness began to advertise that their cans contained "floating widgets." A widget is a small, slippery sphere whose function is to inject carbon dioxide into the Guinness when I open the can. Nevertheless, I still quarrel with the textbook approach.

If I'm introduced to a new client, fresh to the investment business and seeking guidance, I will broach the subject of forecasting commodity prices by pointing out that, no, what you learned in school wasn't exactly wrong, it was, well, *difficult* to implement and, if you *could* implement it, it probably applied to prices averaged over periods of, oh, say, ten years at a time. This isn't a useful time frame for anyone who wants to win a bottle of wine, or a spin around the room with a belly dancer at a Christmas party.

Here's why: The textbook approach assumes that it costs nothing to shut down or re-open a mine or a smelter. However, the gradual usurping of corporate power by governments has meant that companies are now generally required to shut plants in a socially and environmentally responsible fashion. But responsibility is expensive! A company that is operating a money-losing mine may look at the cost of closing 'er down, shake its corporate head, and keep on mining.

What Did the Biggest Business Story of 1998 Have in Common With a Belly Dancer?

In the mid-1980s, copper prices collapsed. Noranda's Chairman, Alf Powis, used to say that he slept like a baby: he woke up and cried every few hours. According to the textbook theory, Noranda and other suppliers of copper should have reduced their output. Few did. Instead, they poked around for new ways to cut costs. The result was a brilliant engineering triumph — the widespread use of a relatively new, cheap way to produce copper called "solvent extraction — electrowinning" (inevitably shortened to "sexy W"). Had costs determined prices, as mandated by textbook theory? No! *Prices* had determined *costs*.

The price of copper, like the prices of other metals, suffered another sharp fall in 1998, providing us with another illustration of producers' reluctance to curtail output. According to the textbooks, Codelco, the world's largest producer of copper, "should have" responded to the decline of copper prices by shutting down its higher-cost operations. Instead, the company announced a plan to reduce costs, from US$0.45 per pound in 1998 to $0.40 per pound by the end of 1999.[236] Again, prices had determined costs.

A second flaw in the textbook theory is that it ignores inventories. Consider a week in the life of the world. The supply of widgets, or copper or nickel available to the world's consumers during that week, is equal to the amount produced in that week, plus the world's stockpiles, or inventories. Typically, the world's inventories of almost anything are equivalent to more than a week's consumption.[237] This means that the availability of widgets, or copper, or nickel in any one week is almost always greater than the amount that the world can consume in one week. Thus, there is no price at which supply and demand are equal in any one week.

Inventories are the key to fundamental forecasts of metal prices. But only fools and think tanks try to project supply, consumption, inventories — and hence prices — more than two or three or more years into the future. To estimate prices more than two or three years into the future, I prefer to assume that historic trends in prices will continue. The figure on the following page shows the estimate of the long-term trend in nickel prices that I made at the end of 1997.

The chart begins in 1972, the first full year in which nickel traded on the London Metal Exchange. "Prices in nominal dollars" are the average prices as reported at the time. "Prices in 'real' (1998) dollars" are nominal dollars adjusted for inflation.[238] I then fitted[239] a trend line to the "real" prices, and extrapolated the trend into the future. My best estimate as to future levels of "real" nickel prices was that, on average, they would lie on this trend line.

Note that the trend line slopes downwards, illustrating the sad fact — well, sad for mining companies, good for consumers — that nickel prices (like most commodity prices) failed to keep pace with inflation.

Trend line analysis of prices tries to anticipate long-term patterns, and is of little use in forecasting commodity prices over periods as short as a year. The usual purpose of trend line analysis is in deciding whether or not a mining company should go ahead with a major investment. A company will usually walk away from an investment that does not give economic rates of return at prices that are on the trend line.

* * * * *

To answer the question posed earlier — Why did forecasters fail to anticipate the sorry slide in nickel prices in 1998? — I will outline how, given the information available at the end of 1997, a fundamental analyst (as opposed to an analyst of price trends) may have made a forecast of nickel prices in the following twelve months.

The first step in a fundamental forecast is to look at the current level of production in the Western world. To this, you would add supply from new mines under construction, and deduct supply from old mines running out of ore. (Analysts often overlook the latter consideration. But it is significant. Imagine: if the average life of a nickel mine was, say, twenty years, you'd need to add 1/20 = 5% more new nickel mining capacity every year just to maintain a steady level of output.) Then add net exports from the former East Bloc. (Even after the collapse of communism, Russia and other former members of the East Bloc generally considered statistics for production of metals to be a state secret. So, forecasters usually considered the former East Bloc economies to be inside a black box, and attempted to estimate the flow of material into and out of this black box.) Finally, add supply from recycling of scrap metal (which, in the case of nickel, is negligible).

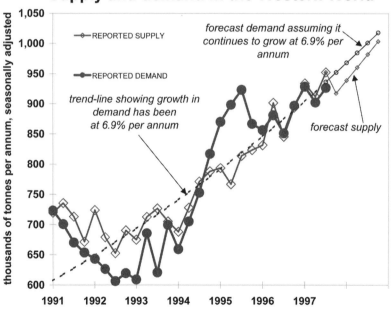

At the end of 1997, a typical forecast for supply of nickel in 1998 was that production from Western smelters and refineries would increase by 57,000 tonnes over 1997's level, but that net exports from the former East Bloc would drop by 15,000 tonnes, for a net 42,000-tonne increase in supply.[240] This forecast of supply is illustrated on the previous page using quarterly data points.

The second step in a fundamental forecast is to estimate consumption. Consumption usually wobbles around either side of a trend line,[241] and the trend line stays in place until there is a shock to the system. (In the previous chart, the trend line is the dashed line representing growth at 6.9% per annum.) If the most recent figure for consumption were to be above the trend line, you might expect consumption to drop down to, and then continue along, the trend line. Should the most recent figure for consumption be *below* the trend line, you might expect consumption to rise to the trend line, then continue along it.

In December 1997, the most recently available consumption number was for the three-month period ending September 30, 1997. This number was almost exactly *on* the trend line, so, to estimate consumption in 1998, it would have been reasonable for you to assume that consumption would continue on the trend line, implying that consumption would increase by 74,000 tonnes from 1997 to 1998.

The third step in a fundamental forecast is to take the most recently reported level of nickel inventories held by the London Metal Exchange and by nickel producers, and to extrapolate them into the future. Do it month by month. Take inventories at the start of each month, add your estimate of supply in that month, and deduct your estimate of consumption.

The final step is to plot the current nickel price and the most recently estimated level of inventories onto a "Pinch-point"™ [242] chart, the same form of chart as the one I introduced to investors in St. John's in June 1995. You've already calculated what inventories should be each month in the future. Use them to plot a trajectory for future prices, assuming that the trajectory will be parallel to the trend of the curve — admittedly a blurry curve — outlined by historic figures.

The end result? The next chart shows that the end result of a forecast made at the end of 1997 would have been that, in twelve months' time, nickel inventories would be at forty-four days' consumption, and that this would correspond to a price of about US$3.70 per pound.

The final chart shows what actually happened in 1998. Note three big differences from the forecast prepared at the end of 1997:

What Did the Biggest Business Story of 1998 Have in Common With a Belly Dancer?

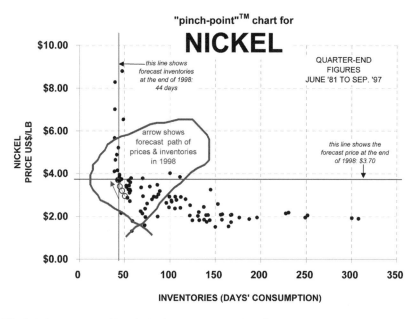

Filled circles represent historical prices and inventories. Open circles represent forecast prices and inventories.

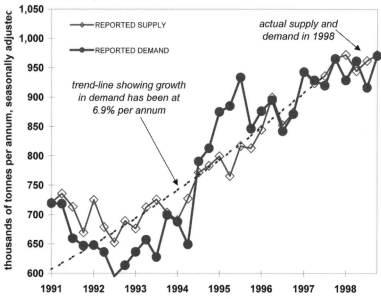

(i) The historical numbers, 1991 to 1997, have been changed from the figures originally reported. This is because clerks with clipboards had updated their estimates of their employers' production and inventories of nickel. (Revisions like this happen all the time.) Nevertheless, the original estimate, that up to September 1997, consumption had been growing along a trend line of 6.9% per annum, remained intact.

(ii) The actual supply of nickel in 1998 was only 20,500 tonnes above 1997's level; not, as forecast, 42,000 tonnes.

(iii) The average level of consumption in 1998 was only 5,000 tonnes above 1997's level; not, as forecast, 74,000 tonnes.

Thus:

(i) The December 1997 forecast overestimated the growth in nickel supply in 1998 by 21,500 tonnes, largely because, as we shall see Chapter 25, the new Australian nickel laterites failed to deliver what was expected of them, and also because the output from existing mines declined by more than forecasters had expected.

(ii) The forecast for consumption, based on simple extrapolation of recent trends, failed to recognize that the Asian crisis had delivered a severe shock to global consumption of nickel. As a result, the forecast overestimated the Western world's demand for nickel by 69,000 tonnes.

(iii) On balance, the December 1997 forecast was too optimistic. It implied that consumption would exceed supply by 21,500 tonnes in 1998. As it turned out, *supply* exceeded *consumption* by 18,500 tonnes. Thus, instead of declining, the Western world's inventories of nickel rose in 1998, and they rose by 18,500 tonnes.

* * * * *

Let's revisit the question posed earlier. Why, at the end of 1997, were forecasters so wrong about the prospects for nickel prices in

What Did the Biggest Business Story of 1998 Have in Common With a Belly Dancer?

1998? Forecasters overestimated supply, but they overestimated consumption even more. As a result, instead of declining, nickel inventories rose in 1998. And, as the preceding charts illustrate, prices and inventories at the end of 1997 were at that critical point, the "Pinch-point"™, where the curve steepens sharply and where a tiny change in inventories can, and usually does, lead to a huge change in prices.

* * * * *

By 2003, nickel inventories had returned to the "Pinch-point"™ and, once again, the members of the Mineral Resource Analysts group were uniformly wrong in their forecasts. But, this time, they were all too pessimistic!

```
Fri January 9 2004 5:52 AM
FROM T.S.Ortslan
M.R.A.G. CHRISTMAS PARTY AND METAL PRICE FORE-
CAST WINNERS
```

M.R.A.G. Christmas Party of Dec 19 had 48 members and special guests in attendance, including our this year's surprise Santa Claus — Robert McEwen, Goldcorp.

Among the contests — the Guess The Santa Claus game had many winners and they will each get Montreal bagels, as promised, from TSO. M.R.A.G. also made a pledge to match the $s and contribute to a cause. On our last trip we were very impressed with the activities and efforts of FAL-CONBRIDGE DOMINICANA FOUNDATION. We are topping it up and a cheque of $500 will be sent on behalf of all M.R.A.G. members to that institution.

The metal price forecast for 2003 (submitted in Dec of 2002) produced the following winners: On the base metal front — a combination of aluminum, nickel, zinc, and copper — as it was very close — Ernie Nutter and Ray Goldie will share the prize. Most participants had the direction of metal prices correct but nobody had pinned the nickel price correctly. Close runners-up were Greg Barnes and Victor Lazarovici.

CONGRATULATIONS TO ALL

CHAPTER 24

SOIRÉE '99

Thursday, April 1, 1999, 8 p.m. (CTV) SOIREE '99 This little shindig is coming to us almost live (taped from a celebration the night before in St. John's). It's 90 minutes of aye-tiddly-aye music, tap dancing, and other carrying on to celebrate the 50th anniversary of Newfoundland and Labrador joining Confederation.
— *Broadcast Week, The Globe and Mail*, Toronto, March 27 1999

Dan Bagi, biotechnology analyst, sits up and casts his eyes around the meeting. "Today," he says, "is a red-letter day for biotech stocks. I want to introduce you to an Amex-listed company with the ticker symbol ORG."

Patricia rolls her eyes and puts down her pen. "I'm not telling this story to my clients."

Dan continues. ORG has done a deal with Novartis, whereby Novartis has taken over ORG's project to harvest skin cells from the foreskins of newly circumcised baby boys.

("I'm really not going to tell this story to my clients!")

ORG is able to grow these skin cells in petri dishes and thereby manufacture hundreds of thousands of 10 centimetres by 10 centimetres patches for sale to burn victims and candidates for plastic surgery.

"The margins are huge!" enthuses Dan.

"I just hope there are no opthalmological applications," says Patricia, enunciating carefully. "Just imagine: all your patients would be cockeyed!"

I am a little suspicious. It *is* April first.

My own meagre contributions to that morning's meeting are a quick update on a nickel exploration play in northwestern Quebec involving a company called Nuinsco, and a reminder that the environmental assessment report for Inco's Voisey's Bay project is due out at noon. I tell the meeting, "I continue to expect that the report will, in general, approve the project. However, there may be a requirement to establish and fund a research institute to monitor the environment in northern Labrador, and some approvals may be made contingent on completion of native land claims negotiations. It is the latter negotiations, and the impasse between the government and Inco with respect to construction of a smelter, which I see as the major impediments to development of Voisey's."

The release time — noon — comes and goes. Nothing appears on the website of the Canadian Environmental Assessment Agency. Humming aye-tiddly-aye music, I try the website of the Newfoundland government. There is a story saying that the provincial Minister of Environment and Labour, Mr. Langdon, has just made a statement in the House of Assembly welcoming the release of the Environmental Assessment Panel's report. "Honourable members of this House," said Mr. Langdon, "may recall that the procedure established to deal with the panel report entailed a thirty-day process of review and consultation ... [however] ... given the anticipated number of recommendations and the complexity of the report, it would be reasonable to allow for a sixty-day period of review and consultation." Hmmm. *Anticipated* number of recommendations. Sounds as if the report still hasn't been released. And does Mr. Langdon's statement mean that the entire process had been delayed by another thirty days? Does his reference to "complexity" suggest that even more delays could be in store? Might the approvals now come too late to begin work before next year? I dash off an email to Inco asking just that question. Then out of my office and over to Donny the trader.

"How are the VBN shares doing?" (I don't have a quote machine in my office, which is actually not a bad thing since it forces me, from time to time, to go and talk to the traders and find out what's really going on.)

"Remind me — what's the ticker symbol?"

"N dot V."

"Up!"

"What? Am I missing something?"

"Maybe what you're missing, Ray, is this story on *Reuters*."

I peer over Donny's shoulder.

TORONTO, April 1 (Reuters) — A Canadian federal environmental review panel on Thursday approved Inco Ltd.'s development of the stalled Cdn$4.3-billion Voisey's Bay mine project in Labrador, Newfoundland, an Inco spokesman said.

"It's a significant milestone in the Voisey's Bay development. It's a positive development," said Inco spokesman Jerry Rogers.

The agency's approval came with a long list of conditions, ranging from Native land claims and marine transport to ice-user safety. The panel ruled that the mine project would not seriously or irreversibly damage the environment as long as these conditions are met ...

A "positive development"? Scratching my head, I wander back to my office to find a response to my email to Inco. It's from the selfsame Mr. Rogers. He doesn't appreciate my concerns that the project could be further delayed:

```
Ray — You're taking an unduly pessimistic view
of the report; from our perspective, it's a very
positive, significant development. The review
process is thirty days and, yes, it could be
closer to sixty days or late June for the
responses from the two governments. In the mean-
time, the report's release, and its positive
tone, could be the catalyst, as both [Premier]
Mr. Tobin and [Inco's President] Scott Hand have
publicly stated, for getting the discussions
going again.
```

The phone rings. Chris Flanagan from the St. John's *Telegram*. "Ray, the report is now on the C.E.A.A. website. Let me know what you think of it. A hundred and seven recommendations!"

"Well, Chris, I don't know what *I* think of it yet, but here's what Inco thinks," I say, reading him my email.

"That's interesting," says Chris. "The comment by Mr. Hand that he refers to was probably the one he made a few weeks ago, when he said that he *hoped* the report would be positive and get discussions going again. And I just asked Mr. Tobin what *he* thought, and he said he was too busy solving the nurses' strike to take a look at it."

I start to download the report from the C.E.A.A. website. Yup. One hundred and seven recommendations. The first ones to come off the printer looked daunting.

Four p.m. "Where did the VBN's close, Donny?"

"Up $1.05! Must be because of that fucking *Reuters* report."

The next day, *The Globe and Mail* follows Inco's line: "Inco gets environmental panel's blessing on Voisey's Bay project." *The Financial Post*, with files from Chris Flanagan, was more cautious: "Report could open way for Voisey's Bay truce. Inco sounds optimistic."

Because of Easter, I have the luxury of three days to compose my thoughts, and ponder if the news was really worth $1.05 per share.

But first, I settle down to watch CTV's "Soiree '99" celebrating the 50th anniversary of Newfoundland's entry into Confederation. The Prime Minister of Canada and the Premier of Quebec are there. Mr. Tobin is not. He blames the nurses' strike. He didn't miss much. It is a surprisingly bloodless affair, lacking in edge and passion, so middle-of-the-road that I expected to see white lines down the performers' backs.

I turn to the Environmental Report and distill my thoughts as follows:

> In January 1997, the governments of Canada and of Newfoundland and Labrador, the Innu Nation and the Labrador Inuit Association established a joint panel set up to examine the potential environmental impact of Inco's proposed Voisey's Bay nickel mine-mill project in Labrador. On Thursday, the panel published its report.
>
> The four parties that established the panel had originally contemplated taking thirty days to review this report. However, because of the complexity of the report, these parties have agreed to extend the period of review to sixty days.
>
> The report is very comprehensive, and will undoubtedly become the model for future reviews of similar projects in Canada and, perhaps, in other countries such as Australia.

The first of the panel's recommendations is that the project should proceed, subject to 106 other recommendations. These recommendations range from the sensible to the neurotic. The most important from an investor's point of view are probably recommendations number 2, 3, 4, and 5.

Recommendation #2 states, in part, that Inco must ensure that the project will operate for "at least twenty to twenty-five years" and that, if necessary, the rate of production must be reduced in order to achieve this. If the provincial government were to adopt this recommendation, it would, I believe, set a precedent. In effect, the scope of the mining plan would be established by legislative fiat rather than by sound engineering practice. The financial consequences could be significant: If, for example, Inco were to mine the planned "Ovoid" open pit over twenty-odd years instead of, say, seven, the project would suffer reverse economies of scale. As a very rough guess, if Inco were to scale down the production rate by 67%, capital costs would drop by only 55%. Furthermore, the Net Present Values of future cash flows would be reduced because they would be spread over a longer period.

Recommendations #3, 4, and 5 state that, before authorizing any construction at Voisey's Bay, the governments and the native groups should reach some tentative agreements regarding land claims, and that Inco should also conclude agreements with the native groups. These recommendations recognize the importance of obtaining the support of Labrador's natives before proceeding with the project. Although Inco and the Innu have disagreed violently in the past, and have yet to resolve their differences, this report could provide a framework for discussions to resolve these differences. However, I believe that the agreements contemplated in these recommendations are probably still years in the future.

The government of Newfoundland and Labrador has demanded that Inco build a smelter in the province. Inco won't — can't — make such a commitment. This dispute is beyond the scope of the panel's mandate and remains a major issue that must be resolved before construction can begin at Voisey's Bay.

In conclusion: the report was harsher than I had expected. It was as if Mother said you could go swimming as long as you didn't get wet. And the biggest surprise is the suggestion that Inco guarantee the life of the project to be "at least twenty to twenty-five years."

The next trading day, Easter Monday, Voisey's Bay Nickel shares lose 45 cents of the $1.05 which they had gained on Thursday. By Wednesday, the shares are down another 50 cents.

From St. John's, Margaret Butt emails me her own distillation of the report:

```
It's as if mother said you could go swimming so
long as you didn't get wet.
```

* * * * *

Investment books often tell us to avoid playing hot tips. Rather, one should buy the shares of well-managed companies when they are cheap, and tuck them away for a few years. This is good advice. Imagine that, on the morning of April 1, 1999, you had believed that the Voisey's Bay environmental assessment report would recommend that the project be stretched out over at least twenty years, and that the report was so complex that the government was going to take an extra month to think about it. Could you have made money on that belief?

I don't believe that *I* could have. I would have failed to take account of the release of the document on a day when Newfoundland's investors were feeling pretty good about themselves because the Prime Minister was in town to help them celebrate. I would also probably have failed to anticipate that very few investors would see the report until after the markets had closed for a long weekend. And I certainly would have anticipated neither Inco's decision to put a positive slant on the report, nor that the Premier would be otherwise distracted.

* * * * *

A routine physical exam shows the need to have some tests. My doctor books an appointment for me at St. Michael's Hospital on April 29, 1999.

First, I have to get through Inco's Annual General Meeting of Shareholders. Inco's annual meetings are like the emergency room when there is a full moon. You could take all the aggrieved, grandstanding, and loud-mouthed dissident shareholders from all of the other mining companies' shareholders' meetings, put them together, and still have less disturbance than that which faces Inco most years. My favourite was in the early 1980s, when a sweet old lady, in the course of a convoluted query, asked Inco's Chairman why the doors in Ottawa were so heavy.

April 28, 1999, in the Metro Convention Centre, Toronto. For a hundred minutes, Inco's Chairman, Mike Sopko, patiently guides the meeting through a series of noisy interruptions. The most active intervenor is a retired employee of Inco who shows up every year to castigate successive chairmen, and to disturb the torpor of those of us who find allure in the subdued lighting and comfortable seating.

I remain sufficiently alert to note two comments by Inco's President, Scott Hand. The first is that, in March, a federal court had rejected the Citizens' Mining Council of St. John's application to require that the environmental review of the proposed mine and mill at Voisey's be combined with a review of any proposed smelter and refinery. The Council had not lodged an appeal. I'd missed this development. It was important because, had the decision gone the other way, the federal and provincial governments would have been obliged to begin a new environmental review process, and Inco would have found itself defending a smelter and refinery project that it insisted it didn't want and couldn't afford.

Mr. Hand also remarks on the report of the environmental review panel. Like me, he had difficulty with the recommendation that the mine plan be adjusted so as to guarantee the life of the Voisey's Bay project. "We are committed to a long-term operation, but we can only work with what we have," says Mr. Hand. "What we cannot do is build a project which might be uneconomic, just to have a twenty-five-year life."

Next morning at 7 a.m., somewhat dazed because I haven't been allowed to eat, I report to the hospital. A friendly nurse advises me to "strip to the waist ... both ways." As I settle into my bed in the pre-op room, I grin when I see the next victim of the asset stripper.

"Mike, this must be your idea of hell, having to share a hospital room with a mining analyst!"

It is Mike Sopko, whom I had first met at a meeting arranged by my former employer, Richardson Greenshields, in 1991.[243] "I usually schedule a checkup after each annual meeting," he explains.

Once he is suitably attired and has been appropriately poked and prodded, Dr. Sopko asks the nurse when he would be out of the hospital. He hopes to attend a board meeting that afternoon, and then a fundraiser for Premier Mike Harris's Conservative party. A look of alarm crosses the nurse's face. "Sssh," she says, looking around for eavesdroppers. "My husband's going to the same fundraiser but, given the Premier's abysmal popularity among health care professionals, it's not a good idea to talk about it here!"

Later that morning, after we have both been poked and prodded, Dr. Sopko adds some background to the Voisey's story. In theory, when the sixty-day review period is up, the provincial government should invite Inco to discuss the environmental review. However, because Premier Tobin had fired his chief negotiator, Bill Rowat, back in December, it was not at all clear that there would be anyone for Inco to talk to. And there are summer holidays to consider. ... Dr. Sopko worries that there might not be enough time to begin mobilizing in the fall for work in the spring of 2000.

On June 1, Premier Tobin spoke to reporters about Voisey's Bay. Perhaps some of the reporters had intended to ask Mr. Tobin about the fate of the environmental panel's report now that the sixty-day consultation period was up. If they did, the Premier successfully diverted their attention. Mr. Tobin said that his government continued to insist that Inco build a smelter, and had urged Inco to form a partnership with other companies, notably Sherritt International, "which are experimenting with hydrometallurgical techniques for extracting nickel."

After the Premier's press conference, several journalists called me asking what "hydrometallurgy" was. Mr. Tobin had clearly been successful in turning the media's attention away from his failure to deliver the results of the consultation process, so I planted a question with a reporter. The reporter called me back a few days later, saying that the government thought that I had misunderstood the "sixty days." That was just the time required for initial consultations, which were now complete. The next step would be to refer the results of these consultations to the executive bodies of the parties involved for their ratification. In any event, I shouldn't expect any news until, at the earliest, July.

Dr. Sopko's fears about slippage of Voisey's Bay's timetable were being realized. I told our morning meeting that I was worried that delays could prevent Inco from carrying out a full program at Voisey's in 2000.

On August 3, 1999, more than four months after the beginning of the "sixty-day" process for consideration of the report of the Voisey's Bay Environmental Assessment Panel, the provincial and federal governments announced that they had released the Voisey's Bay mine/mill project from further assessments. The provincial government also published its decisions on each of the 106 recommendations made by the Panel. At the morning meeting the following day, I analyzed these decisions:

"In April, when the Environmental Assessment Panel released its report, I concluded that, from an investor's point of view, the most important recommendations in the report were probably numbers 2, 3, 4, and 5.

"Recommendation #2 stated, in part, that Inco must ensure that the project will operate for 'at least twenty to twenty-five years' and, if necessary, the rate of production must be reduced in order to achieve this. This concerned me because it could have led to the scope of the mining plan being established by legislative fiat, rather than by sound engineering practice. However, the province sidestepped Recommendation #2. It announced that 'although it accepts the principle of a long-term, sustainable mining project, the Minister of Mines and Energy would set the final terms of the mining lease as appropriate.'

"Recommendations #3, 4, and 5 stated that, before authorizing any construction at Voisey's Bay, the governments and native groups should reach some tentative agreements regarding land claims, and that Inco should also conclude agreements with the native groups. The province made a sensible decision on these recommendations. It offered 'to expedite discussions with' the native groups, but it did not 'agree to make project approval or commencement of construction conditional on' the attainment of such agreements."

Labrador's native groups were disappointed that the provincial government did not implement Recommendations #3, 4, and 5.

"Hypocrisy!" cried Chesley Andersen of the L.I.A. "Premier Tobin is saying the project can hold out for a smelter deal with Inco, but it can't wait for a benefits deal to be finalized with the Inuit."[244] He threatened legal action. So did Daniel Ashini of the Innu Nation,[245] and, on September 3, Mr. Ashini made good on his threat. The Innu Nation filed suit against the federal government in federal court, and announced it would also challenge the provincial government's decision to approve Voisey's Bay. The L.I.A. soon joined the Innu Nation in federal court.

Mr. Ashini was at pains to note that "our fuss is not with ... [Inco]. Our fuss is with the governments."[246] So, a few weeks later, when the Innu and L.I.A. renewed their negotiations with Inco, both groups asked the federal court to suspend their actions as gestures of good faith. The court agreed.[247]

CHAPTER 25

A CHALLENGE FROM AUSTRALIA: ONE MAN AND THE STARTER'S PISTOL

... and what of this laterite nickel nonsense? Back in the good old days, nickel came in big black lumps of sulphide ore and a percentage assay which did not start with a decimal point. Now we have nickel pretenders running around with zillions of tonnes of 0.9% and 0.8% dirt, mines which look like veggie gardens and factories with lots of hot acid — and bugger all nickel! Laterite nickel be damned!
— Australia's *Mining Monthly*, July 2000

* The alpha male in any group is he who takes the barbecue tongs from the hands of the host and blithely begins turning the snags [sausages].

* It is proper to refer to your best friend as "a total bastard." By contrast, your worst enemy is "a bit of a bastard."

* Historians believe the widespread use of the word "mate" can be traced to the harsh conditions on the Australian frontier in the 1890s, and the development of a code of mutual aid, or "mateship." Alternatively, Australians may just be really hopeless with names.

* The wise man chooses a partner who is attractive not only to himself, but to the mosquitoes.

* If it can't be fixed with pantyhose and fencing wire, it's not worth fixing.

* It's considered better to be down on your luck than up yourself.

* *Australians love new technology. Years after their introduction, most conversations on mobile phones are principally about the fact that the call is "being made on my mobile."*

* *The shorter the nickname, the more they like you.*

— Compilation courtesy Joanne Warner, Colonial First State, Sydney, Australia, 2000

"... a nation of shoplifters ..."

— Niall Ferguson, 2000

I'm embarrassed to recall that, in June 1995, I told our clients in St. John's that Voisey's Bay was a threat, a loaded gun that Inco could point at its competitors. Some threat! It was more like a starter's pistol.

In 1995 I believed — and I think Inco's management did as well — that Voisey's Bay would produce a flood of cheap nickel that would make any other new nickel development uncompetitive. And so, I thought, fear of Voisey's would dissuade Inco's competitors from building new mines. Instead, Inco's competitors scrambled to expand, gambling that they could get their new plants built and paid for before Voisey's Bay ushered in an era of low nickel prices.

Australia's audacious bid to dominate the global nickel business featured two natural phenomena: "dry" laterites and a man called Andrew Forrest.

Belts of nickel-rich rocks rim the Pacific Ocean. As an exploration geologist for Kennecott in New Zealand, I walked over kilometres of rock which contained 0.5% nickel. However, in southern New Zealand's cold climate, these rocks are scarcely weathered and the nickel is locked inside silicate crystals, making extraction hopelessly uneconomic. In tropical parts of the Pacific, the same kinds of rocks have been intensely weathered by millions of years of warmth and water, which have converted them into soft crumbly rocks called "laterites." Because many of the other minerals in the rocks have been washed away, leaving nickel behind, these laterites often contain a greater percentage of nickel than their initial 0.5%. And, because weathering releases nickel from its crystalline cage, the nickel in laterites is often in a form amenable to economic extraction. In fact, New Caledonia has produced nickel from laterites since the late nineteenth century.

Western Australia boasts huge tracts of nickel-rich rocks which were converted into laterites by millions of years of tropical weathering. However, because Western Australia is arid, its laterites are different from those that formed in wet places like New Caledonia. For example, Western Australia's laterites are much richer in clay and lower in grade than "wet" laterites. Until the mid-1990s, no one had ever tried to make them into nickel mines.

As Inco was contemplating the development of Voisey's Bay, the Aussies were contemplating building hydromet plants at each of three dry laterite nickel projects in Western Australia: Bulong, Cawse, and Murrin Murrin. Bulong and Cawse were small,[248] whereas Murrin Murrin was big, both in terms of its proposed output of nickel — initially 45,000 tonnes of nickel per year — and in terms of the ego of its promoter, Andrew Forrest.

Mr. Forrest was Chairman of Anaconda Nickel, which owned 60% of Murrin Murrin.

> *Anybody who has ever worked with Andrew '"Twiggy" Forrest will attest to the fact that he is a legendary salesman. Some will spit the description with venom, others will chuckle affectionately at the memory of the deals — some good, some bad, and some just plain extraordinary. "He's got a silver tongue and amazing perseverance," says Albert Wong [a former partner of Forrest]. ...*
>
> *Both [Forrest] and his detractors agree on one thing: that Forrest is driven by more than money. His great-uncle, Sir John Forrest, rode over the Murrin Murrin site in 1874 on his 4,300-kilometre crossing of the continent, from Champion Bay on the west coast, to lay the overland telegraph line from Adelaide to Port Darwin, the first time a route eastwards had been forged. Later Forrest would be a key player in the development of Western Australia. With his faithful engineer, C.Y. O'Connor, Forrest dreamed up the idea of a water pipeline to supply the dry goldfields of Kalgoorlie. The media of the day kicked up such a fuss about the radical plan that O'Connor committed suicide, riding his horse into the waves and shooting himself.*

> *Forrest is unlikely to take the criticism of Murrin Murrin so personally, but he uses the anecdote to illustrate the corrosive nature of what he sees as ill-informed, small-minded analysts and journalists. ... [Forrest] has sold his nickel-plated dream to Anglo, the world's largest mining house, which now holds 26% of Anaconda. ... [His] aspirations have been perhaps assisted by the tension between Anglo and the Swiss commodities house, Glencore International, which owns 21% of Anaconda. ... Meanwhile there's talk that Anglo has appointed BHP's former chairman, Jerry Ellis, to shadow the exuberant Forrest. As one observer says, "You would need a big umbrella, maybe a circus tent."* [249]

Mr. Forrest also sold his "nickel-plated dream" to Canada's Sherritt International, which purchased 8.9% of Anaconda in May 1999. Sherritt had provided some of Murrin Murrin's hydromet technology and, with the encouragement of Brian Tobin, had been trying to interest Inco in applying similar technology to ore from Voisey's Bay.

Western Australia's three laterite projects began production in the late 1990s, thus beating Voisey's Bay into production. All of them featured high-pressure technologies, high-pressure financing, and high-pressure construction schedules. All failed to meet their deadlines, their capital budgets,[250] and their projected output of nickel.

Why were these projects such disappointments?

> *"Anglo-American has a well-read manual that most South African mining analysts possess. It is entitled* The Financial Evaluation and Financing of Projects. *It was produced back in 1985, but is a classic amongst investment research texts. In the manual, Anglo states that one should 'be wary of including in the financial evaluation metallurgical recoveries obtained in laboratory testwork. Results ... can differ significantly from those obtained in the full-scale continuous operation of a plant. Pilot plant results are of course more reliable.'*
>
> *"One wonders how Anglo can now reconcile the investment decision made regarding Anaconda where no pilot plant testing was conducted and whose commissioning woes are now well*

known. ...The selection of pilot plants as opposed to full-scale production facilities may have been a more prudent course of action.

"Perhaps Inco are [sic] showing the way forward now with a more conservative approach — a pilot plant first, as recommended by Anglo-American! At Goro in New Caledonia Inco has spent US$50 million constructing and running a pilot plant. ... No decision has been made until this aspect of the feasibility study is satisfactorily concluded, and the expenditure of US$1.4 billion is dependent on the results from the pilot plant." [251]

The irony was that investors probably would not have been interested in either providing Anaconda with US$50 million to build a pilot plant, nor in waiting several years for results from such a plant while, presumably, development of Voisey's Bay roared ahead. Yet such an investment could have saved hundreds of millions of dollars.

November 13, 2000

"Ray, it's Jack Mergott of Roth Investor Relations in New Jersey. Would you like to have breakfast with Anaconda Nickel on Friday?"

"Hey, sure!"

"OK — see you at 8:00 in the Park Lane room of your King Edward Hotel."

"Great! Thank you."

November 17, 2000

In an elegant room, seventeen analysts and reporters, dressed mostly in Friday casuals, place themselves around a table groaning with fruit, pastries, and juice to listen to smartly suited Michael Masterman, Anaconda Nickel's Chief Financial Officer. I squeeze in next to Harry. "You know, Ray, seeing us dressed in our grubbies in a place like this reminds me of the old joke about Lady Fitzroy," he says, his twirling finger lazily indicating the decorative cornices.

"Hmm?"

"On her wedding night, it seems that the good lady took to love-making with great enthusiasm. During a respite, her shining eyes caught those of her husband, of whom she demanded: 'Is this what they call "'fucking'"?' His lordship wearily conceded that, indeed, it was. 'Well!' said Lady Fitzroy, 'it's too good for the working classes!'"

Before Mr. Masterman begins his presentation, Harry leans toward him at the end of the table and poses the question that is probably on everyone's mind. "If you wanted a blueprint for a problem-plagued plant, your Murrin Murrin project was it. There are rumours that Andrew Forrest cut corners in constructing the plant, and that your partner, Anglo-American, wants to shut it down and rebuild it. You've lost credibility — and money — with all your start-up problems. Don't those problems mean that you are going to face all kinds of niggling little problems in years to come?"

Mr. Masterman squints at Harry's name tag. "Harry, our process for extracting nickel and cobalt from a novel source — dry laterites — works. Our technical problems have been a result of poor decisions by the contractor who built it, Fluor Daniel. Before they started construction, we paid them a $50 million (Australian) fee to guarantee both a fixed price and that the plant would work properly. That's why we've just announced that's why we're suing them for a billion, Australian. That billion dollars is to cover both the extra costs incurred in fixing up the plant to work properly, and to cover the income foregone because the plant has come on stream twelve months late. As for problems in the years to come, yes, you're right that the plant will probably be available to us for less time than we had budgeted, but it looks as if we can offset that lower availability by being able to push more material through the plant when it is in operation."

"Excuse me, sir ..." Ulp. The fruit, pastries, and juice were just for starters. Here come eggs, hash browns, sausage, ham, and bacon.

Mr. Masterman moves into his prepared presentation.

"It is Anaconda's goal to be the world's largest and most profitable producer of nickel and cobalt. We now have 14.71 million tonnes of nickel contained in the resources at our three 'dry laterite nickel provinces' in Western Australia. That compares with only 4.23 million tonnes at Inco and Falconbridge's Sudbury operations. We're even bigger than Noril'sk [Russia], which has 13.09 million tonnes of contained nickel.

"And we are producing nickel from these resources. Our costs are low. Already they're in line with, or under, the figures in our feasibility study. We have huge advantages over conventional underground sulphide nickel mines like those of Inco and Falconbridge in Canada. They typically spend US$36 to pull a tonne of ore out of the ground. It costs us $2.40 a tonne to scrape it off the surface."

"How about energy costs, Michael? Natural gas prices here in North America are now over US$5 a gigajoule. What are your costs?"

"First, we need less natural gas than do conventional sulphide miners — we're targeting 100 gigajoules of natural gas to produce a tonne of nickel, whereas the sulphide guys need 150 gigs. And we have a long-term contract to buy gas at Australian$1.80 per gigajoule. With the Aussie dollar at 50 cents U.S., it's easy to do the conversion these days. Just divide by two; that's only 90 cents U.S.

"Our labour costs are also lower than those for conventional sulphides. And not only are our capital costs lower than those for conventional sulphides, they're also lower than those for some of the new laterite projects that use a technology different from ours — Inco's Goro project, for example."

"Michael, from 2000 to 2010, you're talking about bringing on stream 350,000 annual tonnes of new nickel capacity. Does the world need all that nickel?"

"The answer depends on the growth rate you assume for nickel demand. For the period 2000 to 2010, forecasters are using figures in the range of 3.5% to 4.5% per annum."

I peek at my notes and my own estimates of historic growth rates: the Western world's demand for nickel rose at 7.0% per annum from 1991 until the Asian crisis in early 1996; since then it has been growing at 4.2% per annum, so Anaconda's forecasts seem reasonable.

"That implies the need for some 300,000 to 450,000 new tonnes of annual capacity. We don't think we'll see change in Russia's exports. In the West, we foresee no net new production, either from laterites other than our own, or from conventional sulphide deposits. Any new production will be offset by tired old mines shutting down."

"So, for example, the proposed Ramu River mine in Papua New Guinea won't be coming on stream by 2010?" I ask.

"Ramu River won't come on. At all. It faces high capital costs, an unstable political environment, and the prospect of opposition to marine disposal of its tailings. Incidentally, we think that's a huge and largely insuperable hurdle that most of the 'wet' laterite deposits — like Inco's Goro project — will face. We foresee huge pressure from environmental groups opposed to dumping mine wastes at sea."

I understand that Inco plans to keep its wastes at Goro on land, but I bite my tongue.

"How about Voisey's Bay, a sulphide mine?"

"We think that Voisey's will come on sometime in the second half of this decade, but it doesn't change our view that there will be no net new production from sulphide mines. For example, Falconbridge may be successful at extending the life of its sulphide mines at Sudbury, but Western Mining's sulphide operations in Kambalda, Western Australia, will be largely exhausted by 2010." Mr. Masterman pauses. "So, yes, the world will need 350,000 tonnes of new nickel capacity, and we're going to supply it."

The presentation over, I thank Mr. Masterman and, wondering why he had made the effort to speak to us, asked if Anaconda was considering a listing on the Toronto Stock Exchange.

"In the Internet age, is it necessary to have two listings? Maybe, maybe not. We're open-minded."

A knot of half a dozen mining analysts wanders into the studied opulence of the King Eddy's second floor, agreeing that even if Anaconda doesn't need to list its shares in Toronto, it would certainly have to draw upon North American markets for much of the financing to bring on stream that 350,000 tonnes of new capacity. Provided, of course, that North American investors could be convinced that Anaconda has figured out how to make the process work.

November 27, 2000

Investors in Australia's $50 billion mining sector gained a rare insight into the creditworthiness of some of the industry's sec-

ond-tier companies last week, when Standard & Poor's took the unusual step of publicizing its views on 11 companies to which it had not assigned credit ratings.

Controversial laterite nickel miner Anaconda Nickel Ltd. which, with borrowings of $800 million, ranked as the most indebted company on S&P's list, fared the worst, with the ratings agency describing its business profile as "marginal" and its financial profile as "'very aggressive." ...

S&P said the financial profile of Anaconda, which has suffered well-publicized problems with the commissioning of its Murrin Murrin project in Western Australia, reflected high leverage, poor returns, and weak debt-protection levels.[252]

May 10, 2002

Anaconda Nickel today announced the retirement of Mr. Andrew Forrest as deputy chairman and non-executive director of the company.[253]

September 13, 2002

Anaconda Nickel today ... reported a net loss of [Australian] $919.9 million. The loss represents further significant write-downs in the carrying value of the Murrin Murrin nickel cobalt plant, in order to align the Company's balance sheet with valuations agreed with secured creditors as part of the Company's ongoing debt restructuring and recapitalization negotiations. ... Murrin Murrin produced 28,652 tonnes of nickel for the year ended 30 June 2002.[254]

October 31, 2002

During the third quarter of 2002, [Sherritt International] ... Corporation wrote down its investment in Anaconda Nickel Limited by $37.0 million.[255]

November 20, 2002

> *Production and cost estimates for Anaconda Nickel Ltd.'s Murrin Murrin nickel laterite project in Western Australia were over-optimistic and unlikely ever to be attained, according to a strategic review by the company. In addition, capital expenditure requirements were significantly underestimated, ... James Campbell, Anaconda's chairman, said at the company's annual general meeting.*[256]

December 18, 2002

Another Christmas dinner for the Mineral Resource Analysts Group in Toronto; another belly dancer. As part of his prognostications for nickel markets, Santo Ranieri of Falconbridge Limited comments that Murrin Murrin will never produce at its rated capacity of 45,000 tonnes per year. Eventually, however, it should be able to produce about 32,000 tonnes of nickel per year, but, with cash operating costs of US$2.35 per pound, this would hardly be competitive with conventional nickel operations. And Mr. Ranieri's figures imply that Murrin Murrin's high capital costs would probably dissuade anyone from attempting to expand Australia's output from "dry laterites" anytime in the foreseeable future.

May 5, 2004

> *The joint-venture partners in the Murrin Murrin laterite nickel project in Western Australia will receive Australian $155 million in an out-of-court settlement with Fluor Daniel Corp. ... This settlement brings to an end one of the longest-running private arbitrations in Australian commercial history.*[257]

March 29, 2005

"I've picked up a story from Australia," I tell the morning meeting.

"Inco is to provide most of the funding for a 60% interest in an Australian $1.4 billion nickel "dry laterite" project in Western Australia, which would produce 50,000 tonnes of contained nickel per year. Inco intends to use the hydromet technology it is developing at Goro, New Caledonia. I think that Inco is likely to be criticized for this proposed deal by critics who say that the Goro process will never work, and that it will doubly never work on the kind of laterites which all but defeated Murrin Murrin.

"So, Inco's partner, an Aussie company called Heron Resources, is set to become another 'baby Inco.' Despite the critics, the shares of 'baby Incos' — companies like Altius, Canico, FNX, Jubilee Mines, LionOre, and Skye Resources — have done rather well."

CHAPTER 26

A CHALLENGE FROM SIBERIA: HUGE STOCKPILES OF NICKEL?

There's certainly a risk of a major disruption in supply from the U.S.S.R. and this would have a significant effect on Western nickel markets. There is also, admittedly, a risk that Soviet exports to the West could increase — say, if it were to stop building tanks or if the internal demand for consumer goods were to be throttled. However, it's difficult to imagine this happening.

— Summary, prepared by Richardson Greenshields's Toronto office, of a presentation made by Inco to investors in Toronto, May 23, 1991

We shall not cease from exploration
And the end of all our exploring
Will be to arrive where we started
And know the place for the first time.

— *Little Gidding*, T.S. Eliot, 1942

"Compare and contrast" is a favourite phrase of professors of English Literature. It's also a favourite of professors of ore deposits. By the late 1970s, University of Toronto geology Professor Tony Naldrett had become the world's leading authority on nickel deposits in general and, in particular, those in Inco's back yard, Sudbury, Ontario.

Tony recognized that, just as his knowledge of Sudbury provided him with insights into other nickel deposits, knowledge of other nickel deposits could help him to better understand Sudbury. Noting that Noril'sk in Siberia was a nickel mining district that rivalled Sudbury in size, Tony carefully cultivated contacts with his counterparts in Russia.

His efforts paid off, and he became one of the first Westerners to visit Noril'sk, bring back samples, and publish research on Noril'sk.

Tony's secretary convinced herself that her boss was a Soviet spy and, from 1986 to 1990, regularly reported his activities to the Canadian Security Intelligence Service and the R.C.M.P.[258] Fortunately, her paranoia had no noticeable effect on Tony's career, which he would cap with a term as President of the Geological Society of America.

Like Tony, Inco's management recognized the value of comparing and contrasting the geology of different mining districts. Because Voisey's Bay appeared to resemble Noril'sk more than it resembled Sudbury, Inco asked Tony to take some geologists from Inco and from Diamond Fields (which was then in the process of being taken over by Inco) to Noril'sk.

May 13, 1996, Toronto

Rosie Moore of Diamond Fields has just called. Would I like to visit Noril'sk? Why, yes, very much! "Good," said Rosie. "I think that Tony and I can slip you onto the Inco trip!"

Why do I want to go to Noril'sk? Not only could I see the geology of one of the world's most important mining districts, I could search for clues as to Noril'sk's future capabilities and intentions. Will it — can it — continue to keep shipping nickel to the West? What about the rumours I've heard of vast stockpiles of nickel ore sitting on the surface, waiting to be run through Noril'sk's smelters and dumped onto the market? And what about the rumours that Noril'sk is reinvesting nothing in its operations, which will, as a result, soon grind to a halt?

May 15, 1996, Toronto

"Give me fax number," breathes Olga at the Russian Embassy in Ottawa. I do, and an hour later an alarmingly inquisitive form appears.

The payment schedule for Russian visas is brisk: $60 for fourteen-day delivery, $120 for seven-day delivery, and $150 for three-day delivery.

June 27, 1996, Moscow

I never expected that my first view of Russia, between the clouds as we banked to land at Sheremetyeva airport, would be of a golf course!

Seven Canadian geologists are met at the airport by Nikolai Gorbachev of the Russian Academy of Sciences, and by Tony Naldrett and his wife, Galina "Galya" Rylkova, who is to be our translator. Warning us to be careful, Tony recounts the tale of a visit to Moscow two years earlier. Within a few minutes of his arrival, someone used a razor to steal his money pouch ... and his money, tickets, and passports.

Then into a battered little school bus, on to our hotel, then downtown by subway.

Travellers' stories had led me to expect a grim, crumbling city full of contrasts between the flash and wealth of a few and the grinding poverty of everyone else. But grey, wet Moscow looks remarkably similar to any large northern European city.

We sit outside under umbrellas, getting to know each other over plastic tablecloths and draft beer. I'm impressed by big, bearded Daniel Lee, who, with Bruce Ryan, was one of the first geologists to have mapped the Voisey's Bay area. He is now working for Chislett and Verbiski's company, Archean Resources, under contract to Diamond Fields. Dan prefers to buy his beer in bottles, explaining that he collects beer bottles — *empty* beer bottles — of the world.

Although beer costs US$20 a pitcher, one of our contingent is able to drink enough to be obliged to find relief among the rain-sodden bushes around Red Square.

MOSCOW AEROSTAR HOTEL

Dear Guest

Please choose your favourite pillow from our wide selection. When you are staying with us at the Moscow Aerostar Hotel — Just bring yourself — we will make you feel like home.

June 28, 1996

In anticipation of the presidential runoff election on July 3, Moscow's streets are full of posters showing Moscow Mayor Yuri Luzhkhov shaking hands with Boris Yeltsin. These posters are intended to benefit Mr. Yeltsin because the mayor is an immensely popular man. He has been shipping out of town anyone who does not have the documents permitting him to reside in Moscow.

Up to now, all the Russian men we have seen look either like Canadian men in Toronto's financial district on a weekday, or in a hardware store on Saturday morning. But tonight we see shabby, shiny-suited men with shoddy shoes, like a guidebook's description of stereotypical Russians. Hundreds of them in a ragged procession streaming into the Kremlin: farmers who have come to visit Mr. Yeltsin. Mr. Yeltsin, regrettably, is unavailable.

There are rumours of food shortages in Noril'sk, so Tony recommends we visit a supermarket to stock up on staples: sausage, cheese, vodka, and Guinness.

June 30, 1996

We were supposed to have spent the night aloft. Instead, we spend it on the floor of the airport. That's OK — a daylight flight will let us see the view.

"So what was the highlight of Moscow for you, Rosie?"

Her eyes light up. No hesitation. "Front-row centre seats at the Bolshoi!"

In a Transaero Boeing 757, it's a three-and-a-half-hour flight to Noril'sk, across the Arctic Circle and through four time zones. Just before landing, we see the port of Dudinka on the east bank of the Yenisei River. The Yenisei flows north into the Arctic Ocean. There is a railway between Noril'sk and Dudinka, Noril'sk's only surface link with the rest of the world. There is no road out.

We drive into Noril'sk in another school bus, past grim, black open-pit coal mines, gleaming white anhydrite mines, and the Nadzezdha smelter, built by the Finnish firm Outokumpu Oy.

Twenty-five kilometres to the northeast, we can see Noril'sk's twin mining town, Talnakh.

Noril'sk: massive, rectangular, brick buildings finished with incongruously delicate neoclassical devices, all sadly shabby with paint sandblasted by blizzards; triple doors to keep out the cold; a town ringed by smelters, each billowing noxious brown and white clouds; perpetual construction of new buildings to replace old ones whose permafrost footings have melted.

At the Noril'sk Hotel, we meet leather-jacketed Alexander "Sasha" Stekhin, newly minted Chief Mine Geologist and Mr. Fixit Extraordinaire. Sasha explains that the Noril'sk Kombinat, which is a subsidiary of the Noril'sk Nickel Company, is owner and operator of the mining and metallurgical facilities at Noril'sk and Talnakh. The Kombinat has taken over the Noril'sk Expedition (formerly part of the Ministry of Geology) and the Zapolyarsky (Polar) Party/Expedition. So the Kombinat now has two exploration arms, organizations which historically have been rivals.

Although the weather in Noril'sk is brilliant, in contrast to rain, rain, rain in Moscow, a gloomy mood has settled over the group. It's not just the industrial squalor of the approaches to Noril'sk after the lively opulence of Moscow; nor is it just that the vodka, originally destined for Noril'sk, was depleted during the long night waiting for our plane. It is also the surprise announcement, made by the Noril'sk Kombinat's tour organizer, that the cost of mine and surface tours is US$860 per person, payable in cash. The request for payment is supported by a document written, Galina tells us, in old and flowery language. It details such items as "guided tour of mine, use of clothing and change facilities, US$110."

I now give credence to recent *Reuters* stories that suggested that, despite the fact that Noril'sk is one of Russia's biggest earners of foreign exchange, little of its earnings are reinvested and that, as a consequence, the Kombinat is suffering a severe shortage of cash.

Tony has visited Noril'sk many times before, but this is the first time he has encountered such a situation. Few of us have cash sufficient to meet this demand. We decide to respond to the tour organizer tomorrow: we'll pay — but we can do it only by credit card, bank draft, or invoice.

There's clearly no shortage of food in Noril'sk. The streets are full of kiosks brimming with fresh fruit (including, if the box labels are to be believed, New Zealand apples). Dan is astonished at the variety of beers on display. Curiously, the one beer he'd most like to add to his collection — Noril'sk beer — is unavailable. Does it exist?

Noril'sk in late June: midnight sun; piles of dirty snow still lying untidily in odd corners; young women in delicately embroidered white blouses and wearing crucifixes and astonishingly short skirts, walking arm in arm and squinting in the sunlight; a woman stealing earth from the median of the wide main street; bluish, snow-streaked mesas in the distance.

July 1, 1996

Morning ablutions in Noril'sk: shave quickly before the planned power shutdown at 8:00 a.m., no hot water, foul-smelling brown soap embossed with a palm tree and, on the wrapper, a price of 20 kopeks (at this price and current exchange rates, $40 would get you a million bars), a bath towel of the size and consistency of a dishtowel. But, surprise! There is a roll of toilet paper!

Galina has the difficult task of delivering our "ultimatum" to the Noril'sk Kombinat's tour organizer. It seems that the Kombinat is to ask a banker to pursue the possibility of obtaining payment via VISA; alternatively, we will visit an ATM on our return to Moscow and somehow deliver the cash advance to Noril'sk.

It's Monday morning and, where the woman was stealing earth last night, teenagers in red safety vests are enthusiastically attacking the road median with shovels. Sasha points out that behind the enthusiasm is the disappointment that, because their parents haven't been paid for six weeks, they're stuck here. No vacation in Moscow or on the Black Sea this summer! However, as soon as the kids are old enough to leave town for good, they will — provided they can afford the airfare. Jobs are being cut drastically, and Noril'sk now has an embarrassing overcapacity of nurseries and elementary schools.

At the headquarters of the Zaporlyarsky Expedition in Talnakh, we review the geology of the Noril'sk-Talnakh district. The Expedition's geologists tell us that the cut-off grade — that is, the dividing line between ore and waste — is 7% sulphide minerals. More than this, it's ore. Less than 7%, it's waste. Because most economic minerals are sulphides, but not all sulphides are economic, we press for more details. What are the grades — per cent nickel, copper, and other metals — of the material that is mined? Sorry, we can't reveal them, they're a "commercial secret." But we can tell you that the ratio of nickel to copper in the most valuable ore type, "massive" ores,[259] is about 0.85:1, and about 1:1 when averaged across all ore types.

We also discover that it is not just grade that determines whether or not a piece of rock is ore or waste. Grain size is also important. Some of the pentlandite (a nickel-rich mineral) at Noril'sk and Talnakh is so fine-grained that it is lost during processing, and gets dumped into a tailings pond along with other wastes. The Inco people glance at each other appreciatively. Voisey's Bay's mineralization is famously coarse grained, and processing it should be a met dream.

Noril'sk and Talnakh have "significant" potential reserves of "disseminated"[260] mineralization with low grades of nickel, but relatively high grades of platinum, that are accessible to open-pit mining. However, it will be "quite a while" before they run out of nickel-rich ore. How long a while? "At least 20 years of massive ore remain, and maybe seventy years or more of disseminated ore." Looks as if, no matter when Voisey's comes on stream, Voisey's will face competition from Noril'sk.

We take our school bus into the hills behind Talnakh to enjoy the sunshine and the view southwest across the Siberian plains to the clusters of chimneys that mark the town of Noril'sk's three smelter complexes: the old nickel smelter, the old copper smelter, and the Nadezhda nickel and copper smelter built by the Finnish company Outokumpu. Noril'sk is shrouded in dense sulphur dioxide fumes, the filthiest air I have seen around any smelter other than the El Teniente copper smelter in Chile. Noril'sk and El Teniente are sombre warnings of what Voisey's Bay's smelter would look like if there were no environmental movement in North America.

Nine or 10 kilometres to the east, we can see the surface facilities of the Skalisty mine, which started production four years ago. It is to produce 50,000 tonnes of ore this year, 100,000 tonnes next year, and, ultimately, 200,000 tonnes per annum (t.p.a.) from a 1,150-metres deep shaft. (For comparison, the nearby Oktyabr'sky mine produced

500,000 t.p.a. at its peak.) All of Skalisty's ore is of high grade. Construction appears to be proceeding on schedule.

Sasha claims that Skalisty's miners excavated a drift (tunnel) to the Komsomolsky mine so that, when they were unable to meet their planned production rates, they stole ore from Komsomolsky. Komsomolsky's miners eventually found out and filled in the drift.

Back to the hotel past two construction projects: Noril'sk's first church and first mosque.

Into the bar at the hotel. "Do you have any Noril'sk beer?" asks Dan hopefully. "Nope," says the hefty lady behind the counter, "just Mexican." We toast Canada Day with Tecate, Corona, and Dos Equis. At 9:00 p.m., the barkeep shows us to the door, saying we've drunk everything she has.

Monday night in Noril'sk: elegantly coiffed, beautifully dressed women sporting sunglasses navigate stony, puddly sidewalks in spike heels.

July 2, 1996

Back to Talnakh for a visit to the Komsomolsky mine. As we dress to go underground, we are at a loss as to what to do with the two rectangles of white cloth laid out for each of us beside boots, hard hats, and overalls. "Well," mutters our chaperone, "you have less imagination than the Cubans, who thought they were bandanas. Let me show you." She expertly wraps our feet, Russian Army-style. "I think they're onto something," says Dan. "My socks never stay up inside miners' boots."

Descending, we share the mine cage with carefully made-up, brightly lipsticked women, who protect their coiffed hair with turbans under their hard hats.

I stoop and fold myself into an electric train to be hauled off to the stopes — mining excavations — where I gaze in awe at the remarkably thick, golden, glistening, high-grade nickel-copper-platinum-palladium-rhodium-osmium-silver-selenium-tellurium ore.

Back to the surface for the water treatment: shower, sauna, and dubious-looking plunge pool, followed by a visit to Sasha's favourite spa to take the local mineral waters. As we sit enjoying the sun and feeling sorry for a nearby bear that has been caged for the alleged educational value it confers on those who torment it with sticks, we ask about two events reported recently in the Western press: a shakeup in Noril'sk's management and a wildcat strike in the Nadezhda smelter. Sasha explains that Noril'sk's workers haven't been paid since April. April and May's wages and salaries will be paid next February at 7% interest; June salaries are to be paid soon. Noril'sk's workers earn about US$800 per month, perhaps two to four times that of other Russians, and they get three months' holiday per year.

"That's nice, Sasha, but if you haven't been paid, how do you buy groceries?" Sasha whips out his wallet and shows us his Noril'sk Nickel smart card with embedded chip — good in Noril'sk's stores (but not its travel agencies!).

Noril'sk in the week between the end of snow cover and the beginning of mosquito season: scrublands full of sun-worshipping bodies; Sasha finally doffing his brown leather jacket; Nikolai, the eternal romantic, reciting love poetry.

July 3, 1996 — Runoff Election Day

A polling station: fresh flowers in vases, bright red curtains on the booths; rival parties distributing campaign literature outside the booths. Tony recites his favourite Russian political joke:

> "Mr. Yeltsin, I have good news and bad news."
> "What's the bad news?"
> "Mr. Zuganov got 55% of the vote."
> "What possible good news could there be?"
> "You got 65% of the vote."

Election days are holidays in Russia, so it is very gracious of our hosts to provide us with a tour. Our visit is to Bear Creek, a huge — 1.5 kilometre by 1.2 kilometre by 360 metres deep — open pit south of Noril'sk. The Bear Creek mine director has pictures of both Lenin and Tsar Nicholas II in his office.

He gives a remarkably frank presentation, including an acknowledgement of the misjudgment that led to collapses of the pit walls in March and in June of 1992. Before these misadventures, his crew was mining 4.2 million tonnes of ore per year. Now he can pull no more than 0.3 million tonnes from the pit each year. And he tells us the grade of the ore: it's 0.23% nickel and 0.28% copper; pretty low.

Did the pit wall collapses undermine Russia's ability to compete with Western producers of nickel, like Inco? I play with some numbers, and estimate that Bear Creek's reduction in output would have represented a loss of only about 8,000 tonnes of finished nickel per year, or about 4% of Russia's total exports to the West. That's equivalent to less than 1% of the West's annual consumption of finished nickel.

In the bar afterward, over Mexican beer, we convince ourselves that a similar failure at the Voisey's Bay open pit would be most unlikely: Bear Creek's collapse was in soft bedrock sediments, which are lacking at Voisey's; Voisey's pit will be smaller and hence more stable; and, we tell each other, our computer modelling and monitoring of the stability of pit walls is much superior to that of the Russians. Right.

And on to the headquarters of the Noril'sk Expedition. As we tramp through the corridors, one of the Expedition's employees translates a graffito for me. A sign that originally read "Cash Office" now reads "No Cash Office."

The Expedition's Chief Geologist, Vladimir Kunilov, tells us about the logistics of running Noril'sk. Noril'sk's residents feel so isolated that they consider themselves to live on an "island" — the rest of Russia is "the continent."

There are two surface routes from the port of Dudinka to "the continent." One is up the Yenisei River to Krasnoyarsk, which is on the Trans-Siberian Railway. This route can be used only from around the end of May until August. The second route, downstream to the Arctic Ocean, can be used all year except when the ice is breaking up in late May and early June. It is much cheaper to bring food and other supplies in through the Arctic than via Krasnoyarsk.

The only food grown locally — in greenhouses — is parsley, onions, and cucumbers. The Noril'sk Kombinat also produces milk, cottage cheese, beer, and sausage.

Beer! Dan perks up. Perhaps he isn't chasing a phantom after all.

The Kombinat is looking for oil and gas in the Lower Yenisei lowlands. As well as metals, the Kombinat mines coal, anhydrite (to use as a cement for backfill), sandstone (for smelter flux), shale (for bricks), and basalt (for construction aggregate).

Will Voisey's Bay have ancillary mines, too? asks Mr. Kunilov. Well, reply the Inco people, the only mining at Voisey's will be of the nickel ore itself. Oh, and we will quarry sand and gravel for construction. Backfill? If mining does eventually go underground, we would probably use tailings for backfill. It would be pleasing to have a local source of anhydrite, as at Noril'sk, to cement those tailings, but, as far as we know, there isn't one, so cement is something we'll have to barge into Labrador.

Mr. Kunilov gives me some figures to toss around. Noril'sk has produced about 5 million tonnes of nickel metal and 9 million tonnes of copper metal from 500 million tonnes of ore. Assuming that 82.5% of the nickel in the ore and 90% of the copper were recovered, the average grade of that ore would have been 1.2% nickel and 2.0% copper. Remember that our ore is also rich in platinum metals, Mr. Kunilov adds. For comparison, Voisey's Bay's star performer, the "Ovoid" deposit, contains 32 million tonnes grading 2.8% nickel, 1.7% copper and 0.1% cobalt. But Inco hasn't found any platinum metals — which is one of the reasons for our visit. Nickel-copper ore bodies usually have platinum as well. If there *is* platinum at Voisey's, can Noril'sk's geology give us any clues about where to look for it?

July 4, 1996

Today, we tour the Komsomolsky mine's neighbour, Oktyabr'sky. The ores are just as impressive as Komsomolsky's, and the grades run up to 4% nickel and 15% copper. I stagger out of the shaft carrying a sample to put on my desk. (Even after Noril'sk's technicians have kindly sawed it down to a manageable size, it is still so massively rich in metal that it would later trigger a mildly unpleasant experience with security officials at Heathrow.)

While reviewing mine plans and sections, I mention to one of Oktyabr'ksy's engineers that I've heard rumours that Noril'sk has huge stockpiles of unprocessed nickel sitting on the surface.

"For fifteen years," he replies, "we have been storing pyrrhotite concentrate in an artificial pond. It's for future use. We can't process it now because we would have had to build the Nadezdha smelter twice as large, and we couldn't afford that. This concentrate contains about 2% nickel with a little copper, but the main value is in the platinum metals."

Pyrrhotite is a mineral that is poor in nickel and rich in sulphur. In Sudbury, to avoid the costs and consequences of removing the sulphur, Inco sends pyrrhotite straight to waste dumps. I surmise that, if the prices of platinum metals were to rise sharply, Noril'sk might send some of its stockpiled concentrate to be smelted. But doing so would displace some of Noril'sk's more nickel-rich smelter feed, resulting in a drop in the amount of nickel coming out the other end of the smelter.

Sasha bustles in, excited. The new "Director" (what we'd call "Chief Executive Officer") of the Noril'sk Kombinat, Mr. Abramov, is in town and has asked to meet a few of us after lunch. "Hurry, hurry," urges Sasha, not wanting to keep his boss waiting. (Actually, as it turns out, wanting to give his boss an opportunity to keep *us* waiting.) We race back to the hotel where I thrust myself into my suit, and we drive downtown to the Kombinat's head offices, which would not be out of place in Frankfurt or Zurich.

Mr. Abramov asks us about nickel developments in Canada, noting that Russians are confused by the North American practice of referring to production and reserves of *ore*: the Russian practice is to refer to *contained metal*. This puts us on the defensive, allowing Mr. Abramov to bully the Inco representatives, whom he accuses of unwarranted secrecy in concealing Inco's true reserves of ore. (His accusations are not entirely without merit — at the time. Inco, inexplicably, and unlike most of North America's mining companies, did not report ore reserves for individual operations.)

Afterwards, Sasha counsels the Inco people not to worry about the abrasive tone of the meeting. "I don't think Mr. Abramov will be around for long. He doesn't have the right political connections."

And on to the Noril'sk Expedition's offices for a helicopter ride to the lake district east of Noril'sk. The helicopter has evidently been recently used to transport fish, and I wish I'd had time to change my suit.

The helicopter sports twelve portholes, which you can open for a clearer view. The pilots fly low and slowly, so I am able to take marvellous photographs of Noril'sk's serried rows of grim Stalinesque apartment blocks and spectacularly filthy air, boggy barrens strewn with rusty waste, then the town of Talnakh, and then remarkable Arctic scenery: lakes whose shores are jostled by gleaming, white polygons of ice, flat-topped, steep-sided mountains with bare brown grass on their upper slopes, and huddles of trees below.

We stop at a fishing lodge on Sobach'ye (Dogs) Lake for raw fish and smoked reindeer. Sasha just happens to have a bottle of vodka in his briefcase.

Back in Noril'sk, we come across a dozen men, each dangling a grubby, empty, four-litre bottle or two. They are lined up at a cylindrical tank, mounted on a two-wheel trailer and marked "ПИВО." Beer. Dan, maybe that's why you can't find a bottle of Noril'sk beer. Maybe it doesn't come in bottles. Maybe it's available only in bulk. Dang.

July 5, 1996

Fifty employees of the Kombinat file into the auditorium of the Noril'sk Expedition to attend our group's presentations on Voisey's Bay. After several hours of translating with no one to relieve her, Galina, exhausted, is momentarily stumped. Our presenter is outlining a giant S-shaped structure that may be an extension of the mineralization at Voisey's Bay. S — how do you translate S? There is no S in the Russian alphabet. A stroke of brilliance: "Like a giant dollar sign," says Galina. An appreciative laugh from the audience. Dollar signs they understand. Afterwards, Galina tells us that the Russians who questioned her after the presentation were interested mostly in how Canada's system of mineral claims works, and how much money geologists and engineers earn in Canada.

Lunch in a typical Noril'sk building: a shack on the outside (albeit with polished stone steps at the front entrance); a palace inside.

We try to thank our hosts by organizing a reception. As we shop for the party, Dan makes a wonderful discovery. Noril'sk beer! Two labelled bottles of Noril'sk beer! Sasha and his colleagues select the venue for our party: a banya (sauna). Ladies first; have fun, Rosie! No mixed bathing, please — this ain't Germany, and they swamp our rather muted contributions to the party by laying on lavish gourmet foods and bottles of ice-cold vodka, and present to every inebriated one of us a breathtaking collection of polished and mounted samples of ores and rocks from Noril'sk. I recall stumbling outside afterwards, clutching our prizes, for group photographs in the 2 a.m. sunshine.

July 6, 1996 — Noril'sk to Moscow

We can't check out. The hotel won't take U.S. dollars. Rubles, please. Panic, bewilderment, despair. But ... the desk clerk happens to run a small money-changing business. Problem solved? Not quite. Another wave of panic and trading currency amongst ourselves as we learn that Russians often refuse U.S. bills that have been stamped, folded, written on, or otherwise marked.

We are as amused as we can be, in our hungover condition, to see Sasha stride up the steps of the hotel wearing a Diamond Fields shirt and a huge smile, waving a bottle of champagne. He opens it, the cork flies over the bus, and, to groans, passes around the bottle.

Our flight to Moscow is in an Ilyushin 86. The safety video ends with the encouraging words "Don't worry! Be happy!" Interior is huge, nine seats across, ceiling high enough for a basketball game. The fuselage has two storeys; you enter the lower one and ascend a flight of stairs. The kitchen is contained within a large elevator. Vases of cut flowers on the drinks wagons. Washrooms are whiffy but work. Be careful not to trip over small dogs as you walk down the aisle.

Tomorrow we must pay for our tour. I take my copy of the bill from my wallet. "Galina, what's this item here — US$150?"

"Oh it's for — let me see — 'polished and mounted samples of ores and rocks from Noril'sk.'"

July 6, 1996 — Moscow

Canadians standing in front of an ATM, each withdrawing $860 in U.S. bills and handing them to a grim-faced representative of the Noril'sk Kombinat who will, presumably, fly back to Noril'sk with them.

Red Square: wedding couples, all with attendants clad in crimson, lining up to be photographed in front of Lenin's tomb.

Our first sunset in a week!

July 7, 1996

Dan is despondent. The chambermaid has chucked out his collection of beer bottles.

July 8, 1996 — BA837

"Ladies and gentlemen," says the British Airways purser, "we remind you that taking photographs is forbidden in Russian airspace."

July 10, 1996 — Morning Meeting, Toronto

"Welcome back, Ray. What were the investment implications of your trip to Russia?"

"I've brought back some thoughts about nickel markets. Analysts who are bullish on the price of nickel suggest that production at Noril'sk will soon collapse because there has been no reinvestment of capital in the business. And that, because Noril'sk is such an awful place and workers haven't been paid for months, there'll be massive labour unrest.

"Analysts who are bearish on the price of nickel suggest that Noril'sk is stepping up production from new, high-grade mines, and that it has huge stockpiles of nickel, which it can dump on the Western world, depressing prices.

"From what I saw, they are reinvesting in the business, but not much more than enough to replace the output of older mines which are running out of ore. There *are* large stockpiles of unprocessed low-grade material, but Noril'sk's output of nickel is limited by the capacity of its smelters, not by the amount of feedstock. I don't think any future labour unrest will last long. Sure, workers haven't been paid cash in the hand, and sure, there have been wildcat strikes. But

Noril'sk's workers are much better off than most Russian workers. They can buy most of what they need — except airline tickets out — with their company credit cards. I suspect that, in the event of a strike, those cards would mysteriously stop working.

"My best guess is that we should make our forecasts of future nickel supply assuming that Noril'sk's output remains steady for years to come."

June 2003 — Toronto

The seventh anniversary of our visit to Noril'sk has prompted me to look back at the forecasts I made in July 1996.

The "large stockpiles of unprocessed low-grade material" to which I referred caught the attention of Osmium Holdings, an obscure company owned by British and American investors. In late 1996, Osmium signed a deal with Noril'sk to upgrade 11 million tonnes of this material at Noril'sk and ship it to Italy where it would be further refined. Osmium hoped to produce 17,000 tonnes of nickel per year, which would have been about 1.7% of the Western world's supply. However, new management took over the Noril'sk Nickel Company in 1997 (fulfilling Sasha's forecast that Mr. Abramov would not last long). The new management stalled shipments in order to review the agreement and to determine whether it could do the job itself. Osmium's shareholders were understandably "furious at Noril'sk's failure to honour legally binding commitments."[261]

However, even if Noril'sk had delivered the material to Osmium, I'm dubious that Osmium could have pulled the nickel out of it. Osmium planned to refine the material at Crotone, which is a *zinc* smelter/refinery that the Italian government shut down, for both economic and environmental reasons.

The people at Noril'sk, however, seemed to believe that Osmium would have applied exotic biotechnology to their nickel. "Noril'sk was interested in the deal because it involved heat-loving bacteria that could not function at Noril'sk's frozen headquarters north of the Arctic [Circle]," said Noril'sk spokesman Anatoly Komrakov.[262] "Because of our geography, we have to take the ore to the microbes, not the microbes to the ore."

But the deal died. It died, not because Noril'sk decided to do the job itself, not because of Osmium's inability to turn Crotone into a nickel smelter, and not by a failure to develop novel biotechnology. As Mr. Kromakov said, "The concentrates contained precious metals whose export by companies was forbidden under Russian law."

In 2001, Noril'sk Nickel signed a deal under which Outokumpu would modernize and expand ore concentrators at Noril'sk. By 2005, the old plants of the Noril'sk district would become available to treat material like the "unprocessed low-grade material" sought by Osmium.[263]

My forecast of labour relations at Noril'sk appears to have been accurate. Since my visit, there have been only occasional wildcat strikes, resulting in little loss of production. It's tougher to assess my forecast that Noril'sk's output of nickel wouldn't change much. Part of the problem in assessing Noril'sk's output is that reporters sometimes fail to distinguish between the Noril'sk Kombinat, which owns and operates the facilities in the Noril'sk district, and the parent company, Noril'sk Nickel, which owns the Kombinat and other operations.

The Noril'sk Nickel company, now known as MMC Norilsk Nickel, owns two smaller complexes that also produce nickel: Severo and Pechenga, both in northwestern Russia near the border with Finland.

Another part of the problem is that definitions of "output" vary. For example, in 1996 our hosts in Noril'sk told us that although the Skalitsky mine had been in operation for four years, its output wouldn't reach its full potential for several more years. However, Russian accountants don't seem to count output from mines that are not yet in full production. Thus, at the end of 1997, MMC Norilsk Nickel reported that it had begun development at Skalitsky, but that Skalitsky was not yet in production and wouldn't be in production until 1998.[264]

The figures that I have compiled for MMC Norilsk Nickel's output from the Noril'sk district reflect this confusion. In 1997, the company reported that these operations produced about 93,800 tonnes of nickel in 1995, 100,000 tonnes in 1996, and that it expected to continue to produce at the latter rate.[265] In early 1999, MMC

Norilsk Nickel confirmed that it expected to continue to produce 100,000 tonnes of nickel per year. However, an analyst at Standard Bank Group, South Africa, said that output from the Noril'sk district would be "closer to a range of 70,000 to 80,000 tonnes."[266]

It's easier to count tonnes of nickel when they cross Russia's borders than it is to count them as they move inside the country. Perhaps, then, the best approach for a Western analyst is to consider individual operations as representative of the whole, and to measure that whole from customs data. On that basis, output has been declining modestly. The chart below shows that, from the time of my visit to Noril'sk in 1996 until the end of 2002, net nickel exports from the former East Bloc (of which Norilsk's Siberian operations contribute the largest portion) fell at a rate of 1.1% p.a.

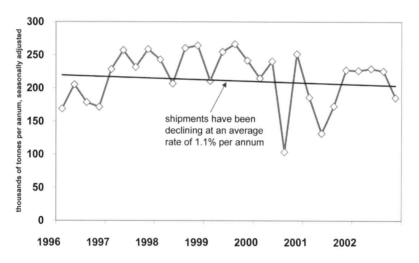

June 1, 2004 — Moscow

Michael D. Prokhorov, General Director and Chairman of the Management Board of MMC Norilsk Nickel, posts Norilsk's Annual Report for 2003 on the company's website. For the first time, the annual report carries details of Norilsk's ore reserves and resources, calculated by Western geologists according to Western standards. In the Noril'sk and Talnakh districts, total reserves and resources comprise 17.965 million tonnes of contained nickel and 34.147 million tonnes of contained copper. Platinum and other precious metals are still a secret.

CHAPTER 27

A CHALLENGE FROM QUEBEC: VOISEY'S II?

The light which experience gives is a lantern on the stern, which shines only on the waves behind us.
— *Recollections*, Coleridge, 1831

Go slowly and attend to your work, live a godly life, and avoid mining shares.
— Sir William Osler's recipe for longevity

For decades, Douglas Hume enjoyed modest success as a mining promoter. A measure of his peers' respect is that he served a term as President of the Prospectors and Developers Association of Canada. In January 1999, when his company, Nuinsco Resources Ltd., reported spectacular drilling results, it was a pleasure to contemplate that, perhaps, near the end of his career, Doug had made the big score that had long eluded him.

The first results from the first hole into Nuinsco's Lac Rocher project, 120 kilometres northeast of Matagami in northwestern Quebec, were exciting: 3.2 metres of mineralization grading 10.8% nickel. Noting that the local geology had similarities to that of both Noril'sk and Voisey's Bay, I inferred that the mineralization was likely to be sheet-like and continuous.

With Nuinsco's shares trading at $2.30, I enthusiastically reported to our morning meeting on January 25, 1999 that Nuinsco's shares were "a roll of the dice," but a worthwhile one. I even speculated that, should Lac Rocher emerge as a producing mine, it could encourage further deferral of development of Voisey's Bay. My rationale was that Inco might prefer to assist the development of a nickel mine closer to its hungry smelters than Voisey's Bay, and that it might be politically less difficult to develop a mine in Quebec (which already had an operating nickel mine and had no objections to export of concentrates) than in Newfoundland and Labrador.

In the following weeks, Nuinsco reported the results from 9 drill holes, which I gleefully plotted up. Just like the old days following Diamond Fields's drill results with Liz! With less glee, I watched the price of the stock drop, despite the flow of good news, from $3.15 in mid-March to $0.98 by the end of March. On April 1, 1999, after Nuinsco's shares had dropped to $0.98, I told the morning meeting that:

> *Nuinsco has examined, by diamond drilling, about 150 metres of a 1-kilometre long geophysical anomaly. Typical drill intersections have been tens of metres of material with [Net Smelter Returns] of about $38/tonne, and 2 or 3 metres with N.S.R.'s of about $530/tonne. Assuming each intersection to be representative of the material within 25 metres, assuming a relative density of 3.5 tonnes per cubic metre and a cut-off grade [267] of $25/tonne, and assuming that the material is diluted by 15% during mining, I estimate that Nuinsco may be able to demonstrate 3 million tonnes of material grading $37.20/tonne in the area tested so far.*
>
> *If it were to cost $25/tonne to extract and process this material, it would have a net value of 3 x (37.2-25) = $36 million or $0.69 for each of the 53.3 million shares outstanding.*
>
> *Admittedly, this figure is before any allowance for taxes and capital costs. However, it gives an idea of Nuinsco's sensitivity to any future discoveries (noting that only about 15% of the anomaly has been tested so far and, geologically, it appears likely that Nuinsco will discover more of this material as it drills further to the south).*
>
> *I also note that Nuinsco has a fully-funded, well-planned program for exploration of the rest of this anomaly. Accordingly, I have a "Speculative Buy" recommendation on the shares of Nuinsco.*

But the next twenty holes, which Mr. Hume published on April 26, 1999, were duds. In his press release, Mr. Hume commented that he was "encouraged by the drilling results," but that efforts to trace the mineralized zone had been "complicated by faulting ... that truncates the massive sulphide mineralization."

June 2, 1999

Twenty-one more holes. All duds. Mr. Hume remained "encouraged by the drill program." I recalled that Donny once told me, "When the company says it 'remains encouraged by' its property, it's time to sell!" With Nuinsco's shares at $0.58, I sadly told our morning meeting that the Lac Rocher play had been a losing gamble. Whoever had been selling his shares in the second half of March had been right in his assessment of the property, and I had been wrong.

Nuinsco continued to explore Lac Rocher but, by the end of 2000, even Doug Hume conceded that it was probably a lost cause. I meet him on November 30, 2000, and ask him why he thought that the Lac Rocher discovery was such a disappointment. Had the mineralization been cut off by erosion? Faulting? Or was it never more than just a little pod?

"We have no idea, Ray. Tony Naldrett's a nickel expert. I think you know him?" I nod. "The Quebec Government hired him last summer to look at it, but he can't explain it. Western Mining out of Australia, Falconbridge, Inco — they've all looked at it and can't explain why the deposit was so small. We hope we'll be able to use Inco's new geophysical exploration technology, which is proving so successful for them at Sudbury, to find an answer. I'm very optimistic on the prospects of further nickel discoveries in the Lac Rocher area, and Inco's technology would be the best way to make those discoveries."

I shake my head. "I'm not sure you'll be able to, Doug. Inco's Vice-President of Exploration made a comment on that at Inco's analysts' conference yesterday. He said that 'Inco does not own exploration technology. It is not our business. Owning exploration technology ultimately destroys value.' This is pretty cryptic, but presumably he meant that Inco does not want to rent out or license its exploration techniques."

I walk out into a cold, grey evening, wondering if I'd learned anything from the Lac Rocher play.

I decide that I hadn't.

A set of tools I use for judging exploration plays is "the four P's" — Property, People, Politics, and Pricing.

Property: does the geology suggest that the property could host a significant ore deposit?

People: are the people running the show credible and scrupulous, and are they competent technically, in their ability to promote their story to investors and in their ability to fund continuing exploration?

Politics: is the project likely to be sidelined by lawsuits, or by government action — or inaction?

Pricing: is there room for an investor to make money, or is the stock priced as if the company had already discovered significantly more mineralization than it has found so far?

Nuinsco's Lac Rocher play had passed these tests, and while the tests reduced the chance that an investor would lose money, they were no guarantee of success.

And I reflect back on Voisey's Bay. Voisey's also had its disappointments. The geology of Voisey's Bay is similar to that of other nickel deposits, such as those of Noril'sk, but Voisey's Bay has thus far failed to show any sign of the rich concentrations of platinum group metals found elsewhere. And the "big dollar sign" at Voisey's had promised much but delivered little.

CHAPTER 28

A CHALLENGE FROM NEW CALEDONIA: TROPICAL NICKEL

Few men who come to the islands leave them. ... No part of the world exerts the same attractive power upon the visitor, and the task before me is to communicate to fireside travellers some sense of its seduction ...
— *In the South Seas*, Robert Louis Stevenson, 1908

Both Inco and its scrappy crosstown rival, Falconbridge Limited, sponsored the construction of "Science North," a hands-on gee-whiz display case for science and architecture in Sudbury, Ontario.

In front of the entrance to Science North are two parabolic reflectors facing each other, like a giant pair of headphones. If you stand on a little platform and whisper into the focal point of one of the reflectors, your words are spread out, reflected across the parking lot, and reassembled by the other reflector. A confederate with his ear at the other reflector's focal point can hear you clearly.

In late April 2000, 22 mining analysts from the northeastern corner of North America spread out on trajectories which converged on the other side of the globe. All of us took different routes. Most of the Canadians flew west. The Americans preferred to fly east, through Europe, reasoning that they had tailwinds all the way. Nevertheless, each of us took more than thirty hours to reach the focal point: Makassar, which is on Sulawesi, a swastika-shaped island in the middle of Indonesia. A twenty-third analyst, Joanne Warner, joined us from Sydney, Australia. Our host was Inco, which had invited us to see its nickel mining properties in Indonesia and New Caledonia.

Inco Comes to Labrador

Inco chartered a plane to take us from Makassar to Soroako, the home of Inco's 59%-owned subsidiary, PT Inco. From Makassar, on the southwestern arm of the Sulawesi swastika, we fly across damply reflective paddies, open ocean, and then thick forest, which looks like very dark green broccoli. Then, gashes of orange-brown soil, converging plumes of dirty grey steam from a bank of chimneys mounted on a fortress-like industrial plant, and a hint of shimmering silver lake. Welcome to Soroako, 550 metres above sea level.

The pilot seems pleased with our uneventful arrival. "We weren't sure the strip could take a plane this big, so yesterday we flew this plane here for the first time, just for practice."

In claustrophobic bunkhouses, we pay down part of our sleep deficits, then dress for dinner. Airy dining room, inspired by local architecture; exquisite entertainment from Sulawesi dancers and musicians. Our turn. Our turn? For what? Entertainment? Analyst John Redstone steps up and leads a small group of his colleagues in a stirring interpretation of that cherished Canadian folk song "Can't buy me love."

"Just when I could use a beer," he sighs afterwards in his world-weary English accent, "I find there isn't any." A reminder that most of PT Inco's employees are Muslim.

PT Inco produces a black, sandy material called nickel matte, which the company sends to Japan for further processing. The day after our arrival, we follow the beginning of the matte's path to market. It travels by truck down a mountain road to a river port, then onto barges and out to ocean-going vessels moored a dozen kilometres offshore in the shallow waters of Usu Bay. At the port, pale, jet-lagged analysts shamble into the back of a boat for a trip down the river. Our boat slows to cut its wake as we pass canoes precariously loaded with bundles of leaves to be used as roofing material, and propelled by smiling, waving paddlers.

Despite the awkwardness of getting its product to market, PT Inco is one of the world's most efficient producers of nickel. Just as high electricity prices had helped to kill Inco's interest in constructing a nickel smelter at Argentia, Newfoundland, the prospect of cheap power was one of the reasons that attracted Inco to Sulawesi. The company's own dams generate electricity at a cost of only 0.2 U.S.

cents per kilowatt-hour, and this electricity fires the furnaces that process Soroako's ore. After driving us back up into the mountains, Inco shows off its dams by treating us to lunch atop one of them. I'm grateful that someone had thought to supply tents: it is raining seriously. We speculate that Inco had arranged the rains to dispel concerns about the water shortage that had plagued PT Inco's operations for the preceding two years.

"Ray, when did you first become aware of the Goro project?" asks Harry, who has to shout to be heard above the sound of rain on canvas. He sports a gaudy, slightly damp Indonesian silk shirt thoughtfully provided by PT Inco.

Goro is the next part of our South Seas tour, a site in southern New Caledonia where Inco is contemplating the construction of a nickel mine and a hydrometallurgical processing plant. I finish masticating a spicy skewered piece of chicken, um and er, and admit that it seemed to have been there in the background for some years and I'd only really noticed when the Voisey's Bay negotiations were going badly.

"I remember speculating, oh, last August," I say, "that the development of the Australian nickel laterite projects might worry Inco that it was being left behind by new technological advances in hydromet. I thought that Inco might respond by devoting more attention to developing hydromet plants at its own nickel laterite projects here in Indonesia and at Goro. So the result could be Voisey's Bay being temporarily sidelined."

"Have you ever been to New Caledonia?"

"No, this will be my first trip. When I was growing up in New Zealand, a trip to New Caledonia was the rather dubious prize for taking French in the Sixth Form. New Caledonia was a sort of ersatz Paris, only with worse political problems, a few hours' flight away. I never did French in the Sixth Form, but the kids who went there seemed impressed by only three things: they drove on the wrong side of the road; their miles were shorter than ours; and everything was covered in red dust!"

"Did you see this?" he asks, pulling a crinkled and slightly damp newspaper clipping from his bag: *The Toronto Star*, April 18, 2000. I confess that when I read the *Star*, it is only on Saturdays, and for the comics.

"Let's see," I say, adjusting my glasses. "'Tobin-free zone ... Inco's Goro site on New Caledonia is a safe haven from the many trials of developing a nickel mine in Canada.' Gosh, Harry, 'safe haven'? New Caledonia was on the brink of civil war in the mid-1980s."

"Read the rest, Ray."

"'Peter Garritsen, President of Inco's Goro Nickel Co., says, "We don't have to worry about icebergs"' ... referring not so much to [Newfoundland's Premier Brian] Tobin as to the geographical benefits of the new project. ... Once Goro gets the green light, it means Inco will have to wait until at least 2006 to bring Voisey's Bay on-line because it would want to avoid a nickel glut that would drive down prices.'"

"Not to mention ruining its balance sheet," adds Harry.

As the rain roars, I reflect that Mr. Tobin must believe that Toronto has a cruel fascination with skewering him. The *Star* article, which unfavourably compares Newfoundland with a colonial jurisdiction where whites and Melanesian natives had been slaughtering each other only a dozen years earlier, has followed hard on the heels of Seymour Schulich's attacks.

A dash through the warm rain back to the bus and on to Soroako for a tour of PT Inco's mines. In shallow open pits, trucks and shovels move gingerly over pads of crunchy slag, placed to prevent them from bogging down in the slippery, slick, red ore.

I put a question to Ted Hodkin, PT Inco's Chief Operating Officer. "Ted, I understand that you have material here — limonite — a lot like that Inco proposes to mine at Goro. Your plant here can't take it. So, why not build a Goro-type here to treat it? Admittedly, it seems to be lower grade — I've heard 1.35% nickel versus 1.6% at Goro — but you have a lot of sunk costs and cheap electricity here. Why not build a plant here instead of Goro?"

"You're right, if we didn't have Goro, by now we probably would have begun work on the limonite here," says Mr. Hodkin. "But the main reason for choosing Goro limonite over Soroako limonite is political diversification — spreading the risk."

"Speaking of political risks," asks Harry, "Indonesia has been through a lot of civil unrest lately. Any signs of it here?"

A pause. "No."

And back in the bus for a tour of the Soroako townsite. In most Canadian mining communities, the mine manager lives in a big house on top of the hill, with the residences of lesser functionaries below. (Geologists, commonly viewed by engineers as the lunatic fringe of the mining industry, tend to seek homes in unlikely and secluded spots.) Soroako's houses are also topographically ordered, with the better class of houses also having the best views. Even so, in order to avoid any ambiguities, the class of the house you inhabit is emblazoned on the front: "A" — there's only one "A" — with "B," "C," and "D"-grade houses disposed on decreasingly attractive sites.

From Soroako, a charter back to Makassar; Makassar to Bali; Bali to Sydney; Sydney to Nouméa.

Nouméa, New Caledonia

In Nouméa, I rinse some of my clothes and, with some hesitation, hang them to dry on my hotel balcony, recalling my Sixth Form classmates' experience with nickel smelter dust. But, next morning, no discolouration! As we were to learn later, touring Eramet's facilities in Nouméa, the smelter has cut emissions of dust by more than 90% over the past ten years.

Dinner with Goro's Peter Garritsen. Fine French food, casual attire. Mr Garritsen claims that ties are forbidden on the island.

Mr. Garritsen is enthusiastic about what would probably be his last assignment of a long career in mining. One of his first challenges is to establish Inco's hiring policy. The labour situation in New Caledonia reminds me of that in Chile. The biggest mining companies in both countries — Eramet in New Caledonia and Codelco in Chile — were each, to some degree, controlled by their governments. Each dominated its industry. In Chile, Canada's Rio Algom decided that it could staff its Cerro Colorado project either with employees lured away from Codelco, or with mining virgins. The former would require much less training, but had the reputation of having been inculcated with the culture of a stifling bureaucracy. Furthermore, would it be a good idea to piss off Codelco? In the end, Rio Algom decided it would not be a good idea to piss off Codelco, and hired and trained its own fresh young people. Mr. Garritsen, noting that Goro had, per-

Inco Comes to Labrador

haps, a 100-year mine life, had made a similar decision with respect to Goro.

I bring up the topic of Brian Tobin. Mr. Garritsen points out that one of Mr. Tobin's most recent set of demands was for Inco to guarantee that, whatever processing technology it chose to apply to Voisey's Bay ore, it would work.

"I don't think I've ever seen a new technology applied to mining which *did* work right the first time," I reply.

"Yes, that's why we think the attitude of the government here is much more reasonable. We hope to produce 54,000 tonnes of nickel per year using somewhat novel technology. But, rather than sign any guarantee that it's going to work, we're spending US$50 million on a pilot plant that can produce at a 54-tonne-per-year rate and, if that works out OK — and, so far, it *is* working out OK — we'll scale up from there, learning as we go.

"Right now," he continues, "we own 85% of the project — the French government has the rest — and it looks as though the whole thing will cost about US$1.3 billion, so we'd like another partner to share the risk."

Next morning, mining analysts meander over the beach outside our hotel, a beach whose uninhibited dress code brightens a feature in the current issue of *National Geographic*. Male eyes dart from side to side, seeking undressed women. But it is only 7:30. Spot the Englishman in the tropics: John Redstone in a beige trench coat, muttering, "Just my luck, all the toplesses are still asleep. I bet just as soon as I've gone the beach will be covered with them."

And on to Club Med's dock to board the *Mary D Princess*, chartered by Inco. Spot Goldie, would-be diver, dragging mask, fins, and wetsuit.

"One of our plans is to buy a catamaran to take our employees from Nouméa to the project," explains Maurice Solar of Inco.

"How long a commute would that be?"

"About an hour. And you could fish on the way!"

Arrive at Goro's dock, bus to the pilot plant. Lots of pipes, tubes, and tanks. Very exotic plumbing: in places they use titanium-rhodium alloys. Observing that rhodium is trading at around US$1,600 per ounce, one of the analysts asks if there was any scrap tubing around so that he can one-up his friends with a set of titanium-rhodium golf clubs.

Then off to see the nickel deposits. There's a prevalent myth among Canadian geologists that Mother Nature put all the good ore bodies at the bottom of bogs. It's true at Voisey's Bay and it's true at Goro, so the best vehicle for a quick overview of Goro is a helicopter. As we swirl over the future mining fields, we are unaware that the bogs conceal some nasty problems, which will cause a crisis two and a half years in the future.

Geology explains why nickel laterites favour flat, swampy areas. Nickel laterites are soft, crumbly deposits formed by weathering. Areas which have been recently uplifted to form ridges, or that have been incised by streams to form valleys, are likely to have lost, to erosion, their cover of weathered rocks. Old, deeply weathered rocks are best preserved in flat-lying, uneroded areas.

Back on board the *Princess* for a leisurely return to Nouméa.

"How leisurely? Leisurely enough that I can go diving along the way?"

"No, Ray. There have been shark attacks in the lagoon lately. Our insurance policy's a bit tight. Go dive on your own time, not ours."

Falconbridge Limited also has a nickel project, Koniambo, in New Caledonia. When Falconbridge heard of the Inco trip, its management, perhaps under pressure from some of the analysts participating in the Inco tour, invited us to spend a day looking at Koniambo project.

The current owner of the Koniambo deposit is SMSP, a corporation majority-owned by the North Province. In order to earn a 49% interest in Koniambo, Falconbridge is obliged, by January 1, 2006, to make a commitment to developing the mine and to build a smelter. SMSP would own the remaining 51% of Koniambo.

SMSP, one of the world's largest miners of laterite nickel ore, has no processing facilities and sells all of its ore to third parties. This situation makes SMSP's future uncertain. I suspect that SMSP sees Falconbridge as its key to realizing a long-held ambition of owning its own smelter.

Our day with Falconbridge, May 6, 2000, starts with a one-hour flight up New Caledonia's mountainous spine. I chat with my seatmate, a charming lady who is to act as translator between English and French. We land in tiny Koné, the newly established capital of the

North Province. Our group files into the provincial legislature. Clean lines and exposed wood create a modern expression of a traditional Melanesian meeting place.

The meeting in the legislature, café et croissants, is well-attended for a Saturday morning. Most noticeable are the Melanesian politicians: large and physically impressive, with the slightly uncertain air of those who had been struggling outside the system for years. Their demeanour reminds me of press descriptions of the legislature of Canada's Nunavut Territory during its early days.

We keep Madame Translator busy. The Falconbridge people speak. Representatives of local, provincial, and French governments speak, all indicating their warm support for the project. Then it is the turn of Raphael Pidjot, a Melanesian activist who has become President of SMSP. The General Manager of SMSP, Jean-Pierre Lapous, follows.

Like many of Canada's government-owned corporations, SMSP appears to suffer from mild schizophrenia. It has a mandate both to make profits and to act as a force for social good. Thus, Mr. Pidjot refers several times to "rééquilibrage," a process whereby Falconbridge is to help North Province to obtain its fair share of New Caledonia's economic activity.

Falconbridge whisks us away for a helicopter tour. As we rise above Koné, to seaward we can see mangrove swamps, then a lagoon with a wharf, which is served by a narrow channel cut into the fringing reef. We turn inland and fly up valleys choked with waste rock from small mines last worked in the 1940s, and across the fairy forest on the top of Koniambo massif, touching down in one of the old pits for a geology lesson.

Back to Koné for lunch in the hotel's restaurant. The local politicians and Messrs. Pidjot and Lapous continue to express their great enthusiasm about having found a rich partner to develop their "treasure." Local TV crews draw aside some of the analysts. I ask Harry about his interview.

"They wanted to know why we were here, and it was kinda difficult to explain that we were in New Caledonia essentially because Inco had invited us. I got the impression that they thought we are international bankers with big cheques in our pockets."

The restaurant is hot and the meal and speeches endless. My colleagues begin to drift outside in search of fresh air. I eventually join them. We agree that the people of North Province want this project. They want it very much. We worry that they want it too much.

On the flight back to Nouméa, I sketch out in my head what I would put in my fax to Donny, to be read at our morning meeting.

I was impressed by Inco's Goro project. The first results of the pilot plant at Goro have been encouraging. Inco seems committed to the project and expects commercial production in 2005. Inco's current estimate of Goro's capital cost is US$1.3 billion (which I think is more likely to be exceeded than to fall short). Hence, even if Inco were to be successful in its search for another partner, Inco's balance sheet may not support simultaneous development of both Goro and Voisey's Bay.

That implies to me that Voisey's Bay shares (N.V.; $7.10) are still overpriced.

Saturday, in the North Province's provincial assembly, Falconbridge met with local, provincial, and national politicians and with the visiting analysts. Falconbridge gave the impression that it was already committed to developing the Koniambo project. (The project manager, seconded from Falconbridge, has been quoted by a local newspaper as saying "the question is not 'if' but 'when.'") The politicians seemed to have great expectations of the project. As a provincial official said, "We've set our hopes on this project to allow our people to live decently."

Under the current set of agreements, Falconbridge must commit to build a 54,000-tonne/year nickel pyrometallurgical plant by January 1, 2006, or lose Koniambo. This concerns me, because it forces Falconbridge into a timetable, a technology, and a plant size which may not be optimal.

Falconbridge's presentation reminded me of Inco's press conference in St. John's, Newfoundland, a few years ago, at which Inco announced it would build a smelter at Argentia.

I conclude that investors should switch from Falconbridge to Inco.[268]

In hindsight, the switch recommendation was a good one. The shares of Inco and Falconbridge both went up in the week following our visit to New Caledonia, but Inco's shares went up more.

The day after our trip to Koniambo, most of the group flies out. I say goodbye to John Redstone in the lobby. "Ray, I'm a little peed off," he says. "This month's article on New Caledonia in *The National Geographic* talks about the glamorous champagne life, and all I experienced was an empty beach and the Japanese tourist in the room next to me throwing up all night. So much for the bloody glamorous high life. I suppose as soon as I've gone the toplesses will all come out serving champagne." Still in his trench coat, he clambers into a taxi muttering. "All the airline connections on this trip have gone perfectly so far. Mark my words. Something will go wrong before it's over."

Four or five of those of us who remain take Inco's advice and go scuba diving on our own time. No sharks, but lionfish, rays, and turtles compensate. Not to mention that, now that Mr. Redstone has gone, the beach is covered with undressed women.

```
email
From: John Redstone, Scotia Capital, Montreal
To: Raymond Goldie
June 6, 2000


"Life styles of the rich and famous"

Not only did our little jaunt to bare boobs land
turn out as I predicted but my other fearless
forecast that "something will go wrong before my
trip ends" was eerily precise.

After wandering through Western Australia (no sign
of any kangaroos), and chasing around Hong Kong and
Tokyo (the latest fad in the Ginza — Italian Food
!!! "Oh Redstone san please to try lasagna"), I
found myself in Toronto (after a 12 hour flight)
awaiting the final take off for Montreal. They had
closed the door and pulled away from the gate — all
systems go. Then came the ominous announcement:
"Eh, ladies and gentlemen there is a small storm
approaching the airport, we will have to wait until
```

it clears before taking off." Well, that "small storm" turned out to be the mother of all thunderstorms and did not finish until 1:30 a.m. (by which time I was sitting in a bar listening to a young woman tell me how she could only be satisfied by two men at the same time !!). Regardless of the erotic talk, I slept on the benches of Terminal 2 Toronto and made it back to Montreal the next day, a much chastened traveler. If only I could predict the copper price with such accuracy!!

email
From: Raymond Goldie
Sent: Tuesday, November 21, 2000 01:43
To: Joanne Warner, Portfolio Manager, Global Resources, Colonial First State Fund Managers, Sydney

Dear Joanne:

I recently heard from an Inco employee in Toronto that, only a few weeks before our tour, some laid-off PT Inco employees had held senior managers hostage at Soroako.

Ray

From: Warner, Joanne
Sent: Tuesday, November 21, 2000 2:21 AM
To: Raymond Goldie

I heard something like that. It didn't seem good manners to go on about it at the time, but I'm told it made the local papers in Jakarta.

email
From: John Redstone, Scotia Capital, Montreal
To: Raymond Goldie
November 21, 2000

```
If it were not for our splendid rendition of
"Can't buy me love," the locals would never have
let our group go home.

Good luck with your book. Please have Pierce
Brosnan play me in the movie version.
```

— PLATTS METALS ALERT —

Helicopter crash off New Caledonia kills seven —
(AFP)—28Nov2000/137 a.m. EST/637 GMTT

A total of seven people were killed Tuesday when a helicopter crashed in a mountainous area of the French Pacific territory of New Caledonia, the high commissioner's office said. Security forces found the wreckage and the cause of the crash was under investigation, it said.

Four of the victims were officials from a major nickel mining firm in the territory including the chief executive, a company spokesman said. Raphael Pidjot, 40, head of the *SMSP* mining company, the firm's general manager [M. Lapous], technical director and finance director perished in the crash, which was initially attributed to bad weather. *SMSP* is the top exporter of nickel from New Caledonia, which has close to a third of the world reserves of the mineral.

December 18, 2002

Falconbridge's new chief executive officer, Aaron Regent, tells the Mineral Resource Analysts Group in Toronto that development of the Koniambo project has been slower than expected. And, as a result of the tragic loss of much of SMSP's senior management, Falconbridge has been obliged to take greater control of the project than it had originally expected.

CHAPTER 29

BUY ON MYSTERY — SELL ON HISTORY

In an efficient market, publicly available information cannot be used to generate abnormal investment profits. The authors find that the Toronto Stock Exchange may not be efficient in this sense. They show that stocks being accumulated by insiders generally outperform both stocks being sold by insiders, and the market as a whole. This is so even after this information has been standardized and distributed to the clients of a brokerage firm.
— Suret and Cormier, 1990

Remember, don't just follow the lone insider. If an insider says he is selling to pay for his daughter's wedding, no problem. ... But if six insiders tell you their daughters are getting married, the company may be in trouble.
— Amy Dunkin, *Business Week*, August 7, 1995

Humans are reluctant to concede that anything might be beyond their comprehension. The ancients responded to mysterious events by creating myths. Modern financial communities respond to mysterious events by creating rumours. An analyst's task in assessing rumours is not necessarily to uncover truth; it is to attempt to anticipate the effects of those rumours on share prices.

May 24, 2000

"I've updated my valuation of Inco's VBN shares," I tell the morning meeting. "Because the Goro project now looks more attractive than Voisey's, Inco is likely to keep Voisey's on the back burner. If

Inco were to delay the start-up of Voisey's Bay until 2008, the VBN's would have a net asset value of only $2.95 per share. I'm changing my recommendation on them from "'Reduce' to an outright 'Sell.'"

August 9, 2000

"Hey, Goldie!" Donny the trader, peering at his screen, vigorously chewing what I hope is gum. "Still have a fucking sell recommendation on Inco's VBN shares?"

"Yessir."

"Then why are they up so fucking much — $8.55 bid? Could've bought them for $7.45 a week ago."

When in doubt, ask a question. "Well, you're closer to the clients than I am, Donny. What are you hearing?"

Donny begins to pace back and forth. "I'm hearing that Seymour Schulich has sold his shares to Inco."

Seymour Schulich is Chairman of Franco-Nevada, a canny company that focuses on buying resource royalties. It has become the largest shareholder of the VBN shares, holding 9.576 million shares, 37% of those outstanding. (A royalty interest in an operation is the right to receive a small proportion, typically a figure like 3%, of the revenues from that operation. Since revenues are the top line on an income statement, a royalty interest is often called "a little bit off the top." The VBN shares, however, represented an interest not in the revenues thrown off by Voisey's Bay, but in the amount of cash it generated, after expenses.)

"I'll get back to you, Donny — my phone is ringing."

"Hi, Ray, it's Nancy." Nancy Walsh, CBC Radio, St. John's, Newfoundland.

"Hi, Nancy!"

"What are you hearing about Voisey's Bay?"

"Ah, yes, the VBN shares are having a good day, aren't they?" I say, scrambling to pull up the right screen on my computer in order to verify what Donny has just told me. "Um, the rumour on Bay Street is that Franco-Nevada, their biggest shareholder, has just sold them back to Inco."

"Now why would they do that?"

"If they've done it, it could be partly because of the dividend. When they bought those shares, one of the reasons was that the dividend on the VBN shares was almost as good as the yield on government treasury bills. But sometime last year[269] Inco stopped payment of dividends."

"Do you think there's any truth to the rumour?"

"Well, I know one way to find out. Franco-Nevada is an insider of both Inco and the Class VBN shares, so if they *have* sold, they'll have to report it to the Ontario Securities Commission within ten days of the end of whatever month they sold them in. The O.S.C. would take a week or two to publish this report, so I guess we'll know for sure by the end of September."

"The end of September? Ray, I have to file a story in less than an hour. Anyway, the rumour down here is that Inco and the government have resumed talks."

"Hmm. I'll get back to you, Nancy! Have to jump."

I hope that Sandra Scott is in town. She isn't, but Stuart Feiner, Inco's General Counsel, is.

"Stuart, we've heard a couple of rumours about Voisey's."

Silence.

"One was that the VBN shares are up because Franco has sold its block to you. "The other is that you've started talks with Mr. Tobin again."

Chuckle. "No truth to either rumour, Ray. And there is a third rumour."

"Oh, what's that?"

"That a third party is interested in buying all of the VBN shares, thereby gaining control of the Voisey's Bay project."

"Which is surely incorrect."

"It's certainly incorrect. The only influence anyone could obtain even by buying all of the VBN shares would be the right to name two members of Inco's Board of Directors."

"Right away?"

"It's on the expiry of the terms of the two directors nominated by VBN's shareholders. ... Let me check ... those terms expire in April 2002."

"Thanks, Stuart!"

The next time the phone rings, it is Liz to tell me that the "real new rumour" is that Brian Tobin will be stepping down as premier and going back into federal politics. A new premier would be unlikely to be as much an obstruction to Voisey's as was Mr. Tobin.

"That's quite a story," I say. "Let me think about it for a minute. Yes, there has been speculation in St. John's that Mr. Tobin might be reluctant to face the next provincial election against either of two likely contenders to be leader of the opposition [Danny Williams and Vic Young], and I'll concede that Mr. Tobin gives the appearance of grooming Paul Dicks as a successor.

"Let's assume your rumour is true, Liz. Would it make it any easier for Inco to cut a deal with the Newfoundland government? Hmm. Mr. Dicks, the Minister of Mines and Energy, appears to be committed to Mr. Tobin's tough stance against Inco. In fact, there are rumours that one of the reasons Mr. Dicks got the job in Mines was that his predecessor, Roger Grimes, may have been too willing to compromise with Inco. And, because Mr. Dicks appears to be less personally popular than Mr. Tobin, I think that a Premier Dicks would be unlikely to begin his administration by overturning popular policies ... and Mr. Tobin's stance on Voisey's *is* a popular one."

"Maybe, if Tobin were to step down, he wouldn't be able to impose Mr. Dicks on the province, Ray."

"Well, even if Tobin steps down and someone other than Paul Dicks takes his place, a lot of the pressure on the government to do a deal with Inco has dissipated. A smelter at Argentia would've been an ideal task for the guys who built the Hibernia oil platform just across the peninsula from Argentia. Now that Hibernia's built, and the crew has dispersed, the pressure's off. Not only that, but oil and tourism are starting to bring in big bucks."

Later, I am talking with Harry about the Mineral Resource Analysts group. Harry mentions Voisey's Bay. "Ray, you got the wrong rumour. The real reason VBN's shares ran up is that the Government of Newfoundland bought Franco-Nevada's block. How did you miss that?"

Back to the trading desk.

"Donny?"

"Yes, Ray."

"I really can't explain the rise in VBN's share price. But I still think that the ultimate block to development of Voisey's Bay won't be the government. It is more likely to be the native groups. I'm going to keep telling our clients to switch from the VBN's to Inco's common shares."

"OK, but the tape [i.e. the movement in the stock price] is telling us fucking something."

"It is, Donny, but I don't know what!"

August 23, 2000

CBC Radio News, St. John's, Newfoundland:

Rumours about Premier Brian Tobin's future have been circulating around Bay Street recently. The people picking up on the rumours aren't interested in where Tobin may be going ... just as long as he goes. Some investors see Newfoundland's premier as an impediment to development of the Voisey's Bay project. So, rumours of his imminent departure from politics may have driven up the value of Voisey's Bay shares on the stock market.

August 31, 2000

Inco's VBN shares close at $8.75, up $1.30 since the end of July.

September 6, 2000

INCO PRESS RELEASE

Inco Limited (Inco) announced today that, subject to certain conditions, it intends to make an issuer bid, in accordance with applicable regulatory requirements, to purchase all of its outstanding Class VBN Shares.

> The consideration to be paid by Inco for each Class VBN share under the issuer bid will consist of Cdn$7.50 in cash (or at the holder's option the equivalent in U.S. dollars) and a fraction, 0.45, of an Inco Common Share purchase warrant. The Class VBN Share price has averaged on a weighted basis Cdn$8.06 per share on the Toronto Stock Exchange over the past thirty trading days. ... Said Scott Hand, Inco's President ... "Given the nature of the Class VBN Shares, situations concerning the development of Voisey's Bay could create potential conflicts between the financial interests of the Class VBN holders and our other shareholders. The retirement of this Class will eliminate these potential conflicts, simplify our capital structure, and maximize our strategic options."

"You're right, Donny, the tape *was* telling us something ..."
"You're fucking right!"
"You know, Donny, if the word 'fuck' didn't exist, you'd be a mute!"
"Hey, I'm an emotional kinda guy!"

Unlike the situation on January 11, 2000, when Inco's Class VBN shares plunged several hours before Inco announced the failure of its talks with the Government of Newfoundland and Labrador, there was no indication that the Toronto Stock Exchange was examining trading in the VBN shares.[270]

October 5, 2000

Inco's VBN shares close at $10.50, following a Canada Newswire story that reports that "angry investors, calling Inco's surprise buyback of its Voisey's Bay Nickel (VBN) class shares 'unfair,' are opposing the tender."

I think that Inco's offer is the best that shareholders could expect and, the next morning, I publish a comment advising investors to "take the money and run."

I subsequently receive an email, evidently from one of the "angry investors" described by Canada Newswire.

email
From: Mitchell L. Shnier
[mailto:ssch@idirect.com]
Sent: Saturday October 20 2000 12:44 AM
To: rgoldie@firstassociates.com
Subject: Inco Voisey's Bay
Importance: High

Dear Mr. Goldie:
Having seen you quoted a number times regarding Inco's attempted purchase of the outstanding shares of Voisey's Bay class shares, I must ask you who are you working for. Surely not investors, as your remarks are anything but misleading. An example would be that the expire of 2006 represents the loss of VB shares 80% portion of Inco common dividend, not as you mislead, the entire interest to the VB holdings. In 2006 Inco has the option to convert these shares at a 20% premium. Those are all facts, your quotes do not relate this information or the reporter who wrote this information should be corrected. I frankly do not know who you represent, but while your welcome to your opinion I doubt you have enough facts to make judgment. Do you know how much ore exists, no, Inco has not provided shareholders with any information. Why has Inco left these assets at cost on their books, suggesting each time there is no need for a write down yet they expect to pay out the outstanding shares at a 75% discount, have you asked them. Lastly the dividend we hopefully can agree on will be returning to Inco shareholders within the next year, a dramatic support to all Inco shares. With respect to developing VB, challenges yes, years away maybe. With such value already accounted for, a dividend while we wait and Inco having to pay a premium to the common, why would one sell based on a poor offer of price and warrant. At Inco's present price using your 2008, with 2006 option and the 20% premium with dividend for a few years what are you talking about, the value is far greater than 7 bucks and warrant that will be worthless.

```
    If you are to be in a future article, I sug-
gest you represent all the facts. If you intend
to mislead I will raise a complaint with the
O.S.C. regarding you and your firm.

    Sincerely,
    Mitchell Shnier
```

Copy to our firm's counsel, copy to my file, no reply.

I brood for a few weeks — not on Mr. Shnier's email, but on the fact that my "sell" recommendation on Voisey's Bay shares in August 2000 had been wrong.

Keith Ambachtsheer's "simple process" hadn't warned me that Inco was about to buy back the VBN shares, nor that Inco would be willing to pay a premium price in order to eliminate what it saw as potential conflicts of interest. In fact, my estimate of the discounted value of the VBN shares had been only about $3.00 per share.

However, I recall that Keith's tastes in valuation methods were eclectic, and that he had introduced me to another stock-picking technique, a technique that might have allowed me to anticipate what was going to happen to the VBN shares: analysis of insider trading.

Donny had eloquently hinted at one form of insider trading, trading based on information that has not been released to the public. Such trading is illegal. However, a second form of insider trading is both legal and useful to ordinary investors.

December 2000

Inco's VBN shares trade for the last time, at $10.70.

Summer 1978

Keith Ambachtsheer pokes his head into my office. "Ray, can you come into the boardroom for a minute?"

"Certainly, Keith."

"Ray. I'd like you to meet David Fowler, from McGill." A dapper man stands there, hand extended.

"Pleased to meet you, Professor Fowler."

"Pleased to meet you, Ray." English, I think. As I discover later, English accent, yes, but born in Argentina.

"Ray," says Keith, "we've been funding some work David's been doing on insider trading. His results so far are interesting, and we'd like to use this work to help our clients pick stocks. That is, we'd like *you* to use David's work — and before he completes his study, since we're paying for it, is there anything you'd like him to look at more closely?"

My face expresses my surprise.

"Don't worry, Ray, trading by insiders is perfectly legal as long as they don't trade on specific information before it has been made public," explains David. "Since 1967, insiders have had to report their trades on the Toronto Stock Exchange to the Ontario Securities Commission. My colleague, Harvey Rorke, and some students have been braving the dusty archives of the Commission gathering information so that we can evaluate the performance of stocks after the publication of those reports."

"Actually, my surprise was, Keith, that you've always been such a staunch advocate of disciplined fundamental analysis. This seems so ... arbitrary ... superficial."

"Well, Ray, two totally unrelated valuation techniques — if they work — are worth more than two different, fundamental techniques, if only because fundamental techniques that look different often turn out to be capturing much the same information."

I turn to David. "Professor Fowler, Keith said 'if they both work.' Does insider trading 'work'? Surely, if markets are efficient, by the time the insider reports are published, whatever information they contain will already be reflected in the stock price?"

"We think that markets are *almost* efficient," gently interjects Keith.

"Ray, does insider trading 'work'?" says David. "The answer is a very clear 'yes' ... subject to some qualifications. Which surprised me as I started this study with the idea that I'd find what you just said — you know, 'by the time the reports are published, they're reflected in the stock price.'"

"What are the qualifications?"

"Well, some insider trading activity has no predictive value. Here's what doesn't count." He hands me a sheet of paper.

> ... trades in securities other than common stocks, less than board lot [i.e. 100 shares] trades, trades which occurred more than two months before release of the Ontario Securities Commission Bulletin in which the trade was published, purchases for employee profit-sharing plans, purchases by the company for a retirement plan, gifts, bequests or inheritances, exchange or conversions, rights exercises, initial reports, internal transfers, qualifying shares, redemptions, stock dividends, splits, and distributions.

"After eliminating these trades, what we did in our study — well, what two students did for us — was to count the numbers of insiders buying and selling in each month. If there were more buyers than sellers, we recorded a 'Buy' signal. If sellers exceeded buyers, we recorded a 'Sell' signal. The size of the transaction doesn't seem to matter. If the fellow with the green eyeshade is buying a hundred shares, it's just as strong a signal as the Chairman buying 100,000. We count noses, not stocks."

Some weeks later, I call David at his office at McGill. "David, Keith has given me a paper by a teacher at Ecole Polytechnique, across the mountain from you. This fellow, Roger Morin, concluded that the Canadian stock market is really two stock markets: one for the shares of mining and oil — resource — companies, and another market for the shares of non-resource companies."

"Right."

"I think that the reason for the existence of this division is that the market for Canadian non-resource stocks is largely domestic, whereas resource stocks generate strong interest by foreign investors. Anyway, would you be able to split your results into those two groups?"

A pause, a slight aspiration of breath. "Very well, I'll mail you a list of stocks and you tell me which you consider to be mining and oil stocks and which you consider to be non-resource stocks."

Several months later, David sends us the results of his split study. In the six months following the Ontario Securities Commission's publication of insider trades, he calculated the following average rates of return:

Average returns (% per annum) gained through dividends and price appreciation

	Resource stocks	Non-resource stocks
Stocks receiving "Buy" signals	7.4	13.7
Stocks receiving no signals	2.8	4.0
Stocks receiving "Sell" signals	6.8	-4.2

The biggest surprise is that resource stocks went up in price after they had received "Sell" signals. I scratch my head and conclude that, perhaps, resource insiders underestimate the persistence of public sentiment when it turns in favour of investing in the companies of which they are insiders.

As I make preparations to begin publishing a monthly report on insider trading as a means of picking stocks, another pair of researchers, Messrs. Baesel and Stein of York University, release the results of their own investigation of the predictive value of insider trading in Canada. These two researchers wanted to find out not only if insiders did better on their investments than non-insiders, but also whether those insiders who belonged to "the Canadian Corporate Elite" are better investors than ordinary insiders. In terms of Fowler and Rorke's dictum of counting noses, not stocks, Baesel and Stein wished to know if some noses were worth more than others.

Baesel and Stein decided that the best definition of Canada's corporate elite was that it comprised the directors of Canada's major chartered banks. Baesel and Stein found that, in the twelve months following their trades, insiders who were also bank directors tended to beat the market by an average of 7.8%; "ordinary" insiders beat the market by an average of 3.8%. Thus, bank directors appear to do twice as well on their trades as ordinary insiders.

"How's RITA coming along, Ray?" Keith likes cute acronyms, and RITA stands for "Report on Insider Trading Activity."

"Fine, Keith. I'm combining both Fowler and Rorke's and Baesel and Stein's studies into a scoring scheme. Here's what I've come up with."

In any one month, give a stock +1 if more "ordinary" insiders are buying than selling, -1 if more "ordinary" insiders are selling than buying and zero if equal numbers of "ordinary" insiders are buying and selling. To this score add a bonus of +2 if the number of insiders who are bank directors and who are also buying is greater than the number of bank directors who are selling. If the reverse is the case, subtract 2.

There are two exceptions to these rules:
(1) For resource stocks, "Sell" signals cannot be considered bearish, so don't count them. As a result, the scores for resource stocks should never be negative.
(2) In the financial services industry group, bank directors are treated as ordinary insiders and no bonus points are applied.

Then, average these scores over the most recent six months, putting the most weight on the most recent months, using what the accountants call the "sum-of-years-digits" — e.g. multiply the most recent month's score by 6, add the previous month's score multiplied by 5, then the previous month's score multiplied by four ... all the way to the score six months earlier, multiplied by one. Finally, divide the sum by 21 (i.e. 1+2+3+4+5+6), to give a Confidence Index, or "C.I." for each stock.

I look up.
"Keith, I wasn't sure I was right in ignoring sales by insiders of resource companies. David's results suggest that resource stocks *sold* by insiders do almost as well as stocks *bought* by insiders."

Keith pats my arm. "I think you're doing the right thing, Ray. It would be hard to tell our clients that they should be buying a stock because the insiders are selling it."

I produced RITA every month for the next sixteen years. The biggest boost to its reputation came in 1990 when two academics — Jean-Marc Suret and Elise Cormier of L'Université Laval — published a study that concluded that stocks, reported in RITA as having positive C.I.'s outperformed those with negative C.I.'s. I was gratified by this result.

In 1995, my boss took me aside and said, "Ray, you're a mining analyst. This insider trading shit is muddying your image and it's making it harder to market your work to investors. I suggest you stop it." Always sensitive to the finer nuances of the word "boss," I did.

But in September 2000, after Inco had announced that it was buying back the VBN shares, I wondered if insider trading could have provided an early warning. So I trudged across Yonge Street to the offices of Micromedia, the company that stores back issues of the Ontario Securities Commission's publications, and tested the patience of the clerk as I plowed through the O.S.C.'s weekly "Bulletins" with a pencil and a list of bank directors at hand.

I tabulated my results, and calculated the C.I.'s for all of the base metal mining stocks on the Toronto Stock Exchange in the six months before Inco's announcement. I found no purchases of VBN shares. (I did find, however, two sales by insiders in March 2000, suggesting that maybe there was something to Fowler and Rorke's discovery that insider selling of resource stocks was a positive indicator!)

One stock's C.I. did stand out: that of Rio Algom Ltd. Immediately before August 22, 2000, when Noranda launched a bid that began a takeover battle for Rio, Rio's C.I. was 0.76, the second highest of the fifteen base metals stocks I surveyed. And, in the following nine months, the seven stocks in this group with the highest C.I.'s rose, on average, by 57%, whereas the unweighted average rate of return on all fifteen stocks was 27%.

I concluded that insider trading can *often* help investors pick takeover candidates, but not in the case of the Inco VBN's.

And to return to Nancy's question — why would Franco-Nevada have sold its shares back to Inco (which is what eventually happened)?

In mid-2001, I called David Harquail, Senior Vice-President of Franco-Nevada, and asked him.

"Ray, including brokers' commissions, we paid an average of $8.43 for our VBN shares. Before Inco's offer, the shares were trading below our cost. Inco's offer allowed us to make a profit."

He sighed, "Diamond Fields, Falconbridge, and now Franco-Nevada have all made a profit out of Voisey's; so have Inco's management and directors. The only losers have been the holders of Inco's common shares, the taxpayers of Canada, and the thousands of good jobs that would have been created."

"Well, maybe, David, I should turn the question around. Why would Inco offer to buy back its VBN shares from Franco-Nevada — and other shareholders — at a premium price?"

"I was one of the two members of Inco's Board who was appointed by the holders of the VBN shares. To show you what I mean, imagine that one of Inco's competitors — say, Anglo-American — had offered to buy the entire Voisey's Bay project for, say, half of what Inco had paid to Diamond Fields. That would have been worth $14 per VBN share.

"If this proposal had been put to the ballot, I believe that the institutional shareholders would have voted in favour, to realize more immediate value out of the VBN shares. But the responsibility of the board is to all classes of shareholders. Keeping the project out of the hands of competitors is of value to the common shareholders but is clearly oppressive to VBN shareholders. The VBN buyout has resolved that conflict."

And, perhaps, it removed Seymour Schulich's desire to lecture the members of the government with whom Inco was attempting to negotiate.

October 16, 2000

News release, Government of Newfoundland and Labrador (Executive Council)

The following statement was issued by Premier Brian Tobin:

Good Afternoon Everyone,

Thank you for joining Jodean and I at this press conference this afternoon. I have just met with the cabinet and caucus of the Liberal Government of Newfoundland and Labrador. I have informed my colleagues, as I am now informing the people of this province, that today I have submitted my resignation as Premier of Newfoundland and Labrador to the Lieutenant-

Governor, Max House. In addition, I have further submitted my resignation both as leader of the Liberal Party of this province and as MHA for Straits-White Bay North to the President of the Liberal Party and to the Speaker of the House of Assembly respectively.

CHAPTER 30

GRIMES TAKES CHARGE

There was a time not long ago when you could walk around the old [U.S. naval air station at Argentia], look through the fog at the concrete stairs that led to nowhere, walk the edges of the empty foundations and see the crazy-quilt of broken glass in the doors on the front of the huge hangars. ... Time and place create strange situations. ... Argentia is on the edge of a plan to save a provincial political party ... it's Voisey's Bay nickel and the requirement that it be processed in this province that are on the table. It is a time to be careful. Of all of the possible places where the Grimes government can be seen to be taking charge, this is the spot where the provincial government's hands are most free, where the administration has the most possibility to effect change without having to depend on another government. The clock is ticking on the two years Roger Grimes has to prove himself, and he needs a deal with Inco in a way Brian Tobin never did. Dangerous times.
— Russell Wangersky, St. John's *Telegram*, March 13, 2001

I think it's great, in a number of ways, that Brian [Tobin] is going to Ottawa.
— Inco President Scott Hand, Inco Technology Conference, Sheridan Park, Ontario, November 29, 2000

October 26, 2000

Literary types, CBC veterans, Newfoundland professionals, and professional Newfoundlanders gather in the Great Hall of the University of Toronto's Hart House to celebrate the life and mourn the recent death of one of their own, Sandra Gwyn.

Professional Newfoundlander John Crosbie speaks admiringly of Ms. Gwyn's patronage of Newfoundland arts. "She took struggling painters, writers, and musicians under her wing and gave them a good boot in the arse." Mr. Crosbie then hits up two bank presidents for contributions to a foundation set up in honour of Ms. Gwyn.

After mummers have woken up the crowd, Pamela Morgan and Anita Best perform Ms. Gwyn's favourite song, "She's Like the Swallow." Then the noted introvert Mary Walsh bursts on stage, backlit by a video that roasts Newfoundland and Labrador's recently retired premier, Brian Tobin. Perhaps in his future political campaigns, she suggests, he could redeploy the slogan that he used when he ran for president of the Student Council at Memorial University of Newfoundland: "Every gram is a weighed gram." The audience laughs knowingly.

But Mr. Tobin is not in the audience. Soon after he resigned from both his post as premier and his seat in the provincial House of Assembly, the Prime Minister called a general election. On October 26, 2000, Brian Tobin is in Corner Brook, Newfoundland, campaigning to be elected as a Liberal to the federal House of Commons in Ottawa.

Mr. Tobin won his seat, the Liberals returned to power, and Prime Minister Chrétien appointed him to the Cabinet as Minister of Industry. Inco's management was delighted. The company's President, Scott Hand, said that he thought it was "great, in a number of ways, that Brian is going to Ottawa."[271]

I presumed that Mr. Hand was thinking that it was unlikely that Newfoundland and Labrador's next premier (who was to be chosen at a convention in early February 2001) would be as inflexible as Mr. Tobin; that as federal Industry minister, Mr. Tobin would probably champion Inco's application for federal funding for research and development of hydromet, and that Mr. Tobin might even be able to convince the federal government to change the equalization formula that had bedevilled Inco's negotiations with the government of Newfoundland.

Inco's management seemed to decide to send a signal to investors that it still believed that it would one day develop Voisey's Bay, but not on Mr. Tobin's terms, and that, while it waited, it was investigating the properties of Voisey's Bay ores.

On November 29, 2000, a grey Toronto day, Inco herds fund managers and financial analysts onto buses and drives us to the company's technology centre in the manicured wilds of Oakville. We split into small groups and enjoy the enthusiasm of scientists in white coats and safety glasses explaining the workings of tubes, pipes, and vessels, and the meanings of arcane computer displays and amazingly detailed microscopic images.

"We are working on a new hydrometallurgical process for the direct recovery of nickel, cobalt, and copper from Voisey's Bay nickel concentrate — a process that does not involve a prior smelting step," explains Eberhard Krause, Director of Process Research. "We anticipate that this process will have capital and operating costs about 30% lower than conventional smelting and refining." And it would recover 50% more of the cobalt in the concentrates, adds Ashok Dalvi, Process Manager. How soon? Perhaps within three years Inco could begin to build a pilot plant, perhaps in Newfoundland. It would take about a year to build and a year to test it.[272]

Meanwhile, in Newfoundland, Ed Byrne resigned as leader of the opposition Progressive Conservative party on June 12, 2000, in order to spend more time with his family. In December, lawyer Danny Williams announced that he'd like the job. Because of his successful business dealings, which had included selling his interests in the cable television business to a crowd up in Toronto when the "convergence" mania was at its dizzy height, and perhaps also because of his impressive collection of speeding tickets, Mr. Williams was known locally and affectionately as "Danny Millions."

As he campaigned for the leadership, Mr. Williams said that he was likely to be more flexible with respect to Inco and the Voisey's Bay project than was former premier Tobin.

On Wednesday, January 31, 2001, there being no other candidates, Mr. Williams won the leadership of the Progressive Conservatives by acclamation.

The following weekend the governing Liberals were to meet to select their own new leader. Whoever they chose would automatically become the new Premier of Newfoundland and Labrador. At our Thursday morning meeting, I tip Roger Grimes as winner, adding that, even though he and the other two candidates seemed to be outdoing one another in their promises to be intransigent in their dealings with Inco, Newfoundlanders suspected that Mr. Grimes harboured flexible views towards Inco.

"So," asks Patricia, "are you worried about your bets that Voisey's Bay won't be on stream before 2008?"

"No. Before Voisey's Bay can go ahead, the native groups have to settle their land claims with governments." I also remind the meeting that Inco has settled into a multi-year research program to methodically investigate the application of hydromet to Voisey's Bay ores, and that it appears to be in no hurry.

"Well, Ray," says Patricia, "some of my clients are worried that, if Mr. Grimes were to win, he would make a deal with Inco, and Inco would make an early start of Voisey's Bay, stretching its balance sheet and putting an oversupply of nickel on the world market."

"Actually," I reply, "that points to another reason why I think Inco's in no rush on Voisey's Bay. The Goro nickel project in New Caledonia seems to be making increasing demands on Inco's balance sheet and on the attention of its management."

Mr. Grimes wins. The following Monday, investors speculate on the implications of the election result. "The most recent scenario for the future of Voisey's Bay is that Inco would begin construction of a $745 million mine and mill in Labrador by as early as May," reports *American Metal Market*, adding breathlessly, "Voisey's Bay could conceivably be turning out concentrate by mid-2002."

Nancy Walsh calls me from CBC Radio in St. John's. "Don't you think our new premier will see Voisey's Bay developed any sooner?" she asks.

"No, Nancy!"

"Ah, you're probably right, Ray. However, I do think that the fact that Inco is doing this mini-pilot plant testing indicates it must have made some sort of arrangement with the government regarding nickel development."

The day ends with enthusiasts trumping skeptics. Inco's share price closes 3.2% higher than it did on Friday, despite a 1.0% drop in the price of nickel.

The next day, Tuesday, February 6, Inco's management meets with analysts. The analysts have spent the past three weeks coping with a flood of press releases from mining companies reporting their year-end results. We sit at Inco's meeting, arms folded, as if to say "OK, so surprise us!" Inco obliges.

First, Mike Sopko says that, on April 25, he will step down as Inco's CEO and that President Scott Hand is to take his place. Peter Jones is to become the new President.

Then, in his first speech as CEO-designate, Mr. Hand sends a message to Premier-Designate Grimes. "We're ready to return to the negotiating table." I abruptly unfold my arms when he adds, "With the cleaning up of our capital structure with the Class VBN share redemption, we have more flexibility to bring in a partner."

Mr. Hand continues. "Does it make sense then for Inco to do both major projects — Goro and Voisey's Bay — more or less at the same time?" He answers his own question in the affirmative, and goes on to envision a future in which both Goro and Voisey's Bay are up and running by 2006.

Question time. I raise my hand and an usher passes me a cordless microphone. After congratulating him on his new job, I ask Mr. Hand, "Is this the first time Inco has said that it is open to the idea of a joint venture at Voisey's Bay?"

"Yes, it is, Ray."

Mike Sopko adds, cryptically, that he himself is "still looking for a partner."

On Wednesday, Nancy Walsh calls and asks me who would be a likely partner for Inco. I can't think of one, but I tell her that some of my clients are speculating that it would be Falconbridge.

"After all, by battling Inco for control of Voisey's Bay, they argue, Falconbridge was the only other nickel producer to have shown a clear interest in the project. And, way along the coast from Voisey's Bay, Falconbridge is already mining nickel at Raglan. Raglan's product sails right by the site of Inco's proposed smelter at Argentia on its way to Sudbury. But I think that's a red herring. At Sudbury, Falconbridge recovers about US$0.80 worth of precious metals for every pound of Raglan nickel, but the technology Inco is testing for the treatment of Voisey's Bay concentrates at Argentia is unable to extract precious metals. So that makes it likely that Falcy is no longer interested in using whatever plant gets built at Argentia.

"Nancy, I think that Falcy's main interest in Voisey's Bay was to replace its short-lived reserves and keep its hungry smelter at Sudbury full. Mr. Tobin made it pretty clear that Newfoundland is not in the business of feeding hungry Ontario smelters. I think you can count out Falconbridge."

Tuesday the following week, after Roger Grimes is sworn in as premier, reporters crowd him. Would he respond to Mr. Hand's invitation to talk? "My new Mines and Energy Minister, Lloyd Matthews, and I plan to contact Inco within the next week or so to try to hammer out a deal," replies Mr. Grimes. He goes on to suggest that his approach will not be as rigid as that of his predecessor. Mr. Matthews adds that he hopes to reach a deal with Inco before the next provincial election.[273]

Early the following month, March 2001, the Premier and Minister Matthews fly to Toronto to meet Inco to see if there might be a basis to proceed to more formal negotiations.[274]

March 5, 2001

Nancy Walsh calls. "Ray, Mr. Grimes has been to Toronto. Now he's back and he's calling a press conference today."

I seize the opportunity to hop on my hobby horse.

"You know, Nancy, we haven't heard much about native land claims lately. I hope he tells you how things are going with the L.I.A. and the Innu Nation. Oh, and another thing. The Ontario Court of Appeal recently ruled that Ontario's Metis — let's see, I have it here — are 'full-fledged aboriginal people with constitutional rights that compare to those of Indians.' I wonder if this ruling put pressure on your provincial government to recognize the Labrador Metis as having native title."

Nancy phones back after the press conference. "Lots of stuff, Ray! As you might have expected, he announced that he'd asked Lloyd Matthews to continue the talks."

"OK."

"Then someone asked about hydromet. Grimes made it sound as if Newfoundland was pushing hydromet on Inco and not the other way around! He seems to want Newfoundland to have the technology of the future — more efficient, more environmentally friendly, even though you could expect less than half the number of jobs than with an old-style pyromet smelter."

"What if hydromet doesn't work?"

"Someone asked him that, but he dodged the question. Someone else asked if he'd allow ore to leave the province unprocessed, but he dodged that question, too! Ah, what else ... oh yes. Even though Roger Grimes is hoping for an outcome of the talks by August 31, there's a reporter here with *American Metal Market*, Aaron Smith. He believes construction of a mine and mill could begin this summer, and we could even see production as early as 2003!"

"How about the issues with the native groups?"

"Oh, yeah, they'll be on my report."

Later, I download her report from the CBC's website, and I hear Mr. Grimes say:

"The L.I.A.'s claims are proceeding. The Innu claims are not quite as advanced, but some work has been done as well."

And:

We've committed to the Metis Nation of Labrador that we would try to work with them ... but ... we have not expressed any willingness to ... having discussions about a land claim with them.

In the following months, Mr. Matthews popped up from time to time and talked about Voisey's Bay. His government brought him to the Prospectors' Convention in Toronto on March 13, 2001: Newfoundland's sixth mines minister since Voisey's Bay was discovered less than eight years earlier.

On April 11, Mr. Matthews told a business lunch in St. John's that formal talks with Inco would begin "probably next month," and emphasized that any deal with Inco would have to include a fully-integrated operation, from mine to smelter, in the province.[275] He told reporters, "It's time to roll up our sleeves ... and try to reach a deal."[276]

At the North Atlantic Mineral Symposium in St. John's on May 29, he said that, as well as negotiating a Voisey's Bay deal with Inco, the "government will renew its mineral rights tax and develop an overall mineral policy framework." Fine words and, at the Mineral Symposium, fine music as well, supplied by Newfoundland's Gayle Tapper and her harp. But no sign of talks with Inco and, given the brevity of Labrador's construction season, Aaron Smith's schedule had slipped back into the realms of fantasy.

On June 15, 2001, Lloyd Matthews finally announced that he had opened formal talks with Inco on the possible development of Voisey's Bay. Recalling that Newfoundland's previous negotiating team had disbanded when Bill Rowat left to become the Chief Executive Officer of the Railway Association of Canada, Mr. Matthews appointed his Deputy Minister, Brian Maynard, to head discussions, adding, "There will be a media blackout during the talks."[277]

"Grimes is hoping to wrap it up by August 31," Nancy Walsh told me later.

The market did not seem to mind that the negotiations were proceeding at a leisurely pace. Inco's shares closed on June 15 at a price of $26.90, which was 4.4% above their level immediately after Mr. Grimes won the leadership, despite a 2.3% decline in nickel prices in the same period. The strength in Inco's share price worried me, not because of my views about Voisey's Bay, but because my charts of global demand for base metals were showing signs of slippage. On June 18, I told clients "Don't buy Inco's shares now. You should be able to buy them more cheaply in late summer."

The signs of slippage became stronger and, from June 18 to September 10, 2001, nickel prices declined 22.1%, to US$2.31 per pound. Inco's share price dropped 8.5%, to $24.80.

Then come the horrors of September 11. Our trading desk stops trading. I watch a screen hanging over the desk, not believing that I am seeing the destruction of two buildings I have visited many times since they were first occupied in 1971.

Ed Pennock and I are working together again. With flagging enthusiasm, Ed urges us back to work. After the second plane hits, the Toronto Stock Exchange closes and Ed sends everyone home. I stay, too numb to think, mechanically transcribing notes for this book.

It is weeks before I am sure that none of my colleagues, competitors, and clients in New York had been victims.

And I watch Inco's share price drop as low as $17.90 in late September while nickel prices bottom out just below US$2.00 per pound.

Meanwhile, Inco and the government had been negotiating. Mr. Matthews visited Goro in June, on his return taking pains to point out that the province, not Inco, had paid for the trip.[278] The purpose of his visit was probably to assess the New Caledonian government, which was competing with his own jurisdiction for Inco's attention and investment. Had Mr. Matthews wanted just to see a hydromet plant, he could have found one at Fort Saskatchewan, Alberta, which was not only closer to home, but also a full-scale commercial facility. Goro boasted no more than a pilot plant.

On July 24, 2001, M. Pierre Frogier, President of New Caledonia, paid a visit to Toronto. Inco invited Toronto's financial community to meet M. Frogier at a reception amid Inco's exhibits in the Royal Ontario Museum. In a speech, which seemed to be directed more at Mr. Matthews than Mr. Frogier, Scott Hand praised New Caledonia's welcoming attitude to investment, its tax holidays, and access to preferential financing.

August 31, 2001, Roger Grimes's target date, came. "There is nothing to report ... we don't want to put a time frame on this," said a government spokesman.[279] Mid-September, still no word. Inco's subsidiary, Voisey's Bay Nickel Company, completed the exploration program at Voisey's Bay, which it had begun in August 1996 after Inco took over Diamond Fields, folded up camp and left behind only a four-person security and maintenance team.[280]

On October 11, Inco announced that the events of September 11 had increased economic uncertainty, and that it had agreed to extend its negotiations with the province until the end of the year. Despite warnings from Lloyd Matthews that the province saw nothing magic about the year-end, and that "it will take as long as it takes,"[281] reporters immediately dusted off their rumours of a spring 2002 start to construction,[282] and Inco's share price notched up 5.2%.

Despite the media blackout, Inco reported that the key issues that remained unresolved were:[283]

(i) "The scope of the guarantee covering processing in the Province" and its implications for "[m]ovement of ... concentrate ... to the company's existing Canadian operations";
(ii) "Financial participation by the Federal government";
(iii) The extent to which the province would allow "flexibility in the timing ... and financing" of the project.

As far as Inco was concerned, point (i) was key. In Voisey's Bay's early years, said Scott Hand, Inco required that feed from Voisey's Bay would supplant some of the feed from Inco's mines in Ontario and Manitoba. Only when Voisey's Bay's smelter came on stream would Voisey's Bay represent new production.

As far as the government was concerned, point (ii) was the key one. "The people of Newfoundland and Labrador [are] worried about another major sellout of a major resource," thundered Danny Williams, the new Leader of the Opposition. He complained that the government should never have let Inco "export" 29 tonnes of drill core samples to be assayed outside the province.[284] Premier Grimes, he said, was poised to surrender too much to Inco Limited.[285]

No, we're not! responded the Premier. "Inco must agree to build a traditional smelter in the province if new hydromet processing technology doesn't work ... if that doesn't happen, there won't be a project. Now we don't have that guarantee from Inco, but that's always been the position of the province and still is."[286]

In St. John's, CBC Radio's Lee-Anne Power didn't believe the bluster. On December 5 she reported, "It's widely known among those close to government and industry that the date for a deal is set. Two of those sources tell CBC Radio that the province and Inco plan to sign an agreement on Voisey's Bay on the 21st of this month. They say the only party not in agreement right now is the Labrador Inuit Association. Another source says Inuit people are worried about the impact of winter ore shipping on the coastal ice they use for transportation. They're also concerned that the compensation for land use offered by the company will be good enough."

The CBC posted Ms. Power's story shortly before my publication deadline, so I dropped it into our morning letter to clients. I was probably the only analyst to have caught the story, so it took several hours for it to spread through the market and to be reflected in the price of Inco's shares.

At 11 a.m. Eastern time, I phone Ms. Power to congratulate her on having added $150 million to the value of Inco's shares.

"Oh, shit, and I didn't buy any first!"

"I know you wouldn't have, Lee-Anne!"

By December 21, the supposed deadline, the market seemed to have forgotten about it. There was no news from St. John's. Inco's share price did rise about 1% that day, but it was probably because of a similar move in the price of nickel.

As 2002 began, the fate of Voisey's Bay was still in limbo. Although I was willing to concede that the odds of a deal between Inco and the province were better under Roger Grimes than they had been in Brian Tobin's time, I thought it unlikely that Inco would be able to begin construction at Voisey's Bay in 2002.

Despite Brian Tobin's move back to Ottawa, there was no news about federal financial support for the project. And, before it could break ground, Inco had to achieve agreement not only with the province but also with the L.I.A. and the Innu Nation. And I continued to be concerned that native groups other than the Innu Nation and the L.I.A. could make a legal claim which would block development.

The Innu had attempted to tie their negotiations with Inco to their negotiations with the province. In March 2001, the President of the Innu Nation, Peter Penashue, had told CBC Radio[287] that he would "oppose the Voisey's Bay project until the Innu reach a land claims agreement-in-principle with Newfoundland and Canada."

Lloyd Matthews had conceded that "there is a possibility that land claims could be a stumbling block."[288] Nevertheless, there had been some promising signs of improvement in Inco's relationships with native groups, especially the Innu. On May 29, 2001, while Gayle Tapper played her harp to the delight of the Irish delegates at the North Atlantic Mineral Symposium in St. John's, some Voisey's Bay Nickel Company employees told me that they had noticed a marked improvement in their relationships with the Innu Nation.

"Ever since Tobin turned them over to federal jurisdiction," said one, "the purse strings have tightened and the Innu have had to give much more detailed accounting of how they are spending government funds, especially on things like legal interventions in Voisey's Bay. Ray, I think it's unlikely now that the Innu would try to stop the project in future."

"That's encouraging," I replied, "even though I don't quite follow the logic!"

"Well, it's personalities, too. The influence of the hard-liners in the Innu Nation has been falling while that of Peter Penashue has been rising. Penashue is university-educated and seems to embrace both the 'back-to-the-land' traditionalists and the 'we-want-jobs' factions. He's more conciliatory. You'll notice that Penashue has not insisted that there be a full and final land claims deal with the government before we can go ahead at Voisey's."

A couple of months later, Inco again had hinted, this time in public, that its discussions with the native groups were going surprisingly well. Scott Hand said that he expected that Inco would be able to make interim agreements with the Innu Nation and with the L.I.A. However, Stu Gendron warned the natives of further delays if they were to make development contingent on settling their land claims with the government.[289]

On September 7, 2001, there had been another straw in the wind. Peter Penashue, as President of the Innu Nation, signed a deal to allow a junior exploration company, Donner Minerals, to work on what the Innu regarded as their land, land from which the Innu had ejected Donner only two years earlier. "Our agreements set the standard for building respectful relationships between the mining industry and aboriginal people," said Mr. Penashue.[290]

For months thereafter, we heard nothing more from the native groups.

On December 5, 2001, Mr. Penashue told CBC Radio in St. John's in a telephone interview, "We've been in negotiations with Inco for a number of years right now and things are progressing quite well, and as soon as the province and Inco sort out their differences, I'm ... we're pretty confident that we can conclude our agreements."

Mr. Penashue then disappeared from view. No CBC reporters could find him.[291] He stayed out of public view for more than six months, and when he reappeared it was to unveil a surprise.

CHAPTER 31

DEAL!

One difference between this time and previous discussions [with the Government of Newfoundland and Labrador is that] ... we've gotten to know each other better.
— Scott Hand, CEO, Inco Ltd., presentation to analysts and investors in Toronto, February 5, 2002

They [the provincial government] are being more flexible this time. For instance, when Brian Tobin was the premier of the province, he said, you know, there'll be no concentrate shipped out of here. Now we're discussing how many kilotonnes of nickel-in-concentrate we can ship out in the early stages of the development.
— Peter Jones, President, Inco Ltd., Morgan Stanley conference in New York, March 12, 2002

I get on pretty well with Roger Grimes.
— Scott Hand, at Inco's Annual General Meeting in Toronto, April 17, 2002

On January 4, 2002, more than five years after Inco had announced that it would build a smelter and refinery on the north side of the former U.S. naval base at Argentia, the federal government handed the property over to a local body, the Argentia Management Authority. Finally, Inco would be able to have access to the site. I ticked off the removal of a potential obstacle to the development of Voisey's Bay.

On January 14, 2002, Brian Tobin resigned his post in the Federal Cabinet and his seat in the House of Commons and quit politics. Only 12% of those responding to an Internet poll, conducted by the St. John's *Telegram*, believed his explanation that he wanted to spend more time with his family. I ticked off a second potential obstacle to the development of Voisey's Bay: a federal cabinet minister whom I suspected of undermining his successor as premier.

On February 5, 2002, Inco hinted that its negotiations with the native groups were becoming more complex. Scott Hand said that[292] land claims settlements between the native people and the federal and provincial governments must "appropriately" deal with the Voisey's Bay project. I told the St. John's *Telegram* afterwards that "I've never seen [Inco] say that that was a concern of theirs. ... I think they're telling us that the land claims have become part of Inco's negotiations with the provincial government."

The last I'd heard about the negotiations between the L.I.A. and the Province was that, although the parties had initialled an agreement in May 1999, ratified it in July 1999, and "formally and officially initialled it in June 2001,"[293] a final agreement was still "a year or two" away.[294] As for the Innu nation, it had been almost a year since we'd heard anything about the progress of their land claims. If Inco was indeed tying the fate of its own talks with the native groups to the progress of the land claims negotiations, it risked waiting years for the outcome.

I concluded that negotiations with native groups remained a formidable obstacle to the development of Voisey's Bay.

On April 17, 2002, Inco holds its annual general meeting in the Toronto Convention Centre. Eight giant posters, each depicting a representative employee of the company, decorate the brutal concrete walls. With the broad, bearded face of Voisey's Bay pioneer Dan Lee beaming down at us, Mr. Hand tells us that he is "pleased to report this morning that we have made significant progress in negotiations with the government of Newfoundland and Labrador." And, when a shareholder asks how negotiations with the Innu Nation are going, Mr. Hand says "we're making very good progress."

In St. John's, Roger Grimes is quick to downplay Mr. Hand's optimism.[295] "We were surprised that Hand came out with such strong language," indicating a deal was likely, adds a spokesman for the mines ministry.[296] And Peter Penashue huffs, "I don't know where they get the idea things are going smoothly. We haven't met with them for about six weeks. We don't get the sense things are pushing forward to wrap up a deal."[297]

Time is tightening. In order to commence any substantial work at the mine site that year, Inco needs a deal by June. Nancy Walsh phones me on May 15. "A deal is imminent, Ray. I'm hearing that the engineering firm SNC Lavalin has been in talks with the Building Trades Council aimed at getting Voisey's Bay declared a Special Construction Site under provincial legislation. That designation is given to large projects to streamline labour regulations. The people and companies have been told to keep it quiet for now."

Later that day, Premier Grimes reveals that he is also planning what to do if there should be a deal. Although he has previously said that he would go ahead and sign a deal with Inco before releasing any information to the public, he has changed his mind. The House, he says, will be allowed to vote on it. And if it's rejected, the deal's off.[298]

The Leader of the Opposition, Danny Williams, retorts that, if it is rejected, it could lead to a huge lawsuit. Says Mr. Grimes, "It won't be rejected!"

Wednesday, May 22 feels like a replay of early December 2001. CBC Radio in St. John's again tells us that "the Opposition and a lot of other people seem to think that" a deal is almost done and, again, Inco's share price begins to rise. And, again, I cynically expect that nothing will happen.

The next piece of news is not good. CBC Radio reports that the L.I.A. appears to be far from signing its own Impact Benefit Agreement with Inco.[299] The two parties do not seem to have found any common ground on the issue of winter shipping. Inco wants to ship concentrate year-round, whereas the Inuit believe that this would hurt traditional hunting. Why should this be a deal breaker? At Falconbridge's Raglan mine in far northern Quebec, the company stops shipments for a few weeks each spring and each fall on the advice of, and to the evident satisfaction of, the local Inuit. I'm puzzled, but I'm also more comfortable with my view that no deal is imminent.

But the next day, May 23, 2002, I am astonished. Mr. Penashue announces that the Innu Nation has reached a tentative agreement with Inco, spelling out the company's commitments to environmental protection, to training and providing jobs for Innu, and to a compensation formula. The full membership of the Innu Nation must ratify the deal by a vote on June 12. Reporters think that ratification is a foregone conclusion.[300] I feel as if I have come to work to find that, overnight, the vacant lot across the street had been replaced by a completed building with tenants moving in.

Another surprise. William Barbour, President of the L.I.A., announces on May 24 that he has signed a tentative benefits agreement with Inco on development of Voisey's Bay, and that on June 24 the 5,000 members of the Association will vote on ratification of the package.[301]

The Innu Nation later postpones its own referendum because of several deaths in the community,[302] and holds it on the same day as the L.I.A.'s vote.

Another day, another set of vacant lot has disappeared, there's another new building across the street. Is the timing a fluke, or is there someone co-ordinating events? Mr. Penashue pops up again, hinting that yes, someone is — it's the premier. He tells the CBC that "Roger Grimes and his government announced to Inco and Voisey's Bay Nickel Company that nothing was going to happen without Impact and Benefits Agreements with the aboriginal groups, such as the L.I.A. and the Innu Nation."[303]

Over the following weeks, the CBC obtains a copy of the L.I.A.'s deal with Inco.[304] The big-ticket items are for Inco to pay the L.I.A. $123.5 million and to spend nearly $3 million to train 170 Inuit to work at the mine.

Leaning against the door of my office, Patricia says, "$123.5 million sounds like a lot, Ray."

"Yeah, but the leak says that it's to be spread over thirty years, so it would cost Inco only —" tap, tap, tap on the calculator "— U.S. 1% per share per year. Well, make that 2%, because Inco has probably made a similar commitment to the Innu." As Patricia walks away, I realize that if the leaked details are accurate, Inco must have agreed to stretch the mine life over thirty years, which implies a smaller project than the company had originally envisioned.

* * * * *

One of the great debates about stock markets is to what extent they are "efficient": that is, does the price of a stock incorporate everything that is known, publicly and privately, about it? And one of the reasons that it is unlikely that this debate will ever be resolved is that it is devilishly difficult to determine whether or not a particular piece of information has been captured in the price of a stock. I ponder this puzzle on Friday, May 24 after Inco's shares have closed at a price of $33.82. In the previous three days, the Innu Nation had announced a deal with Inco. The L.I.A. had announced its own deal with Inco. And CBC Radio in St. John's, admittedly a source of market information that is not usually monitored by either Wall Street in New York or Bay Street in Toronto, had predicted that a deal between the provincial government and Inco was imminent. Yet Inco's share price had risen only 4.4% in those three days. Why such a modest move? Is it because markets were inefficient and these events had not yet been incorporated into Inco's share price? Or is it because markets *are* efficient, and there are almost as many investors who believe (as I do) that the imminent development of Voisey's Bay would be, on balance, bad for Inco as there were investors who thought it would be positive?

Events on the following Monday, May 27, do not resolve the ambiguity. The Saturday *Globe and Mail* had carried a story[305] that Inco had hired a contractor to manage construction work at the Voisey's Bay site, with a sidebar that screamed, "Mine and mill to begin production by 2007." However, before the stock markets open on Monday, Mines Minister Matthews tells CBC Radio, St. John's, that "there is no basis for a deal [with Inco] as we speak." Inco's share price closes the day at $34.99, up 3.5% from Friday.

On Tuesday, while "rumours of an imminent deal ... dominate discussion in the province's coffee shops and the radio call-in shows," Lloyd Matthews announces that Inco had presented him with an offer the previous week, but that he had turned down the proposal because its wording was "too vague."[306] "Over the next few days, maybe a week or two," he says, " we will be bringing this to some sort of conclusion."

On Wednesday night, Inco celebrates its 100th anniversary of incorporation by throwing a party in the geological section of the Royal Ontario Museum in Toronto. Deftly weaving between big chunks of rock, Sandra Scott gives me a big, bright smile. "I think we caught you by surprise last week, Ray, with those Impact Benefit Agreements!"

"Yes you did, Sandra."

"Are you still confident you'll win your bets that Voisey's Bay won't start up before 2008?"

I grin. "Not as confident as I was! But CBC Radio in St. John's is saying that 'people close to'" — I make the quote signs in the air with my fingers — "'your negotiations with the government say '"it's still 50:50."'"[307] Then there was that piece in the *Globe* on the weekend saying that production would start in '07 if there's a deal now. ... It's pretty easy for me to imagine something gumming up the works and delaying that schedule by a year."

Sandra shakes her head. "I don't know where the *Globe* got that story."

Dan Roling, a Merrill Lynch analyst visiting from New York, joins us. "I've been meaning to ask you, Dan," I say. "I think that if there were to be a Voisey's Bay deal today, it would be an overall negative for Inco — a strain on nickel markets and a strain on Inco's balance sheet. Some people here seem to agree with me, some don't.[308] What's the New York view?"

Intense blue eyes. "I, and I believe other U.S. analysts, Ray, would see the achievement of a Voisey's Bay deal as a strong positive."

I raise my eyebrows. "Hmm! Thanks, Dan!"

Lloyd Matthews and his team resumed their discussions with Inco in Toronto. Mr. Matthews returned to St. John's on Tuesday, June 4, amid intense media speculation that he would announce a deal with Inco.[309] But Mr. Matthews briefed the premier in private and kept quiet in public. Starved for a story, CBC reporter David Cochrane commented, "It's very different from when Brian Tobin was premier. Every time they went to Toronto something would be leaked to the national media and we'd get a full briefing here on their return."

Nevertheless, newspapers that week confidently reported that Inco and the government had come to an agreement.[310]

"A tentative deal has been reached," reported *The National Post*.[311] "The deal is done," cried *Reuters*.[312]

Said *The Globe and Mail*, "Mr. Grimes began circulating [on June 6] a thick report to his Liberal Party caucus that outlined the proposed terms of what is being called a 'tacit agreement, reached this week with Inco Ltd.'"[313]

Canadian Press published the boldest and most confident story: "Members of Newfoundland's governing Liberal caucus huddled at a remote location yesterday [Thursday, June 6] to hear details of a proposed deal with Inco. ... The secret briefing, held at a home on the south shore of Conception Bay, was called to persuade reluctant backbenchers that the deal won't become a political liability when Premier Grimes calls an election, probably early next spring."[314]

On Thursday evening, Premier Grimes emerged from a $500-a-plate Liberal Party dinner at which he was the keynote speaker. Reporters hounded him.

"Is *The National Post* right or is *The National Post* wrong? Is there a tentative agreement or not?"

"No," replied the premier, "we don't have a tentative agreement ... despite our best efforts we don't have a deal ... there is no agreement of any kind. No, repeat, no deal."[315]

At lunchtime on Friday, reporters asked the same question of Lloyd Matthews. "These are stories written by others," he said, "from a basis of which I am not aware."[316]

Inco's share price ended the day at a price slightly lower than that of a week earlier, even though nickel prices had risen slightly. The market was probably as confused as me. Was there really a deal? If so, was it good news for Inco's shareholders, or bad news?

Over the weekend, some tens of kilometres southwest of St. John's, residents of Conception Bay South noticed a fleet of cars and government vehicles parked awkwardly in their streets. Someone called a reporter, who quickly determined that at the centre of the cluster of vehicles was the house of Jim Walsh, a Liberal backbencher. Journalists pounded at his door.

"I'm having some friends over for tea," he explained.

Not completely satisfied, the journalists hung around. Eventually, Mr. Grimes and twenty-six of his twenty-seven-person Liberal caucus emerged from Mr. Walsh's house. All but the premier were tight-lipped. And Mr. Grimes would say only, "We haven't taken any decision about any matter." *The Globe and Mail* was able to reach someone at Inco, but could elicit no comment.[317] However, in St. John's, CBC Radio's David Cochrane found some Liberal insiders who told him that there was an agreement on the table, but that a proposal to let nickel concentrate leave the province was provoking concern and debate.

"The whole issue is ... a tough one politically: it's a shift away from the election promises of 1999. ... Some caucus members weren't comfortable with the wording ... they fear it wasn't strong enough to force Inco to replace the nickel concentrate it will export to Ontario and Manitoba while it builds a nickel processor in Argentia. If Inco agrees to tighten that language, the deal will go ahead. ... This last-minute haggling has delayed things for at least twenty-four hours, meaning the Voisey's Bay saga will last till tomorrow." Assuming Inco does agree, he concluded, the government and the company planned to announce the deal at 10 a.m. at the Fairmont Hotel on Tuesday.

At Monday's morning meeting I summarize David Cochrane's report and somewhat self-consciously conclude that the odds on a deal are now better than 50:50. A few salespeople raise their eyebrows. Later that morning, *American Metal Market* reports that Scott Hand is scheduled to arrive in St. John's that day. It sounds as if Inco has agreed to, in David Cochrane's words, "tighten" the language of the deal. From a dusty corner of my computer, I retrieve my financial model of Voisey's Bay and prepare to update it.

Tuesday, June 11, 2002

I am up early and anxious, eat my granola and yogourt too fast, and hiccup on the subway. Just after 7 a.m. I step into my air-conditioned eyrie on the 52nd floor of the Toronto-Dominion Tower and switch on my computer. As I stare at the screen, an email arrives from Inco.

> Inco Ltd. and the Province of Newfoundland and Labrador jointly announced that they have entered into a statement of principles on the development of the Voisey's Bay nickel-copper-cobalt deposits in Labrador.

A shiver down my spine. *After all this time.* My eyes flick from phrase to phrase.

> The non-binding statement of principles provides for development of a ... mine and mill ... at Voisey's Bay, and a ... research and development program in

hydrometallurgical processing, including a demonstration plant at Argentia. ... The next step for Inco and the Province is completion by the end of September 2002 of one or more definitive agreements. ... Before proceeding to complete such agreements the statement of principles is subject to approval in the provincial legislature. ... Inco also confirmed that the Government of Canada has identified ... up to $150 million that could support activities in and around the Voisey's Bay project. ... The statement of principles provides for shipment of ... Voisey's Bay nickel-in-concentrate to Inco's operations in Ontario and Manitoba ... during development of [a hydrometallurgical plant]. While Inco remains fully confident in the feasibility of processing Voisey's Bay concentrate with a hydrometallurgical process, in the unlikely event that the technology does not [work], Inco will build a state-of-the-art 110 million pound per annum refinery in the province using proven technology. ... The company said it is also assessing the need to write down the ... value of Voisey's Bay [on Inco's book]. ... Webcast and phone conference call 10:30 a.m. [Eastern time].

On the sales desk, just outside my office, Patricia is sipping coffee and glaring at her screen. Without looking up, she yells, "Hey, Ray, did you see that Inco and Newfoundland have come up with a deal?"

"Yes, I have, Patricia! They pulled it all together! Wow!"

My next thought is that it has suddenly become a lot more important that the Inuit and the Innu both ratify their tentative Impact Benefit Agreements with Inco. What are the rules governing ratification? I dash off an email to Sandra Scott, congratulating her and adding a question on the Impact Benefit Agreements. In order to be ratified, do they have to be approved by a majority of their memberships (which would be a difficult test to meet), or just by a majority of those voting?

Sandra responds almost immediately.

For both the L.I.A. (Inuit) and Innu Nation, ratification requires a straight majority of those who will vote.

OK. Then:

```
Jones is here. Do you still have his bottle of
Scotch?
```

Inco's President, Peter Jones, was one of those whom I had bet, in September 1998, that Voisey's Bay would not be in production before 2008. I reply:

```
I have won several such bottles recently on more
successful   speculations   and   am   keeping   in
reserve, for Mr. Jones, one such bottle. I trust
that Glenmorangie suits his palate.
```

Another quick response:

```
>>>> Jones here. Glenmorangie will be a fine back
up, but if you have some Glen Moray that would be
preferred!
```

At the morning meeting a few minutes later, I outline the deal and point out that it contemplates commercial production beginning in 2006, two years earlier than I had anticipated. However, Inco's commitment to a smaller project, spread over thirty years rather than the 22 years which Inco had previously suggested, alleviates some of my concerns about Voisey's impact on nickel markets and on Inco's balance sheet.

"The next steps," I say, "are, first, ratification of the deal by Newfoundland and Labrador's House of Assembly —" I pause and think of the efforts that Mr. Grimes had reportedly made in order to try to convince his caucus to support the deal. "— and that's unlikely to be a problem; secondly, is ratification of the 'Impact Benefit Agreements' recently initialled by Inco and the two native groups, the L.I.A. and the Innu Nation. I've just learned that these votes will pass if a majority of those voting were to vote in favour. My guess is that they will pass."

If you ask a cab driver in St. John's to take you to "The Hotel," he or she will deliver you to the Fairmont, the former Canadian Pacific Hotel Newfoundland, where I once numbed my bum during the environmental hearings.

At 8:30 (10:00 a.m. Newfoundland time) I take myself to the Fairmont via the Internet. Inco and the government formally announce the deal. The business people and government officials who pack the ballroom give Mr. Grimes three standing ovations. Beaming, he exclaims, "It's difficult today to keep a smile off my face!"[318]

At 10:00 Toronto time, I punch in the numbers for a conference call with Inco's management. Mr. Hand tells us how pleased he is. He opens the lines to questions. Canadian analysts ask about taxes (Inco will pay the same rates as everyone else), electricity costs (Inco will pay the same rates as everyone else), whether Inco can claim their payments to native groups as tax deductions (management couldn't say). But Victor Lazarovici, Nesbitt Burns's mining analyst in New York, seems upset by the proposed construction schedule.

"It seems fairly long to build the initial phase," he says. "Can you explain why it seems to be slipping from three years to four?"

Peter Jones doesn't think there has been any "slipping" in the schedule. "We've always talked about a thirty-six-month construction period," he says, "and essentially that's what we've got because we would aim to be starting up in the first half of 2006."

"Remember," adds Scott Hand, "what you're faced with in the north is having to deal with the logistics of the ice coming in December and not leaving until the end of June."

Stu Gendron notes that the ice will continue to affect the operation once it is in production. "Providing they [the L.I.A.] ratify the Impact Benefit Agreement ... we will winter-ship with two periods of about six weeks in the fall and the spring when we won't ship." Which, as Mr. Hand points out, "is similar to what Falconbridge does at Raglan."

I want to make sure I've understood the agreement about the price Inco will pay for electricity, so I register a question. "Will you be forced to carry some of the capital cost of the new electricity capacity?"

"When we first got into the project, there was some suggestion that we would pay a higher power rate," replies Mr. Hand.

"That's right!"

"And we wanted to be sure that we were not discriminated against ... and the province has confirmed that."

John Redstone is next up. In his matter-of-fact, common-sense English accent, he observes that Inco is no longer talking about taking a partner at Voisey's Bay.

"I've shown a lot of blood, sweat, and tears, as have other people, to get this project going," sighs Mr. Hand. "Sorry, John, I had to say that! So, no partner."

"Fair enough!"

Terry Ortslan chimes in with a question about Voisey's Bay's effect on nickel markets. "I want to hear ... that with all these project dates and the way the phases are working, there will not be any major, net addition from Voisey's Bay to the markets. The world is still going to struggle, I guess, with the issue of the bottlenecks, as well as the gap between supply and demand."

Inco's senior nickel marketer, Peter Goudie, pauses, no doubt to digest what he's just heard, then replies. "It is still our belief that by the year 2005 ... there is going to be a gap [with demand exceeding supply]. If you go into 2006, when Voisey's Bay starts up, there are no other significant projects that we would see coming into production ... so we believe that the market needs this nickel."

The next day, Wednesday, June 12, I come to work a lot less excited than I had been twenty-four hours earlier. Reading the *Globe* in the subway, I realize that Mr. Grimes and Mr. Hand had run their deal very close to the wind.

"According to sources familiar with the negotiations, talks reached a critical impasse on Saturday when Newfoundland made a last-minute demand that Inco extend the life of the planned processing plant by importing nickel concentrate from other Inco operations. ... 'We were caught totally off guard' ... says one person close to Inco. ... 'The first reaction was to draw the line and say, '"That's it. No more."' ... But Inco's senior management decided Sunday night to acquiesce because Mr. Grimes's potential successor, Danny Williams, would probably have taken a much harder line."[319]

When my turn comes at Wednesday's morning meeting, I observe that the prices of nickel and of the shares of nickel producers had dropped the previous day, probably because investors had judged that the emergence of Voisey's Bay would increase the world's supply of nickel. But, whereas Falconbridge's share price had fallen by only 1.7%, about the same as the drop in the price of nickel itself, the price of Inco's shares had dropped by 4.2%. Evidently, there was some aspect of the deal that the market did not like. Was it:

Inco's announcement that it was considering a writedown of an unspecified amount?

Hardly. A writedown is only a book entry. Not only would it have no economic effect, it had also been widely expected.

The realization that the project had been scaled down and stretched out over thirty years?

Possibly, although the CBC's leak of Inco's agreement with the Inuit had previously revealed the stretched schedule.

Disappointment that Inco would not begin mining at Voisey's Bay until mid-2006?

Probably.

"Other analysts seemed to have underestimated the difficulty of construction in northern Labrador," I say to the meeting, "and had been expecting a construction time shorter by one or two years."

I return to my office to find another whisky vulture circling. David Davidson, an analyst with whom I have also bet that Voisey's Bay would not be in commercial production by 2008, has sent an email:

```
Barring a last-minute hitch, such as some wayward
politician recognizing the difference between a
refinery and a smelter, any bottle of Ardbeg would
suit me just fine.

Cheers
Dave
```

In Newfoundland, the leader of the opposition Conservatives, Danny Williams, did recognize that the deal gave an ironclad guarantee only of a refinery, not of a smelter and refinery. He also believed that the province's share of Voisey's Bay's revenues was inadequate, "only $1 for every Newfoundlander [per year]." "This deal is so flawed," he thundered," you could drive a truck through it!"[320] And what about the ore that would be shipped out before a plant was up and running in Mr.

Manning's district? "Four hundred and forty thousand tonnes of nickel, representing a profit of $3 billion, cannot fit on a spoon!" he cried.[321]

Although the point of Mr. Williams's rhetoric was to remind the world of Brian Tobin's promise that "not one spoonful of ore will leave the province," it seemed odd that a smart businessman would confuse profits with sales revenues. To Stewart Gendron of Voisey's Bay Nickel Company, it seemed more than odd. According to Premier Grimes, Dr. Gendron called Mr. Williams "a smooth liar."[322]

Mr. Williams's opposition to the deal with Inco put Fabian Manning in a difficult position. Mr. Manning was a member of Mr. Williams's party. But he also represented Placentia and St. Mary's in Newfoundland and Labrador's House of Assembly. Placentia and St. Mary's included the Argentia area. His constituents seemed pleased with the agreement with Inco because it would deliver a long-awaited plant and good long-term jobs to the district.

In the House of Assembly, the Liberals urged Mr. Manning to cross the floor. "No," he replied, "I'm comfortable where I'm to. I was a blue baby[323] and I expect to be a blue corpse."[324] He decided that the best way to preserve his political career was to poll his constituents by sending postage-paid ballots to every household in his district, and for him to vote according to the results of that poll.[325]

On June 18, 2002, Mr. Grimes initiated a three-day debate on the tentative Voisey's Bay deal. Fabian Manning's constituents had voted "yes" and so, at the end of the debate on Friday 21, 2002, Mr. Manning, alone in his party, voted "yes,"[326] the Liberals voted "yes," and the House of Assembly of Newfoundland and Labrador approved the Voisey's Bay deal by 28 to 18. Mr. Grimes pointed out that "the legal text [of the Voisey's Bay deal would] be drafted behind closed doors by a team of lawyers from Inco and the provincial government by September 30th but it [wouldn't] be up for debate."[327]

Why was Mr. Grimes in such a rush? Could it be to make legitimate the mobilization that Inco had already begun? The leader of the third party in the House of Assembly, the NDP's Jack Harris, had another theory: Mr. Grimes's goal was "to pressure the Innu and Inuit to ratify their benefit agreements on June 24."[328]

On June 24, 2002, 1,952 Inuit, representing 51% of the Labrador Inuit Association's membership, voted 82% in favour of their deal with Inco; and 563 Innu, about 30% of the membership of the Innu

Nation, voted 68% in favour of their deal. Innu dissident Daniel Ashini angrily vowed to continue his fight against Inco with a legal challenge or protests on-site.[329]

Todd Russell, President of the Labrador Metis Nation, added another voice of protest. The Metis Nation, he reported, had held its own referendum — 1,222 of its members had voted, 96% of them against Inco.[330]

The native groups' votes were no surprise to investors, or maybe they just went unnoticed. Inco's shares ended June 25 at a price of $33.14, barely changed from their level on June 20, the day before the vote in the legislature.

On July 9, John Tumazos, an analyst with Prudential Securities in New York, took a look at the deals which Inco had made with the government and native groups, and pronounced that he was disappointed. The deals, he said, contemplated costs that were higher than he had been expecting.[331] The next day, Inco's share price dropped 8.2%.

Inco held a conference call on July 23, 2002, to announce its results for the second quarter of the year. As promised, the company revealed the amount by which it had written down its investment in Voisey's Bay: US$1.55 billion.

Are you "seeing a much smaller project than you saw in 1996?" asked one analyst.

"Yes," replied Chief Financial Officer Farokh Hakimi.

The bigger the change in the scale of the planned project, the bigger the writedown. But it's difficult to tell whether or not investors were surprised by the change in the scale of the project or by the size of the writedown. Yes, the price of Inco's shares dropped 4.7% that day, but perhaps this move was simply a response to the price of nickel, which had dropped 5.6%.

By August 2002, 200 men and women were working at Voisey's Bay building gravel roads, a dock for ocean-going vessels, and an airstrip.[332] Labrador's Metis showed their displeasure by preventing a barge from unloading at Happy Valley, Labrador.[333] Meanwhile, Inco and its consulting engineers, SNC-Lavalin, were working on a feasibility study that they hoped to complete by the end of 2002.[334]

And in Toronto and St. John's, lawyers continued to shape the agreements that governed the project. Unlike the construction workers, the lawyers were not impelled by the approach of Labrador's winter, so the definitive agreements were not ready to be ratified by the House of Assembly until October 7, 2002.[335]

Labrador's Metis were not the only people unhappy with developments at Voisey's Bay. Chris Verbiski, who with Al Chislett had discovered the deposit, was upset with a bill introduced to the House of Assembly to amend the Mining and Minerals Rights Tax Act. Chris Daly, Chief Financial Officer of Verbiski and Chislett's company, Archean Resources, complained that, under the amendment, its 3% royalty interest in Voisey's Bay's net revenues would be taxed at a rate of 57.3%. By imposing such "obscene" taxes on Archean's income, he said, the government was continuing a decades-old policy of mitigating the effects of rape-and-run resource development. "John C. Doyle, [a] financier, ... fled to Panama in the 1960s. Since the Newfoundland government couldn't tax Doyle's income, it opted to tax his iron ore royalties from the Wabush Mines [in Labrador] at source."[336] Mr. Daly began to plan a campaign to appeal to public opinion and force the government to back down.

CHAPTER 32

WHOA, GORO!

Southern Grande Terre [the location of Inco's Goro project] is mainly an iron plateau, 250 metres high ... a fascinating area of shrubland, waterholes, and marshes ... you better be prepared for some rough terrain.
— L. Logan and G. Cole, 1997

It's a damned long, dark, boggy, dirty, dangerous way.
— *She Stoops to Conquer,* Oliver Goldsmith

December 6, 2002

"You stayed late last night, Ray?"

"Yeah, Patricia, Inco's conference call didn't even start until 5, then I had to figure out what it meant."

"This was the New Caledonia announcement?"

"Yes. It's the Goro nickel project. Back in September, Inco was suggesting that the capital cost of Goro could be as much as 15% above its previous estimate, which was US$1.45 billion. Now, a 15% overrun in the capital cost of a project is not a big deal. But last night Inco announced that capital costs could be *30% to 45%* higher than US$1.45 billion, and that the project would be delayed at least six months while the company stopped construction to review ways of saving money."

"Why," Patricia asks with eyebrow raised, "such a huge increase in the cost?"

"Hmm. The number one reason they gave was 'geotechnical conditions.'"

The eyebrow remains raised.

"They said ... 'driven by ground conditions at plant site.' Which seems to mean that the bedrock surface is more irregular than they thought. Look, Goro's flat and swampy. Imagine that, magically, the swamp disappears, leaving behind the hard bedrock underneath. What does it look like? Inco thought that it would be pretty flat. Now that they've done more detailed work, they know it's not flat. There are cavities and caves, bumps and pillars. So, to put buildings onto that swamp is going to take a lot more concrete and steel reinforcements to support them. That alone apparently accounted for about $200 to $300 million."

Patricia's face expresses surprise.

"And they found they'd have to put better-quality nurglers in the heat exchange columns: another $35 million."

"You made that bit up, Goldie."

"Well, the explanation was something like that. I'm not an engineer."

"And that six-month delay," continues Patricia, "from when to when?"

"The old start-up date was at the end of 2004. In September they were talking about a 'slight slippage' in this date. So I guess, until last night, the expected start-up date was early 2005."

"So what does this do to your recommendation on Inco's shares, Ray?"

"Before last night, I had a target price of $49.35 and a 'Buy' recommendation. If I assume a worst case of a 45% cost overrun and a nine-month delay in start-up, that knocks $2 off the target price. But Inco's shares closed yesterday at $32.05, so even with a target price reduced to $47.35, the shares are still a 'Buy.' Plus, you gotta admire Inco for having the courage to say 'let's stop and think about this!' Most other companies faced with cost overruns just plow right on. And just think, a delay in Goro should mean higher nickel prices for Inco's other projects — like Voisey's Bay."

That day, December 6, with nickel prices unchanged, the stock market knocked $1.81 off Inco's share price. The day after, another $0.94. Although Inco took pains to point out that the review of Goro should not affect the schedule for Voisey's Bay, Newfoundland and Labrador's Opposition Leader, Danny Williams, seized on Inco's willingness to halt Goro as evidence that Inco could walk away from Newfoundland and Labrador if the project were to face technical problems.[337]

A year later, at Inco's meeting with **M.R.A.G.** on December 5, 2003, as I heard the company's management concede that Goro's "start-up will not occur before second half of 2006, at the earliest," I recalled Canadian cabinet minister C. D. Howe's dictum that "a late train gets later."

CHAPTER 33

ENTER ALTIUS

From a nickel market perspective, the future has China's name written all over it.
— Peter Jones, President and Chief Executive Officer, Inco Limited, quoted in *American Metal Market*, August 5, 2002

Nobody pays the taxes we pay — nobody.
— Chris Daly, Chief Financial Officer for Archean Resources, quoted by Moira Baird in *The Telegram*, St. John's, November 19, 2002

In January 2004, Terry Ortslan reviewed the forecasts that the members of Toronto's Mineral Resource Analysts Group had made at the end of 2002, and concluded that we had all been surprised by the heights to which nickel prices had risen. As 2004 began, it was becoming clear that the world was facing a shortage of nickel and that there weren't any big new sources of supply in the next few years, other than Voisey's Bay and Goro. Voisey's Bay would not ship concentrate before mid-2006 and Goro had been delayed until, at the earliest, the second half of 2006.

The Prospectors and Developers Association of Canada invited me to talk about nickel at the Association's annual convention in Toronto in March 2004. I focused on what I believed to be the most important issue facing the nickel industry: looming shortages. On March 10, I mounted the podium in a huge underground concrete bunker, shielded my eyes from the brilliant lights, and began to list the reasons for the shortage. Firstly, I pointed out, the demand for nickel had been growing strongly, thanks in large part to the Chinese economic juggernaut. Then I talked about the social history of nickel.

"Let me take you back ten or fifteen years to the late 1980s and early 1990s. At that time, we saw an increase in the public's worries about the dangers of germs. People were growing more and more concerned about AIDS. Lucien Bouchard lost his leg and Muppeteer Jim Henson his life to antibiotic-resistant superbugs. Books and movies dealt with gruesome plagues like Ebola. Diners stopped sharing utensils. 'Seinfeld' portrayed the urban angst visited upon a pizza maker who didn't wash his hands after visiting the bathroom, and on a chip eater who dipped again in the communal bowl after already having taken a bite. Demand for Lysol, which was traditionally a down-market product, soared when its manufacturer introduced an antibacterial version. Sales of bar soap plummeted; sales of soap pumps soared.

And stainless steel began a massive invasion of the domestic kitchen. What are the first words you think of when you think of stainless steel? For many people, the answers are words like 'cleanliness,' 'hygiene,' 'surgical sterility.' Guess what! Stainless steel is the single major end use of nickel, accounting for about two-thirds of total consumption. Although I will not give microbe mania all of the credit for having increased the Western world's growth in consumption of nickel from 3.5% p.a. in the 1980s to 5.6% in the 1990s, it was a factor.

"The last few years have been a little like the late 1980s and early 1990s. There has been a resurgence in concern about public hygiene, prompted by outbreaks of SARS, West Nile virus, Norwalk virus, and bird flu. These concerns should ensure that stainless steel kitchens are not a short-lived fad like the Avocado and Harvest Gold appliances of the 1970s. Stainless should continue to move down-market, and it should continue to replace plastics, ceramics, mild steel, and brass. Over the next ten years, we may even see stainless steel invade the domestic bathroom."

At this point, as I flashed on the screen a picture of a stainless steel toilet bowl from an upmarket bathroom, I overheard a fellow from the Nickel Institute whisper to his neighbour, "Upmarket? That's prison issue!"

"In the nickel markets of the next two or three years," I continued, "demand from China will be even more important than our growing fear of germs. Like so many speakers at this convention, I can't overstate China's importance." I threw in some statistics about the phenomenal growth in stainless steel demand in China, and concluded that "China will follow Japan's path, and enjoy several more decades of sustained strong growth in consumption of nickel."

My presentation turned to the supply side and looked at the reasons why there had been so little increase in nickel production in the preceding years: the flood of nickel from the former Soviet Union in the early to mid-1990s, and the threat of early and massive production of nickel from Voisey's Bay and the Australian laterites. "All three," I said, "had discouraged companies from investing in new nickel mines."

In the late 1990s, Inco had recognized the possibility that there could be a global shortage of nickel in the following decade. Inco also recognized that the weakest link in its production chain was its mines.

I recall a conversation with Liz in mid-2003. She'd asked why Inco was so keen to develop new mines like Goro and Voisey's Bay while it had resisted, kicking and screaming, adding new smelting and refining capacity in Newfoundland. I answered her question with another question.

"What do you think is the average life of a nickel mine, Liz?"

"I don't know what the average life of a nickel mine is, Goldie! Is this a trick question?"

"I suppose it is. I don't even know the answer myself. Humour me and guess."

"OK — twenty years."

"OK, so if it's twenty years, that means that, on average, 1/20, 5%, of the world's nickel ore reserves is falling off the table every year." With one hand, I pushed the other off the table of Liz's boardroom. "So, you have to add 5% to your new ore reserves every year and then develop those reserves just to keep your production steady. That's a lot of running just to stay in the same place. But a nickel smelter is like the dog teams I used to see in northern Quebec in the winter: throw them a few frozen fish and they just keep going."

* * * * *

In order to find and develop new sources of nickel ore to feed its smelters, and to do so on a limited budget, Inco's management came up with an imaginative plan. The company decided to create a nursery for "baby Incos." Inco helped provide some of the money that

Jubilee Mines NL and LionOre Mining International Ltd. needed to bring nickel mines into production in Australia. It sold some tired old nickel properties in Sudbury to FNX Mining Company Inc. and Dynatec Corp. in the hope that the latter companies could finance further exploration and bring the shut-down mines back into production. It optioned its laterite nickel properties in Brazil and Guatemala to Canico Resource Corp. and Skye Resources Inc., respectively. Without any prompting from Inco, another baby joined the nursery: Altius Minerals Corporation.

* * * * *

While Roger Grimes was charming Irish miners with his earthy language at the North Atlantic Mineral Symposium in Dublin in 1999, some of his compatriots were manning a trade show booth. Brian Dalton, an engaging and disarmingly young President and Chief Executive Officer of Altius, was displaying his company's wares. Dalton had grown up in Cape Broyle, on Newfoundland's Southern Shore (which is really its eastern shore), south of St. John's; he studied geology at Memorial University in Newfoundland and entered the mining exploration business during the exploration rush that followed Al Chislett and Chris Verbiski's discovery of Voisey's Bay. In 1997, Dalton formed a team that included Roland Butler, a geologist whom he had met at university, Geoff Thurlow, an old hand at Newfoundland geology, and John Baker, a St. John's lawyer. Mr. Baker was the cousin of Max Baker, who had been my field assistant when I worked for Kennco in 1970.

Dalton's group formed Altius to carry out mineral exploration in Newfoundland with the idea that Altius would acquire properties, then make deals whereby well-heeled senior mining companies would pay Altius to explore them. In return, the senior companies would earn interests in the properties but not in Altius itself. This is an admirable business model for two reasons.

Firstly, it enables a junior company to have interests in many active exploration programs without either diluting its shareholders' interest in the company or running the risk of a "take-under."[338]

Secondly, if one major company were to be a big shareholder, it might inhibit the junior company's ability to do business with other majors.

The model is not easy to implement but, in Altius's first five years, Dalton and his team signed twenty-nine deals of this type. I'm not entirely sure how they did it, but I suspect that charm, good timing, local knowledge, and technical expertise went a long way.

At the end of 2003, one of my clients, who managed a flow-through fund[339] and was looking for investments, remarked wryly that Altius was so efficient at spending other mining companies' money that it had no need of his.

Despite the success of Altius's business model, in 2003 Mr. Dalton was trying to convince his partners that they should waive its principles, just this once, in order to pursue a seductive and prestigious opportunity.

As Brian Dalton's team was building Altius, Archean Resources was fighting to have the government of Newfoundland and Labrador reduce what it termed the "obscene" (57.34%) rate at which the government would tax Archean's royalty payments from Voisey's Bay.

After a five-year legal battle, the courts rejected Archean's claim that it should be exempted from the "J.C. Doyle" tax on royalty payments. Archean sought leave to appeal to the Supreme Court of Canada. However, the government brought in a bill to clearly establish the "J.C. Doyle" tax in law, making an appeal pointless, so Archean began a publicity campaign to shame the government into amending the bill.

"We're the highest-taxed company in all of Canada, according to Ernst and Young," Archean's Chris Daly told anyone who would listen. "Why should we pay more than Inco?"[340]

The Newfoundland and Labrador Chamber of Mineral Resources lobbied on Archean's behalf, but Mines Minister Lloyd Matthews was unmoved. "The people of the province, the owners of the resources," he said, "will be served better ... by getting more rather than less taxes from these major resource funds [like Voisey's Bay]." Mr. Matthews's colleague, Finance Minister Joan Aylward, was more specific and more emphatic. The government should, she said, "tax the recipient of the royalty paid by the mine operator and allow a deduction to the company that builds the mine." The 'J.C. Doyle tax'

... has been in place for almost thirty years. ... [It] will apply to all mineral rights and mining rights."[341] She shed no tears for Archean which, to her, appeared "to have negotiated a net-smelter royalty contract in 1993 without determining the tax consequences of the transaction."[342]

On January 13, 2003, Chris Daly called me, suggesting that Archean was interested in becoming a public company. At his request, I ran some numbers through my financial models to determine what Archean was worth, then referred him to my colleague, Rodger Gray, a corporate financier who had begun his career as an underground miner with Inco in Sudbury and who had had some experience with taking companies public. On January 20, Rodger strolled into my office, scanned the windows of the hotel rooms across the street for signs of activity, toyed with my sample of aluminum ingot, and, glasses askew on chubby face, came to the point.

"Ray, I'll go and see these fellows — Daly and what? Verbiski? — but the reality is they probably shouldn't go public."

"Why not, Rodge?"

"If Archean really does have to pay a tax rate of about 57% on its royalty revenues, those revenues would be worth more to lower-taxed Inco than to Archean, so it would make more sense for Archean to sell the royalty to Inco than to the general public through an IPO.[343] But don't worry, Ray, I'll go. How long can a trip to Newfoundland take anyway?"

Rodger left Toronto for St. John's at 7:10 a.m. on February 3, 2003. I next saw him on February 5.

"How did it go, Rodge?"

"Ray, you wouldn't believe it. A gem in the annals of fuck-updom. We were about to take off from Toronto when a passenger stood up and declared that this plane wasn't leaving the ground. When a stewardess rushed over to get her to sit down and shut up, the passenger said to her, 'But listen!' The stewardess stopped and listened and I don't know what she heard — I couldn't hear anything unusual — but it was enough to make her rush to the cockpit. Eventually, two annoyed pilots marched back, cocked their ears, shook their heads, walked back, and drove the plane back to the terminal. I don't know who the passenger was, or what she heard, but it must've been serious 'cause we waited three hours while they found a mechanic, then waited for him to fix the problem."

"Scary!"

"Yes, Ray, but it gets better — er, worse. We had to stop in Halifax. More delays. Just as we were about to take off from Halifax ..."

"Another mysterious passenger?"

"No, one of the cabin staff announced that, because of the delays, by the time they arrived in St. John's they'd've exceeded their union-mandated maximum hours of service. So the pilots took the plane back to the gate and we passengers were treated to the surreal sight of our crew walking off and waving goodbye. It was hours before they found another crew willing and able to work. Ray, I was pretty hungry by that time."

"You didn't eat while you were waiting at the terminal?"

"No, we stayed in the plane each time. Our last crew was sympathetic. They thanked us for our patience and said they'd reward us with a free drink once we were aloft. Big whoop! 'Course, it was only once we were aloft that they discovered that the previous flight crew had neglected to pack any drinks at all."

"OK, did your meetings with Archean go any better than your encounters with Air Canada?"

"Oh — delightful guys. St. John's was a hoot. I still don't think Archean should go public anytime soon but, if they do, we should be part of it."

Three months after Rodger's epic flight to St. John's, on April 21, 2003, Brian Dalton calls me to ask if I might be interested in some potential corporate finance business. Sure, I am interested, and after I agree that the discussions would be confidential, Brian, a couple of our corporate financiers, and I hold a conference call. Brian reveals that Archean Resources has approached him offering to sell Altius part of its 3% royalty interest in the Net Smelter Returns (NSR) from Inco's deposits in Labrador, both known deposits and those yet to be discovered.[344]

"Why you? Why Altius, Brian?"

"It's in part because, through exploration, we are generating Newfoundland tax credits that can be used to reduce the tax burden on the royalties. It's in part, too, I think, because Chris Verbiski knows me and trusts me. He once taught me gold panning at a prospectors' course, and I've worked for him. I got reacquainted with him when I helped the Chamber of Mineral Resources lobby the government on behalf of Archean Resources."

Dalton and Archean had agreed that Altius would issue 750,000 common share warrants to Archean and pay $9.75 million to Archean. In return, Archean Resources would pass to Altius a 7.5% share of its Labrador royalty, with an option to buy another 2.5% in the next four years. Dalton is putting together a group of investment dealers to raise the $9.75 million by selling shares of Altius to the public. He asks if we are interested in becoming part of the group.

"Could Inco block the deal, Brian?"

"They do have a right of first refusal on buying the royalty, but I was talking with Stuart Feiner, Inco's chief in-house lawyer. They seem inclined to conserve cash and let us go ahead. I'm surprised at how quickly they've responded."

"What would you do with the cash coming in from the royalty?"

"In part, at least, fund exploration. It's always been too expensive for us to operate in Labrador. This could open up Labrador to us."

My corporate finance colleagues take a close look at Dalton's proposals but decide to pass, preferring to work on larger deals.

On June 3, 2003, Altius announces that it has agreed to purchase an interest in Archean Resources' interest in Voisey's Bay. Archean was to put the royalty into a limited partnership, then sell a 7.5% interest in the partnership to Altius with an option for Altius to buy a further 2.5% interest by November 2006.

On July 10, Altius consummates this acquisition. The stock market now has, once again, a play on the development of Voisey's Bay other than that represented by the common shares of Inco.

CHAPTER 34

AHEAD OF SCHEDULE

"We've had our differences with the Innu in the past, but now we're like this," he said, holding up two intertwined fingers.
— Scott Hand, CEO, Inco Ltd., presentation to Toronto's Mineral Mineral Resource Analysts Group, December 5, 2003

I think it's worked out pretty well.
— Former Premier Brian Tobin, on Voisey's Bay, quoted by Wendy Stueck, *The Globe and Mail*, Toronto, June 17, 2004

Peter [Penashue] is one of this country's most promising and gifted young leaders. He was recently selected as one of Canada's Top 40 Under 40 Leaders.
— Brian Tobin, 2002

The splendid task will soon be fulfilled.
— Motto of Labrador, as translated by White, 2003

December 3, 2002: Peter Penashue, President of the Innu Nation, stands quietly beside Scott Hand and Sheshatshiu Band Chief Paul Rich on the stage of the former trading floor of the Toronto Stock Exchange. Under gilded Art Deco renditions of early twentieth-century resource developments in Canada, he listens to jocular jousting between John Crosbie and Brian Tobin. When it is his turn to take the microphone, he immediately changes the mood of the meeting. He reminds us that the purpose of the gathering is to promote the Innu Healing Foundation, whose goal is to build sports facilities for the Innu of Natuashish (the new name for the relocated community of Davis Inlet) and Sheshatshiu.

"No jokes from me," he says, "because I'm a very serious person." He explains that seeing his father regularly beat his mother has made him that way. "Innu parents have failed their children, so I'm very guarded in what I say."

Mr. Penashue and Mr. Hand had met a few months earlier when Mr. Hand and Premier Grimes flew into Voisey's Bay to see the new road, the new airstrip, and the people who were building them. Mr. Grimes presented Mr. Penashue with a $750,000 cheque for the Innu Healing Foundation.

William Barbour, President of the Labrador Inuit Association, also met Messrs. Grimes and Hand at Voisey's Bay. Mr. Barbour was pleased that, of the 140 workers on-site, 81 were from Labrador and 48 were members of the L.I.A. He affirmed that the Inuit were committed to the Voisey's Bay project and, in a verbal nudge to Mr. Grimes, added that the Inuit looked forward to completing their land claims deal. Mr. Grimes replied that he expected that his government would initial the deal that fall, and that he hoped the federal and provincial legislatures would give their final approvals by the spring of 2003.[345]

Fall 2002 ended without a deal. December came. Still no deal, but the native groups saw the first financial fruit of their Impact Benefit Agreements with Inco. The L.I.A. put its cheque into a trust fund to be administered by a board that would consider applications for compensation should the Voisey's Bay project infringe on traditional activities such as hunting. The Innu Nation distributed its payment to its members, telling them it had to be spent on furniture or vehicles.[346]

Spring 2003 came and went. No word of a final deal for the Inuit. Finally, on August 29, 2003, Premier Grimes announced that his government, the L.I.A., and the Government of Canada had that day initialled a deal to settle the L.I.A.'s land claims and to allow the Inuit a limited form of self-government. Mr. Grimes pointed out that the agreement had not yet been ratified by either the Inuit or the provincial and federal governments, and he wisely refrained from speculating when these events might occur.

The agreement set two important rules for the ratification vote by the Inuit.

Firstly, all individuals — not only members of the L.I.A. — *all* individuals with at least one-quarter Inuit ancestry (presumably only *Labrador* Inuit ancestry) could vote, regardless of where they lived.[347]

Secondly, to pass, the deal had to be approved by 50%, plus one, of the 4,300 eligible voters — not just those who voted, *all* eligible voters. In other words, no vote was a "No" vote.

On May 26, 2004, three-quarters of the eligible voters voted in favour of the deal.[348] The next steps would be to obtain provincial and federal ratification. Newfoundland and Labrador's minister responsible, Thomas Rideout, announced that he looked forward to introducing ratification legislation to his parliament that fall, and he hoped that the federal government would do the same after the federal election on June 28, 2004.

September 22, 2003

I point out to the morning meeting that, on September 19, the Supreme Court of Canada ruled unanimously that "the Metis people are a distinct aboriginal group." This judgment, "the Powley case," had given the approximately 300,000 Metis people across the country a status similar to that of native Indians and Inuit.[349] It could mean, I speculate, that the Newfoundland and Labrador government will now direct Inco to reach an agreement with the Labrador Metis Nation similar to its agreements with the Innu Nation and the L.I.A. The cost to Inco? Perhaps US$0.01 per share per year.

October 8, 2003

In a press release, the Progressive Conservative Opposition Leader, Danny Williams, affirms, "Our commitments to the Labrador Metis are solid. ... A PC government I lead will acknowledge that the recent Supreme Court of Canada decision in the Powley case does indeed apply to Metis in Newfoundland and Labrador."

October 21, 2003

Election day in Newfoundland. When the votes are counted, Danny Williams's Progressive Conservative Party has defeated Roger Grimes's

Liberals. PC Fabian Manning, who had polled his constituents asking for permission to defy his party's policy by voting for Roger Grimes's deal with Inco on Voisey's Bay, scores 65% of the votes cast in his riding.

Newfoundland and Labrador's new Minister of Natural Resources will be Ed Byrne, who had led the PC party between 1998 and 2001.

Inco's Scott Hand isn't worried that a party that had been opposed to Inco's deal with the former government was now in power. "Nothing could change as a result of the new government in Newfoundland," he declares. "We have had a definitive agreement since last October."[350]

February 5, 2004

"Look at this, Patricia. I had to read it three times to figure it out." I thrust a Newfoundland and Labrador government press release towards her.

"'Premier Danny Williams stands by commitment that the Powley decision applies to Section 35 Metis in the province,'" she reads. "Sounds clear to me, Ray."

"Yeah, my first reaction was, 'well, good for him!' But read the rest, Patricia."

"'Based on the province's legal view of Powley, it is our assessment that members of the Labrador Metis Nation do not meet the criteria put forward by the Supreme Court to determine who may be Section 35 Metis and enjoy aboriginal rights.'" Patricia now looks perplexed.

"Section 35 is the section of the Canadian constitution dealing with the rights of aboriginals."

"So ..." says Patricia slowly, "despite the headline, the premier thinks that the Powley decision does *not* apply to the Labrador Metis."

"That's the way I read it." I pause. "The way Mr. Williams handled this story reminds me of the old story about how a politician would formulate the laws of thermodynamics."

"I'll bite, Goldie."

"Well, the first law of thermodynamics says you can never get as much out of anything as you put in. So, a politician wanting to get elected will campaign on the second law, which says, well, you *can*; at a temperature of absolute zero you *can* get as much out as you put in. But once in office, he'll invoke the third law, which says you can't get to absolute zero."

"So, no pressure on Inco to make a deal with the Labrador Metis Nation?"

"Right — and just to stick the knife in a little further, you'll see that Mr. Williams goes on to say that 'The Labrador Metis Nation land claim has never been accepted by the federal government.'"

April 3, 2004

One of the other aboriginal groups excluded from the formal agreements at Voisey's Bay, the Innu of Quebec, bring attention to themselves by illegally hunting caribou in Labrador. "I am appalled," says Minister Byrne. Peter Penashue adds that he thinks that the Quebec Innu are trying to establish claims to resources in Labrador.[351]

* * * * *

February 4, 2003

One of the analysts participating in Inco's conference call asks Scott Hand about the labour situation at Sudbury. Mr. Hand replies that the union's contract with Inco doesn't expire until May 31 and that formal negotiations won't begin until March. "Since we signed the last contract three years ago," he says, "we have taken on 1,200 new employees at Sudbury. As a result, this time around wages should be more of an issue and pensions should be less of an issue."

March 20, 2003

Inco issues a press release that includes, three months later than originally promised,[352] a summary of its feasibility study for the Voisey's Bay mine and mill. I walk to the trading desk. Donny is just reaching for the phone. He freezes when I call his name.

"Donny — Inco. Do you care?"

His hand drops.

"Ray, even a fuckin' research guy must know that the market's just opened. Put it in a fuckin' email!"

"'K."

```
MEMO
To: Sales/Trading
From: Ray Goldie
Re: Inco

Conference call 11 a.m. to discuss:
(a) US$77 million increase in capex for Voisey's
Bay;
(b) warning (without giving EPS estimates) that
costs in the first quarter of 2003 would be high-
er than previously estimated.

Comments:
(a) Cost increases at Voisey's Bay shouldn't be a
surprise. They are due largely to inflation since
the last estimates, made in 1999 in expectation
of what then seemed to be imminent commencement
of construction. In my own modelling, I've used
the 1999 figures, but added escalation in line
with the CPI.
(b) First quarter cost increases also shouldn't
be a surprise. They are due largely to a higher
$Cdn and higher oil prices than previously
expected. Inco also reminded investors that
changes in their realized prices lag changes in
the LME (by about six weeks). As I've pointed out
in the past, this is overlooked surprisingly
often.

Conclusion: although most of this news shouldn't
be a surprise, the market is likely to treat it
as such.
```

By the time Inco's conference call begins, the company's shares have dropped by $0.88, to $29.40. Inco's management does not reassure investors shaken by the press release. By the time the call is over, the stock has lost another $0.10.

June 17-19, 2003

There's no better way to travel from Toronto to Montreal than by train. March down to the bowels of Union Station, stride up the steps past the long line of coach passengers, and flash one's Club Ticket. Every seat is a window or an aisle; no need to find a cab and endure traffic congestion out to the airport, no lining up to obtain a boarding pass, no lining up to clear security, no need to juggle boarding pass, carry-on bag and government photo ID while lining up to board the plane, no need to line up getting *off* the plane, no need ...

As my train bores through fresh Ontario summer scenery, I feel increasingly claustrophobic. The gentleman in the seat beside me has laid out a laptop on his tray table and has donned a cellphone headset. With spreading arms and loud voice, he takes a succession of his clients through the process of updating the address-labelling software that he has sold them. Meanwhile, the two businesswomen in the seat in front of me spend most of their trip talking on their cellphones, with the gentleman behind me chiming in from time to time. When the train finally pulls into Montreal, and I walk to the elevator to the Queen E Hotel, I feel as though I have been liberated from a hostage incident in a phone booth.

Patricia had taken the plane. Over the next two days she and I would visit a dozen clients and make a dozen presentations, Patricia in her Montreal outfits: skirts a little shorter and heels a little spikier than in Toronto. Whether over croissants on the first floor of the Queen E, or high in office towers, overlooking the fresh green mountain or newly renovated Old Montreal, the core of each meeting is my message that Inco's shares are out of favour and therefore cheap, and that now is the time to buy them. Since December, I would point out, the market had whacked Inco's shares on three occasions. Each time, investors lost some of their confidence in the company's management.

The first blow had come on December 5, 2002, when Inco announced that the capital costs at its Goro project could be 30% to 45% higher than earlier estimates, and that the project would be delayed by at least six months. Over the next two trading days, Inco's shares had fallen by 8.6%.

Next, on March 4, 2003, Inco had announced that it would issue US$400- to US$500 million of convertible debt. Investors immediately began to speculate: (i) that hedge funds would purchase the new convertible securities, while simultaneously shortening Inco's common shares to the detriment of the price of the common shares; and (ii) that Inco was sending a signal that it was becoming worried about its ability to finance the development of Goro and Voisey's Bay. Over the next two trading days, Inco's shares had fallen by 6.6%.

Then came the nasty surprises of March 20: the release of the Voisey's Bay feasibility study and the announcement of higher costs at Inco's existing operations. During the following five trading days, Inco's share price had fallen by 8.9%.

I reminded my Montreal clients that whenever I had mentioned Inco to them in the first few months of 2003, most of them had become angry. They had wanted to punish the company's management. I had been waiting for a sign that the anger had subsided.

On April 15, 2003, Inco published its earnings for the first quarter of the year. The average of all analysts' forecasts[353] for these earnings had been US$0.20 per share. But Inco surprised everyone with a stellar number: US$0.29 per share. That day, grudgingly, the market had added 1.8% to Inco's share price.

Nevertheless, over the next five weeks, despite rising nickel prices, Inco's share price had fallen 9.2%, bottoming out at $25.15 on May 21. Then the market's sentiment changed. Ironically, what had changed it was a strike. A strike against Inco.

The contract between Inco and the United Steelworkers union at Sudbury, Ontario, was to expire on May 31, 2003. As the end of May approached with no signs of a settlement, Inco's share price rose because, as I had told *The Globe and Mail*,[354] "analysts believe the surge in [nickel] prices will help the stock more than any loss of production will hurt it." By May 28, Inco's share price had moved up to $28.12. On Sunday, June 1, the strike began. The next day, Inco's share price responded by moving up another 2.0%.

I would conclude each of my presentations in Montreal by saying that investors now seemed to have forgotten their gripes against Inco's management, that I couldn't think of any more bad news that could make them grumpy again, and that nickel prices seemed likely to soar.

And so, Madame or Monsieur Client, with Inco's share price around $28, could I please have your order?

Our last client call ends promptly and Patricia and I heave ourselves and our remaining sales materials into a cab on Sherbrooke Street East, run into the Queen E Hotel, pick up our bags, back into the cab and on to the airport. We are booked on the 6:00 plane, but we reach Dorval in time to catch the 5:00.

Visions of an early arrival home vanish when Air Canada cancels the 5:00 plane. I sit back and read a book while Patricia scrounges for a fashion magazine.

Time to call the 6:00 flight. The smartly pant-suited thirty-something lady boarding in front of me is clearly pissed that the airline had cancelled the 5:00 flight. "Air Canada has stolen an hour of my life," she grouses loudly to the grey-haired gentleman who accepts her boarding pass.

"Consider yourself fortunate, Madame. Air Canada has stolen *twenty-four years* of *my* life."

August 26, 2003

Inco announces a tentative agreement to end the strike in Sudbury. Inco's share price declines 0.9%, ending the day at $34.14.

July 20, 2004

"Ray."

My office door is open, and I can hear Patricia calling from the sales desk.

"Yuh?"

"Inco. Seventy-seven."

Donny chimes in. "Another typical fucking Inco disappointing earnings report!"

"Oh."

```
MEMO
To: Sales/Trading
From: Ray Goldie
Re: Inco
```

Inco Comes to Labrador

SUMMARY

DISAPPOINTMENT: operating costs
PLEASANT SURPRISE: Voisey's Bay is six months ahead of schedule

OUTLOOK: it may be September/October before the market recognizes the resurgence in China's economy and regains its enthusiasm for nickel stocks

DETAILS: I had forecast that Inco would earn US$0.92/share diluted, adjusted (i.e. excluding non-recurring items) in the second quarter of 2004. The actual figure was US$0.77/share.

Production and deliveries of nickel, copper and precious metals all exceeded my expectations. The disappointment appears to have been almost entirely on the cost side. Cash costs rose from US$1.90/lb of nickel in the second quarter of 2003 and US$2.42 in the first quarter of 2004 to US$2.54 in Q2. Because costs in the first quarter of 2004 were still affected by the carry-over of costs related to last year's strike, I had been expecting a decline in costs in the current quarter.

Inco attributed its high costs in the second quarter of 2004 to:
(i) higher costs of purchased feedstock for its smelters (because of higher nickel prices)
(ii) the Canadian dollar
(iii) maintenance and repair costs
(iv) employment costs

Well, we knew about the first two before Inco reported its numbers. The last two constitute the unpleasant surprise. Although Inco suggests some improvement in such costs in the second half of this year (because of productivity changes recently implemented) and in early 2006 (because Voisey's Bay is now six months ahead of schedule), I shall be obliged to increase my forecasts of costs and accordingly reduce my forecasts of earnings per share. (It will take a few days because Inco's subsidiary, PT Inco, which accounts for about a third of Inco's output of nickel, will not report for several more days.)

I continue to believe that Inco's shares are a
"Buy," that their prime driver is nickel markets,
and that it may be two or three more months before
the market gets enthused about nickel. The best
news in this regard are the indications that China
is enjoying a new surge of growth.

As I compose this email, I keep an eye on Inco's share price. Down Cdn$1.72 to Cdn$43.30. Ouch. The market doesn't like Inco's surprisingly high costs.

Later in the day, the share price regains most of its loss, probably because investors realize that an early start to Voisey's Bay means that Inco's costs should soon start coming down again. At least, that's what I tell the *Reuters* reporter when she calls.

```
To: Ray Goldie
Subject: Voisey's Bay
Sent: Wednesday, July 21, 2004, 2:10 PM
```

Ray,

I saw your quote in Reuters on Inco's announcement that Voisey's will be in production earlier than expected. Next time you are passing by our office, feel free to drop off that bottle of malt scotch from our bet. I recall your guess was production post Jan 1, 2008.

Feel free to wait until the first ore is mined if you like!!

****

Richard A. Ross
President & CEO
Inmet Mining Corporation

*****

August 19, 2004 — Voisey's Bay, Labrador

Inco's President, Peter Jones, looks over the fifty analysts and fund managers seated before him in the cafeteria of the Voisey's Bay construction camp. "As Gord Bacon told you last night, the research and development program to test the hydrometallurgical process is going very well," he says. In fact, Dr. Bacon had confidently predicted that Inco would have a commercial hydromet plant in operation at Argentia, Newfoundland, by the end of 2011. It would produce 50,000 tonnes of nickel metal per year and 2,500 tonnes of cobalt metal. And, even though the provincial government had decided not to require Inco to smelt and refine copper in Newfoundland and Labrador, Dr. Bacon had added, "I would suspect very strongly that we're going to produce copper [metal] ... at Argentia."

I look around the spartan room, lit by fluorescent lights and by the surprisingly sunny day outside. Hey, there is Wiktor Bielski, the first time I have seen him since the Asian Crisis of 1997 (he must be back in the business); Fraser Phillips, too; there is Terry Ortslan, undoubtedly taking notes on Sandra Scott's superb organization of our tour of Voisey's Bay[355] in order to better plan the forthcoming M.R.A.G. tour of Peru; and there, wearing a bemused expression, is John Redstone, New Caledonia's beach man.

After the presentations, Mr. Redstone and I approached Inco's President Jones.

"Peter," says Redstone, "if a hydrometallurgical plant at Argentia — or anywhere for that matter — produces commercial quantities of metals from Voisey's Bay, I'll show up at the opening ceremony clad only in my trench coat."

Redstone turns to me, sniffs, and adds, "I'm told my backside is quite attractive under appropriate lighting conditions, notably complete darkness."

Peter Penashue, President of the Innu Nation, had spoken after Mr. Jones. "This project," he declared, "has employed 130 Innu who would otherwise be on welfare. The project has given our young people a future. We own 51% of the cafeteria you're in. We own 51% of the airline you came in on, so our young people can now look forward to becoming pilots. We're the biggest employer right now in Labrador. Compare that with where we were four years ago. It's incredible. It's possible because we were able to sign a deal [with Inco]."

The President of the Labrador Inuit Association, William Andersen, had also stood to speak. "The rest of the world destroyed our lifestyle by doing away with the fur trapping and sealing industries ... but now, thanks to our deal with Inco, things are looking very positive for the Inuit of Labrador."

Peter Jones thanked his native partners and outlined one of the concessions that Inco had made in order to secure a deal with the L.I.A. For example, to reduce the danger to Inuit travelling on the sea ice, Inco will suspend shipments from Voisey's Bay during two six-week periods each year: when the ice is freezing; and when it's breaking up. However, Inco will make no concessions to native employees who wish to hunt or fish or have family visit them while they are on-site.

At the back of the room, Dan Lee shows us trays of shiny drill core, and points out, on a wall map, the discoveries that Diamond Fields and Inco have made since Diamond Fields found the Ovoid: Reid Brook; Reid Brook Deep; Southeast Extension; Eastern Deeps; Far Eastern Deeps; and Ryan's Pond. All are Inco's properties and are within 5 kilometres of the Ovoid.

"Hey, Ray," Dan says, his big bearded face lighting up, "Tony Naldrett dropped in just last week! There's been very little grassroots exploration at Voisey's in recent years, but the jump in the price of nickel has brought in a junior, Cornerstone, which has a joint venture with Falconbridge. They're looking for a Voisey's Bay–type deposit just west of here, and Tony is consulting for them."

We spill outside into the sun, grateful that the deerflies, blackflies, and mosquitoes appear to have heeded Scott Hand's admonition that they might participate in our tour only on a "listen-only basis." We squeeze into two dusty school buses. I ask our driver, an Inuk, about his job.

"I live in Goose," he says, "and they send a plane to pick me up every six weeks. It's four weeks on, two weeks off."

He follows a bumpy, unpaved road, Voisey's Bay's only road, past the abandoned site of Diamond Fields's camp. On the hillside above, Diamond Fields's drill core still lies stacked in wooden boxes. We disembark and walk up a hill overlooking the Ovoid. It is no longer under a bog. Shovels and trucks are removing 6 million tonnes of glacial debris. They have just uncovered the first patch of gleaming high-grade ore. Dan Lee points out where he and Bruce Ryan mapped in the mid-1980s. Redstone nudges me.

"Ray — I've got the perfect title for the last chapter of your book: 'Lords of the Ovoid!'"

Sandra shepherds us back into the bus for our last stop, the busy port. As we admire the magnificent view of shining sea and ancient, steep-sided, round-topped, clefted hills, their lower slopes treed, their upper slopes tundra, it is Dan Lee's turn to nudge me.

"Down there," he says, pointing, "is the world's finest fishing spot for Arctic char!"

Peter Jones ambles over.

"Impressed, Ray?"

"Very!"

"Feel free to drop off that whisky anytime!"

* * * * *

November 24, 2004
Wellington International Airport

I approach the clerk at the liquor counter of the duty-free store. "Do you have any specials on Ardbeg or Glen Moray?"

APPENDIX 1
VALUING MINING STOCKS

Traditional techniques which analysts use to value the shares of mining companies include: Discounted Cash Flows; Option Pricing (i.e. treating a mine as an option to produce a commodity); the application of P/E and Price-to-Cash flow multiples and a variant, the Peak Multiple approach; and Break-Up Valuation (i.e. valuing each piece for the company separately and adding up the results). In applying these techniques, I have uncovered anomalies which are both persistent and difficult to explain. For example:

> (1) base metal stocks usually trade at a discount to their option-pricing valuation, suggesting that, as noted in the Preface, "the option-pricing valuation is generally an indicator of the highest share price available under a management policy of auctioning the firm."
> (2) Between 1986 and 1990, when the giant mining company Noranda Inc. owned partial interests in a variety of publicly traded companies, I was able to calculate that Noranda's shares traded at between 61% and 81% (averaging 68%) of their break-up value.
> (3) Stocks which represent a pure or liquid play on a particular commodity often trade at prices higher than traditional valuation techniques would indicate. For example, at a meeting with analysts on December 2, 1996, the management of Cameco, a large producer of uranium, stated that the market valued Cameco's earnings and cash-flows at a premium to those of producers of base metals, but at a discount to those of gold producers.
> (4) Although Inco produces about five times as much nickel as copper, Inco's share price has sometimes tracked the price of copper more closely than the price of nickel.

Because of these anomalies, I often take a pragmatic approach to valuation. At any given time, I may assume that the market is appropriately valuing its expectations of a company's future. Then I ask whether those expectations are more likely to improve or to deteriorate, and rate the stock's potential performance accordingly.

The Class VBN shares of Inco provided a good example of this approach. On March 26, 1996, Inco proposed to issue the Class VBN shares as part of its intended takeover of Diamond Fields Resources, and indicated a valuation of $42.00 per VBN share. However, in the view of Falconbridge Limited (which was also bidding for Diamond Fields), the Class VBN shares were each worth only about $24.00.

I had constructed an elaborate valuation model for the Class VBN shares, based on discounting back to the present, at the historic rate of return on Canadian equities (i.e. Long Canadas plus 560 basis points), a series of cash flows based on the assumption that over 220 million tonnes of ore would eventually be discovered and mined at Voisey's Bay. My model gave a value for the Class VBN shares which was similar to Falconbridge's estimate.

Inco eventually issued the Class VBN shares with an added feature: a stipulation that the dividend on these shares would never be less than 80% of the dividend on the common shares. This improvement added, I estimated, about $1.20 to the value of these shares.

In initial trading, the Class VBN shares changed hands at prices as high as $43.75, demonstrating that the market accepted Inco's indicated price and not Falconbridge's (or my) valuation. Subsequently, however, the price of the Class VBN shares was driven by events which changed investors' expectations about the future of the Voisey's Bay project, notably:

(a) moves in nickel prices;
(b) the realization that Inco's Chairman Sopko had been too optimistic when, in May 1996, he speculated that the mine would be in production by the end of 1998;
(c) the realization that the mine would cost more to build than Inco had originally expected.

APPENDIX 2
PRICE CHARTS

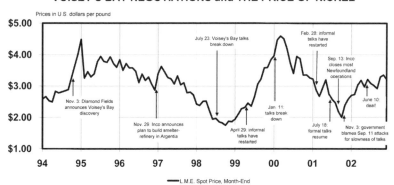

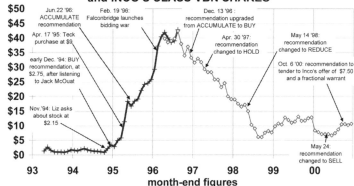

APPENDIX 3

TERRY CREBS'S REMINISCENCES, BY EMAIL, OF EARLY 1995

Before Archean Resources [the company owned by prospectors Al Chislett and Chris Verbiski] and Diamond Fields contacted me, Diamond Fields thought their geophysical anomalies were being caused by a slablike mineralized body that leaned to the south. Al Chislett, however, thought they were being caused by a mineralized body shaped like a doughnut — the technical term is "ring dyke."

Mike McMurrough of Diamond Fields and Al Chislett called me at about 10 p.m. my time in Denver (Jan-10?-95). They must have been worried — hell, it would have been 1:30 a.m. where they were in St. John's! They wanted my assessment of the hole they were then drilling, Drill Hole 6. Drill Hole 6 had gone down 140 metres and had intercepted just a few metres of very weak mineralization at the 70-metre drill depth.

I told them to fax me the geophysical data and I would give them my assessment in the morning. They sent me only the EM data, which indicated to me that Drill Hole 6 was a dud because it had drilled under the conductive zone; therefore, I recommended DFR to stop drilling and move the drill 200 metres to the south to drill the centre of the EM anomaly. I told Mike and Al that, at that location, they would hit massive mineralization at a drill depth of 20 metres. Al protested and said his geologist had told him to continue drilling DDH-6. I told Al to "fire your GD'ed geologist because he's drilling blind," because the EM data could detect conductors only within about 50 metres of the surface.

(As an aside, Al didn't shut down Drill Hole 6 until it had drilled over 240 more metres of barren rock. "Looking at the labelling on the map you faxed me, Ray, I think I can understand now why Al didn't want to move

Appendix 3

the drill to the location I recommended — he apparently didn't know which geophysicist or geologist to believe when it came to interpreting the geophysical data.")

I asked Al if any magnetic data had been acquired over the EM anomaly. Al said "yes," and his description of the magnetic pattern made me quite confident of my recommendation. Al, however, wanted to move the drill 400 metres to the south. I told him that he could miss if he moved the drill too far to the south.

(As another aside, Drill Hole 9 was later drilled about 400 metres south of Drill Hole 6, and it *did* miss the massive mineralization.)

McMurrough later told me that, after that phone conversation, he lobbied hard for my recommendation to Drill Hole 7 200 metres south of Drill Hole 6. And, four days later, (Jan. 15?) I got a conference call from McMurrough, Chislett, and Boulle (who was in Europe). They told me that they had put Drill Hole 7 where I recommended, and congratulated me on the high-grade massive mineralization that they had just hit at 19.6 metres drill-depth.

I congratulated them for following my advice (grin). Because neither the EM system they used nor magnetic data are very good at imaging the bottom of highly conductive and magnetic ore, I was interested to know what thickness of mineralization they had intercepted. They said something like 138 metres, and I dropped to my knees — I knew we'd hit a world-class nickel ore body with Drill Hole 7.

Drill Hole 7 still holds the record for the richest nickel mineralization of any hole drilled in Labrador. Drill Hole 7 was the first hole I spotted in Labrador; therefore, I think the Ovoid is a classic geophysical discovery. The prospectors were good, but there is no rusty rock or any other geological indication over the Ovoid; it's a blind target.

Yup, the Ovoid discovery has been the highlight (technically and financially) of my thirty-two years in mining exploration geophysics. I told Al, Chris, and Mike their Drill Hole 2 was pretty good too, but they never liked being teased by a "GD'ed Yank," heh-heh.

ENDNOTES

1. Goldie, R. and Yedlin, D., *Canadian Investment Review*, Summer 1993.
2. Equivalent to the former Grade 13 of some Canadian high schools.
3. To a rational economist, the only factors that should have determined the discount rate that I chose should have been current interest rates, my expectations about future rates of inflation, and my assessment of Keith's creditworthiness. However, two researchers at McMaster University in Hamilton, Ontario (Wilson and Daly, 2003) have shown the importance of other factors. Their work suggests that, for example, the sight of a beautiful woman can influence men to select higher discount rates, and that the sight of an impressive car may have a similar effect on women.
4. A Canadian subsidiary of the giant U.S. copper company, Kennecott.
5. In the Crystal Lake Gabbro, a mafic intrusion. (Intrusions are bodies formed when molten rock, with a chemical composition similar to that of basalt, cools and freezes below the surface of the earth.)
6. According to White (2003), the original church burnt down in 1921 and was rebuilt in 1922.
7. "Down: Northward along the coast. ... Newfoundlanders have always said 'down' to any place north of where they were living"; Story et al, 1990.
8. "Deer: Caribou"; Story et al, 1990.
9. "Screech: ... a variety of cheap, dark Demerara rum bottled in Newfoundland"; Story et al, 1990.
10. We had sent rock samples to a laboratory for chemical analysis. The laboratory's reports of the concentrations of metals in these samples are called "assays."
11. Molloy, 1977.
12. "Troctolite" is an esoteric name for a specific type of mafic igneous rock.
13. The prices of Diamond Fields's shares in this chapter are before allowance for a subsequent 4:1 stock split.
14. The current estimate is 10,500–11,500 years ago, according to Clark and Fitzhugh, 1991.
15. Goldie and Tredger, 1992.
16. In the chart in Appendix 2, this price is shown as $2.75. This is because, on September 21, 1995, Diamond Fields split its stock, giving its shareholders four split shares for each share they held.
17. See, for example, Haugen and Jorion, 1996.
18. The prices of Diamond Fields's shares in this chapter are quoted before the subsequent 4:1 split.
19. *Hansard*, Newfoundland and Labrador House of Assembly, May 15, 1995.
20. PGE: "platinum group elements" — platinum, palladium, and related precious metals.

21. Ferronickel: an alloy of iron and nickel. Stainless steel producers are able to use, as feedstock, either refined nickel or ferronickel.
22. Raglan: a Falconbridge nickel mine in far northern Quebec.
23. Keith drew this inference from Ibbotson and Sinquefield's 1979 study, which indicated that the standard deviation of annual rates of return on U.S. common stocks in the period 1926 to 1978 was 22.2%. Keith proposed that stocks be classified according to a 10%–20%–40%–20%–10% scheme in Ambachtsheer (1977).
24. "Pinch-point" is a trademark registered to Raymond Goldie.
25. Meaning the Cabinet.
26. Which would have been $153.00 had Diamond Fields not split its stock, four for one, on September 21, 1995.
27. Equivalent to $151.00 before the 4:1 share split.
28. Inco completed fulfillment of this commitment in August 1999.
29. Bloomberg, July 25, 1996.
30. Inco press releases, August 20, 1996 and August 21, 1996.
31. *Hansard*, Newfoundland and Labrador House of Assembly, May 28, 1996.
32. Inco press releases, August 23 and 27, 1996.
33. *Hansard*, Newfoundland and Labrador House of Assembly, March 27, 1996.
34. Bloomberg Business News, September 11, 1996.
35. *The Financial Post*, Toronto, September 30, 1997.
36. *The Globe and Mail*, Toronto, October 31, 2000.
37. This was a reference to a Newfoundland song that warned of the dangers of confederation with Canada ("Come near at your peril, Canadian wolf," Anon., 1869).
38. *Hansard*, Newfoundland and Labrador House of Assembly, March 27, 1996.
39. Dr. Sopko made these comments during the conference call, March 26, 1997, which followed Inco's announcement of its bid to take over Diamond Fields Resources.
40. *Hansard*, Newfoundland and Labrador House of Assembly, March 27, 1996.
41. *Hansard*, Newfoundland and Labrador House of Assembly, December 19, 1995.
42. Inco press release, December 2, 1996.
43. Press release, Government of Newfoundland and Labrador, January 10, 1997 and comments by Stewart Gendron, the President of Voisey's Bay Nickel Company, during an Inco conference call on April 23, 1997.
44. Eileen Houlihan, 1992.
45. Troke et al, 2001.
46. A piece by Pat Doyle in the St. John's *Evening Telegram* of September 18, 1997 supported this view. Mr. Doyle reported that "Colin Janes of the federal

agency Public Works and Government Services Canada, is in charge of the cleanup of Argentia. 'Before any land is passed over to [Voisey's Bay Nickel Co. Ltd.], an agreement must be concluded between Public Works and Voisey's Bay Nickel,' he said."

47. Canada Newswire, St. John's, June 5, 1998.
48. Press release, Government of Newfoundland and Labrador, August 27, 1997.
49. *The Financial Post*, Toronto, September 30, 1997.
50. Allan Robinson, *The Globe and Mail*, Toronto, September 16, 1997.
51. *The Globe and Mail*, Toronto, March 18, 1998.
52. *Platts Metals Week*, October 28, 1996. At Inco's Special and Annual Meeting on May 22, 1996, Dr. Sopko had forecast a 1998 start-up.
53. Inco press release, September 19, 1997.
54. Government of Newfoundland and Labrador press release, September 19, 1997.
55. But he may have – on May 15, 1996, his former Minister of Mines and Energy, Rex Gibbons, speculated in the Newfoundland and Labrador House of Assembly that Voisey's Bay might start production as late as 2000.
56 Paul Bagnell, *The Financial Post*, September 26, 1997.
57. Peter Kuitenbrouwer, *The Financial Post*, Toronto, November 20, 1997.
58. This was the view of Falconbridge's marketing department, and it was supported by a story in the August 13, 1997 *American Metal Market*, New York.
59. At his meeting with the Mineral Resource Analysts Group in Toronto, September 28, 1998.
60. Press release, Inco Ltd., February 11, 1998.
61. Inco conference call, February 4, 1998.
62. Inco's Annual General Meeting of Shareholders, Toronto, April 22, 1998.
63. Inco Ltd. briefing for analysts and media, November 18, 1997.
64. As explained to Liz in in Chapter 3.
65. *Reuters*, June 24,1998.
66. *The Globe and Mail*, Toronto, July 24, 1998.
67. CBC Radio, St. John's, July 3, 1998.
68. Curtis Rumbolt, CBC Radio, St. John's, July 31, 1998.
69. *The Evening Telegram*, St. John's, July 29, 1998.
70. *The Evening Telegram*, St. John's, August 20, 1998.
71. CBC Radio St. John's, September 9, 1998.
72. As noted in Chapter 25, hydrometallurgy or "hydromet" is a process employing giant pressure cookers to extract metals from concentrates using hot water. In contrast, Inco originally proposed using "pyromet" at Voisey's Bay. Pyromet involves handling and separating molten metals.
73. *The Telegram*, St. John's, November 16, 1998.
74. VOCM Radio, St. John's, October 25, 1998.
75. CBC Radio, St. John's, November 2, 1998.

76. Press release, Government of Newfoundland and Labrador, November 17, 1998.
77. *Canadian Press*, November 24, 1998.
78. *American Metal Market*, New York, December 2, 1998.
79. Press release, Government of Newfoundland and Labrador, November 17, 1998.
80. Press release, Government of Newfoundland and Labrador, December 22, 1998.
81. Press release, PC Opposition party, February 3, 1999.
82. State Reception for the North Atlantic Minerals Symposium, Dublin, September 19–22, 1999.
83. Robert Fife, *The National Post*, Toronto, May 23, 2002 reported that Mr. Grimes said, "I come from a family of 12 children. There is a saying in Newfoundland that you either fish or you fuck. I guess my family had a lot of bad fishing seasons." Mr. Fife made the improbable claim that this story had shocked and offended Mr. Grimes's audience.
84. Inco press release, April 27, 1999.
85. Inco conference call, April 28, 1998.
86. *The Telegram*, St. John's, July 13, 1999.
87. Inco press release, July 26, 1999.
88. For example, Merrill Lynch analyst Joyce Bish concluded "no nickel will be produced at … Voisey's Bay … before the end of 2004." And 2004 would be "an absolute best-case scenario" (*Platts Metals Week*, July 5, 1999).
89. *The Telegram*, St. John's, October 24, 1999.
90. Inco conference call, October 25, 1999.
91. *The Globe and Mail*, Toronto, November 16, 1999.
92. *Hansard*, Newfoundland and Labrador House of Assembly, November 25, 1999.
93. Despite Mr. Grimes's comments, Sherritt International's hydrometallurgical plant at Fort Saskatchewan, Alberta, had, in fact, treated concentrates of sulphide nickel ores, including some from Inco. Brett Haugrud of Sherritt International and Roman Berezowsky of Dynatec Corporation have said (personal communications, 2002) that the Fort Saskatchewan plant was originally designed to treat nickel-copper sulphide concentrates from the former Sherritt Gordon mine at Lynn Lake, Manitoba. The refinery was commissioned in 1954 and the Lynn Lake concentrates were treated using hydrometallurgy (ammonia leaching followed by nickel reduction) until 1976, when the mine was exhausted. Sulphide concentrates from Inco's Manitoba operations and from Hudson Bay Mining and Smelting's Namew mine in Manitoba then essentially replaced the Lynn Lake feed. The Inco contract expired in 1989 and the Namew mine closed late in 1993. After that, the plant treated artificial sulphides, produced by adding sulphur to lateritic nickel ore from Cuba. The WMC refinery in Kwinana, Australia, which uses a similar process to the original Sherritt refin-

ery, has also treated concentrates from sulphide ores. Messrs. Haugrud and Berezowsky added that Mike Sopko himself used to run a small (5,400 tonnes of nickel per year) hydrometallurgical plant, which treated sulphide nickel ores, for Inco at Sudbury.

94. *The Telegram*, St. John's, November 25, 1999.
95. PC Opposition critic for Mines and Energy, John Ottenheimer, *Hansard*, Newfoundland and Labrador House of Assembly, November 26, 1999.
96. "Stunned: foolish, stupid, naïve"; Story et al 1990.
97. *Hansard*, Newfoundland and Labrador House of Assembly, December 2, 1999.
98. CBC Radio, St. John's, December 8, 1999.
99. *The Telegram*, St. John's, December 7, 1999.
100. PC Opposition critic for Mines and Energy, John Ottenheimer, *Hansard*, Newfoundland and Labrador House of Assembly, December 9, 1999.
101. Some governments levy royalties as well as taxes on extractive industries. (Taxes are usually calculated as a percentage of some measure of profitability, whereas royalties are a percentage of revenues.)
102. *Canadian Press*, January 7, 2000.
103. Inco President Scott Hand in an Inco conference call, February 11, 2000.
104. Michael MacDonald, *Canadian Press*, January 13, 2000.
105. Press release by the PC Opposition party's John Ottenheimer, January 12, 2000.
106. *Hansard*, Newfoundland and Labrador House of Assembly, January 13, 2000.
107. Press release, PC Opposition party, January 13, 2000.
108. Peter Foster, *The National Post*, Toronto, January 14, 2000.
109. *The Telegram*, St. John's, January 14, 2000.
110. CBC Radio, St. John's, February 17, 2000.
111. Macquarie Equities, cited by *Platts Metals Alerts*, January 26, 2000.
112. CBC Radio, St. John's, February 14, 2000.
113. Richard Mackie and Paul Adams, *The Globe and Mail*, January 19, 2000.
114. *The National Post*, Toronto, January 20, 2000.
115. *The National Post*, Toronto, January 26 2000.
116. Michael MacDonald, *Canadian Press*, January 25, 2000.
117. *The National Post*, Toronto, February 17, 2000.
118. *The National Post*, Toronto, March 3, 2000.
119. *The National Post*, Toronto, March 8, 2000.
120. On January 19, 2000.
121. *The Globe and Mail*, February 1, 2000.
122. Jacquie McNish, *The Globe and Mail*, Toronto, February 19, 2000.
123. Diane Francis, *The National Post*, Toronto, February 17, 2000.
124. VOCM Radio, St. John's, March 8, 2000.
125. Press release, Inco Limited, March 7, 2000.

126. Bert Pomeroy, *The Express*, St. John's, June 21, 2000.
127. *Reuters*, Toronto, September 11, 2000.
128. Press release, Government of Newfoundland and Labrador, September 12, 2000.
129. Canada News Wire, October 5, 2000.
130. "East of the overpass" means "in St. John's."
131. Press release, Government of Newfoundland and Labrador, October 16, 2000.
132. Internet polls conducted by *The Telegram*, St. John's, October 2000.
133. *The National Post*, Toronto, October 17, 2000.
134. Brian Tobin, 2002.
135. Gavin Will, *The Financial Post*, Toronto, January 15, 1997.
136. McManus and Wood, 1991.
137. Oxymoronic but correct. Although *The Evening Telegram* was then being published in the morning, it did not change its name to *The Telegram* until September 11, 1998.
138. Bonnie Belec, *The Evening Telegram*, St. John's, July 25 1997.
139. On December 9, 1997, management of the Come By Chance refinery complained to *The Evening Telegram* that there had been yet another disruption in its supply of power the previous day, and that it would cost the refinery about $1 million.
140. *The Evening Telegram*, St. John's, July 8, 1997.
141. William Hilliard, *The Evening Telegram*, St. John's, August 13, 1997.
142. Chris Flanagan, *The Evening Telegram*, St. John's, November 19, 1997.
143. Tracy Barron, *The Telegram*, St. John's, October 25, 1999.
144. On July 6, 1999, the federal government's National Energy Board released its outlook for the supply of and demand for energy to 2025. This report concluded that an electricity transmission line under the Strait of Belle Isle was unlikely.
145. Mines and Energy Minister Paul Dicks, *Hansard*, Newfoundland and Labrador House of Assembly, April 4, 2000.
146. *Hansard*, Newfoundland and Labrador House of Assembly, March 19, 1997.
147. *Hansard*, Newfoundland and Labrador House of Assembly, April 25, 1997.
148. E.g. O'Hara (1980).
149. *Hansard*, Newfoundland and Labrador House of Assembly, May 13, 1997.
150. PC Opposition Party Press Release, April 25, 1997.
151. Pat Doyle, *The Evening Telegram*, St. John's, September 22, 1997.
152. Chris Flanagan, *The Evening Telegram*, September 25, 1997.
153. CBC Radio St. John's, December 8, 1999.
154. Posted on the website of the Canadian Environmental Assessment Agency, www.ceaa.gc.ca.

155. *Lost Visions, Forgotten Dreams*; Sutherland and McGhee (n.d..).
156. Fitzhugh (1999).
157. Arnold (1976).
158. John Gray, *The Globe and Mail*, Toronto, February 3, 1997.
159. Cominco became part of Teck Cominco Limited in 2001.
160. At the September 11, 1998 Voisey's Bay Environmental Panel Hearings in Goose Bay, Labrador, Todd Russell of the Labrador Metis Nation claimed that there were 5,000 to 6,000 Metis in Labrador. He added that he knew brothers, one of whom was a member of the L.I.A. and the other of the Labrador Metis Nation. On October 30, 1998, Peter Penashue of the Innu Nation told the Panel, in Sheshatshiu, that there were 1,700 Innu in Labrador. And, in 1997, Carol Brice-Bennett estimated that the L.I.A. had 4,000 members (Newfoundland and Labrador's Heritage website, www.heritage.nf.ca.).
161. On October 30, 1998, Peter Penashue of the Innu Nation told the Voisey's Bay Assessment Environmental Panel in Sheshatshiu that there were "several thousand" Innu in Quebec. Zebedee Nungat told the Panel in Goose Bay on May 13, 1997, that there were 8,600 Inuit in Quebec, and that they had a claim to parts of northern Labrador.
162. Judith Pereira, in the *Report on Business Magazine*, *The Globe and Mail*, Toronto, May 2002.
163. CBC Radio, St. John's, July 1996.
164. *The Globe and Mail*, January 27, 1997.
165. Dr. Sopko, during Inco's conference call on April 23, 1997.
166. Comment by Charles Ferguson, Vice-President, Environment, Health and Safety, Inco Ltd., to the Voisey's Bay Environmental Assessment Panel Scoping Study, April 29, 1997.
167. By the time that Inco had substantially completed quarrying sand and gravel for construction at Voisey's Bay, Inco and Archean had still not settled this suit. In April 2005, Stuart Feiner, Inco's General Counsel, told me that "the court action ... concerned whether [Archean] had any rights to receive any payments as a 'licensee' with respect to any quarrying in areas covered by the mining claims Voisey's Bay Nickel Company held for use in connection with the Voisey's Bay project. While this action has not been dismissed, nothing has been done by Archean to advance the proceeding for over five years."
168. *American Metal Market*, September 8, 1997.
169. Press release, Voisey's Bay Nickel Company, September 19, 1997.
170. Judgment re Environmental Assessment of Voisey's Bay Infrastructure, by Marshall, Steel and Green, J.J.A., in the Supreme Court of Newfoundland Court of Appeal, September 22, 1997.
171. *The Evening Telegram*, St. John's, August 11, 1998.
172. Drew and Napier, 2000.
173. Charles Pelley, quoted by Chris Flanagan in *The Evening Telegram*, St. John's, September 10, 1998.

Endnotes

174. The price of nickel was US$1.95 per pound that day and had been $2.07 on July 27, 1998; both down considerably from $3.21 on January 31, 1997, when the Memorandum of Understanding had been signed.
175. Stewart Gendron and Gerry Marshall spoke on behalf of Inco.
176. Voisey's Bay Environmental Assessment Panel, Goose Bay, September 10, 1998.
177. Homer Seguin, representing the Innu Nation, in Davis Inlet, October 16, 1998.
178. *The Sudbury Star*, November 3, 1998.
179. Inco President Scott Hand, Annual General Meeting of Shareholders, Toronto, April 22, 1998.
180. On April 17, 1997.
181. In Goose Bay, Labrador.
182. Hearings of the Voisey's Bay Environmental Assessment Panel, Cartwright, Labrador, November 1, 1998.
183. Voisey's Bay Environmental Assessment Panel, Cartwright, Labrador, November 1, 1998.
184. Voisey's Bay Environmental Assessment Panel, Goose Bay, September 12, 1998.
185. Voisey's Bay Environmental Assessment Panel, Nain, September 17, 1998.
186. V.B.N.C.'s Gerry Marshall, to the Voisey's Bay Environmental Assessment Panel, November 3, 1998 in Goose Bay.
187. Herb Clarke, Voisey's Bay Nickel Company, to the Environmental Assessment Panel, Goose Bay, November 3, 1998.
188. Larry Innes, environmental advisor to Innu Nation, to the Environmental Assessment Panel, Davis Inlet, Labrador, April 19, 1997.
189. Voisey's Bay Environmental Assessment Panel, Goose Bay, Labrador, November 3, 1998.
190. See the headers of Chapter 18.
191. *The Telegram*, St. John's, February 17, 1999.
192. Voisey's Bay Nickel Company press release, September 17, 1997.
193. According to the Innu, Voisey's Bay Nickel Company offered them $70 million, and the "major mining project" to which Inco referred was Falconbridge's Raglan project in far northern Quebec, *The Evening Telegram*, St. John's, September 18, 1997.
194. Penote Ben Michel, to Inco's Annual General Meeting of Shareholders, Toronto, April 22, 1998.
195. Inco press release, October 25, 1999.
196. Which Silpa Edmonds, Director, Tongamuit Inuit Annait, Voisey's Bay alleged before the Environmental Assessment Panel in Postville, Labrador, October 7, 1998.
197. In Nain, Labrador, September 16, 1998.

198. Lionel Johnson of the Freshwater Institute, to the Voisey's Bay Environmental Assessment Panel, Goose Bay, Labrador, September 30, 1998.
199. Bevin LeDrew, consultant to Voisey's Bay Nickel Company, to the Environmental Assessment Panel, Goose Bay, Labrador, September 30, 1998.
200. Reported by Christine Cleghorn of the Innu Nation to the Environmental Assessment Panel, Goose Bay, Labrador, October 31, 1998.
201. Herb Clarke, to the Voisey's Bay Environmental Assessment Panel, Goose Bay, November 3, 1998.
202. Voisey's Bay Environmental Assessment Panel, Sheshatshiu, Labrador, October 30, 1998.
203. The Corporation's Managing Director, Fred Hall, to the Voisey's Bay Environmental Assessment Panel, Sheshatshiu, Labrador, October 29, 1998.
204. Voisey's Bay Environmental Assessment Panel, Nain, Labrador, September 15, 1998.
205. Charlotte Wolfrey, Labrador Inuit Association spokesperson, to the Voisey's Bay Environmental Assessment Panel, Rigolet, Labrador, October 5, 1998.
206. Keith Damsell, quoting "a source close to the negotiations," *The National Post*, January 6, 2000.
207. What I term "challengers of corporate power" were, in this case (according to a flyer posted at the University of Toronto), the Student Christian Movement of the University of Toronto and two other groups, "Canadian Action for Indonesia and East Timor" and "Minewatch."
208. CBC Radio, St. John's, April 25, 2000.
209. Mr. Gauld, of the federal Department of Indian Affairs and Northern Development, made these comments to the Voisey's Bay Environmental Assessment Panel, St. John's, Newfoundland, April 29, 1997.
210. Michelle MacAfee, *Canadian Press*, July 19, 1996.
211. Toby Anderson, chief negotiator for the L.I.A., *The Globe and Mail*, Toronto, January 27, 1997.
212. Chesley Andersen, Mineral Resource Advisor for the L.I.A., to the Voisey's Bay Environmental Assessment Panel, April 16, 1997.
213. Voisey's Bay Environmental Assessment Panel, Nain, Labrador, April 16, 1997.
214. Premier Brian Tobin, CBC Radio St. John's, September 30, 1997.
215. Isabel Pain, a land claims negotiator for the L.I.A., Voisey's Bay to the Environmental Assessment Panel, Goose Bay, November 3, 1998.
216. Government of Newfoundland and Labrador press release December 18, 1998, and story by Natalie Southworth in *The Globe and Mail*, Toronto, January 1, 1999.
217. William Barbour, CBC Radio, St. John's, July 27, 1999.
218. Press release, Government of Newfoundland and Labrador, July 6, 1999.
219. CBC Radio, St. John's, July 30, 1999.

220. Mike Sampson of the Labrador and Aboriginal Affairs Secretariat of the Government of Newfoundland and Labrador, to the Voisey's Bay Environmental Assessment Panel, Goose Bay, Labrador, November 3, 1998.
221. Government of Newfoundland and Labrador press release, January 11, 1999.
222. *The Telegram*, St. John's, March 9, 1999.
223. Government of Newfoundland and Labrador press release, November 3, 1999.
224. *The Globe and Mail*, Toronto, December 7, 2000.
225. CBC Radio, St. John's, November 25, 1999.
226. Kirkby Lethbridge on May 6, 1997.
227. In Goose Bay, May 13, 1997.
228. In Goose Bay, September 11, 1998 and in Cartwright on November 1, 1998.
229. Makivik is an Alaskan-style native corporation which represents the 8,600 Inuit of Nunavik, which is that part of Quebec north of the 55th parallel. Its eastern border is with Labrador. Mr. Nungak made these remarks to the Voisey's Bay Environmental Assessment Panel in Goose Bay, Labrador, on May 13, 1997.
230. CBC Radio, St. John's, Newfoundland, February 4, 2000.
231. According to CBC Radio, St. John's, August 12, 1998, on August 10, 1998, federal Associate Chief Justice John Richard ruled that "the Quebec Inuit must be consulted before a national park can be created in Labrador. Lawyers familiar with the decision say the ruling ... could also affect the land claims of the Labrador Inuit and Innu ... and developments like Voisey's Bay."
232. *Canadian Press*, October 25, 1999.
233. Armand McKenzie of the Innu Committee of Schefferville, Quebec, Band Chief Taddé Andre and another Schefferville Innu, John Meamskum; in Goose Bay, April 23, 1997.
234. My principal sources of data were, for aluminum, the International Aluminium Institute; for copper, CRU International Ltd.; and, for zinc, the International Lead and Zinc Study Group; all in London, U.K. In all cases, I calculated figures only for the Western world because of the absence or unreliability of statistics from the former East Bloc.
235. Which wasn't a bad estimate. From the beginning of the Asian crisis in the second quarter of 1996 to the third quarter of 2000, when "Paasche" indicated the beginning of another sharp downturn in demand for base metals, the Western world's demand for nickel grew at an average rate of 3.2% per annum.
236. *Estrategia,* Santiago, Chile, in February 1999.
237. The most notable exception is electricity.
238. I.e., I multiplied prices in nominal dollars by what I then estimated to be the U.S. Consumer Price Index ("CPI-U"; Bureau of Labor Statistics, U.S.

Department of Labor) in 1998 and divided by the U.S. Consumer Price Index in each year.

239. Using exponential least-squares regression analysis.

240. I have used a forecast of supply which was published by Metals Analysis and Outlook, Exton, PA, USA, in December 1997. (Metals Analysis and Outlook forecast that nickel prices in 1998 would average between US$2.70 and US$2.80 per pound. The actual average nickel price in 1998 was US$2.10 per pound.)

241. Here estimated using exponential least-squares regression.

242. "Pinch-point" is a trademark registered to Raymond J. Goldie

243. Dr. Sopko was appointed President in April 1991. Perhaps because George Richardson was on Inco's Board, Inco asked Richardson Greenshields to arrange a meeting in Toronto to enable Dr. Sopko to meet the financial community. That meeting took place on May 23, 1991. The Board appointed Dr. Sopko as Chairman and Chief Executive Officer in April 1992.

244. CBC Radio St. John's, August 6, 1999.

245. CBC Radio St. John's, August 5, 1999.

246. Daniel Ashini, quoted by Alan Robinson in *The Globe and Mail*, Toronto, September 8, 1999.

247. Inco press release, October 25, 1999.

248. Bulong was supposed to produce 9,000 tonnes of nickel per year and Cawse was supposed to produce 6,400 tonnes per year.

249. Adam Shand, *Australian Financial Review*, Sydney, June 10, 2000.

250. According to Falconbridge, budgeted capital costs were US$145 million, US$156 million, and US$675 million for Bulong, Cawse, and Murrin Murrin, respectively. By 2001, capital expenditures had been US$190 million, US$245 million, and US$969 million, respectively.

251. Russell (2000).

252. Roger Hogan, *Australian Financial Review*, Sydney, November 2, 2000.

253. Anaconda Nickel Limited press release, May 10, 2002.

254. Anaconda Nickel Limited press release, September 13, 2002.

255. Sherritt International Corporation press release, October 31, 2002.

256. *American Metal Market*, November 20, 2002.

257. *American Metal Market*, May 5, 2004.

258. Andrew Mitrovica, *The Globe and Mail*, Toronto, October 20 and 22, 2001.

259. "Massive" ores consist almost entirely of ore minerals. The crown jewel at Voisey's Bay, the "Ovoid" deposit, is composed of massive ore.

260. "Disseminated" mineralization consists of blebs and streaks and veins of ore minerals within rocks that would otherwise be uneconomic. Most of the mineralization outside the "Ovoid" at Voisey's Bay is disseminated.

261. Kenneth Gooding, *Financial Times*, London, July 17, 1997.

262. *Reuters*, July 18, 1997.

263. *American Metal Market*, September 3, 2001.
264. Harriet Forster, *American Metal Market*, December 3, 1997.
265. *Reuters*, January 14, 1997.
266. Philip Burgert, *American Metal Market*, February 24, 1999.
267. Cut-off grade: material with less than the cut-off grade is considered to be waste rock and is not included in estimates of reserves.
268. Quotations translated from French by me.
269. On February 10, 1999, Inco announced in a press release that its Board of Directors had suspended payment of dividends on its common shares. The VBN shares were entitled to a dividend of at least 80% of the dividend on the common shares, but 80% of nothing is nothing.
270. See Chapter 12 for more details about what happened on and after January 11, 2000. According to Robert Cook of the Toronto Stock Exchange, the Exchange had a policy of never issuing press releases about investigations which it may or may not have carried out (personal communication, March 5, 2002).
271. At Inco's Technology Conference, Sheridan Park, Ontario, November 29, 2000.
272. Gordon Bacon, Inco, Inco conference for analysts, February 6, 2001.
273. Brian Dunn, *American Metal Market*, February 14, 2001.
274. Inco spokesman Jerry Rogers, quoted by *Reuters*, February 28, 2001.
275. *Reuters*, April 12, 2001.
276. Craig Westcott, *Voisey's Bay News*, May 2001.
277. CBC Radio, St. John's, June 18, 2001.
278. Ibid.
279. Darrell Mercer, quoted by *Reuters*, August 31, 2001.
280. *American Metal Market*, September 14, 2001.
281. In a speech to the St. John's Board of Trade, October 11, 2001.
282. *Platts Metals Week*, October 11, 2001 and CBC Radio, St. John's, October 12, 2001.
283. Inco press release and conference call, October 23, 2001.
284. Inco conference call, December 14, 2001.
285. *Canadian Press*, St. John's and *The Globe and Mail*, Toronto; November 20, 2001.
286. Speech to the St. John's Board of Trade, December 6, 2001.
287. In Happy Valley-Goose Bay, March 30, 2001.
288. Danette Dooley, *Voisey's Bay News*, May 2001.
289. In response to a question during Inco's conference call to discuss its second quarter results, July 24, 2001.
290. Donner Minerals press release, September 7, 2001.
291. Cathy Porter, CBC Radio, St. John's, February 5, 2002.
292. At Inco's annual presentation to analysts and investors, Toronto; Mr. Hand's first as CEO.

293. Email from Stuart Gendron of Voisey's Bay Nickel Company, July 24, 2001.
294. Karen Blackmore and Bonnie McLean, *Voisey's Bay News*, September 2001.
295. CBC Radio, St. John's, April 17, 2001.
296. Renate Mas, *American Metal Market*, New York, April 25, 2002.
297. Allan Robinson, *The Globe and Mail*, Toronto, April 18, 2002.
298. *Hansard*, Newfoundland and Labrador House of Assembly, May 16, 2002.
299. David Cochrane, CBC Radio, St. John's, May 22, 2002.
300. Will Hilliard and Moira Baird, *The Telegram*, St. John's, May 24, 2002.
301. CBC Radio, Happy Valley-Goose Bay, Labrador, May 24, 2002.
302. Author's conversation with Mike MacDonald, *Canadian Press*, St. John's, June 10, 2002.
303. CBC TV News, Happy Valley-Goose Bay, May 24, 2002.
304. CBC Radio, St. John's, June 4, 2002.
305. By Jacquie McNish and Allan Robinson
306. Michael MacDonald, *Canadian Press*, May 28, 2002.
307. David Cochrane, CBC Radio, St. John's, May 22, 2002.
308. For example, according to Drew Hasselback of *The Financial Post*, May 29, 2002, Griffiths McBurney, a Toronto dealer, increased its target price on Inco's shares from US$22 to US$29.75 because it believed a deal on Voisey's Bay was imminent.
309. On August 22, 2002, Nancy Walsh of CBC St. John's reported that she had found out that, on June 1, Premier Grimes's political staff had started to write the speech that the premier would use to announce a deal.
310. Meanwhile, according to Nancy Walsh's August 22, 2002 story on CBC Radio, Premier Grimes's staff was preparing for the press conference to announce a deal, and writing the brochures which were to be mailed to voters.
311. *The National Post* reporters were Drew Hasselback and Ian Jack, June 6, 2002.
312. The *Reuters* reporter was Roger Bill, June 6, 2002.
313. Jacquie McNish, June 7, 2002.
314. Published around noon, Eastern time, on June 7, 2002.
315. Will Hilliard and Barb Sweet, *The Telegram*, St. John's, June 7, 2002.
316. CBC Radio St. John's, June 7, 2002.
317. Jacquie McNish and Allan Robinson, *The Globe and Mail*, June 10, 2002, and CBC Radio St. John's, June 10, 2002.
318. Jacquie McNish and Kevin Cox, *The Globe and Mail*, June 12, 2002.
319. Jacquie McNish and Kevin Cox, *The Globe and Mail*, Toronto, June 12, 2002.
320. Barb Sweet, *The Telegram*, St. John's, June 19, 2002.
321. Barb Sweet, *The Telegram*, St. John's, June 13, 2002.

Endnotes

322. CBC Radio, St. John's, June 14, 2002, reported that Premier Grimes made this comment to a business group in Corner Brook, Newfoundland.
323. A "blue baby" is usually one born with a congenital heart defect; blue is also a Conservative's colour of choice.
324. Barb Sweet, *The Telegram*, St. John's, June 19, 2002.
325. Will Hilliard, *The Telegram*, St. John's, June 19, 2002.
326. Kevin Cox, *The Globe and Mail*, Toronto, October 21, 2003.
327. Michael MacDonald, *Canadian Press*, June 17, 2002.
328. Barb Sweet, *The Telegram*, St. John's, June 19, 2002.
329. CBC Radio, Happy Valley-Goose Bay, Labrador, and Deborah Thomas, *The Telegram*, St. John's; both June 25, 2002.
330. According to an email to me from the Labrador Metis Nation, the question on which its members had voted was, "Was Voisey's Bay Nickel Company right to refuse the Labrador Metis Nation's offer of agreement for a Labrador Aboriginal Adjacency Program that would benefit the Labrador Metis Nation's membership?"
331. Carolyn Leitch, *The Globe and Mail*, Toronto, July 10, 2002.
332. Moira Baird, *The Telegram*, St. John's, August 26, 2002.
333. CBC Radio, Happy Valley-Goose Bay, Labrador, August 26, 2002, which noted that the barge did not carry any goods actually related to the Voisey's Bay project.
334. Press releases, Inco Limited, October 10 and October 22, 2002.
335. Will Hilliard, *The Telegram*, St. John's. October 8, 2002.
336. Moira Baird, *The Telegram*, St. John's, November 19, 2002.
337. CBC Radio St. John's, December 12, 2002.
338. "Take-under" isn't a generally accepted term. (I've also heard it called the "wither-on-the-vine" technique.) I use it to mean a situation where a senior company earns an interest in a junior company, the interest being sufficiently large to dissuade other companies from attempting to take over the junior. The senior then limits the flow of news from the properties shared by the two companies. As a result, the junior company's stock price sags. As the price sags, the senior company slowly buys more shares.
339. A "flow-through" fund is a fund which invests in companies which spend the money on exploration in Canada. The tax benefits generated by these expenditures are "flowed through" back to the fund (and its investors).
340. *The Telegram*, St. John's, November 16, 2002 and November 19, 2002; Kevin Cox, *The Globe and Mail*, Toronto, November 21, 2002; Darcy Keith, *American Metal Market*, November 27, 2002.
341. Kevin Cox, *The Globe and Mail*, Toronto, November 21, 2002.
342. Darcy Keith, *American Metal Market*, November 27, 2002.
343. IPO: Initial Public Offering (of stock).
344. In April 2005, Stuart Feiner, Inco's General Counsel, commented to me that, at around the same time as it had brought an action against Inco regarding

rights to quarry material at Voisey's Bay, Archean had brought a second action against Inco. The second action covered Archean's "rights to make available to third parties interested in acquiring its net smelter royalty interest in production from the Voisey's Bay deposit certain information it had on Voisey's Bay. This action [was] rendered moot by confidentiality agreements under which Inco agreed that certain of such information could be made available to such third parties."

345. Moira Baird, *The Telegram*, September 26, 2002.
346. Paul Piggott, CBC Radio, St. John's, December 2, 2002.
347. L.I.A. President William Andersen; Government of Newfoundland and Labrador press release, January 27, 2004. Presumably only those of *Labrador* Inuit ancestry were eligible, and presumably minors were excluded.
348. Government of Newfoundland and Labrador press release, January 14, 2004.
349. Kirk Makin, *The Globe and Mail*, September 20, 2003.
350. At an M.R.A.G. meeting in Toronto, December 5, 2003.
351. CBC Radio St. John's, April 3 and 8, 2004.
352. Inco press release, October 10, 2002.
353. As compiled by The Thomson Corporation, and available on www.globeinvestor.com.
354. "Nickel climbs on Inco strike threat," Oliver Bertin, May 29, 2003.
355. For example, Inco had even issued each of us with personalized baggage tags imprinted with Labrador's flag.

BIBLIOGRAPHY

Agricola, G., 1556. *De Re Metallica* (Translated by H.C. Hoover and L.H. Hoover). Dover Publications, New York.

Ambachtsheer, Keith, 1977. "Where are the Customers' Alphas?" *The Journal of Portfolio Management,* Fall 1977.

Arnold, Robert D., 1976. *Alaska Native Land Claims.* Alaska Native Foundation, Anchorage, Alaska.

Baesel, J.B. and Stein, G.R., 1979. "The value of information inferences from the profitability of insider trading." *Journal of Financial and Quantitative Analysis.*

Clark, P.U. and Fitzhugh, W.W. "Postglacial Relative Sea Level History of the Labrador Coast and Interpretation of the Archaeological Record." In Johnson, L.L., ed. *Paleoshorelines and Prehistory: An Investigation of Method.* Boca Raton, Florida: CRC Press, 1991, 189-213.

Cranford, Garry. *The Buchans Miners.* St. John's: Flanker Press, 1997.

Ferguson, Niall. *Empire: How Britain Made the Modern World.* London: Allen Lane, 2003.

Fitzhugh, Lynne. *The Labradorians.* St. John's: Breakwater, 1999.

Goldie, Raymond and Tredger, Peter. "Net Smelter Return Models and Their Use in the Exploration, Evaluation and Exploitation of Polymetallic Deposits." *Geoscience Canada,* 18 (4), 159-171.

Goudie, Elizabeth. *Woman of Labrador.* Halifax: Nimbus Publishing, 1996.

Haugen, R. and Jorion, P. "The January Effect: Still There After All These Years." *Financial Analysts Journal,* Jan-Feb., 1996, 27-32.

Hennessey, Bryan. *Absolutely Frank.* St John's: Killick Press, 1997.

Houlihan, Eileen. *Uprooted!: The Argentia Story.* St. John's: Creative Publishers, 1992.

Ibbotson, Roger G. and Sinquefield, Rex A. *Stocks, Bonds, Bills and Inflation: Historical Returns (1926-1978).* Financial Analysts Research Foundation, 1979.

Johnston, Wayne. *Baltimore's Mansion.* Toronto: Alfred A Knopf, 1999.

Lacasse, C. and van den Bogaard, P. "Enhanced Airborne Dispersal of Silicic Tephras During the Onset of Northern Hemisphere Oscillations, from 6 to 0 Ma: Records of Explosive Volcanism and Climate Change in the Subpolar North Atlantic." *Geology.* 30, 623-626.

LeDrew, B. and Napier, W. "The Voisey's Bay Mine/Mill Environmental Impact Assessment — the Proponent's Perspective." Joint Meeting of the Prospectors Association of Canada and the CIM. Toronto: March 2000.

Logan, L. and Cole, G. *New Caledonia.* Hawthorne, Australia: Lonely Planet Publications, 1997.

McManus, Gary E. and Wood, Clifford H. *Atlas of Newfoundland and Labrador.* St. John's: Breakwater, 1991.

McNish, Jacquie. *The Big Score.* Toronto: Doubleday, 1998.

McPhee, John. *In Suspect Terrain.* New York: Farrar, Strauss, Giroux, 1983.

Molloy, Les. "Red Mountain — National Park or Asbestos Mine?" *Forest and Bird.* Journal of the Royal Forest and Bird Protection Society of New Zealand, Wellington, 1977.

Morin, Roger. "Tests of Efficiency in the Canadian Stock Market." Financial Research Foundation Conference, Montebello, Quebec, October 1978.

O'Flaherty, Patrick. *Old Newfoundland: A History to 1843*. St. John's: Long Beach Press, 1999.

O'Hara, T. Alan, 1980. "Quick Guides to the Evaluation of Ore Bodies." *CIM Bulletin*. Feb. 1980, 87-99.

Rorke, Harvey and Fowler, David. "Do Published Insider Trading Reports Contain Valuable Information?" Financial Research Foundation Conference, Montebello, Quebec, October 1978.

Russell, David, Argosy Minerals Inc. "Doing the Hard Yards." World Nickel Congress, Melbourne, November 2000.

Story, G.M., Kirwin, W.J. and Widdowson, J.D.A. *Dictionary of Newfoundland English* 2nd edition. Toronto: University of Toronto Press, 1990.

Suret, Jean-Marc and Cormier, Elise. "Insiders and the Stock Market." *Canadian Investment Review*. Fall 1990, 87-90.

Sutherland, Patricia and McGhee, Robert. *Lost Visions, Forgotten Dreams Exhibit Guide*. Ottawa: Canadian Museum of Civilization, n.d.

Tobin, Brian, *All in Good Time*. Toronto: Penguin Canada, 2002.

Troke, G. and Janes, C. (Public Works and Government Services Canada, Placentia) and consultants K. Taylor, K., Gale, J., Duerden, F.C. and Keane, S. "Trial Dewatering and Remediation of Shag Pond, Argentia, Newfoundland." Paper presented at Geological Association of Canada Annual Meeting, St. John's, May 2001.

White, Winston. *Labrador: Getting Along in the Big Land!* St. John's: Flanker Press, 2003.

Wilson, Margo and Daly, Martin. "Do Pretty Women Inspire Men to Discount the Future?" The Royal Society, *Biology Letters*, online edition, December 12, 2003.

ACKNOWLEDGEMENTS

I give my thanks to all who are mentioned in this book: to my wife Jo-Anne and our daughters Kate and Alexandra for their love and support; to my parents, Norma and John Goldie, for having me; to Garry, Margo, Jerry Cranford, and the staff of Flanker Press; and to Anne Hart; and Anne Keyes; and Leo Furey; and for the encouragement of Terry Salman and my other colleagues at Salman Partners Inc.

The publisher wishes to thank Leo Furey, author of *The Long Run*, for recommending that Ray offer this book to Flanker Press.

RAYMOND GOLDIE's interest in Voisey's Bay began in 1970, when he was part of the first prospecting team to visit the coast of Labrador to examine its potential for deposits of copper and nickel. In the late 1970s, armed with a Ph.D. in geology from Queen's University, Kingston, he began to work in the Canadian investment industry. As mining analyst, he has followed the fortunes of North American mining companies and mine developments, including Inco Limited and its Voisey's Bay nickel-copper project.

Raymond Goldie is a senior analyst with Salman Partners Inc. in Toronto. However, all opinions and interpretations of historical events expressed in this book are those of the author and do not necessarily reflect the views of Salman Partners Inc. or its associates, affiliates, or any of their respective directors, officers, employees, or shareholders.